Freak to Chic

Freak to Chic

"Gay" Men in and out of Fashion after Oscar Wilde

Dominic Janes

BLOOMSBURY VISUAL ARTS
LONDON • NEW YORK • OXFORD • NEW DELHI • SYDNEY

BLOOMSBURY VISUAL ARTS
Bloomsbury Publishing Plc
50 Bedford Square, London, WC1B 3DP, UK
1385 Broadway, New York, NY 10018, USA
29 Earlsfort Terrace, Dublin 2, Ireland

BLOOMSBURY, BLOOMSBURY VISUAL ARTS and the Diana logo are trademarks of
Bloomsbury Publishing Plc

First published in Great Britain 2021
Paperback edition first published 2023

A catalogue record for this book is available from the British Library.

Library of Congress Cataloging-in-Publication Data
Names: Janes, Dominic, author.
Title: Freak to chic : 'gay' men in and out of fashion after Oscar Wilde /Dominic Janes.
Description: London ; New York : Bloomsbury Visual Arts, 2021. |
Includes bibliographical references and index.
Identifiers: LCCN 2021000734 (print) | LCCN 2021000735 (ebook) |
ISBN 9781350172609 (hardback) | ISBN 9781350248083 (paperback) |
ISBN 9781350172616 (pdf) | ISBN 9781350172623 (ebook)
Subjects: LCSH: Gay men–Social life and customs. | Fashion–History. | Gay culture. |
Gay men–Clothing. | Wilde, Oscar, 1854-1900–Influence.
Classification: LCC HQ76 .J34 2021 (print) | LCC HQ76 (ebook) | DDC 306.76/6–dc23
LC record available at https://lccn.loc.gov/2021000734
LC ebook record available at https://lccn.loc.gov/2021000735

ISBN:	HB:	978-1-3501-7260-9
	PB:	978-1-3502-4808-3
	ePDF:	978-1-3501-7261-6
	eBook:	978-1-3501-7262-3

Typeset by Integra Software Services Pvt Ltd.

To find out more about our authors and books visit www.bloomsbury.com
and sign up for our newsletters.

"Some of us are looking at the stars."
Oscar Wilde, *Lady Windermere's Fan* (1892).

Contents

Illustrations

Acknowledgments

I thank the following libraries, archives, and collections that were consulted in the course of this research:

Birkbeck Library, University of London
Bodleian Libraries, University of Oxford
British Library, London
British Museum, London
Cambridge University Library
Cecil Beaton Studio Archive, Sotheby's Picture Library, London
Columbia University Libraries, New York
Harry Ransom Center, University of Texas at Austin
John Deakin Archive, London
Keele University Library
Metropolitan Museum of Art, New York
National Archives, London
National Fairground and Circus Archive, University of Sheffield
National Library of Scotland
National Portrait Gallery, London
New York Public Library
Syracuse University Library
Tate Gallery, London
University of Brighton Design Archives
University of Kent, British Cartoon Archive
University of Sussex, Mass Observation Archive
Victoria and Albert Museum, London
Wellcome Collection Library, London
Yale University Library

The publisher and I gratefully acknowledge the following permissions granted to reproduce copyright material in this book:

Alamy Ltd, Fig. 2.1.
Beerbohm, Max, estate of, Fig. 2.5.

Bodleian Library, University of Oxford, Fig. 2.5.

Boston Public Library, Fig. 1.1.

British Cartoon Archive, University of Kent, Fig. 7.2.

British Library, Figs 2.2, 2.3, 6.8, and 6.9.

Condé Nast Publications Ltd, Figs. 4.15 and 5.5.

Condé Nast, Figs. 3.14, 4.8, and 7.1.

Copyright reserved, Figs. 3.6, 4.10, 5.6, 6.3, 6.9, 6.11, 6.15, and 7.3.

Crystal Bridges Museum of American Art, Fig. 6.2.

DACS, Fig. 5.8.

Hearst Magazines UK, Figs. 4.16, 5.4, and 6.15.

George Hoyningen-Huene Estate Archives, Figs. 4.13 and 4.16.

Keele University Library, Figs. 2.6, 2.10, 4.2, and 4.6.

Mary Evans Picture Library, Figs. 2.8, 3.1, 3.5, 4.3, 4.4, 4.5, 4.10, 4.11, 4.12, 4.14, 5.1, 5.6, 5.7, 5.9, 5.10, 5.11, 5.12, 5.13, 5.14, and 5.15.

National Portrait Gallery, Figs. 2.7, 4.12, 4.13, and 6.3.

Nottingham City Museums and Galleries, Fig. 5.4.

Philpot, *Jongleur,* owner, Fig. 5.2.

Pd Courtaulds Group, Fig. 6.9.

Punch Cartoon Library/Topfoto, Figs. 1.2, 1.3, 1.4, 1.5, 2.4, 3.2, 3.3, 4.1, 4.7, 6.1, 6.10, 6.12, 6.13, and 6.14.

Revlon Inc., Fig. 4.11.

Rhys, Emilie, Fig. 5.4.

Solo Syndication, Fig. 7.2.

Sotheby's, Figs. 4.9, 4.17, 5.3, and 6.5.

TI Media Ltd, Fig. 6.8.

Wellcome Library, Figs. 5.9 and 7.3.

Ziolkowski, Professor Jan M., Fig. 5.2.

Every effort has been made to trace copyright holders and to obtain their permission for the use of copyright material. The publisher and I apologize for any errors or omissions in the above list and would be grateful if notified of any corrections that should be incorporated in future reprints or editions of this book. I have not been able to identify or contact the owners of the estates of Abdulla Cigarettes, Patrick Bellew, Anne Fish, Charles Henri Ford, Courtauld's Rayon, George Plank, "Tony"/E. Marks Ltd., Olivia Wyndham, and Anthony Wysard. Anyone with information about the ownership of their estates is asked to contact me via Bloomsbury. Third-party copyrighted material displayed in the pages of this book is done so on the basis of fair dealing for the purposes of criticism and review and fair use for the purposes of teaching, criticism, scholarship, or research only in accordance with international copyright laws, and is not intended to infringe upon the ownership rights of the original owners. Permission to quote was obtained from the Trustees of the Mass Observation Archive. I also thank Taylor and Francis for permission to include rewritten material from my article "Early Twentieth-Century *Vogue,* George Wolfe Plank and the 'Freaks of Mayfair,'" *Visual Culture in Britain* 18, no. 1 (2017): 68–83 (https://www.tandfonline.com/).

I thank the following individuals and organizations for funding to cover the cost of archive visits, image acquisitions, and copyright permissions:

Isaac Julien
Keele University
University of the Arts London
University for the Creative Arts.

Several talented friends helped me in the final stages of this project. Prof. John Dunkley and John Lotherington read and discussed a draft of this book. Adam Thorn supplied a series of important suggestions on a later version. Dr. Jacob Bloomfield provided invaluable assistance with referencing and formatting. I am also grateful to Wendy and Gordon Hawksley for information concerning William Ranken. Finally, thanks for a lively discussion in New York on calla lilies in queer American art go to Dr. Jonathan Frederick Walz, who requested that I refer to him as a delicate flower.

Introduction: In Search of Lost Times

The ages live in history through their anachronisms.

Wilde, "Phrases and Philosophies."[1]

In the interwar period, queer styles came into fashion. What had been freakish became chic. This book explains how this came about and why it did not last. Accompanied by bunches of flowers and attending to glamorous women, a select number of homosexual and bisexual men were allowed to dine at many of the top social tables on both sides of the Atlantic in an age when their sexual choices were widely criminalized. On the way, they contributed immensely to the artistic achievements of their times. The design of George Kukor's film *My Fair Lady* (1964), which was based on George Bernard Shaw's play *Pygmalion* (1913), emerged from these milieus. Its story of the transformation of a cockney flower-seller into a glamorous socialite bore some comparison to the rise from middle-class obscurity of Cecil Beaton, who designed many of the film's costumes. As a confirmed bachelor and aesthete, he insisted that his working environment be as beautiful as possible. He pestered the studio for ever more plants and bouquets with which to furnish his Hollywood apartment since "in England, this was the time of the year when I could hardly drag myself from my garden for fear of missing the opening of a bud."[2] For queer men such as Beaton, fine decor, exotic blossoms, and the women who adored them provided a lusciously decorative mask that, by the 1960s, barely concealed their sexual deviance.

Suitors have long been encouraged by florists to "say it with flowers," but in fact blossoms could be employed in poetry and art to hint at a wide variety of thoughts and feelings. They have been analyzed as providing "an alternative model of the production (of meaning) which would take into account what has been rejected and repressed in logocentric systems of thought and knowledge, namely plurality, the feminine, the unconscious and the signifier."[3] Not all flowers were bright and gay: some were dark, strange, and evocative of decadence. Men who dared to explore same-sex desire more openly were drawn by the dramatic power of the contrast between lushly beautiful surfaces and the fleshly truths that they concealed. Beaton hinted at troubling aspects of life through an exploration in much of his work as a celebrity photographer of strange juxtapositions and queer contrasts between beauty and ugliness, the extraordinary and the everyday. His was a carnivalesque imagination that celebrated, like that of his sexual fellow-traveler Jean Cocteau in France, "stars ('the sacred monsters'), the boxers, the clowns, [and] the fashion mannequins [i.e., models]."[4] Other writers and artists who were not dependent, as Beaton was, on the patronage of high society were able to explore contrasts between beauty and beastliness with even greater openness. In France, Jean Genet produced overtly queer books such as *Our Lady of the Flowers* (1943) and *Miracle of the Rose* (1946).[5] In the United States, Tennessee Williams was to write of the intense passions that would tear open the aesthetic camouflage in *Suddenly Last Summer* (1958). The garden of Sebastian the queer aesthete, he wrote, "may be as unrealistic as the décor of a dramatic ballet," featuring "massive tree-flowers that suggest organs of a body, torn out, still glistening with undried blood."[6] At the end of the play, all that is left of Sebastian after a horrific, cannibalistic assault is described as looking like a "big white-paper-wrapped bunch of red roses [that] had been *torn, thrown, crushed!*"[7]

Many people thought that homosexual sex was wrong and that the men who liked it were little better than beasts. Some queer men openly embraced their seemingly ugly deviance in the countercultural mode of Genet, while others denied its existence. But there was another option: to conceal in plain sight. This, essentially, was Oscar Wilde's choice. As the dandy Lord Goring says to the morally compromised politician Sir Robert Chiltern in Wilde's *An Ideal Husband* (1895): "in England a man who can't talk morality twice a week to a large, popular, immoral audience is quite over as a serious politician. There would be nothing left for him as a profession except Botany or the Church."[8] Wilde insinuates that the truly monstrous hypocrite can only survive when he takes spiritual or worldly beauty as his occupation. Oscar Wilde had been one of the most glamorous celebrities of his age. The images that we have of him today have been powerfully influenced not just by his literary works but also by the way in which he performed himself.[9] In his early life, he was both feted and mocked as a willowy aesthete. During his lecture tour to the United States in 1882, he became notorious for his interest in unusual fashions and for his allegedly effeminate fascination with aesthetic style in general and with flowers in particular.[10] A decade later, *The Star* reported that he had appeared at a theater premiere in the company of a "suite of young gentlemen, all wearing the vivid dyed carnation which has superseded the lily and the sunflower."[11] By that time, his body had expanded from svelte to corpulent, and he was being lampooned as a gourmand. Rumors concerning his sexual interests had been spreading in London for many years before his trials made him the most notorious sodomite of the age.

This book does not explore the reception of Oscar Wilde's literary works. It does, however, examine the ways in which images associated with his life and style became constitutive of constructions and perceptions of male homosexuality. It likewise follows the queer pattern of Wilde's own life by focusing on fashionable society in London seen in connection with metropolitan milieus across the Atlantic and in Paris. The book aligns with the trend identified by the American historian of gender and sexuality Regina Kunzel that "queer histories are increasingly [seen as] transnational, tracing the global circuits of sexual ideas, practices, politics and subjects."[12] Forms of queer transatlantic modernism developed as Anglophile Americans influenced cultural life in London and men from the UK had made increasingly frequent visits to New York. Wilde's lecture tour of the United States in the early 1880s was a precursor of this process. This book, therefore, is a case study focused on a particular city, but one that invites related engagements with queer fashion in other locations around the globe.[13] John Potvin, in his study of queer bachelordom, has talked of the "omnipresence of Wilde" in early-twentieth-century Western culture.[14] Even though Wilde was widely reviled, he became a figure against which evolving standards of normative masculinity were measured. He thereby became associated with a heady combination of ugliness and aestheticism, disgrace and fashionability, freakiness and chic.

That last term—chic—has been established in English since at least the mid-nineteenth century. It refers to skill, style, and taste and was acquired from French, where it was originally regarded as slang, and may have in turn been derived from the German word *schick*. *Fin-de-siècle* modes of dandyism had a powerful influence on the formation of queer styles of male self-expression during this period. While the sexually assertive woman—the vamp—flickered alluringly across the screens of movie theaters, the styles of Wilde were re*vamped* for new groups of seemingly androgynous men who proclaimed themselves to be "gay" in the sense of happy. This book tells the story of how queerness in the sense of gender ambiguity came—albeit briefly and precariously—into fashion in the 1920s. However, this style and those who generated it swiftly fell out of vogue in the 1930s as the sexual content of that queerness became the subject of popular derision. These were decades that saw a dizzying pace of cultural change that involved, for some people at least, greater opportunities for sexualized self-expression. *Freak to Chic* explores the birth of the queer culture that would in time lead to lesbian and gay liberation and new forms of sexual identity. It centers on the question of how freakery and fashion came briefly into alignment in the form of "freak chic."

The word "freak" was sometimes used in quite explicit ways to refer to same-sex desire, including by people of color, as in Harlem Hamfat's song "Garbage Man—or The Call of the Freaks," or "Freakish Man Blues" by George Hannah.[15] But the word was also used in a much wider sense to refer to countercultural behavior, especially by wayward and often fashion-conscious youth. In this sense, the interwar period prefigured a similar process of appropriation of freaks and freaking by the counterculture of the 1960s and 1970s.[16] In 1978, the American rhythm-and-blues band Chic released a hit disco song "Le Freak" on their new album *C'est Chic*. It was inspired by their experience of failing to meet with Grace Jones on New Year's Eve after being turned away by bouncers at the hot new nightclub Studio 54, which had just opened in New York. The record was a huge commercial success, becoming the best-selling album for their label, Warner Music, prior to Madonna's "Vogue" (1990). In 1995, John Galliano titled a fashion show in Paris "Le Freak C'est Chic," in which "giants, identical twins, fat women, bodybuilders, old men and dwarves" were sent down the catwalk.[17] Such individuals are no longer exhibited to the paying public in freak shows, but they can be paraded for their shock value in the promotion of luxury commodities.

Wilde's visit to the United States marked a key moment when the world of the freak show collided with the world of aesthetic culture and fashion. It was even rumored—falsely—that the great impresario of circuses and freak shows Phineas Taylor ("P. T.") Barnum had offered Wilde £200 if he would ride the famous elephant Jumbo down Broadway in New York with a lily and a sunflower grasped in either hand (Figure 1.1).[18] Cartoons of the time regularly depicted Wilde as a bizarrely dressed, flower-obsessed impersonator of the mores of European aristocracy. The world of popular entertainment included strong traditions of blackface minstrelsy that influenced the ways in which the performances of Wilde and his aesthetes were mocked, particularly in the United States.[19] Many of these American representations were explicitly racialized, depicting people of African or Asian ethnicity as ridiculous for supposedly aping the pretensions of the visiting Irishman.[20]

There had, however, been a tradition of parodying Black dandies in London since the eighteenth century. One print published in 1772 depicted Julius Soubise. He had become famous as the former slave and close companion of the

Figure 1.1 Clark's O.N.T. Spool Cotton, *Jumbo Aesthetic* (New York: Buek and Lindner, *c.*1882). Reproduced courtesy of Boston Public Library Arts Department.

Duchess of Queensberry, who had named him after a courtier of Louis XV of France.[21] Even though those who shaped Western fashion have often been White, the ways in which they were critiqued could still draw on racial prejudice. Celts, for instance, were not always thought of as being quite the same shade of pale as Anglo-Saxons. If queerness is understood as having been constructed through contestation between opponents and proponents, then it will contain within it elements with which we may be uncomfortable, including some that are racist, misogynist, or self-shaming. Elspeth Brown, in her *Work! A Queer History of Modeling* (2019), raised the concern that queer approaches might sometimes lead to neglect of other important markers of identity. This book, unlike hers, does not explore case studies of people of color. Nevertheless, the study of relatively privileged white men such as Wilde and Beaton need not mean that classed and gendered intersectionality is eclipsed in the pursuit of insights into sexuality.[22] Elite lives can tell us a great deal about the systems of classification and control in which they were enmeshed.

The word "queer" usually meant strange or freakish in the first half of the twentieth century. However, it was sometimes applied in ways that betray some suspicion of sexual peculiarity. An early example of this was the reference to Lord Rosebery as a "snob queer" by Wilde's nemesis, the Marquess of Queensberry.[23] He feared that his eldest son, Francis, Viscount Drumlanrig, had been seduced by Rosebery, and he was equally concerned about relations between his younger son Alfred "Bosie" Douglas and Oscar Wilde.[24] But his phrase also implied that the man who was prime minister from 1894 to 1895 was, like Wilde, a social climber with an unorthodox marriage (his wife was Jewish). The past indeterminacy of queerness is argued by many contemporary writers of queer history to be one of its enduring strengths. Queerness can be seen as involving a challenge to fixed categories of identity, including to the boundaries of sexuality as a category.[25] It is often used in queer theory to apply to circumstances in which normativity is put under pressure and transgressed in relation not only to sexuality but also to other aspects of cultural life. Thinking queer, therefore, implies far more than a search for homosexuals in history.

This study complements works that have focused on other aspects of queer experience, such as the history of sexual desire between women and their role as customers and friends.[26] Laura Doan's *Fashioning Sapphism: The Origins of a Modern Lesbian Culture* (2001) and *Disturbing Practices: History, Sexuality, and Women's Experience of Modern War* (2013) have provided important sources of methodological inspiration.[27] The first book offers a model for engaging with the cultural history of a sexual minority group in ways that pay close attention to the politics of dress and visual culture. The second book was highly innovative in that it sought to be informed by, while also critiquing, history written with a focus on identity politics. That approach, she argued, risked reading contemporary categories and understandings of sexuality anachronistically into the past. Historians would benefit from engagement with the critical stance offered by queer theory approaches even though these had often been pioneered within literature departments. However, the theoretical understanding of queerness as the sexualized subversion of norms could itself provide another opening for contemporary expectations to distort our understanding of the past. In a series of case studies from the First World War, Doan put into practice her belief that historians need to acknowledge that the queerness expressed in the primary sources often consists in their lack of conformity to twenty-first-century taxonomies. Indeed, their very queerness might be best approached by abandoning expectations that there should be a binary division between what was "normal" and what was "queer."[28]

Taken to an extreme, this might lead us to assume that past concepts of same-sex desire were essentially inchoate. It may be that the sources do engage with taxonomies and normative expectations, but these do not always fit those that we are expecting to find.[29] In this current book, therefore, I critically engage with expected sexual categories while appreciating the unevenness and inchoate nature of the evidence as a key aspect of its intriguing queerness. Doan's work and its influence need to be seen in the context of a growing body of historical work that is both critical and queer in its stance.[30] I am also, finally, in debt to the vast range of excellent research on Oscar Wilde's life and work by historians, literary scholars, and queer theorists, even though little of this focuses on his influence—both as an exemplar and as a warning—on queer men in the early twentieth century. He is, therefore, not so much the subject of this book as its inspiration.[31]

The period that this study covers, from 1901 to 1939, was one in which many of the terms for same-sex desire now familiar in English were coming into widespread use. It is important to stress the multivalent nature of such terminology. A wide range of terms, from the negative (such as "queer" meaning freakish) to the positive (such as "gay" meaning cheerful), could be used with or without sexual reference, depending on the period and social circumstances. Just because most people continued to use the word "gay" to mean cheerful into the 1960s, that did not mean that it had not begun to acquire secondary, subcultural meanings. When the fashion magazine *Vogue* reported in 1917 that Paris was "gay with the uniforms and flags of the allied nations," it was implying anything but effeminate transgression.[32] But this was, nevertheless, a kind of gaiety that could have sparked same-sex desire on the part of men such as the American artist Marsden Hartley, who is noted for his fetishistic *Portrait of a German Officer* (1914).[33]

Some interwar uses of the word "gay" were, however, much more tightly connected with same-sex desire. One example of this was the American novelist Harry Hervey's *Ethan Quest* (1925), which was published in Britain as *The Gay Sarong*. His protagonist delights in dressing in exotic clothing—including a "gay sarong"—and moves to the South Sea Islands to spend his life with a native boy.[34] In a world of closeted desire where open expression was dangerous, queer meanings were frequently established through ambiguous terminology or through objects such as clothes that acted as proxies for the desiring and the desired body. It is probably impossible to establish precisely when and where the term "gay" in Britain and the United States was first used to mean "homosexual." It was identified as being in widespread use, albeit "almost exclusively by homosexuals to denote homosexuality," in an American study published in 1941.[35] Thus, we simply cannot be sure whether knowing eyebrows were raised by the claim published in *Vogue* in 1933 that "London is the gayest place in the world at midnight."[36] The article was illustrated by the society artist Cecil Beaton, who knew all about the post-theater suppers that were openly celebrated in the accompanying text and the homosexual possibilities that were not. Moreover, as has recently been argued, "the lack of a specific word to describe an experience does not mean that the experience does not exist."[37] It is for these reasons of queer indeterminacy that the word "gay" appears in quotation marks in the subtitle of this book.

Elite tastes and lives played a hugely important role in shaping culture and events in premodern Europe, but how relevant were they to the development of modern forms of sexual identity? In seeking to answer this question, it is helpful to draw a distinction between styles that aped aristocratic mores and the social origins of those who employed them. Cecil Beaton was born into a solidly middle-class family in north London in 1904. By dint of hard work and social climbing, he became one of the most important glamor photographers of the twentieth century. He provides a focal presence in this book as a counterpart to the influential absence of Oscar Wilde, who had died in poverty in Paris in 1900. Beaton was also a central figure in bringing aspects of queer style into fashion during the later 1920s.

London in the interwar period has a very important place in the development of gay/homosexual/queer (sub)cultures. This might seem surprising since that city has usually been seen as more culturally conservative than New York, Paris, or Berlin at this time.[38] However, Florence Tamagne's *Histoire de l'homosexualité en Europe (Berlin, Londres, Paris, 1919–1939)* (2000) came to a different conclusion. In this work, she surveyed the evidence for homosexual lives in three of Europe's most important metropolises. As was perhaps inevitable in such a wide survey, her results were based on a process of sampling in which only certain sets of police reports and runs of newspapers were consulted.[39] She found evidence of vibrant, if divergent, patterns of queer life in the three locales. The France that emerges from her pages is one in which there was a clear divide between claustrophobic oppression in the provinces and sophisticated tolerance in the capital.[40] Tamagne's word for this latter phenomenon was "individualism."[41] By this she meant that, in a country that had effectively decriminalized male homosexuality in 1791, there was a strong current of opinion that most sexual preferences were not a matter for state regulation. Queer men and women moved to Paris not simply from the French countryside but from many other countries across Europe and the wider world.[42] Fashionable circles in the city became known for the presence of gay women sporting masculine styles, and gay men sporting feminine ones.[43]

Legality, however, did not equate to respectability, and as understandings of same-sex desire developed in France, so did attempts to identify and combat it.[44] Cross-dressing performances on the cabaret stage declined in the early twentieth century with the rise of a panicked awareness of the potential for such acts to indicate sexual nonconformity.[45] Individuals and venues could face harassment by the police, and the "scene" could best be described as semi-clandestine.[46] Queer lives intersected with the artistic avant-garde, but they cannot be seen to have challenged the mainstream. Queer culture also flourished in Berlin, but there the partying was accompanied by sustained and partially successful attempts to repeal paragraph 175 of the German constitution, which outlawed male homosexuality. At the same time, as was also the case in France, a range of other laws were at the disposal of the police in order to control related phenomena such as male prostitution.[47]

Britain presented a third pattern. In that country there was no substantial movement for the reform of the criminal law, but there was a widespread fascination with queer expression among parts of the cultural and political elite that amounted to what Tamagne terms a "cult of homosexuality."[48] This concept was advanced by Noel Annan, who claimed that this cult was specific to England, where homosexuality was "more pervasive than anywhere else in Europe."[49] One can, Tamagne argues, "even speak of a 'homosexualization' of the leading classes, explained by the prevalence of single-gender structures (homosociality) and the emphasis on the value of relationships between men."[50] Moreover, in her view this prevalence of same-sex desire was not simply restricted to the elite who had attended same-sex public schools but "it seems reasonable to conclude ... affected the whole of society."[51] Furthermore, if, as she also contends, "during the 1920s, homosexuality was all the rage" in all three capitals, it was London that stood out.[52]

Since the publication of Matt Houlbrook's *Queer London: Perils and Pleasures in the Sexual Metropolis, 1918–1957* (2005 hb; 2006 pb), it has been clear that London did indeed possess a distinctive pattern of same-sex activity that encompassed the full social range. The city possessed, he wrote, "a distinctly *queer* urban culture. What do I mean by this? It was distinctly queer in the sense of being unfamiliar to a twenty-first-century observer. The world mapped in this book is not a *gay* world as we would currently understand it."[53] In particular he stressed the importance of cross-class relationships—of butch working-class men who did not regard themselves as queer even though they might have had homo-sex encounters, and of queens who presented themselves not simply as effeminate men but sometimes as women.[54] While there was public concern about immorality and degeneration, legal enforcement was considerably less intense than it was to become after the Second World War.[55] There was also, he argued, relatively little investigative attention paid to queer life in London by the press.[56] The city that emerges from Houlbrook's study bears some similarity to that depicted in George Chauncey's *Gay New York: Gender, Urban Culture, and the Making of the Gay Male World, 1890–1940* (1995). In these cities, "real" men who sold their sexual services to other men were known as "rent" or "trade". The transatlantic counterpart of the queen was the fairy.[57] The term "gay" appears to have been used by fairies to refer to each other's taste in clothes and bars.[58] The word was also used there and in Britain in reference to prostitutes, who were known as "gay ladies" or good-time girls (Figure 4.2). The fairies themselves, in turn, were referred to as "fags" by people who regarded themselves as sexually normal, while masculine-seeming men who desired other men were referred to as "queers."

As in London, the origins of these identities could be traced back to the nineteenth century, as evidenced, for instance, by the drawing of a fairy with a limp wrist, curvy hips, and tight jacket that appears on a New York map produced around 1870.[59] Fairies became known as "pansies" during the interwar period, and there was even a slumming phenomenon called the "pansy craze" in which tourists flocked to Greenwich Village and Harlem to watch queer men and women drinking and performing in bars.[60] The nightlife of the city emerged from clandestine illegality into a regime of steadily increasing, morally inspired surveillance after the end of prohibition in 1933 and the re-imposition of liquor licensing.[61] Queer New York did not collapse in the manner of its counterpart Berlin in the face of fascist repression, but the 1930s still saw a noticeable decline in homosexual visibility when compared to what had been seen in the previous decade. A similar process took place in Britain, where queerness had a more prominent presence in high society but then fell out of fashion. Indeed, it was not simply queer style that fell out of fashion but also many of the "gay" people who had promoted it.

The Arts and Media

In July 1928, Herbert Farjeon, a playwright working as an arts critic for *Vogue*, attended a London performance of the Ballets Russes. His attention was distracted, however, from what was taking place on the stage by the presence of "young freaks" in the audience. He tells us:

> The corridors of His Majesty's Theatre are crowded with sweet seasonable young men … It takes all sorts to make an audience, but it takes only one sort to make that audience distinguished … the *clientele* for the Russian Ballet may now be distinguished by the beautiful burgeoning boys who seem to recline on art like Madame Récamier on her couch and to regard the dancers and the *décor* as a kind of personal adornment. Indeed, they might even be said to wear the Russian Ballet like a carnation in their buttonholes.[62]

This puts a queer perspective on the androgyny on show in "If We Ordered Our Lives after the Manner of the Russian Ballet," a cartoon by Claude Shepperton that was published in *Punch* in 1920. This depicted fashionable London as a camp spectacle, complete with policeman pirouetting, and ladies and gentlemen greeting one another in front of the statue of the nude, heavily muscled Achilles that stood in the city's Hyde Park.[63]

Lynn Garafola has argued that, with the foundation of the Ballets Russes by Sergei Diaghilev, dance "became a privileged arena for homosexuals as performers, choreographers and spectators. It was a feat unparalleled in the other arts, and for gay men (to use a modern term) it was a revolution."[64] Dancers such as Vaslav Nijinsky presented the young male body as aesthetically, and indeed erotically, desirable. Queer members of London's intellectual Bloomsbury Group such as John Maynard Keynes and Lytton Strachey duly took an interest.[65] Tirza

True Latimer has contended that "neither the legibility of gay-specific innuendo in the productions nor the visibility of a cohesive base of support in the emerging gay community guaranteed historical notice of early modern ballet's significance as both a product and a producer of gay culture."[66] I will go on to argue that the same could be said to varying degrees of a range of art forms in the early twentieth century.

Communities of queer men, therefore, began to use the word "gay" as code to refer to styles and locales appealing to certain sorts of homosexuals. In the course of the 1920s, these subcultural forms began to influence the modish mainstream in ways that ranged from the tacit embrace of homoerotic performance at the ballet to a fashion for "slumming" in bars that put on drag shows. There was an aspect of modernism—it has been referred to as queer modernism—that found inspiration in the sexual lives and practices of bohemian subcultures. Literature, particularly that produced by the circle of the poet W. H. Auden during and after the 1930s, has long been acknowledged as an important locale of queer modernist expression. However, I shall be focusing on various forms of performance and display that crossed between popular and elite youth cultures. These spread during the 1920s not because they were widely read as expressing same-sex desire but because they were understood to evoke individuality, personality, and eccentricity. This was the world of Auden as a student in Oxford between 1925 and 1928, when he was known for writing only by electric light, carrying a loaded pistol, and wearing bizarre hats.[67] This book is, therefore, not about fashion in its narrower sense of costume but in its wider sense of self-fashioning.

Britain, unlike many other European states, survived the First World War with its governing and social structures intact, but traditional values were often held up to scrutiny by the younger generation. Laura Doan has drawn attention to what she terms the "cultural topsy-turvydom" of the postwar years, which extended to an "utter confusion about gender."[68] A long history of misogynistic prejudice against alleged male effeminacy had created an association between androgynous styles and same-sex desire.[69] The new uncertainty about gender roles provided an opportunity for creative play that hinted at unorthodox sexual interests. The cultural forms of the *fin de siècle* provide the backdrop to the queer modernism of the 1920s because that latter era saw a turn away from the earnest and dutiful self-sacrifice of the generation that had fought the First World War. While some wished to see the rebuilding of the fraying patriarchal structures of Europe through modern science and pseudosciences such as eugenics, others looked to their radical and playful deconstruction in the pursuit of new forms of pleasure and opportunity.[70]

Important elite sources for the spread of notions of gender and sexual nonconformity included the German literature of sexology and the French literature of decadence. Aspects of such literatures were brought to wide public attention, if sometimes in confused and jumbled forms, in the reportage of celebrity trials such as those of Oscar Wilde in Britain in 1895 and the series of courts-martial and civil cases that enshrouded members of Kaiser Wilhelm II's cabinet and entourage in scandal from 1907 to 1909.[71] There have been those who have wanted "the literatures of decadence safely quarantined in the 1890s."[72] However, decadence is now understood to have also played an important, if paradoxical, role as a "critically antimodern tendency within modernity" in which the aristocratic styles of the past were reinvented as models for individual taste and discrimination.[73] What Christopher Reed has called the "echoes of aestheticism" hung about such works as T. S. Eliot's "The Love Song of St. Sebastian" (1914), which has been interpreted as an elegy for a deceased male lover. Its author's taste for wearing green face powder (as reported by Osbert Sitwell) likewise seems somewhat decadent.[74] Furthermore, it was not simply that certain writers and aesthetes reanimated the aesthetic of the 1890s in 1920s Britain but also that they "transmitted this enthusiasm for the Yellow Nineties across the Atlantic."[75]

The source material for this current book is not, in the main, literature and art, but is composed of items of popular culture such as fashionable magazines. Publications such as *Sketch* and British *Vogue* provided venues for the discussion and depiction of female beauty, but they also glamorized the landed elite. Photographers working for such publications aspired to the status of artists in a way that was quite different from their counterparts in popular newspapers, whose task was to create a documentary record.[76] High society in the interwar period was, in reality, composed of a mixture of people from old and new money who competed for media attention. Individuals sought to stand out through distinction of birth or beauty or through personal idiosyncrasy. The operation of democratic politics meant that even royalty was not immune to the pressures of public opinion and sought to manage how it was depicted in the press.[77] For a brief period in the 1920s, the youthful elite could publicly flirt with transgressions of class and gender, even to the extent of imitating aspects of groups as marginalized as performing freaks. But as social deference progressively declined, what had once been flaunted as aristocratic foibles started to be perceived as evidence of sexual deviance.

Criminalized desires could, therefore, be hinted at more or less subtly through visual and material media. The reason why these cultural forms are such a rich source of evidence has been explained by the art historian Michael Camille in his

introduction to a set of essays on queer collecting practices: "it is not just that the
unmentionable nature of same-sex desire has often meant that the subject had to
communicate the 'secret' in a coded language, but the fact that this language was
a system of objects. What could not be said could be spoken through things."[78]
I shall be focusing on the social lives and roles of creative people and the ways
in which they and their works were viewed. This involves looking at alternative
or critical responses to the development of modernism that may suggest either
anti-modernism or queer forms of modernism that embraced the strange and
the abject.

The book follows on from my earlier study *Oscar Wilde Prefigured: Queer
Fashioning and British Caricature, 1750–1900* (2016), albeit with the inclusion of
a wider range of source material. Cartoons in magazines do, however, continue
to provide valuable evidence not simply for the mockery of queerness but for its
construction. Contributors to the leading humorous magazine *Punch* regularly
projected the worlds of modern art and contemporary fashion as queer and
freakish. An example of this was George Stampa's cartoon of 1930 that was
captioned as follows: "*Advanced Artist (to Model).* 'This Is Great. You're Just the
Type I've Been Looking for for Years'" (Figure 1.2).[79] The joke is that the model

Advanced Artist (to Model). "THIS IS GREAT. YOU'RE JUST THE TYPE I'VE BEEN LOOKING FOR FOR YEARS."

Figure 1.2 George Stampa, "*Advanced Artist (to Model).* 'This Is Great. You're Just
the Type I've Been Looking for for Years,'" *Punch* 178 (1930), 144. Reproduced by
permission of Punch Cartoon Library/TopFoto.

is beautiful but she is being painted to look grotesque. Innuendo concerning transgressive behavior became more obvious as public knowledge grew about the (homo)sexual lives of a range of leading writers and artists. Such innuendo lurks in another cartoon caption:

"Well, what do you think of my new flat, Uncle John?"
"H'm, too much futurist bric-à-brac about."
"But I must put something on the walls."
"Ah, I was speaking of what you put on the carpet" (Figure 1.3).[80]

Lewis Baumer's satirical comparison between modern art and the masculine-dressed woman needs to be seen in light of the recent banning of Radclyffe Hall's lesbian novel *The Well of Loneliness* (1928) and newspaper publicity concerning its author's personal appearance. On occasion the connection between fashionable modernism and transgressive sexual desire was made explicit. Vanessa Bell, in the course of a letter written to the bisexual artist Duncan Grant in 1914, commented, "I believe distortion is like sodomy. People are simply blindly prejudiced against it because they think it is abnormal."[81]

Figure 1.3 Lewis Baumer, "'Well, What Do You Think of My New Flat, Uncle John?'" *Punch* 178 (1930), 216. Reproduced by permission of Punch Cartoon Library/ TopFoto.

It is important to point out that trends in modern art in Britain had long been associated with freakish practices of bodily deformation, as in the allegedly wasted androgynes appearing in works of Pre-Raphaelite medievalism. Parody of aestheticism in the 1870s and 1880s was similarly replete with intimations of gender transgression (assertive women/weak men) that were freighted with implicit concern about sexual roles.[82] In the nineteenth century, painting and painters of the modern variety had sometimes been associated with sexual scandal, but this had typically been focused on the fear that men would take advantage of their female models. However, explicit connections between same-sex crime and art in Britain surfaced with the arrest and disgrace of the Pre-Raphaelite painter Simeon Solomon in 1873. He seems to have embraced a marginalized life, for example, accompanying cross-dressed young men to the theater.[83]

Solomon was also notable for the series of works that he produced that featured androgynous images of priests and acolytes. Both artists and preachers were precursors of modern homosexual men in terms of mockery and stereotype. It was not only in the thought of Oscar Wilde, such as his notion that Christ was a type of artist in the ancient world, that these two categories can be seen to have overlapped.[84] The original basis for *Patience*, Gilbert and Sullivan's 1881 satire on the aestheticism that Wilde would be dispatched to publicize in the United States, was the competition between two excessively mild prelates.[85] Protestant critique of Roman and Anglo-Catholics focused on the supposed effeminacy of their religious and personal performances in ways that sometimes implied homosexual transgression. As will be seen, there was some truth to these assumptions since many figures associated with the decadence of the nineties were, or became, Catholic, and some even entered the priesthood. One such was John Gray (Wilde's former lover), who maintained a lifelong celibate relationship with the writer and homosexual apologist André Raffalovich. The interiors of the priest house that Gray inhabited in Edinburgh, where he kept copies of decadent literature with their spines turned to the wall, can be read as spaces of the ecclesiastical closet.[86]

Another figure that was alleged to combine glamor and gender transgression was that of the poet. What has been referred to as "Byronism" made its appearance in the nineteenth century.[87] This term refers to the practice by certain dandified social climbers of posing as sexually ambivalent poets. It was a way of capitalizing on the fame of Lord Byron. Bad poets, dubious priests, and posing connoisseurs were combined in the parody of the aesthetic movement of the 1870s and 1880s by such cartoonists as George du Maurier. Suspicions of the general moral unhealthiness of earlier Pre-Raphaelite art, poetic mawkishness, and Catholic devotion ripened into increasingly blatant innuendo concerning sodomy. It has been argued that by the eve of the Wilde trials of 1895, the work of du Maurier in particular was so influential that "the sexual deviancy that he had helped to attach to this community had, for many, become a fact rather than a slur."[88] By the interwar period, the queer subcultures of major cities such as New York, London, and Paris were being employed by a number of artists as sources of creative inspiration. Prime among these was Marcel Duchamp who, as Rrose Sélavy, cross-dressed as a form of performance art and who elevated a urinal—evocative of public toilets as locales of queer sexual desire—to the status of art in *Fountain* (1917).[89]

A major role in the development of freak chic was played by photography. Even though the camera was widely regarded as an inferior form of creative self-expression, it exerted a steady and intensifying influence on the development of visual perception during the nineteenth century and was one of the key factors shaping the development of modern art.[90] Photography embraced the freakish and the abject in a number of ways, the most obvious of which was the widespread practice of taking pictures of exhibited members of freak shows. These shots sometimes domesticated the freak in ways that troubled the gendered boundaries of everyday life. One example by the American photographer Charles Eisenmann showed the bearded lady Madame Devere with her husband who, it was immediately apparent, was an ordinary-looking man.[91] Other photographers explored freakishness through the use of the photographic medium itself, as when the British-born Canadian Hannah Maynard made use of multiple exposures and mirroring effects, with results that were dismissed by others as "freak photography."[92]

Mia Fineman in *Faking It: Manipulated Photography before Photoshop* (2012) puts such developments in a wider perspective by arguing that image manipulation was intrinsic to the history of photography as a medium from the time of its origins in the 1840s. The use of multiple exposures when still in the camera or through combination of images during the printing process was widely employed, as were photomontage, overpainting, and retouching of the negative or the print. These techniques were important for interwar photographers who were interested in queering appearances, such as Cecil Beaton. The perverse possibilities of such "touching up" were parodied by the *Punch* cartoonist David Louis Ghilchik. He depicted the young persons of "Joie de Vivre on the Beach at Brightsea" unconvincingly transformed into the men of "Rugger [rugby] is Now in Full Swing" (1927) (Figure 1.4).[93] Fineman argues that there was a waxing

Figure 1.4 David Louis Ghilchik, "This Charming Photograph, Which Was to Have Been Called 'Joie de Vivre on the Beach at Brightsea,'" *Punch* 173 (1927), 431. Reproduced by permission of Punch Cartoon Library/TopFoto.

and waning of belief in photography as an ideal medium with which to capture the "true" appearance of things or, conversely, as a strikingly artificial form with astonishing potential for the creation of intriguing effects. She places twin high points of belief in photographic realism at the middle of the nineteenth and of the twentieth centuries. Those who, like Cecil Beaton, were keen advocates of the manipulated image in the interwar period were therefore looking back to the late nineteenth century, which was notable for its enthusiasm for "freak" or "trick" images.[94] These, Fineman explains, "work in much the same way as magic tricks; they generate a pleasurable incongruity between what we see and what we know; they elicit wonder and surprise, along with skepticism and curiosity about the artistry behind the illusions."[95] By looking back to such methods, interwar photographers including Beaton were rebelling against a call for what had been hailed in 1904 as "straight photography."[96]

The designer and art director Mehemed Agha looked back on these developments in a *Vogue* article of 1937 in which he commented that there was a craze after the First World War in which people "wanted to photograph strange, weird, grotesque things."[97] This remained a dissident strand in relation to modernist aesthetics, as is clear from the comments made in 1928 by Theodore Dreiser concerning the Russian artist and photographer Alexander Rodchenko. It was alleged that the latter "specializes in freak photography only. All his photographs were at queer angles. I cannot imagine the positions he and his camera must have taken to secure them."[98] Beaton wrote about his freak photography early in his career. This situates his work in relation to a battle that was taking place over the direction of modernism between seriousness and playfulness.

Freak styles of photographic representation could be applied to individuals who dressed themselves in outré attire.[99] Some aspects of high-society freaking, such as cross-dressing, played directly with gender ambiguity in ways that were related to subcultural traditions of sexual parody and "drag." The term "to freak" was used initially to refer to fashion because it could mean to act humorously or on a whim. The presence of such a taste for visual and material excesses would appear to have run counter to the stripped-down aesthetics of functional modernism. Jane Stevenson, building on the work of Stephen Calloway, has referred to this "alternative style" as a form of "baroque" and recognized that it was "to a significant extent a queer style."[100] Yet it is important to recognize that heterosexual women played a significant role as customers and patrons. Much of the glamorous iconography of the interwar period was composed of exoticized images of women created by queer men. I shall be discussing this process in terms of "diva worship," which was sometimes inspired by images of the Madonna and in which the cult of celebrity can be seen as a form of what has been referred to as "weak religion."[101] The resulting imagery spoke a language of "nonverbal rhetoric" that had considerable queer potential.[102] Queer men bonded through camp appreciation of feminized cultures of consumption and through their shared identification with the diva as a figure desired by men.[103]

Self-Expression

The model of inversion was very prominent in Britain in the late nineteenth and early twentieth centuries. It implied that homosexual men were mentally female and that they thought of themselves essentially as women. This is, in fact, much closer to later notions of transsexuality than it is to homosexuality. Work has been carried out by Katie Sutton into trans identities in Weimar Germany and the contemporary use of terms corresponding to transvestism.[104] She makes the important point that systems of categorization were not precise and that we should reflect on how contemporary understandings map onto the diversity of past human experience.[105] Another approach is to identify "transgender-like" phenomena in the past.[106] This can facilitate affective connections across time.[107] However, not all British queer fashioners who were men performed femininity; only some of them cross-dressed, and only some of those who did were doing so out of motivations that might enable them to self-identify as (to use more recent terms) transsexual or transgender.[108] Indeed, parodic aspects of drag, which Beaton adopted on many occasions, rely on a clear awareness of *not* being female. However, it is important to recognize that some individuals may have in effect been trans before that category became known as an identity. This is indeed what Quentin Crisp claimed late in life. He became famous for describing his early years as a makeup-wearing queen in interwar London in his book *The Naked Civil Servant* (1968). He wrote, just before his death in 1999, that his look had not been drag. This, he said, he had only worn once. Moreover, he continued, "at the age of ninety it has finally been explained to me that I am not really homosexual, I am transgender. I have accepted that."[109] Some caution does need to be exercised when using this source as printed since it was compiled by the editors from a variety of previously unpublished materials.[110] Earlier in life, however, Crisp believed that his nonconformity was sexual, and that was the case with the majority of the individuals whom I have been studying.

There is evidence that queer men were able to imagine themselves in the relatively disempowered position of women under patriarchy and could relate sympathetically to women. However, fascination with female beauty, I shall argue, is best understood as an aspect of aestheticism in which men exercised their queerness through what was then held to be an "effeminate" fascination with fabrics, frocks, and flowers.[111] The resulting acts of queer fashioning need not have been related to conscious efforts to assert a precise identity taken from a sexological tool kit.[112] The primary aims of the queer creativity that I shall be discussing were to create opportunities for social and economic improvement, such as what Cecil Beaton talked of as his "uprise."[113] Meeting those of like mind on the way was, of course, very much a bonus, but the establishment of some sort of "gay identity" in the 1970s sense was neither their aim nor their expectation. These were largely closet arts that aimed to draw attention to oneself first and foremost in ways that were "gay" in the sense of amusing and "queer" in the sense of strange, and only implicitly "gay/queer" in the sense of homosexual. The result was the production of homosexuality as a more or less open secret.

Sexual nonconformity required the development of care in the presentation of the self. Same-sex desire needed to be signaled in order to meet like-minded friends and partners, but such signaling needed to be coded in order to avoid undue public exposure. Queer dandyism, therefore, involved skill in finding a balance between confession and invisibility, of knowing when to make the grand gesture and when to be subtle. Such dilemmas are apparent in Jack Yeats's cartoon from 1914 "Hints to Artists and Writers Who Need to Advertise Themselves by Some Eccentricity of Costume" (Figure 1.5).[114] The joke here is that full-on freak dress (leopard-skin and lady's parasol) would not attract attention, while a tiny adjustment in a gentleman's coat would. The knowledge of precisely how to avoid and how to gain attention was immensely valuable not only for those living lives

Figure 1.5 Jack Butler Yeats ["W. Bird"], "Hints to Artists and Writers Who Need to Advertise Themselves by Some Eccentricity of Costume," *Punch* 146 (1914), 295. Reproduced by permission of Punch Cartoon Library/TopFoto.

in the homosexual closet but also in the wider milieus of social competition that characterized fashionable society.

In an age when rank was decaying into celebrity, the challenge in high society was how to stand out as an individual. In 1922 *Vogue* gave its view in an article on "Public Opinion and Personal Liberty" that "the bourgeois' ambition is to be exactly like everybody else, but the aristocrat holds up the standard of eccentricity in the face of popular prejudice."[115] Tramps and artists, the piece continued, are the two other groups that are able to stand out from the crowd. Thus, it was to the depths and heights of society—to the gutter and the stars, as it were—that one must look for innovation. Interwar queer cultures were indeed well placed to contribute to the development of innovative forms of alternative styling because they encompassed two phenomena that troubled class boundaries: the eccentric aristocrat and the working-class queen.[116] Yet the men involved in this process via their work as photographers and fashion and interior designers were themselves often from suburban middle-class backgrounds, as indeed was Quentin Crisp.

Eccentricity occupies a peculiar place in British—though in this case it is probably more appropriate to say English—culture. In Georgian Britain, eccentricity could be associated with extremes such as genius, madness, and monstrosity.[117] Both fear of and fascination with eccentricity, notably as an inheritable quality, flourished during the nineteenth century.[118] The mental eccentric was a close cousin of the physical freak, and in both cases such characteristics might involve a propensity for queer transgressions of gender and sexuality. Jack Halberstam's *In a Queer Time and Place: Transgender Bodies, Subcultural Lives* (2005) begins with an evocation of "wilfully eccentric modes of being."[119] In congruence with this concept, John Timbs's *English Eccentrics and Eccentricities* (1866) introduced, under the category "Wealth and Fashion," William Beckford (perhaps the most famous sodomite of his times), George "Beau" Brummell (the most famous dandy—who was, I think significantly, unmarried), and Hannah Snell "the Female Soldier."[120] The "Ladies of Llangollen" (in other words, Eleanor Butler and Sarah Ponsonby, who formed a possibly chaste same-sex relationship) appeared under the heading of "Delusions, Impostures, and Fanatic Missions." While the category of "Strange Sights and Sporting Scenes" included the more conventional freak-show fare of midgets, giants, and those who were extraordinarily fat.[121] Timbs may have been sensationalistic but he was not condemnatory, and he contended that "with oddness of character may yet co-exist much goodness of heart; and your strange fellow, though, according to the lexicographer, he be outlandish, odd, queer, and eccentric, may possess claims to our notice which the man who is ever studying the fitness of things would not so readily present."[122] This, in fact, is similar to the rationale behind queer modernism: that the peculiar is worthy of notice, or may even be so worthy of emulation as to represent the future of modernity itself.

British promotors of eccentricity played at various times on a sense that the liberties of the island realm validated singular behavior and that those freedoms were threatened by totalitarian variants of modernism emanating from the Continent.[123] It was in this spirit that Clive Bell argued in *On British Freedom* (1923) for London as a "great civilized capital ... full of queer contrasts and odd professions, anomalies and eccentricities."[124] This call to British traditions of particularity and peculiarity reinforced notions of cultural continuity between the past and present. Edith Sitwell in *The English Eccentrics* (1933) linked the queer present to the past. She juxtaposed a cover illustration drawn by the queer surrealist Pavel Tchelitchew with a frontispiece quotation by the originator of eighteenth-century gothic literature, Horace Walpole, who was another significantly unmarried man.[125] The term "eccentric" was also sometimes used to refer more directly to lesbians and gay men.[126] When the Caravan Club in London's West End was raided by the police in 1934, they arrested a variety of individuals, including many men wearing makeup. Jack Neave, who was one of the organizers of the Club, stated that the people who went there were "eccentric."[127]

The cult of eccentricity was inegalitarian in that it was based upon disdain for commonplace opinions and everyday practices, but it was meritocratic to a degree in that it honored those of slender means so long as they had audacious ideas.[128] It drew inspiration from prewar figures such as Wilde but flourished as part of the interwar social phenomenon of the "bright young things." These people have been characterized as a "coterie of top-drawer blue bloods and down-at-heel bohemians" and have sometimes been derided as party people who did little more than dress in outrageous costumes and scandalize their elders and betters.[129] But I argue that there is more to the phenomenon than that. The bright young things were notable not simply for their high-society antics but also for being involved in the fashion for slumming, which had developed through the later nineteenth century before reaching a peak in cities such as London and New York in the early 1930s. Fashionable visitors to "low" bars that featured musicians of color and cross-dressed artistes could be regarded as patronizing tourists from another world. But some members of this milieu, which included Cecil Beaton, went a step further in that they gained aesthetic inspiration from the experience.

The queer potential of slumming had been clear back in the Victorian period, when young priests from respectable families had sought positions in the urban slums where they could work with young men. An account of such slumming asserts that the "leaders of the men's settlement movement were acutely aware of the paramount importance of policing the uncertain boundaries separating male friendship-love [*sic*] from homosexuality."[130] Some visitors who noted the homosexual practices of certain slum dwellers pointed to them as evidence for the need for reform (as was the case with George Orwell's *Down and Out in Paris and London* of 1933).[131] Slumming literature from both sides of the Atlantic shows a wide variety of positions between visceral horror and erotic fascination. Thus, to take just one example, the novel *Nigger Heaven* (1926) by the bisexual American writer and photographer Carl Van Vechten can be seen as a voyeuristic outsider text. Yet he was self-aware concerning the ethical problems inherent in slumming and tried in his book to stress the value of (homo)eroticized negro culture on its own terms.[132]

The bright young things not only dressed up but also dressed down and sometimes cross-dressed.[133] Clothes mattered to their generation as crucial accessories in the production of sexualized self-identities.[134] So where once American *Vogue* had talked in 1907 of "freak styles" as being those dreamed up by designers that were too extreme ever to be adopted as fashions, the bright young things started to employ the term "freak" in Britain to mean modern and chic.[135] By the end of the twenties, the queer writer and critic Robert Byron was authoring pieces in the same magazine—illustrated by Cecil Beaton—that related, albeit with tongue in cheek, how "freak parties" were conquering London society.[136] These events were the extreme expressions of what has been termed an "epidemic of fancy dress" during the interwar years.[137] The craze for extravagant eccentricity in fashion did not long outlast the decade. As homosexuality came increasingly to be identified as an attribute of freaking so the latter fell out of fashion. Freak, no longer chic, was pushed back into the developing gay subculture while, at the same time, the cultural world of the homosexual became associated with a seemingly bizarre blend of gay cheerfulness and queer monstrosity. This did not mean, of course, that gay men ceased to busy themselves with fashion, flowers, and interior decor after the Second World War; but, when they did so, they were increasingly positioned as the passé exponents of cultural cliché rather than the bearers of radical new ideas. Imagining oneself "anew in the vicinity of specific furnishings" became the epitome of naïf as the sixties turned into the seventies and "gay" forever ceased to mean cheerfully acquiescent and turned into an angry challenge to older forms of self-identification.[138]

After Oscar

Two men have a sustained presence through the various sections of this book. The first is Oscar Wilde and the second is Cecil Beaton. I refer to both of them as queer rather than bisexual because their predominant sexual drives were toward members of their own sex. Beaton's greatest long-term passion was for the art patron Peter Watson, who would only allow his admirer to sleep with him platonically. In February 1930, Beaton wrote that he longed to escape from effeminate homosexuality: "I have always hated fairies collectively … I am sure I shall turn mean about fairies because they frighten and nauseate me and I see so vividly myself shadowed in so many of them and it only needs a little grip and dash to get oneself out of that sad and ridiculous predicament."[139] He did have some sexual affairs with women, notably with the notoriously promiscuous Doris Delvinge, Countess Castlerosse, who was very much up for sex with all manner of unlikely men.[140] Hearing of her affair with Beaton, her husband commented, "I never knew Doris was a lesbian"![141] Such gambits seem to have been embarked upon primarily in reaction to Beaton's deep feelings of sexual shame.[142] His greatest—and probably unconsummated—attempt at a romantic liaison with a woman was with that epitome of the unobtainable diva, Greta Garbo.[143] On April 21, 1935, *The Sunday Dispatch* reported, "**Garbo wants to be a man. Her whole life is lived by masculine standards.** On her dressing table there is [*sic*] none of the usual feminine appliances such as scent, powder, bottles—just a battered comb and two men's hairbrushes … Greta Garbo's one ambition—she wants to play a man's rôle on stage."[144] It would have been quite a marriage.

Because this book is focused on the twentieth century, Wilde appears as a spirit of aestheticism and decadence past. Before the First World War, his ambiguous legacy contributed to the construction of the closet, but after 1918 some, if not all, aspects of his visual deviance came to influence a new generation with a taste for decadence. In the process, the Victorian period was rethought as a space for queer inspiration. This played an important role in challenging what could be categorized in retrospect as heteronormative currents in modernism. Beaton was a central figure in this project of queering the era before 1914, and he did so in ways that built on the cultural legacy of the older man. Other studies have explored the afterlife of Wilde's literary works and of his reputation in intellectual circles.[145] This book does something different. It aims to move the debate forward from an earlier focus on Wilde's trials of 1895 as the defining event when, as expressed by Alan Sinfield in his study *The Wilde*

Century: Effeminacy, Oscar Wilde and the Queer Moment (1994), the modern homosexual persona can be seen to have been in formation. In *Oscar Wilde Prefigured* (2016), I explored earlier images of men that informed the public reception of Wilde as a homosexual. *Freak to Chic* will now look at the ongoing development of that tradition. This story is less about the authentic "truth" of Wilde's life and his importance in the formation of sexual identity than it is about the way in which he was reinvented and the degree to which he was central to the origins of gay culture.

To sit in a movie theater and to turn off our mobile phones as the house lights dim is to be transported back to the world of twentieth-century media. The glamor of that age was bound up with the power of still and motion photography. This can still fascinate us with its visual force, despite the homophobia that abounded in the culture that produced it. That problematic attitudes persist was made clear to me when I attended a screening of Clint Eastwood's film *J. Edgar* (2011). The homosexual kiss between Hoover, the first director of the FBI, and his deputy was greeted with laughter in parts of the audience. At the end of the film, I questioned the raucous people seated near me. They were offended that I even questioned their reaction. How could they be homophobic, they said, when they worked in fashion? I could only assume that they were familiar with glamorous gay men but found it hard to take same-sex affection seriously when those involved appeared aging and unattractive. The overweight figure of the middle-aged Wilde likewise presented a problem for queer men of the first decades of the twentieth century. His last years were emblematic of mental and bodily collapse. It was the young Wilde, he of the lily and the sunflower, who was regarded as eccentric, amusing, and inspiring. Even so, his later associations with sexual opportuning and bodily monstrosity haunted the bright young things with the dark implications of the freak show.

That gay men have, or had, a distinctive "culture" is a key argument of David Halperin's *How to Be Gay* (2012). The term as I employ it encompasses a range of cultural traditions—including the appreciation of the pose as gender pastiche—that become particularly associated with homosexual men. I want in this book to shed new light on the origins of that culture and to explain how marginal styles became, if briefly, central to sophisticated living. I also want to salute forms of self-expression that range queerly past both hetero- and homonormativity.[146] This book is also a call to look beyond the normative assumptions of our own day and to learn from queer history. Building notions of the sexual self through engagement with the past has been termed "retrosexuality."[147] This can be understood to operate as a reparative practice of engaging with the inevitable trauma of growing up and growing old in a society that privileges heterosexual experience. It can, perhaps, address the angst highlighted in Alan Downs's *The Velvet Rage* (2005) as being generated by the suspicion that one is an isolated freak rather than a representative of a parade of fabulousness.[148] Tony Kushner's epic AIDS play *Angels in America* (1991) found queer meaning in the execution of Ethel Rosenberg in 1953, and many lesbians and gay men during the Cold War took inspiration from the movies and songs of the 1930s. The interwar generation looked back to the Victorian era, and Oscar Wilde himself found inspiration in the Regency, when freakish dandies were often referred to as "monstrosities."[149]

From the point of view of mainstream modernist thinking, all this represents an obsession with outdated kitsch. But, as has been argued in a case study of the development of modern architecture in Britain, this stance has led to a bullying denigration of styles that playfully deviate from contemporary orthodoxies of taste.[150] I am not calling for a new queer style that makes new claims to superiority.[151] Rather, I think that a proliferation of queer expression is one way to further LGBT visibility without privileging a particular segment of those communities.[152] I agree with the call made by Victoria Pitts in her work on body politics for "the freak and 'queer among queers'" who will "express an ironic twist of already prescribed meanings, promote genders and sexualities that highlight heteronormative limits, and attempt to refute them through irony and flagrancy."[153] This book is both a history of same-sex-desiring men in and out of fashionable society and an exploration of the opportunities and limitations of their visual styles. Appreciating the complex, strange, and— yes—queer development of gay culture out of "gay" style helps us to see it as representing more than a simplistic set of calls for liberation or equality— vital though those demands were and are. There is radical potential in the remembrance of things past.

Freak Shows

One should always be a little improbable.

Wilde, "Phrases and Philosophies."[1]

The word "freak" is often used today, as it was a century ago, to indicate something strange and possibly monstrous. Individuals who belong to sexual minorities have frequently been depicted as strange and freakish. Such jibes followed Oscar Wilde through his career, from the time when he crossed the Atlantic to lecture on aestheticism in the early 1880s, and were to return with renewed force during his trials of 1895. However, in the Victorian period, the term was also used in a variety of more or less humorous ways. It did not need to refer to a person but could be employed in relation to any especially peculiar circumstance, as in the title of Sabine Baring Gould's study of extreme mysticism *Freaks of Fanaticism and Other Strange Events* (1891). A freak could also be used to refer to an eccentricity or a whimsy, as in James R. Bayard's three-volume novel *Lord Garlford's Freak* (1880). In this chapter, I shall be looking at the persons and lives of those who were displayed in freak shows. It will be seen that certain characteristic types of freaks, notably skeletal dandies, bearded ladies, and exaggeratedly muscled strongmen, have particular relevance to histories of gender transgression and queer performance. In subsequent chapters, I shall move the focus from bodies to clothing and look at the way in which androgynous styles and cross-dressing could be claimed to be passing fancies and thus freakish in a less alarming sense. Freak chic drew particularly on this latter tradition of amusing performativity while hostile critique insisted that what was being enacted was a modern(ist) version of the freak show.

Exhibited freaks were primarily those perceived to be strange-looking individuals, those whose appearance or attributes were such that people would pay to stare at them. The poet Wordsworth wrote, concerning the specimens on show at the summer Bartholomew Fair in London in 1802:

All out-o'-the-way, far-fetched, perverted things,
All freaks of nature, all Promethean thoughts
Of man; his dullness, madness, and their feats
All jumbled up together to make up
This Parliament of Monsters.[2]

He was speaking figuratively since, in English law, those who were merely deformed could not be formally categorized as monsters.[3] Those on show were in general legally responsible persons with whom an enterprising showman could sign a contract of employment. Interest in commercialized freak spectacle intensified in the course of the nineteenth century. In 1847 *Punch* duly satirized what it termed "Deformito-Mania."[4]

Freak shows became big business when in P. T. Barnum they found their transatlantic impresario. Barnum founded his "American Museum" in New York in 1841. Three years later, he made his appearance in Britain, bringing with him "Tom Thumb," who was a celebrity midget with his own drag persona, Mary Ann.[5] Barnum's fame increased as the century rolled on. His traveling wagons took his shows from town to town, not just in the United States but also across Europe. The spectacles on offer combined those of the circus, the variety theater, the sports arena, and the freak show. Deformed bodies could be viewed next door to magnificent specimens of manhood employed in displays of ancient Greek wrestling (although modesty demanded the use of loincloths). Striking variations of race, gender, and health were put on display.[6] Freak performers, therefore, only provided one element of the spectacles that Barnum promoted. While there were many other static and traveling shows that specialized in freak entertainment, other freaks made their living as part of an ensemble of performers that were billed to appear in circuses, music halls, and variety theaters.

That extremes of human embodiment were at the core of the fascination of the freak show can be seen from an undated early Victorian print—"Fairground Showman at a 'Freak Show' Booth"—in which a picture of an enormously obese woman is presented to the crowd to entice them inside.[7] It might at first appear obvious that people such as these were only "freaks" because of popular prejudice and that they should be seen as the suffering victims of commercial exploitation. Recent critique, without rejecting this concept entirely, has complicated the picture. The popularity of such shows ensured that human deviance was rendered into something valuable.[8] Some freaks became celebrities and were richer than many of the people who came to gawk at them.[9] The very monstrosity of the freaks relied for its thrill on the notion that they retained a degree of agency and could, potentially, take revenge on the "normal," as shown in Tod Browning's pioneering horror film *The Freaks* (1932).[10] Others were not truly deformed in any way but simply made a living as "freak impersonators."[11] Photographs were sometimes sold by the freaks themselves to earn extra money, and in such cases it has been argued that the "subjects actively and willingly participated in photo sessions."[12]

Freak shows did not create a clear definition of what a freak was, and as a result performers and audiences effectively engaged in the shared construction of the shifting boundaries of what was viewed as normality.[13] It can be argued that the freak show played an instrumental role in the very creation of the category of the "normal" since the role of the freak was to act as an "other" for the members of the audience.[14] Those who viewed such displays lost awareness of the differences between themselves and their fellow attendees when face to face with exemplary cases of difference. Such exhibited prodigies as the "feejee mermaid" (the taxidermied top half of a juvenile monkey sewn onto the bottom end of a fish) have been reinterpreted as a species of "queer art illusion" in which "the precise distinction between the representation and object remained largely unresolved and actively debated among viewers."[15] A recent study has even claimed to "investigate freakery not solely as the victimization of a disenfranchised minority but rather as a highly specialized and potentially liberating form of performance art."[16]

The legality of these shows lent otherwise suspect spectacles and practices a degree of legitimacy. In nineteenth-century San Francisco, laws were passed against cross-dressing in the streets. This legal prohibition was launched as part of an attempt to restrict situations in which there was an overlap between female prostitution and its imitation by men. And yet, in at least one instance, this policy had the unintended result of validating the presence of gender deviance in the freak show. This was the case with Milton Mason, a "female bodies man," who was arrested cross-dressed. On his release, he was offered a contract to sit in a freak show in his frock.[17] Barnum was eager to stress, however implausibly, that his productions were instructional and morally improving. In keeping with this, he preferred to use the term "prodigies" rather than "freaks." Such spectacle was, however, widely condemned precisely because it did not clearly impart moral lessons of right and wrong. As *The Times* pointed out, "visitors resort to it to be impressed, without mental friction … If anyone insists on extracting a purpose from the bearded woman and the legless vaulter, Mr. Barnum is not to be accounted responsible."[18]

Talk of "abnormality" emerged through the interwar years in publications such as Stanley Roger's *Freak Ships* (1936), in which freaks are identified as "abnormal productions."[19] The concept of the "normal" has its own fascinating history. The term was used in medical discourse before the twentieth century to refer to bodily functioning and anatomical regularity. It was employed by late-nineteenth-century sexologists such as Richard von Krafft-Ebing to refer to sexual relations in which the man was active and the woman passive. It has been argued that in his work "abnormal sexualities varied in degree but not in kind from their normal manifestations. The normal and abnormal were not squarely opposed to one another but overlapping regions situated within a dynamic field of possibilities."[20] It is concluded, with reference to the ideas of Freud, that "becoming normal was a difficult business at the start of the twentieth century. It required a great deal of work and attention, and it could never be ultimately or definitely achieved. No one could be perfectly or consistently normal. Everyone was somewhat perverse."[21] This may help to explain why audience responses were sometimes highly sympathetic toward freaks. An example of this was provided by the theater critic of the *Daily Mirror* in response to Arthur Wing Pinero's play *The Freaks: An Idyll of Suburbia* (1918). This play focused on the reactions of members of a local community to the visit of five circus freaks to a suburban home. "Who were the *real* freaks?" asked the journalist. "Were they those physically abnormal people or were they, on the other hand, the mentally and morally abnormal people who affected to patronise them?"[22] The legalized objectification of freaks seems to have spurred, at least in some quarters, a desire to empathize with them as subjects. The parade of people, objects, and images that made up the freak show therefore stimulated a remarkably wide range of responses, both positive and negative.

No training was needed to spot gender and sexual unorthodoxy in the freak-show lineup, since that had always been a major element of the entertainment that it offered. The exhibition of intersex individuals as "hermaphrodites" problematized gender boundaries.[23] Those who mingled physical attributes of both sexes might become the object not so much of horror as of erotic desire, as Wilkie Collins indicated in his novel *The Law and the Lady* (1875). This featured Miserrimus Dexter, who was born with no legs. Nevertheless, that deformity notwithstanding, he was

> an unusually handsome and unusually well-made man. His long silky hair, of a bright and beautiful chestnut colour, fell over shoulders that were the perfection of strength and grace. His face was bright with vivacity and intelligence. His large clear blue eyes and his long delicate white hands were like the eyes and hands of a beautiful woman. He would have looked effeminate but for the manly

proportions of his throat and chest, aided in their effect by his flowing beard and long moustache.[24]

This description of Dexter's body explicitly mingles elements of attraction and repulsion.[25] Not only the erotic potential but also the private lives of freaks were frequently a matter for public fascination since marriages between freaks were not uncommon.[26] Particularly lurid speculation hovered over the possible private lives of Siamese twins or over possible relationships between people of very different physiques. There was ample potential for queer (in all senses of the word) speculation concerning the partnership of men such as George Auger ("the Cardiff Giant" who was 8 feet 6 inches tall) and Tom Sodrie (who was 2 feet 5 inches tall).[27] One photograph of the pair, taken when they worked for Barnum and Bailey, showed the latter as if popping out of the former's rear (Figure 2.1). Fictional accounts of strange alliances circulated, such as one telling of the romance between a male giant and a bearded lady.[28]

In 1903 George Ives, a pioneering British advocate for penal and homosexual law reform, pasted into his latest scrapbook a photograph of a recently deceased woman who had made her living as a Barnum bearded lady. He positioned this image just above a newspaper report of a homosexual court case.[29] Such apparently bizarre juxtaposition of material led the editor of a set of excerpts from these scrapbooks to refer to Ives as an "Edwardian eccentric" (though he was born in 1867 and died in 1950).[30] A photograph of a pair of Siamese twins was employed as the centerpiece of the cover illustration of this edition. The original scrapbooks were not randomly assembled but were bricolages that aimed to preserve the traces of evidence for queer lives. Issues of gender transgression such as women with beards were seen by Ives as relevant to his attempt to record the evidence for variations in sexual behavior.

The bearded lady was a well-known sub-type of freak. Her role was to perform genteel femininity—but with a beard.[31] As Arthur Goddard commented in his article "'Even as You and I': At Home with the Barnum Freaks" (1898), "a bearded lady might well be expected to differ from the rest of her sex in more than this respect; and it is therefore pleasant to find Anne Jones, the 'Bearded Woman,' finishing a lesson on the mandoline [*sic*]."[32] It hardly needs emphasizing that the potential for gender confusion in the case of bearded ladies was considerable. Were they, the spectator might ask, real women with fake beards? Or might they have real beards and in fact be men? The latter situation appeared in a newspaper story of 1883, when it was reported that "after a hand-to-mouth existence, the celebrated character known as the 'Bearded Lady' has met with a mysterious

Figure 2.1 *George Auger and Tom Sodrie, c.*1916. Reproduced courtesy of Science History Images/Alamy Stock Photo (HRKNYB).

death in Sheffield. The deceased was not a woman, but a man, named Ratcliff, and for years dressed as a woman, had appeared at fairs under the above title."[33]

Another freak-show figure was the man–woman (Figure 7.3). One such was Henry Caro, who had been born in France in 1899 but was exhibited in

America as Albert–Alberta.[34] Audiences were led to believe that such he–she beings were hermaphrodites whom nature had disgraced with attributes of the two sexes on the left and right sides of their bodies, respectively. Some of these performers were intersex, but Caro was what might be termed a demi-female impersonator. Hair was shaved from one side of his body, and he wore a single fake breast. Unlike the bearded ladies, he claimed that his supposed physiological peculiarity prohibited him from marriage with either a man or a woman. He inhabited his character both on- and offstage and was buried in full makeup and costume in 1963.

Freaks were sometimes regarded with condescension as inferior beings who, like children or non-whites, were often treated as sources of amusement. Thus, in 1880, *The Times* reported in connection with a display of "pygmies" in London's West End that it was once a "freak of fashion" for great households to keep a midget as a servant.[35] A similar mode of class-based condescension was deployed in 1889, when Barnum showed a troupe of his freaks in London. It was said in the humorous periodical *Funny Folks* that:

> Barnum's curiosities have their Sundays to themselves, and are going to take advantage of the holidays to see London. The Fat Lady and Boy, the Legless Man, the Tatooed Nobleman, the Skeleton Dude, the Bearded Lady, the Circassian Beauties, the Armless Man, "Krao," the Midgets, and the Giant Cowboys may be expected at Church Parade in the Park on Sunday next (Figure 2.2).[36]

This caption and its associated cartoon "Oh, Limp Here!" mock the visitors with the thought that they might think themselves equal to mingling with fashionable society. The title of the cartoon alludes to the Olympia exhibition hall in London, which first opened to the public in 1886 and which was to become a frequent target for conservative attacks on the alleged vulgarity of modern commerce.

In 1833–4 Thomas Carlyle published *Sartor Resartus*, which was to become a highly influential attack on male dandyism. In this he explicitly condemned the failure of men of his own time to see dandies as freaks: "May we not well cry shame on an ungrateful world ... which will waste its optic facility on dried Crocodiles, and Siamese twins; and over the domestic wonderful wonder, a live Dandy, glance with hasty indifference, and a scarcely concealed contempt."[37] Things had moved on by the later decades of the century. At the center of the *Funny Folks* cartoon stand a "bearded lady" and a "skeleton dude." A dude was the American equivalent of the dandy and in his homeland was regarded as somewhat English in manner.[38] This dude was a specific individual, namely J. W. Coffey, who had been born in 1852 and was known for his monocle

Figure 2.2 Detail, "Oh, Limp Here!" *Funny Folks* 15, no. 782, November 16, 1889, 364–5. Reproduced courtesy of the British Library (MFM.M77825 [1889]).

and cane (Figure 2.3).[39] In *Oscar Wilde Prefigured* (2016), I suggested a queer reading of a cartoon by W. K. Haselden that was published in the *Daily Mirror* in 1906.[40] This showed a stick-thin dandy being kicked out of a window by John Bull as the embodiment of British manliness. In the aftermath of the

MR. J. W. COFFEY, THE SKELETON DUDE.

Figure 2.3 *Mr. J. W. Coffey, the Skeleton Dude*, in Arthur Goddard, "'Even as You and I': At Home with the Barnum Freaks," *English Illustrated Magazine* 173, February 1898, 493. Reproduced courtesy of the British Library (P.P.6004.gld.).

Wilde trials, such a cartoon evoked the sodomitical implications of aristocratic posing. That possibility haunts Arthur Hopkins' cartoon *Cut Short* of 1896, in which an "affected young poet" is seemingly about to ask "Miss Bella" for her hand in marriage. She, looking at him knowingly, responds, "I know what you're going to say. You want me to lend you a hair-pin!"[41] Similar associations of same-sex perversity had underlain a variety of depictions of male weakness and effeminacy since the eighteenth century, and Wilde's behavior was also, on occasion, conceptualized as sodomitical well before his trials. The figure of the "skeleton dude" from 1889, therefore, benefits from being considered in the same light.

Flipping through the pages of *Punch* makes it quite clear that mockery of male effeminacy and of the supposedly increasing similarity of the sexes was rife in the late Victorian and Edwardian periods. Anyone who thinks that the fashionable cult of androgynous bodies for men and women was only the product of the 1920s should take a look at cartoons such as Lewis Baumer's "The Sex Question (a Study in Bond Street)" from 1911, in which a dandy's tight-fitting trousers and a fashionable woman's "hobble skirt" are drawn so as to look almost identical (Figure 2.4).[42] The young man and woman's rake-thin bodies are wrapped in close-fitting overcoats, and her cloche hat is almost indistinguishable in appearance from his bowler. Popular interest in bodily health meant that suspicion was directed toward men with too little—and, as will soon become apparent, too much—muscular development. Caricaturists drew Oscar Wilde either as extraordinarily thin when a youth or as spectacularly corpulent when he reached middle age, the latter state evoking enormity of appetite not only for food but also for sex.[43]

Max Beerbohm recalled his shock on seeing a drawing he had published of Wilde pinned up by the police as evidence of the man's criminal monstrosity at the time of his trials (Figure 2.5).[44] The cartoonist's intention had been to depict his friend as a physical freak but one who was, at the same time, the epitome of high fashion. Lewis Farnell, who was Vice-Chancellor of the University of Oxford from 1920 to 1923, wrote in *An Oxonian Looks Back* (1934) that he had regarded Wilde as merely a "humorous and objectionable freak" because he had been ignorant of the man's "evil notoriety and posthumous popularity."[45] Wilde was singled out by Max Südfeld—writing as Max Nordau—in his influential study of *Entartung* ("Degeneration") of 1892, and the figure of the homosexual subsequently became widely viewed as a freak of nature.[46] In 1905 the American phrenologist Edgar C. Beal turned his attention to photographs of Wilde. Beal claimed that male inversion was not simply a matter of mentality but also of

THE SEX QUESTION.
(A STUDY IN BOND STREET.)

Figure 2.4 Lewis Baumer, "The Sex Question. (A Study in Bond Street)," *Punch* 140 (1911), 235. Reproduced by permission of Punch Cartoon Library/TopFoto.

physicality since he believed that it left freakish signs of effeminacy on the male body and marks of undue masculinity on the female body.[47]

Wilde is celebrated today for his stylistic innovations, but other aspects of his life and legacy have become problematic. He was, after all, a privileged white man who loved to be paid a great deal of money. This does not always sit well with a narrative of LGBT emergence from oppression.[48] One way out of this bind is to focus on camp production as an ironic practice that subverts aspects

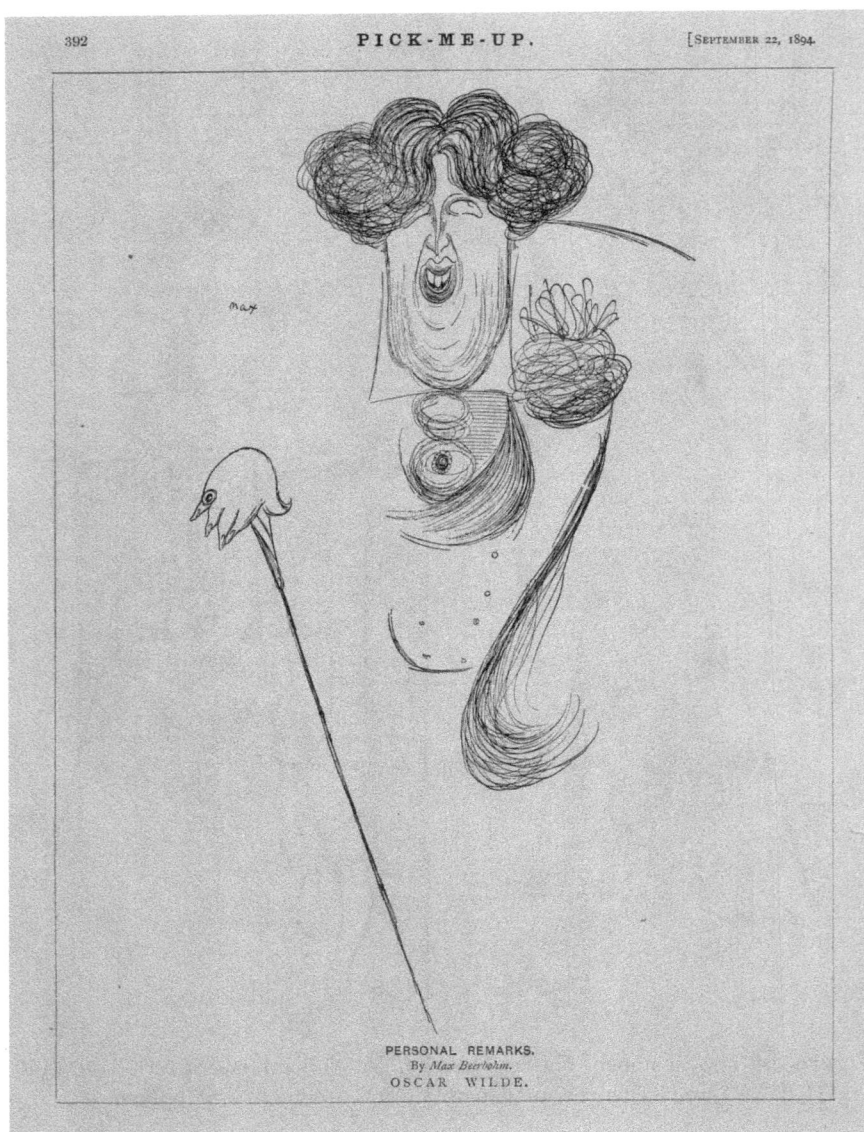

Figure 2.5 Max Beerbohm, "Personal Remarks. Oscar Wilde," in *Pick-Me-Up*, September 22, 1894, 392. Reproduced by permission of The Bodleian Libraries, The University of Oxford (N. 2706.d.24) and © the estate of Max Beerbohm.

of the capitalist practices in which it is embedded.[49] Wilde was a precursor of the interwar queer styles and commercialized freak images that I shall be exploring in the later chapters of this book. He spent much of his life creating an aristocratic aura around his performances of dandyism, but the money to achieve this owed much to his commercial self-cultivation as a celebrity. He worked for a time as the editor of *Lady's World,* a fashion magazine that he renamed *Woman's World.*[50] Rather like Dorothy Todd, the lesbian editor of British *Vogue* in the early 1920s, he mixed material on art and literature with more conventional information on attire.[51] He was also a pioneer of floral aestheticism and was fascinated by Catholic style. He was therefore a pioneer of a range of aesthetic stances that were to inform lives of queer creativity in the interwar period. His disgrace only meant that these modes were given an additional level of queer significance.

Wilde first rose to public fame as a result of lecture tours that took him across the United States in a promotional effort orchestrated by Richard D'Oyly Carte that involved "exploiting, packaging and exhibiting him like one of P. T. Barnum's freaks."[52] He was duly dogged by accusations that he was only pretending to have talent in order to make money through imposture. Barnum's enterprises were viewed in Britain as evidence of a peculiarly American tendency to seek to extract money from any source, no matter how strange or disreputable. When a stock flotation for a Barnum subsidiary was launched in London in 1899, it was reported that a jocular rumor was going around the stock exchange that a bearded lady would be given out with every 100 shares. The cartoonist Alfred Bryan amused himself with the thought of freaks as stockholders, and there were attacks on "Barnum and Bailey Ltd" as a "freak company."[53] In 1915 the American industrial magnate Henry T. Ford was parodied as a new Oscar Wilde in Leonard Hill's *The Tug of Peace* (Figure 2.6).[54] Ford crossed the Atlantic in a ship named *Oscar II* in an attempt to broker a peace settlement between Britain, France, and Germany. Ford/Wilde is shown by Hill as presiding over his ridiculous enterprise amid a freak-show circus of media men and Irish aesthetes. The boat itself has been renamed the *Barnum.* The figure of Wilde, therefore, had become expressive of the way in which many in Britain viewed American commercial modernity as a queerly dubious enterprise. There are also implications in this cartoon that pacifism exhibited a suspicious deficit in manliness. From another point of view, however, American models of production and self-invention offered alternatives to outmoded visions of British imperial greatness that were sinking under the weight of Victorian moralism.[55]

Extreme body shapes were, therefore, capable of evoking associations with aspects of same-sex desire. Extreme thinness was linked with a physical (and mental) weakness that was, supposedly, more appropriate to a woman than to a man. Effeminate men might be thought of as boys who had never managed fully to mature. Their example recalled the alleged androgyny of youths in a society where the pretty boys of the public schools were widely reputed to

Figure 2.6 Leonard Raven Hill, "The Tug of Peace," *Punch* 149 (1915), 483.
Reproduced courtesy of Keele University Library.

indulge in disreputable modes of affection.[56] However, in the early twentieth
century, queer writers in both London and Paris began to hint that same-sex
desire was to be found not only in the case of obviously effeminate men but
also in those who appeared to be quite their opposite. For example, as I have
explored in *Picturing the Closet* (2015), Marcel Proust developed the character
of the Baron de Charlus as exhibiting the "spectacle of the closet."[57] This drew
the attention of the reader to same-sex desire as the obvious truth of effeminate,
camp men, but also implied that many of those who displayed an overtly (or
perhaps "overly") masculine demeanor might share the same interests. In
Britain similar intimations of same-sex desire appeared in the writings of
Lytton Strachey, notably in his queering of the character of General Gordon in
Eminent Victorians (1918), who was portrayed as priggish, highly strung, and
interested in boys rather than women. Strachey also hinted in his life of Queen
Victoria that Prince Albert had been homosexual.[58] The notion that masculine-
seeming men were sometimes queer was promoted by the logic of the idea of
inversion. Thus, when the American writer Edward Prime-Stevenson published
a private edition in London of *The Intersexes: A History of Similisexualism as*

a Problem in Social Life (1908), he noted that "many great military men have been Uranians." This might strike the reader as unlikely but, he argues, the military profession is one that is "most highly aesthetic and nervous."[59] Talk of the "intimacies of specially fine psychic fibre between men" might appear to represent a confusion between homosociality and homosexuality, but the concept of the exquisitely refined military officer found support in the earlier practice in the British army of the purchase of commissions as an aristocratic perquisite.[60] Aristocrats might stand suspected of maneuvering their way into positions in which they could lead and influence platoons of young, attractive, working-class men.

Queer relationships in the army were therefore predicated on differentials of class and wealth. These even took specific forms of embodiment, as can be illustrated by a photograph taken in 1919 of Edward Dudley ("Fruity") Metcalfe, who was to be the best man at the wedding of King Edward VIII (Figure 2.7).[61] While the classic masculine physique of our own times emphasizes broad shoulders and narrow hips so as to form a downward-pointing triangle, Metcalfe is tailored in a way that produces the reverse impression of narrow shoulders and splayed hips. We might assume that this would be the body shape that was associated with allegedly effeminate dandies, but it is in fact the other form that was mocked in cartoons such as Alfred Bryan's *Eclipsed: A Regent Street Study in the Slack Season* (1907).[62] The dandy here is notable for the way in which he has been tailored so as to accentuate the slimness of his waist and his comparatively broad shoulders. What was most extensively mocked in caricatures of dandies such as this was alleged social climbing on the part of those who attempted to clad attractive lower-class bodies in upper-class clothes. The broad-shouldered body with a narrow waist was associated with the rank and file of the army. They were expected to be muscular since they were men socially destined for manual labor, and they were tailored accordingly. The result was that "two distinct body types were promoted through the design of uniforms."[63] Dandy styles were often close-fitting in imitation of military dress. George Ives drew queer conclusions from such sartorial choices, as can be seen from a clipping in his scrapbook from the *Daily News* of April 14, 1920, which featured a "modern Beau Brummell, spotted in the Row" who created "something of a sensation." Rotten Row was, and is, a track along the south side of Hyde Park that was used as a place for fashionable promenading. Ives annotated the clipping in his album: "not so bad."[64]

Fit young men with tight waists were to be spotted at military parades, but they were also available to view at shows by Barnum and his fellow impresarios.

Figure 2.7 Bassano Ltd., *Edward Dudley ["Fruity"] Metcalfe*, 1919. © National Portrait Gallery, London (x83717).

Even though freak shows, as such, began to decline in popularity during the earlier part of the twentieth century, individual freak performances continued to take place at circuses, as *The Sketch* highlighted when it reproduced a photograph of "a very charming spider to be seen at the Bertram W. Mills Circus at Olympia" (Figure 2.8).[65] Going to the circus became chic in the course of the 1920s, and women were openly noted as taking increasing delight in watching male acrobats and wrestlers.[66] The fact that high-society journals such as *The Sketch* and *Vogue* were interested in highlighting such spectacles indicates that circuses were not just popular as lowbrow entertainment but had become fashionable in artistic and literary circles. The figure of the clown, for example, which was derived ultimately from the *commedia dell'arte* figure of Pierrot, has been identified as an icon of decadent modernism that challenged ideals of active masculinity.[67]

The queer potential of the circus was apparent to Oscar Wilde. He wrote in "London Models," an article published in the *English Illustrated Magazine* (1889), that "besides the professional posers of the studio, there are the posers of the Row, the posers at afternoon teas, the posers in politics, and the circus-posers. All four classes are delightful, but only the last class is ever really decorative."[68] What he was referring to here was the fact that it was only at the circus that

STRANGE — BUT TRUE: THE BOGEY MEN AND THE BEAUTY SPIDER.

Figure 2.8 Photopress and "E. P.", "Strange—but True—the Bogey Men and the Beauty Spider," *Sketch*, January 9, 1929, 47. © Illustrated London News Ltd/Mary Evans.

one could reliably expect to view muscular young men with few clothes on. He continued:

> If an ancient Greek were to come to life now ... he would be found far oftener at the circus than at the theatre. A good circus is an oasis of Hellenism ... If it were not for the running ground at Eton, the towing-path at Oxford, the Thames swimming baths, and the yearly circuses, humanity would forget the plastic perfection of its own form, and degenerate into a race of short-sighted professors, and spectacled *précieuses!*[69]

Fit young women did perform as acrobats and even, on occasion, appeared in *poses plastiques* tableaux, clad in pink body stockings that gave the illusion of nakedness, but the reference here to "Hellenism" makes it quite clear that Wilde was talking about the opportunity to view the bodies of men.[70] The traveling lives of circus people meant that, along with gypsies, they were set apart from respectable bourgeois society. And indeed it is notable that the queer argot known as "Polari" was originally associated with lowlifes and circus people who wished to communicate among themselves in ways that could not be understood by censorious officialdom.[71] The term "circus" itself was sometimes employed in the United States to refer to sex shows, such as those reported by Mae West in her novel *Babe Gordon* [aka *The Constant Sinner*] (1930): "Near the club rooms of the Negro Vaudeville Artists' Association were the 'circuses' or 'peepshows' where if one had the price he could watch the antics of blacks, and blacks and whites, in the tortured postures of cruel, will-destroying, soul-naked passion."[72]

A variety of individuals have been hailed as "the tallest man in the world," and Franz Winkelmeier, at a reported 8 feet 9 inches (2.67 meters), may well have been. He was presented to Queen Victoria on June 22, 1887, during his stay in Britain, when he was billed to appear on stage at the London Pavilion Theatre in Piccadilly each day at 10:45 p.m. The publicity materials for his performances show him easily overtopping a British guardsmen, who might be understood as the epitome of military manhood (Figure 2.9).[73] The only slightly shorter George Auger was to be employed by the U.S. Army in campaigns to encourage enlistment during the First World War (Figure 2.1).[74] Members of the British regiments of guards were well known in London's queer community for being available for sexual services, in which they typically played the role of "trade" (masculine men who were willing to prostitute themselves for money).[75] Bearing in mind that speculation was rife about the marital—and therefore sexual—lives of freaks, it is not hard to imagine that Herr Winkelmeier may

Figure 2.9 *London Pavilion, Piccadilly, W.: Every Evening at 10.45: The Tallest Man in the World: Herr Winkelmeier, c.1887*, poster. Reproduced courtesy of Wellcome Library (General Collection EPH ++53).

have attracted a queer following, particularly among those curious about his supersized endowments.[76]

In 1893 Max Beerbohm wrote in the Oxford student periodical *The Spirit Lamp* (edited at that point by Lord Alfred Douglas) that the well-tailored trouser leg should be cut so as to ensure that the "the muscles of the 'strong man' are veiled from our frightened eyes."[77] Some homosexual men of a variety of ages were attracted to slim youths, but others focused their attentions on displays of mature muscularity. Interest in bodybuilding appears unexceptionable from the perspective of the twenty-first century. However, in the Victorian age, ostentatious muscle tone was widely thought of as freakish. Strongmen were displayed alongside human skeletons, just as midgets were paired with giants. A number of fashionable slummers frequented circuses in order to feast their eyes on displays of muscle. Going to the gym became so normalized in the course of the twentieth century that it is hard for us to imagine today how exotic a practice weight training once was. An early popularizer of this practice in Britain was Friedrich Wilhelm Müller. He was a circus athlete, who took the name Eugen Sandow as his stage name. He not only performed acts of strength but also posed to show off his muscles (which could be touched for an extra fee). In 1898 he launched *Physical Culture* (renamed *Sandow's Magazine of Physical Culture* the following year) which is widely regarded as the world's first bodybuilding magazine. Its popularity was driven by a rising tide of popular concern for physical fitness at a time when fears of racial degeneration were widespread. That fact notwithstanding, competitions in the magazine, such as those that invited readers to send in muscle shots of themselves, invited interest from those whose concerns were less with fitness than with voyeurism. Sandow married in 1896, but it has been suggested that he did so as a closet gesture in the wake of the Oscar Wilde trials of the previous year.[78]

William Alden had noted in *Among the Freaks* (1896) that giants had to exercise lest they become round-shouldered and slump.[79] It has been said of Sandow's achievements that "the strong male physiques that up to now the masses had encountered at funfairs had been regarded as freaks rather than as the result of an intense regime of fitness."[80] But this did not mean that extravagant muscularity suddenly became normalized. In particular, it is notable that overlaps between interests in muscular development and those in aesthetic and artistic pursuits seem to have set alarm bells ringing. This was apparent from the reaction to the inclusion in the first volume of Sandow's magazine of an article by the luxuriantly coiffed Polish pianist Ignacy Jan Paderewski (who later became the prime minister of Poland and, as such, a signatory to the postwar Treaty of Versailles). His statement that "it is highly desirable that he who strives to attain the highest excellence as a performer on the pianoforte should have well-developed muscles" brought forth Charles Harrison's "Awful Prophetic Picture of How M. Paderewski Will Appear Next Season" (1898) in *Punch*.[81] This represented the pianist as looking more fat than muscular, but either way his massive arms looked peculiar when employed in the delicate activity of playing the piano. Piano playing was also thereby queered as an effete, un-muscular practice. Much the same joke was applied to Sandow himself in a *Punch* cartoon of 1911 that showed him "in the throes of light verse—which we understand he varies with a little needlework or delicate embroidery" (Figure 2.10).[82] The narcissistic element of bodybuilding was made plain in yet another cartoon, this time by J. H. Dowd. In "Portrait—When Composing Elusive Answer to Challenge" (1909), the pumped-up protagonist struggles with the arts of composition while before him on the writing table, in the place where one might expect to see a portrait of a wife or lady friend, there stands a bosomy self-portrait.[83]

All of this suggests that Leslie Wilson's cartoon "The Regeneration of the Johnny," which appeared in *Physical Culture* in 1898, was far from successful in proving that muscles would instantly redeem the effeteness of the modern dandy.[84] Having taken a course in weight training, the "Johnny" can now bend a lamppost so as to light his evening cigar. He can also, albeit in evening dress, model himself in the same pose as a classical Hercules. Men who worked hard to look like the heroes of Greek antiquity found themselves suspected of harboring aesthetic concerns that were shared by their allegedly effeminate counterparts. It was the irony of this situation that inspired Max Beerbohm to draw a humorous comparison between his own drooping form and a muscular statue in his "Homage to Praxiteles Paid by Max" (undated).[85] It also informed an Arthur Wallis Mills cartoon from 1926 that showed a camp, stick-thin art historian in the act of critiquing the extravagant muscle tone of figures in a painting.[86] Sandow's brand of self-conscious body art stood out against more widespread practices of focusing on overall bodily fitness rather than overt muscularity.[87] Such tensions persisted through the interwar period and established the highly muscled body as indeterminately positioned between masculine self-assertion and queer self-regard.[88] Even in recent years, bodybuilding has been critiqued as a "freak show" rather than a celebration of prowess.[89] And thus it was that a vulgar youth commented of a muscular acrobat who was whirling wheels on his

CELEBRITIES OUT OF THEIR ELEMENT.—II.

MR. SANDOW IN THE THROES OF LIGHT VERSE—WHICH WE UNDERSTAND HE VARIES
WITH A LITTLE NEEDLEWORK OR DELICATE EMBROIDERY.

Figure 2.10 Edward Tennyson Reed, "Celebrities Out of Their Element.—II. Mr. Sandow in the Throes of Light Verse," *Punch* 140 (1911), 13. Reproduced courtesy of Keele University Library.

limbs while balancing on tiptoe in a Lewis Baumer cartoon of 1936: "Looks a bit affected, don't 'e?"[90] To be "affected" in this sense was to be suspected of a form of artificial performance that was associated both with social climbing and with queer effeminacy.

Decline and Fall

Freak shows were a species of popular entertainment that by the very nature of their mass appeal could be derided by snobs. They declined in the course of the twentieth century and were replaced by other media such as horror movies.[91] A variety of factors can be cited to explain this change, such as the visibility of large numbers of mutilated men after the World Wars. This problematized the display of deformity as a species of entertainment.[92] By the mid-twentieth century, commercial shows had begun to be widely regarded as being in poor taste, and "freaks had become inappropriate for the public eye."[93] Such thinking appears to explain why certain books on this subject are kept at the British Library in a collection of special material that is given the prefix "cup" as its shelf mark. This stands for (locked) cupboard. The original purpose of this was to contain material that was dangerous in some way, notably because it might be considered grossly offensive or illegal. Many of these items are to a greater or lesser degree sexually explicit and range from early modern erotica to such cheeky popular histories as Julie Peakman's *The Pleasure's All Mine: A History of Perverse Sex* (2013), which announces itself as looking at "the gamut of sexual activity that has been considered strange, abnormal or deviate over the last 2,000 years."[94] The presence of books on freaks in the "cupboard" indicates that their contents, particularly their photographs, were regarded at their time of cataloging as in some sense indecent.

The medicalization of freaks played an important role in delegitimizing their employment as spectacle. In the later nineteenth century, there is some evidence of hostility toward medical interventions that sought to cure freaks of their deformity. One example of this occurs in the aforementioned *Among the Freaks* (1896) and its story of the love between a giant and a bearded lady. She agreed to surgery before their marriage, with the result that "all her beard was gone, but in the place of it was a horrible fiery swelling that looked just as if she had been burned with a hot iron. It had become infected and this led to her death" (Figure 2.11).[95] A showman interviewed in 1910 was quoted in the British journal *World's Fair* as saying that "the only way for a freak to make a living nowadays is with the doctors ... by selling yourself to the medical professions, in order that they may study your deformity."[96]

Charles Darwin had argued that random variation was a necessary function for the survival of a species. But while Darwin had once talked about the difference between varieties of monstrosity that do not help survival and those that do, later scientific writers overlaid this principle with the notion of the

"OF COURSE HE WAS DEAD IN LOVE WITH HER."

Figure 2.11 J. F. Sullivan and Florence K. Upton, "Of Course He Was Dead in Love with Her," in W. L. Alden, *Among the Freaks* (London: Longmans, Green, 1896), 184.

extreme variant as the result not of natural development but of pathological processes.[97] The pathologization of freakery fostered the notion of disability and thereby turned freaks, "the erstwhile wonders of the natural world, into diseased subjects who could be treated."[98] Bearing this in mind, it becomes clear that photographs of freaks taken by doctors did participate in practices of control, classification, and objectification of quite another order from those evident in prints sold by the subjects themselves.[99]

Fears of degeneration led doctors at the end of the nineteenth century to confuse bodily (de)formation with sexual perversity.[100] An example of this was *Degeneracy: Its Causes, Signs, and Results* (1898) by the American physician Eugene Talbot. Havelock Ellis, the pioneering British sexologist who had just completed his book on homosexual "inversion," edited the British edition.[101] In the view of one recent commentator, Talbot's work exemplifies "the extraordinary inclusiveness with which medical discourse forged links among diverse social, racial, gendered, and sexual subjects."[102] Freudian notions of the primacy of upbringing rather than parentage in personal development were not in wide circulation until the interwar period.[103] Even then, there was intense speculation on the connections between physical and mental abnormality. It was in this context that an article was published in *Current Psychology and Psychoanalysis* during 1936 in which the writer condemned the rise of homosexual visibility in New York's Greenwich Village as having the effect of turning the neighborhood into "a place of 'Freak Exhibits.'"[104] It has been argued that by this time and "in this context, *freak* describes the allegedly unnatural condition of homosexuality, an affliction that is immediately visible in the subject's appearance and personal demeanor."[105] In order to understand such attitudes, it is useful to think about the important insight of Robert McRuer that notions of able-bodiedness imply heterosexuality.[106] He has further argued that "the sexuality of disabled people is typically depicted in terms of either tragic deficiency or freakish excess."[107] The queer thus came to be identified with the freak, and the freak with the queer.

In the late twentieth and early twenty-first centuries, cabaret, critical theory, and literary genres such as steampunk have reclaimed freakish aspects of the past in ways that are queer-positive.[108] Increasingly sophisticated analyses have been produced on disability, alternative ability, and, in particular, crip self-assertion as "contestatory" modes of negotiating what have often been seen as abject identities.[109] In line with this, I have consciously avoided looking away from what might once have been seen as shameful or embarrassing. It was in that mode that there was a collective desire to look away from the disfigured in Britain after the First World War.[110] The demobbed soldier—crippled, outdated, useless—was a national embarrassment.[111] Matt Franks in his article "Crip/Queer Aesthetics in the Great War" (2019) argues that sodomitical interests were associated with forms of bodily disability. To be penetrated by an enemy's weapon was to be unmanned.[112] Some artists and writers of the following years, notably in Weimar Germany, "claimed disability as an aesthetic and political challenge to militarism's focus on able-bodied perfection."[113] A British compromise was to aestheticize the wounded. This was the strategy deployed in *Gassed* (1919) by

John Singer Sargent, who was a celebrated and possibly queer artist. The work depicts a column of blinded soldiers in the manner of an ancient Greek frieze.[114] A photograph of 1934 by the undoubtedly gay George Platt Lynes that shows an erotized male couple wearing bandages as "lover-soldiers" makes explicit what is implicit in Sargent's work.[115] Such aestheticization still represented a looking away from the realities of war damage, but it did at least challenge a vision of bodily aesthetics that placed "degenerates," including homosexuals, outside the ideal.[116]

Ana Carden-Coyne, in *Reconstructing the Body: Classicism, Modernism, and the First World War* (2009), has argued that there were strenuous public attempts in Britain to rebuild the bodies of men in the interwar period as a way of (re-)creating male potency.[117] This would supposedly purge the national body of degeneracy, but in reality it could at most produce the "appearance of heteronormativity."[118] A move from "German drill" to "Swedish drill" before the First World War had already had the effect of prioritizing general fitness over muscular strength.[119] The trend, therefore, had already been set in motion toward the interwar adulation of the slim young man.[120] Youth as a place of play before the onset of adult responsibilities such as marriage possessed distinct queer possibilities.[121] "Vulgar" milieus such as freak shows provided exciting opportunities for viewing strange and perverse bodies. Ironic cross-class reading between high society and such marginalized groups was to emerge as an innovative form of older traditions of social slumming. Clothe such youths in the outdated styles of the *fin de siècle*, and they could perform the past as an amusing freak show.

Freaks in *Vogue*

The only way to atone for being occasionally a little over-dressed is by being always absolutely over-educated.

Wilde, "Phrases and Philosophies."[1]

In both art and life, clothing is ubiquitous and often goes unremarked.[2] But this was not Oscar Wilde's position. Not only was he known as a dandy, but he intervened in debates on dress reform, as well as spending some time as the editor of *The Woman's World* magazine. Fashion history is now an academic specialism in its own right and it is widely recognized that fashion and self-fashioning in the twentieth century were core components of cultural life. Techniques of factory production made stylistic innovation affordable for the majority of the population in Britain. This, ironically, created something of a crisis for the more affluent since it was increasingly difficult to assert superior status through dress. The fashion industry innovated so as to preserve the viability of both haute couture and off-the-peg reproductions.[3] Meanwhile, various forms of countercultural opinion expressed the view that individual self-expression in dress could be a matter of personal choice that need not depend on following the styles promoted by major fashion houses and brands. When the English rock band The Kinks satirized a dandy of swinging London in their song "Dedicated Follower of Fashion" (1966), they alleged that "he thinks he is a flower to be looked at ... when he pulls his frilly nylon panties right up tight."[4] They therefore implied the effeminacy of such consuming passions.

This song needs to be seen in the context of a long history of British parody on related themes that dates back to the later seventeenth century. After the failure of the Parliamentary experiment in governing without a monarch, Charles II returned to England from France to reclaim the throne in 1660. The country was riven by ideological divides. Ideals of courtly ostentation were widely attacked as ungodly and effeminate. Many Puritans argued, from a misogynistic point of view, that interests in fashion were unworthy of men and indicative of a lack of intelligence and moral fiber. Those of a dandified appearance duly found themselves mocked as being androgynous effeminates and referred to as "beaux" or "fops." This, however, also enabled those men who wished to make a queer virtue of elaborate self-fashioning to craft alternative forms of masculinity.[5]

One of the key themes of this book is the effect in the early twentieth century of creative contributions to fashion and style made by queer men. They not only promoted conventional modes of aesthetic prestige, such as finely cut garments and exotic flowers, but also forms of transgressive freakery that were put forward as amusing evidences of individuality. Interest in fashion in the 1920s—as in the 1960s—threatened to blur the boundaries between men and women as they stood like blooms or flitted like butterflies from party to party, shop to shop, and companion to companion. But it was not only men who have been laughed at for following fashion. Women, too, were frequently parodied for their supposedly witless obsession with innovations in dress that were often expensive and sometimes ludicrous. It was claimed not merely that fashion could produce freakishly extreme designs but that its pursuit was inherently associated with a fascination for bizarre effects. It was in light of this that the term "freaks of fashion" came into use, as in William Barry Lord's *Freaks of Fashion, with Illustrations of the Changes in the Corset and the Crinoline from Remote Periods to the Present Time* (1870), or in an article in *Sketch* on the influence of medieval robes (Figure 3.1). A search through the early editions of the leading style magazine *Vogue* reveals that fashion critics also employed the term against modes that they thought excessive or peculiar. Freak hats of enormous size—"a nuisance to handle and a tribulation to transport"—were condemned in 1909.[6] Consumers were warned off from buying freak patterns from France which, it was alleged, would be unwearable when made up.[7] Other freak styles included those that were lovely in themselves but which were spectacular anachronisms, such as an eighteenth-century-style tricorn hat that was merely "made and worn for effect."[8] In the story "A Butterfly Fancy," which appeared in the magazine in 1907, we find condemned "a pose, a freak, a fancy—anything but a genuine emotion."[9]

Yet there was one area of alleged freakishness in dress that was to be very much on the rise during the *belle époque*, and that was the adoption of more masculine styles for women. New Women dressed in ways that showed their seriousness and self-empowerment. Aesthetes and decadents delighted in the figure of the erotically empowered woman who, featuring in the paintings of the Pre-Raphaelites, was identified by hostile critics with perversity and

Figure 3.1 "'Puck. Modes et Robes': Freaks of Fashion," *Sketch*, December 18, 1907, 10. © Illustrated London News Ltd/Mary Evans.

ugliness.[10] *Punch* magazine had established a reputation for its mockery of aesthetes in the later nineteenth century. Its cartoons, by the likes of George du Maurier, featured intimations of gender inversion, such that men were depicted as narcissistic and passive, or women were shown as ugly and unduly assertive.

It was alleged that the latter sex had changed its demeanor from demure prettiness in the past to assertive forwardness in the present, as satirized in the *Punch* cartoon "The Distressing Decadence of the Fashion-Plate Young Lady" (1912) "as we knew her ten years ago" and "as we know her today" (Figure 3.2).[11] This implies that it was only during the previous decade that mainstream fashion had succumbed to the gender indeterminism of aestheticism.

Not only had the clothes changed, but so had the bodily ideals of women and their stance with regard to men. An important difference from late-nineteenth-century caricatures of aesthetic women, therefore, was that while they had typically been mocked as sexless spinsters, the women of the new century were shown as sexually overt. It is the degree of sexualization that appears in many of the Edwardian representations that is most striking. An example of this is a cartoon of 1909 by Arthur Norris depicting a young couple, an older woman, and child in a carriage on the London Underground. The dandified young man to the left looks lustfully at his inert, overdressed companion while a girl who holds a similar-looking doll says to her aunt, "What a *large* dolly that gentleman's got!" (Figure 3.3).[12] This implies that female passivity was read (by men) as a sexual sign and that, therefore, the problem with the decadent-style woman was not

THE DISTRESSING DECADENCE OF THE FASHION-PLATE YOUNG LADY.

As we knew her ten years ago.   As we meet her to-day.

Figure 3.2 Lewis Baumer and "Violetta," "The Distressing Decadence of the Fashion-Plate Young Lady," *Punch* 143 (1912), 369. Reproduced by permission of Punch Cartoon Library/TopFoto.

Figure 3.3 Arthur Norris, "*Molly (On Her First Visit to London).* 'Auntie! What a *Large* Dolly That Gentleman's Got!'" *Punch* 136 (1909), 161. Reproduced by permission of Punch Cartoon Library/TopFoto.

sex appeal in itself but her usurpation of the supposedly masculine preserve of making the first move. Advanced styles for women progressively simplified the form of dresses and—metaphorically as well as literally—gave women greater freedom of movement.

The media across Britain, including the provincial press, worried away at the thought that ordinary, decent young ladies would be led astray from conventional marriage by "the freaks of cranky new women and queer men."[13] New women were associated with feminist demands for female empowerment and were, as such, parodied as androgynous freaks who were seeking to take power away from their menfolk. Yet, by the eve of the First World War, it appeared to some reformers at least that "the masculine style of dress" was "ideal" for everyday use and it was the hyper-feminine dress of the past that was impractical.[14] Even before women went into uniform during the First World War, it was reported in *The Daily Mirror* that "trouser skirts with hip-pockets have recently been shown as a freak fashion" by an "inventive dress designer."[15] The tensions of the time were neatly expressed by the cover of the same newspaper on June 16, 1914, in which an article on the "Suffragette Bomb Explosion at St. George's, the Famous

Wedding Church" was juxtaposed with another on "Freak Fashions Seen at the French Derby." Freakishness was, for better or worse, increasingly being viewed as an attribute of modernity. Another report from the same newspaper in the same year signaled that "freak telephones"—in which the apparatus was concealed within a vase of flowers, a doll, or a stuffed toy animal—were becoming popular.[16]

It would appear that it was not only the influence of "cranky women" but also that of "queer men" that had led to supposedly androgynous styles moving more and more into the mainstream. There was nothing novel about the figure of the allegedly effeminate dressmaker or man-milliner, but what was new was the appearance of such fashion designers as celebrities. Paris was the center of European fashion in the nineteenth century, and there the copying of court modes was replaced by a focus on social competition between the members of the bourgeoisie. One of the first such designers was Charles Frederick Worth, an Englishman who worked in France, who has been hailed as the "founder of the patently modern and gay-dominated art/business of haute couture."[17] There is no direct evidence that he was homosexual, but his tastes in novelty, posing, exoticism, and excess have been interpreted as not merely prefiguring aspects of modern gay culture but as increasingly "beginning to signify homosexuality" in the later nineteenth century.[18] French culture was widely associated in Britain with effeminacy and sexual license. Wearing ostentatious female attire in the form of "drag" was implicated in homosexual subcultures, as evidenced by the trial of the middle-class cross-dressers Ernest Boulton and Frederick Park on charges of sodomy in 1871.[19] Female dresses of the following years incorporated structures that accentuated the bottom and have been associated with anal eroticism: bustles were referred to at the time as "pouffs," which was also slang for effeminate sodomites.[20] These modes carried gaily on past the trials of Oscar Wilde in 1895. All of this helps to explain why, even if Worth's work and that of his immediate successors were not inherently queer, they could be received as such in his home country.

Around 1900 the *couturière* Lucile installed a curtained recess and ramp in her London shop on which, accompanied by music and limelight, models paraded.[21] Similar displays were on offer in Paris, notably at events staged by Paul Poiret, who was one of the most important of the next generation of fashion designers. He arranged parties in the years before the First World War that seem to have provided the inspiration for the first fashion shows that were put on by *Vogue*. Poiret was also a pioneer in his use of artists such as Paul Iribe, Georges Lepape, and Erté (in French "R. T."—the nickname of Roman Petrovich Tyrtov), who had a genius for producing fashion plates that disguised the vulgar commerciality of the sales process through their evocation of aristocratic excess and exoticism.[22] Fashion, it was claimed, was itself an art.[23] These men reveled in camp excess. "I managed to get hold of the most extravagant dress in the whole collection," recalled Erté of a show in 1913, "together with a fantastic ermine-and-red-velvet coat, which I believe was called 'Eminence.' I wore the dress and coat, with a red velvet turban (no wig), long red gloves, and huge earrings."[24] The world of couture and design was one in which men had a remarkable level of license to play at queer self-fashioning. It was this milieu that enabled Cecil Beaton, a young, queer socialite from a humdrum suburban background in north London who had no formal art training, not only to design for a ball at Claridge's but to see the results published in *Vogue* in 1928 in an article on "The Frock of the Future."[25]

The British of the previous decade had been primed to look askance at fashion because of the conditions of wartime. In Lewis Baumer's cartoon *"Le Mot Juste"* (1915), a girl says to her mother of a passing fashion victim, "I don't like to see a lady dressed like that, do you, Mum? It makes her look so *suspicious*."[26] The plebeian term "mum" (as opposed to "mama" or "mother") indicates that concern at elite ostentation and self-indulgence was being brought into play at a time when national resources were being devoted to the war effort. British women, if not in uniform, were dressing more plainly. They had to achieve a look that avoided male ascription of vulgar feminine sexualization on the one hand and supposedly masculine self-assertion on the other. The First World War was, however, to have an important impact in that it provided legitimation for the simplification of women's costume. There was rising awareness that women might wear uniform and retain their feminine charm, although this was a question that was much debated at the time. It was also the case that female over-dressing was increasingly seen as unpatriotic. This was therefore a challenging time to launch a pioneering new fashion magazine in the UK, as the American publisher Condé Nast did with *Vogue* in 1916.

The British market had already caught the eye of one of Nast's greatest rivals, William Randolph Hearst, who had set up offices in Fleet Street for his National Magazine Company in 1911 as a bridgehead for his commercial ambitions in the country.[27] *Vogue* had been founded in 1892 but only became America's premier fashion magazine after it was bought by Condé Nast in 1909. Having been an advertising manager on the popular magazine *Collier's Weekly*, Nast gained his entrance to New York's high society by marrying the socialite Clarisse Coudert. In the following years, *Vogue* became spoken of as essential reading for women who had, or sought to claim, social status in America and the UK.[28] A Paris edition was launched in 1920, with Lucien Vogel as its artistic director. He had previously started the *Gazette du Bon Ton* in 1912, which had had the aim of raising the status of fashion in France to the same level as that of the *beaux arts* of painting, drawing, and sculpture.[29] A range of French illustrators found themselves published in the various editions of *Vogue* since some of the content was shared between them.[30] A Spanish-language edition published in Havana was launched in 1918 and a German one in 1928, but neither was a success and both were soon closed.[31] "Brogue" (as British *Vogue* was known informally in the company) and "Frog" (French *Vogue*) were not money-making in themselves—the highest advertising revenues were always generated in the United States—but they provided essential international expertise and *cachet*.[32] The surviving three editions were sufficient to project the image of the magazine as central to the international fashion scene in the eyes of its main, English-language market.

The world of fashion was changing rapidly in these years. Glamorous women used to have gowns made up for relatively little in Paris and then wore them in public in order to generate publicity for dressmakers, but now professional models were employed.[33] It was in this context that the woman who became editor-in-chief of *Vogue* in 1914, Edna Woolman Chase, staged what are generally understood to be the first recorded fashion shows. These took place in Paris in aid of French war charities. Models, at this time, were not seen as celebrities in their own right but as essentially interchangeable bodies. They were referred to as mannequins. Nevertheless, bespoke clothes were presented as individual creations, a fact that set up a tension between aspects of feminine allure that were universal and those that were based on individuality.[34] Designers such as Paul Poiret dared to produce designs without corsets and others that were heavily inspired by orientalist fantasy.[35] The results were disseminated across the various editions of the magazine.

It took a while for British *Vogue* to find its feet. It worked closely with its sister publications. Cover illustrations and carefully touched-up photographs of beauties crossed the Atlantic in both directions.[36] Yet, despite its extensive international connections and financial backing, its circulation remained under 9,000 copies. Of course, it was meant to be a prestige as opposed to a mass-market publication, but it seemed at times that the cultural exclusivity of the European contributors was threatening to make it commercially unviable. The British edition, for example, developed close links with the artistic and literary avant-garde.[37] Trendy young writers such as Aldous Huxley, Osbert Sitwell, and Alec Waugh, who spent their evenings watching experimental cabaret at venues such as the Cave of Harmony night club in London, were to be found penning columns for British *Vogue* that had no obvious connection with costume at all.[38] The result, if hardly a radical critique of the cultural and political status quo, still enabled members of the intelligentsia, including prominent members of the Bloomsbury Group such as Virginia Woolf, to gain a striking degree of international media exposure.[39] The resulting publication included articles on a wide range of aspects of social, visual, and material culture, including flower arranging and interior design, art, literature, and the theater. The aim was to produce a highly attractive magazine that was elegantly laid out and that balanced high-quality illustrations with stimulating text. The key audience was women who had, or wanted to have, money and social position. It engaged with fashion in a much broader sense than simply clothes, although they were of course of great importance. The magazine therefore aimed to inform the reader about the latest practices in smart society and as such combined social conservatism with a degree of cultural radicalism.

If there is one quality that strongly suffuses the early years of British *Vogue*, it is a sense of the performative theatricality of fashion and the idea that style was never just about dress but extended across a variety of realms of self-fashioning. The position of men who worked in this field was an interesting one. On the one hand they might be seen as heterosexually driven to obsess over female beauty, or on the other hand they might appear to be so interested in the female realm that they wanted to be women themselves. From that point, it was but a small step—and one that was strongly established by the 1930s—to link such individuals with sharing not only women's taste in clothing but also their choice of sexual partners. As the British social research program Mass Observation was to opine in 1940, the fashion designer has "an unusual sympathy and understanding of women, and often his own outlook is more feminine than masculine, and if not actually homosexual, possesses a mind more sensitive and receptive than the average man."[40] There is indeed evidence that homosexual men, and indeed lesbians, were attracted to careers in design. Clues as to why this was the case can be gleaned from some of Matt Cook's work into queer domesticity and the queer interior.[41] Interior decoration was a job that was considered respectable for single women, and it attracted a number of lesbians who identified with the challenge of how to furnish "a room of one's own."[42] Homosexual men and women had to think carefully about how they presented themselves and how they were perceived by others. They also faced the further challenge of attempting to communicate their own sexual identities to potential friends and partners while avoiding the hostile gaze of strangers.

They needed to craft private realms and public performances and were thus preprogrammed to appreciate fashion as a performative activity.

In so far as it documented wider spheres of culture and design, it is hardly surprising that not merely hints of homosexuality but a queer cultural agenda can be identified within the covers of British *Vogue* in the 1920s. That this might be the case rests on a compelling body of work put together by the American art historian Christopher Reed. He developed his ideas in *Bloomsbury Rooms: Modernism, Subculture, and Domesticity* (2004) and in a pair of articles that I shall now discuss in more detail.[43] In the first of these, "Design for (Queer) Living: Sexual Identity, Performance, and Décor in British *Vogue*, 1922–1926," Reed argues that not only have sexual identities been marginalized in many art historical studies, but so has the world of mass culture as an "effeminate 'other'" of modernism associated with "unproductive gossip and transient role playing." He maintains that the result of this has been that "the few scholars who admit to examining British *Vogue* have scurried to assert their critical distance from what they study."[44] Startlingly, Reed finds that "almost every page of the arts and culture coverage in British *Vogue* during the 1920s is queer—intriguingly, delightfully, powerfully queer. I intend 'queer' here in its broadest sense, to indicate an attitude that delighted in destabilizing institutionally sanctioned hierarchies."[45]

The implication of this is that what at first glance appears to be an elite publication for the rich turns out, on his reading, to have been all about establishing high fashion as a radical force in ways that included—even if this was not always made explicit—transgressions of norms of gender and sexuality. Reed terms this *Vogue*'s "amusing style" and sees it as having been fueled by a "queer sensibility" that led to its erasure from what he sees as the sexually normative canon of artistic modernism.[46] Moreover, the fact that the magazine implied, rather than openly proclaimed, the value of sexual and gender nonconformity has meant that its achievement has been ignored by those primed to privilege overt identity politics over "closet creativity."[47] This is the reason, Reed argues, why various scholars have failed to discern *Vogue*'s queerness in the absence of overt images of homosexuality.[48] Thus, Jane Garrity thought that "the magazine depicts no trace of Bloomsbury's ... homosexuality" because she was not seemingly thinking in terms of interwar queerness with its slippery elisions between transgressions of gender and sexuality.[49] Reed, by contrast, highlights "the androgynous *Vogue* ideal" and argues that the publication "relished gender-bending as a form of performance linked with other kinds of modern aesthetics" and was fascinated with "disjunctions between appearance and reality."[50]

In a second article, "A *Vogue* That Dare Not Speak Its Name: Sexual Subculture during the Editorship of Dorothy Todd," Reed focused on this lesbian pioneer as the key inspiration behind the queering of the magazine. It was under her tutelage that readers learned "how to recognise and take queer pleasures."[51] Todd had briefly edited the London edition before being moved to New York, but it was during her second term, from 1922 to 1926, that the magazine "inducted readers into the sensibility now identified by the term 'camp.'"[52] Edna Woolman Chase noted that Todd returned to Britain "and not only to London, as it turned out, but to a very specialized district thereof."[53] Todd lived with her lover—and assistant at the magazine—Madge Garland in a house in Chelsea, where she gave parties that were attended by various members of the Bloomsbury Group, including Virginia Woolf, whom Todd persuaded to write for the magazine.[54] The homosexual ballet dancer and choreographer Frederick Ashton lived at the same address. In 1926 he produced a ballet, *A Tragedy of Fashion*, which included a butch, cigar-smoking character based on Todd.[55] It may have been homophobia that got Todd sacked, or it may simply have been that her highbrow literary tastes were not shared by all of her readers since, as has been mentioned above, the finances of the British edition were not strong in this period. Garland walked out when Todd was dismissed, but she returned as fashion editor from 1932 to 1941. It has been observed that "the creative partnership of Todd and Garland also helps to explain why the assertively masculine dandy style favored by a number of twenties lesbians went uncriticized because it was fashionable: *Vogue* had played a role in defining what was fashionable in the first place."[56] This situation only broke down with the public furor that surrounded the banning of Radclyffe Hall's novel *The Well of Loneliness* in 1928. Her lover, Una Troubridge, was to write in *The Life and Death of Radclyffe Hall* (1961) that "I told her to write what was in her heart, that so far as any effect upon myself was concerned, I was sick to death of ambiguities, and only wished to be known for what I was and to dwell with her in the palace of truth."[57]

Much of the intellectual debate in Britain about homosexuality in the early years of the twentieth century was not dominated by doctors and psychologists but by cultural critics. At Cambridge the young Lytton Strachey and John Maynard Keynes held debates about what they termed "the higher sodomy."[58] Keynes, once he was installed as a fellow of King's College, Cambridge, had his rooms repainted with male nudes by friends and fellow members of the Bloomsbury Set, including the bisexual Duncan Grant.[59] Virginia Woolf once claimed that "my only interest as a writer lies ... in some queer individuality," and it was this quality that Bloomsbury appears to have contributed to *Vogue*, not without, it should be said, certain snobbish reservations about the world of the market.[60] British *Vogue*'s modernism therefore had a romantic, queerly retrospective quality (recalling, perhaps, that of Woolf's *Orlando: A Biography* of 1928) and did not embrace the ethos of efficiency in designs for living.[61] It did not dwell on the homoerotic possibilities of same-sex comradeship.[62] Rather, it tended to emphasize the mingling of male and female qualities, as well as the value of the polymorphous over sexual typologies and of subjective taste over identity politics.[63] This was a world of the smart allusion and the "open secret" (rather than one of earnest campaigns for reform), and of aristocratic entitlement with a fashionably leftish slant.[64]

It was under Dorothy Todd that aspects of feminist cultural influence were felt most strongly in British *Vogue* in articles such as "Why the Wedding Ceremony Ought To Be Revised" (1924), which displayed open hostility to normative structures of patriarchy.[65] Such radical views were less in evidence from the mid-1920s onward, but the playful side of Bloomsbury—that associated more with, say, Lytton Strachey than Virginia Woolf—continued to make itself felt. Indeed, it could be argued that the magazine's openness to Bloomsbury queerness was prefigured by its heavy investment in camp in the previous decade. Camp is a central concept in relation to supposed effeminacy, but the nature of its relationship to same-sex desire has long been controversial. Its appearance in the critical literature is often credited to Susan Sontag's short essay "Notes on 'Camp,'" which appeared in 1964.[66] This was a highly personal and idiosyncratic piece of work, which has been interpreted as a coded expression of Sontag's ambivalent feelings toward her own sexuality and upbringing. The literary critic Terry Castle thinks that this is why this piece, which Sontag dedicated to Oscar Wilde, effectively mocks camp for representing the tastes of a "fey cohort of (pseudoaristocratic) patron-connoisseurs."[67]

Ironic recuperation of otherwise outdated modes and styles could, however, be seen in more positive terms as acts of creativity that combined self-mockery with strategies of self-expression.[68] Such self-fashioning employs knowing reference to both historical and contemporary styles in the construction of new forms of visual expression. Furthermore, such activity that acts to problematize normative assumptions of gender and sexual desire can be identified and lauded even when its originator cannot be easily classified as homosexual. The case for the queerness of the camp deployed in *Vogue* is reliant on reading between its visual and literary content and the lives and what we may deduce to be the intentions of its contributors. Reed argues that "the culture of *Vogue* and the Sitwells, costume parties and camp, re-emerges as crucial to the history, not just of Bloomsbury and modernist aesthetics, but of sexuality."[69] The resulting "amusing style" should, he thinks, be re-evaluated as a neglected form of modernism that once "seemed a viable alternative to Art Deco and the International Style."[70] This was a style that challenged convention not by sweeping it aside but by regarding it with sophisticated irony. It was a style that relished the playful juxtapositions of bricolage.[71]

The amusing style of British *Vogue*, finally, needs to be seen in its international context. For sheer effeteness, it is hard to beat the contributions of Georges Lepape, such as that illustrating the old custom in which "slices of the wedding cake were put through the wedding ring and laid on the pillows of virginal beds, that the fair occupants might dream of lovers-to-be—of some resplendent young man, rosy-cheeked, blue-eyed, with hair of curling gold, and a moustache rivalling that of d'Artagnan."[72] Lepape was married and had a son, but nonetheless brought a startlingly camp sensibility to the depiction of men and women, and one that was inspired by the decadent artist Aubrey Beardsley.[73] Nast signed up a bevy of artists including Lepape who had worked on the aforementioned French fashion magazine *Gazette du Bon Ton*.[74] His counterpart at William Randolph Hearst's rival publications was Erté, who was sexually queer.[75] Camp was also employed by American artists employed by *Vogue* such as Anne Harriet Fish and, as I shall go on to explain, George Wolfe Plank.[76] The use of camp by artists such as these predated Todd and the 1920s, and it is to that earlier period that I now turn.

George, Georgie, Georgino Mio

In the past, it was sometimes thought that sexuality was an incidental aspect of creative professionals' lives or even, when it took the form of same-sex desire, detrimental. By contrast, I shall present an example of queer creativity in which the artistic work in question can only be understood, and indeed be fully appreciated, when seen in the context of its creator's personal life. George Wolfe Plank was an American artist who, although little known and studied today, was once famous as a leading designer of *Vogue* magazine covers. He was born in Gettysburg, Pennsylvania, and taught himself to draw and paint, before moving to Philadelphia in 1907. Plank worked for *Vogue* from 1911 to 1936. For most of this time, he lived in Britain, having moved there in 1914 with two close friends, James and Mildred Whitall, who helped him make connections in London society. His life was very much that of a genteel American expatriate, but his friends and associates included leading modernists such as Hilda Doolittle ("H. D."), who is best known today for her modernist poetry. She had moved to London in 1911, and her bisexuality is openly discussed in her correspondence with Plank, which is archived at the Beinecke Library at Yale University.[77] Her sexuality, it has been argued, may well indeed have been a reason why her "preoccupations with questions of aesthetic beauty gesture backward towards decadence."[78] Thus it can be argued that H. D. was heir to the aesthetic, androgynous tradition of the *fin de siècle* and so too was Plank.[79] Plank spent most of his time in England in Sussex and, in 1927, moved into a house that had been designed for him there by Edwin Lutyens. The architect had previously collaborated with Plank in a commission for a royal dolls house, for which the latter designed the king's bedroom. Plank became a naturalized Briton in 1945 and died twenty years later in a nearby nursing home.

George Plank's work as an artist for *Vogue* has importance not only for those interested in fashion but also for those focused on the transatlantic history of sexuality. Some of the material from the British edition of *Vogue* made it across into the American version, and nowadays it is more accessible there because only the latter has been digitized. What is notable is that the amusingly camp style preceded the editorship of Todd in at least one key respect: the magazine's covers. These were far from being realistic depictions of the latest modes. In the period from 1916 to 1922, George Plank offered the viewer more or less outré fantasies of feminine insouciance. This led one later commentator to opine that there was a "certain shadow" on his work. This consisted of an aura of *belle-époque* decadence and a delight in "bizarre and improbable" clothing.[80] Voluminous frocks and etiolated bodies were a feature of various Beardsley designs, and they appear to have inspired Georges Lepape's first *Vogue* cover— that of October 1916—which showed an impossibly tall woman with a furled umbrella. A similar effect was to appear on the June 1923 cover of *Monsieur* (a pioneering French fashion magazine for men) in which a gentleman in a huge dressing gown peers at himself in a mirror.[81]

The origin of the amusing style may have lain as far back as 1887–9 and the illustrations commissioned for *The Woman's World* by its then editor, Oscar Wilde, from the queer artist Charles Ricketts, which were aesthetic statements first and fashion documents second.[82] Ricketts shared a home and life with another artist, Charles Shannon. They were both products of the aesthetic movement and, as Matt Cook has documented, scrimped on necessitates in order to "purchase arts, collectibles, and ('exotic,' 'queer dear') plants and flowers."[83] They were referred to by Wilde as an orchid and a marigold, respectively.[84] While Ricketts's long relationship with Shannon is well documented, no such equivalent has been known for George Plank. However, the fragmentary evidence of his life that survives is, I believe, sufficient also to position him as having contributed to the development of the queerly "amusing style."

In 1916 the prolific writer E. F. (Fred) Benson published yet another book. His output averaged at least one novel a year, but this one turned out to be one of his more interesting productions. *The Freaks of Mayfair* is a set of satirical sketches of snobbish characters in London's high society. It should be seen in the context of concerns about the war effort. On the one hand there was nostalgia on the home front for more pleasurable times, but on the other there was suspicion of those who continued to enjoy lives of aristocratic ease. This had the effect, for those who eschewed hard-line moralism, of giving an amusingly decadent cast to social activities that had once seemed unremarkable for the elite, such as dressing in high fashion and attending the theater. Plank, who was moving in such circles in London at the time, provided the volume with a set of illustrations that were strongly influenced by the style of Beardsley. The women, like those on his *Vogue* covers, were shown wearing frocks that were out of line with the narrowing silhouettes of their day and, in fact, evoked the atmosphere of the end of the nineteenth century. The layout of the pages, with very wide margins, also recalled that of publications of the 1890s such as *The Yellow Book*.

The style of the social satire applied in *The Freaks of Mayfair* and its focus on the phenomenon of snobbery place it, textually speaking, in a line of descent from the work of William Makepeace Thackeray. We are introduced to a range of society eminences and aspirants, including a fan of spiritual séances, a male gossip, a widow of utter respectability, an unsuccessful debutante, men and women who refuse to grow old gracefully ("grizzly kittens"), and various social climbers both successful ("perpendicular") and less so ("horizontal").[85] Plank's illustration of successful social ascent shows women lavishly dressed at a performance of the Russian Ballet (the queer tone of which I discussed in Chapter 1). They are remarking on "the most wonderful gown in shades of orange that was ever seen."[86] This bears a striking resemblance in its employment of camp, extravagance, and whimsy to Plank's *Vogue* covers, such as one showing a woman wearing a most impractical costume for playing the piano as an accompaniment to birdsong (Figure 3.4).[87] Visual analogues to these images come not so much from conventional fashion plates as from camp theatrical photographs, such as one that appeared in *The Sketch* in 1904 showing "Miss Marie Dainton—'Resting'" (Figure 3.5).[88]

Men who appear not to be of the marrying kind make repeated appearances in the various chapters of the book. We are introduced to a trendy society reverend (unmarried) and to the phenomenon of young men ("Piping Bullfinches"): "a large quantity of young or youngish unmarried men who, living in bachelor chambers or flats, find it both more economical and pleasanter to sing for their dinner ... and they are therefore prepared to make themselves extremely

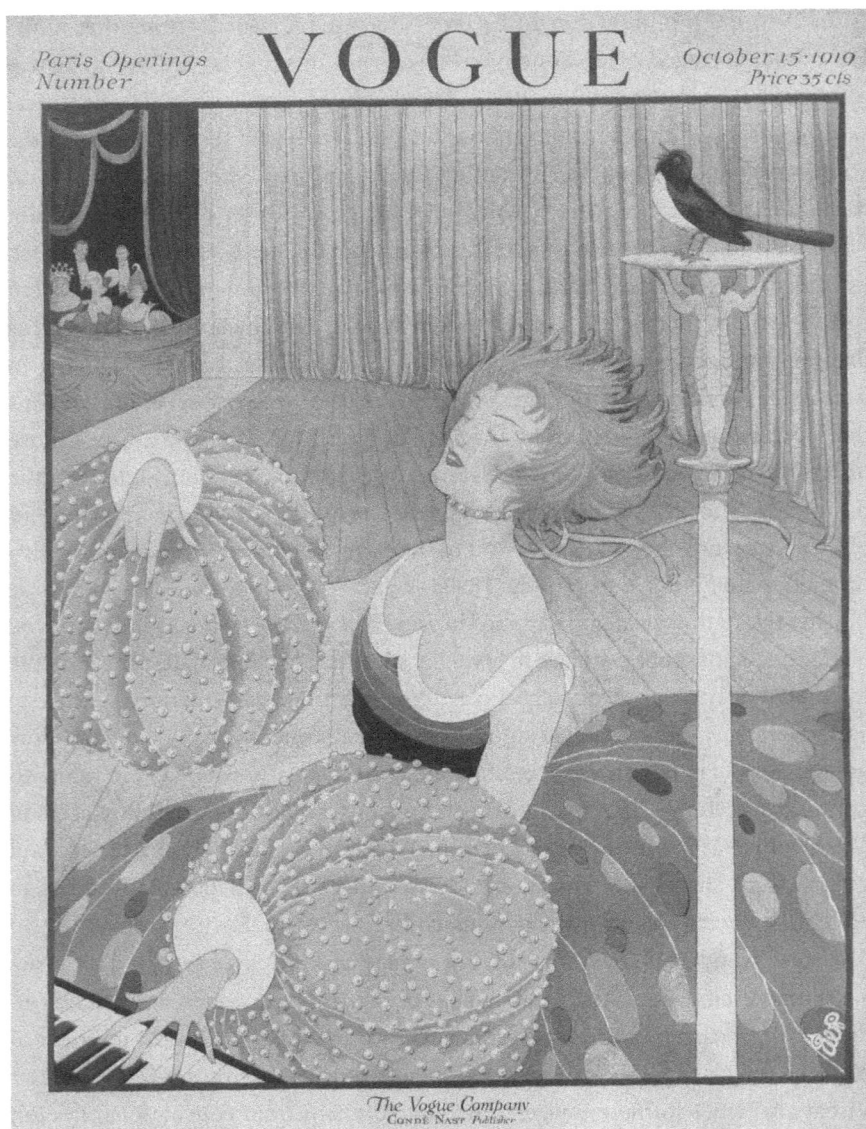

Figure 3.4 George Wolfe Plank, *Vogue* cover with coverlines: Paris Openings Number, *Vogue* (US edn) 55, no. 8, October 15, 1919. Vogue © Condé Nast.

agreeable for the price of their food."[89] Such activity, it is made clear, is a form of work. Of one such young man it is commented that "he has no intention at present of marrying, since even a rich wife would interfere with his career, and he is certainly incapable of falling in love with a poor one."[90] Then there is "Aunt

A FAVOURITE OF THE LYRIC STAGE.

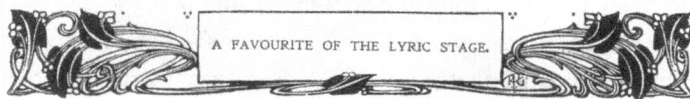

MISS MARIE DAINTON—"RESTING."
Photograph by W. and D. Downey, Ebury Street, S.W.

Figure 3.5 W. and D. Downey, "A Favourite of the Lyric Stage: Miss Marie Dainton—'Resting,'" *Sketch,* August 3, 1904, supplement, 6. © Illustrated London News Ltd/Mary Evans.

Georgie" who is presented, in essence, as an invert (a person with a man's body but a woman's mind): "He was in fact an infant of the male sex according to physical equipment, but it became perfectly obvious even when he was quite a little boy that he was quite a little girl. He played with dolls rather than lead soldiers, and cried when he was promoted to knicker-bockers."[91] It is made clear that he was not, physically speaking, an androgyne—"He did not like boys' games, but being tall and strong and well-made, and being forced to take part in them, he played them with considerable success"—but Plank nevertheless depicts him in a manner that is rooted in deep-seated British stereotypes of male effeminacy (Figure 3.6).[92] Bearing in mind that Benson was in the habit

Figure 3.6 George Wolfe Plank, "Aunt Georgie," in E. F. Benson, *The Freaks of Mayfair* (London: Foulis, 1916), opposite 40. © Reserved.

of writing to George Plank as "Plankino dear," it seems very possible that he was the inspiration not only for Aunt Georgie but also for the later character of Georgie Pillson in Benson's famous Mapp and Lucia series of novels, who was often referred as "Georgino."[93] That these characters were all categorized as "freaks" might imply Benson and Plank's hostility to "queer" characters in society. However, their own personal lives suggest, by contrast, that we are being given sympathetic parody rather than moralistic satire.

Fred Benson's life, in contrast to that of George Plank, is well documented, not simply as a result of his copious writings but due to his family connections. He was the son of Edward White Benson, who was first headmaster of Wellington College and then archbishop of Canterbury. Benson studied at Oxford, where he moved in the circle of Lord Alfred Douglas, and can be located on the fringes of the decadent literary scene. From 1892 to 1895, he worked as an archaeologist but following on from the success of his first novel, *Dodo*, in 1893, he established himself as a writer in London. He made the capital his home until the latter part of the First World War, after which time he lived for most of the year at Lamb House in Rye, Sussex, which had been the home of Henry James. Plank's friend, the essayist and critic Logan Pearsall Smith, wrote during a stay in October 1913 that the house was "very neat and old-maidish and quiet and comfortable, and exactly the sort of place that Henry James ought to live in."[94] Smith knew the members of the Bloomsbury Group, and it has been argued that the character of Nick Greene in Virginia Woolf's novel of gender transformation *Orlando* (1928) was partly based upon him.[95] Benson held the position of mayor of Rye from 1934 to 1937, and died three years later.

It should be remembered when judging Benson's early novels that Britain in the aftermath of the trials of Oscar Wilde was not a place that was amenable to the open expression of same-sex desire. It is perhaps as a result of this that he lived a carefully closeted life and specialized in writing camp social satire. It is important to stress, however, that his sensibility was shaped by the world of aestheticism.[96] And it may also have been strongly influenced by his own family, bearing in mind that none of his siblings married and his mother, his sister, and his brothers have been associated with same-sex desire. For example, Mary, his mother, had an intense relationship with Lucy Tait, daughter of the previous archbishop of Canterbury. E. F. Benson's entry in the Oxford Dictionary of National Biography opines that he lived alone at Rye, "never married and many of his novels suggest that he had a generalized dislike of women."[97] A recent book on these people has concluded that the Bensons were "a very queer family indeed."[98] They were no easier to understand in their own times than they are today. The historian Steven Runciman, who was himself homosexual, knew Benson in the 1920s and said that he found the older man hard to connect with.[99] The characters in Benson's satirical novels are not always presented in ways that invite emotional empathy and sexual identification.[100] Their universe is frequently one of amoral scheming achieved within the realm of a stylized comedy of manners.[101]

Elements of homoeroticism surfaced from time to time in Benson's fiction, but the overall impression of closeted discretion is reinforced when juxtaposed with his volumes of autobiography and cultural commentary. Thus, in Benson's *As We Were: A Victorian Peep Show* (1930), Oscar Wilde appears neither as a disgrace nor as a hero, but rather as something of an eccentric—or, one might conclude, as a "freak of Mayfair."[102] Benson's recollections in this book of holidaying on Capri before the war are suffused with something of a glow, but one that fails to illuminate the queer aspects of the island's life at this time in anything other than very general terms.[103] The novelist Compton Mackenzie was, by contrast, inspired by the prewar ambience of the island to write two novels in the postwar period whose characters were based on various lesbians and homosexual men who lived and vacationed there.[104] Benson had a particular friendship with the aesthete John Ellingham Brooks, and in 1913 the two teamed up with the writer W. Somerset Maugham to lease Villa Cercola on Capri.[105] The atmosphere there was one of homosocial insouciance, as in the conversation that Benson had with Brooks, with whom he was wont to go swimming, on hearing of the assassination of Archduke Franz Ferdinand in 1914 in Sarajevo:

> Never heard of it … I want to go to Monte Salaro after tea. Do come. Those tawny lilies should be in flower.
> "Too hot," said he. "Besides, I must water the garden."[106]

The clearest evidence of a love affair in this material is the platonic one that Benson enjoyed with his mother.[107]

It has been suggested that the discreetly queer life that Benson lived at Lamb House was inspired by that of Henry James.[108] Benson's biographer Brian Masters has, however, noted that a letter survives to George Plank that was signed off "best love," a salutation not apparently granted to others.[109] It is intriguing, therefore, to find no overt mention of Plank in Benson's *Final Edition: Informal Autobiography* (1940), which was published in the year of his death. This may be contrasted with the testimony left by E. F. Benson's brother, Arthur Benson, sometime master of Magdalene College, Cambridge, who in his diary confessed to having fallen in love with the scholar George "Dadie" Rylands. Masters concludes that "Plank's total exclusion from Benson's memory is suspicious, but of course one can draw no conclusions from it, as Benson made sure one would not."[110] However, examination of George Plank's surviving correspondence strongly implies that not only did E. F. Benson and Plank share an (at least emotionally) passionate relationship but that those years helped to shape their literary and artistic careers.[111] In what follows, I shall lay out some of the key evidence and leave it to the reader to come to their own view on the nature of the relations between these two men.

Much of the correspondence in the Plank archive consists of letters sent by the artist to his sister Amy Plank Cocke (Mrs. Charles Hartwell Cocke, Jr.), who remained in the United States. George Plank designed a considerable number of bookplates. One that he produced for his sister, which shows a decidedly un-cute cat scratching on a tree trunk, implies that she was an assertive woman.[112] At the time of his arrival in England in 1914, Plank is found writing to her of his delight at the enthusiasm shown by Ricketts and Shannon, aforementioned artists and same-sex couple, toward his *Vogue* covers.[113] By the following year, Plank had embarked on an intense correspondence with Mary Benson, who wrote to him on March 28, 1915, to say how pleased she was that he had got to know her son Fred, especially since "you understand him so well."[114] At this time, Mary Benson was seventy-four, Fred Benson—"adorable, witty, childlike"—was forty-seven, and Plank twenty-two.[115]

A smudged postal stamp appears to assign a letter from Plank to his sister to February 11, 1916, in which he talks about a set of drawings that he has recently made for Benson. These show "snobs, climbers, scandal-mongers, High-Church fiends, and the usual lot of asses that infest any great city. My drawings are in black and white and rather cruel in their satire but oh, such fun!" He and Benson, we hear, giggle over them.[116] In Benson's *Final Edition* we read that, subsequent to Henry James's death, Lamb House

> was let to an American lady, and she, being obliged to winter in the south, left her housekeeper there, and asked a very intimate friend of mine to occupy it if he wished for a month or so, and he in turn asked me to share his tenancy ... Lamb House began faintly to assume a home-like aspect, for coming back [from London] on Friday afternoon I knew I would find my friend there. He was of neutral nationality, an artist of whimsical and imaginative work.[117]

It seems likely, therefore, that this unnamed artist was George Plank and that it was he who brought Benson into residence at Rye.

On March 22, 1916, Plank wrote to Amy of his own delight at being not only in James's house but also at having the use of the great writer's personal effects: "His wonderful library is there, all his beautiful furniture, plate and linen."

Benson, it is then noted, has come up with a plan to rent the place himself. The writer was full of schemes, such as for the two of them to go on holiday together to Capri or to enjoy "winter sports" in the Alps (ideas that were as romantic as they were impractical in wartime).[118] Amy, meanwhile, was told that "I am so much in love with the house and garden, with the village and all the country about that I feel like staying here for ever and ever."[119] Mary Benson wrote to Plank later that month in a letter addressed to Lamb House to say that she had only just learned that he had been down there with her son "all this time."[120] Early in the new year, Plank wrote to Amy to say that he was also seeing Benson "all the time" in London and would be "lost without him."[121] Plank, it seems, was in love with England, with Lamb House and, perhaps, with Benson. On May 14 he told Amy, "spring is here with all its magic, and there is an intimacy and gentleness and luxuriousness in England at this season that is beyond belief." The house was like "one happy family," and he felt "so lucky to be in the country in this lovely house with a good friend."[122]

Something, however, seems to have gone wrong with the relationship in the course of the summer of 1917. By September 27, Plank was reporting that Benson wanted to take Lamb House permanently: "He wants the house but said he wouldn't take it unless I went there with him." He then related his concern that he could not afford the expense that this would involve and that Benson was becoming increasingly stressed.[123] By the end of the year, Mary Benson was writing—perhaps significantly to Plank's London address in Thurloe Square—to complain that he had ceased to write to her.[124] Through 1918 affectionate letters arrived for the artist from Benson, including one that concluded: "I send you my love, if I may make so bold."[125] On March 27, Benson invited Plank to stay with him again in Sussex.[126] Two months later, Mary Benson was dead. In her last letters to Plank, she often mentioned her son, as if she wished the two of them would get back together.[127] Fred appears to have spiraled into depression that autumn in a way that triggered a degree of boredom and irritation in the younger man.[128] Still, on April 6, 1919, Benson signed off a letter to Plank with the words, "I want you."[129] The two did spend time together that summer, including during August at Cley beach in Norfolk, where they bathed naked in the sea and then "baked … with no clothes on" once or twice a day.[130] By the fall, however, the affair was coming to its close. On November 7, Plank wrote to his sister to say that Benson was pestering him to stay at Lamb House and demanding that they go on long walks in bad weather.[131] Plank agreed to come down for occasional weekends, before ceasing to visit entirely. Finally, on May 20, 1921, he wrote to Amy to say that Benson had become peculiarly religious and snobbish, had become given to "unbalanced views about things and people" and, pretending to be an aristocrat, was wont to rail against the lower classes. Plank, we read, planned to give him "a pretty wide berth" in London.[132] We cannot tell from the evidence whether this relationship had ever been physically sexual, but it was clearly one of great emotional significance to both men. Equally plainly, by 1921 it was at an end.

The evidence of the archives shows that Plank was not merely the commissioned artist for *The Freaks of Mayfair* but that that book, in the form in which it was published, was a collaborative enterprise. Benson was familiar with the circle and mores of Oscar Wilde, and so was Plank, albeit at a generation's remove. He referred to Wilde circumspectly along with the artist Edward Burne-Jones as "great and interesting personalities."[133] On the face of it, Benson and Plank produced a stereotype of the homosexual as an effeminate invert in the character of Aunt Georgie. As I discussed in *Picturing the Closet* (2015), Eve Kosofsky Sedgwick characterized such representations as making a "spectacle of the closet" and as being fundamentally oppressive.[134] Indeed, it is hard not to think in terms of internalized homophobia when reading the following of Aunt Georgie:

> When he entertained at his own house, his guests were chiefly young men with rather waggly walks and little jerky movements of their hands, and old ladies with whom he was always a great success, for he understood them so well. He called them all, young men and old ladies alike, "my dear," and they had great gossips together, and they often said Georgie was very wicked, which was a lie.[135]

And yet it is worth thinking about what American *Vogue* said in its review of Benson's book—namely, that it turned "the searchlight of a humorous and not unkindly satire on the shams and absurdities of London society … with that quiet enjoyment of the foibles of one's neighbours which adds so much to the joy of life."[136] In other words, the reviewer believed it did not matter much that many people of fashion were eccentric "freaks" or even inverts. It has also been suggested that the relationship between Benson and Plank may have surfaced, albeit in heterosexual form, in the former's novels *Up and Down* (1918) and *Pharisees and Publicans* (1926).[137] Aspects of Plank's style appear to have been instrumental in providing a model for queer characterization in Benson's work that contributed to the success of novels such as *Queen Lucia* (1920) and *Miss Mapp* (1922).[138] Plank, too, was to enjoy his greatest period of artistic success during and immediately following the relationship with Benson. For it was at this time that he produced a steady stream of vibrantly camp and amusing cover images for *Vogue* that closely aligned fashion with a queer sensibility.

There are good reasons for championing the queer qualities of Plank's and Benson's work. Aunt Georgie, for instance, is not shown as the sole representative of queer life but merely as one manifestation of it, and his foibles are presented via indulgent satire. Plank, it seems, was self-aware about the nature of his camp images and performances. It was undoubtedly with a strong—albeit, perhaps, rueful—sense of irony that he wrote in *Vogue* of his relationship with the magazine in 1923 that "my emotions are beyond any expressing: what CAN I say?—We have been happily married for more than eleven years and 'I' (literally) could not live without you!"[139] Likewise, the needlework that the real-life George produced for *Vogue* was, in contrast to the delicate productions of Auntie Georgie and Georgie Pillson's thimble-fingers, conspicuously modern. Plank's sampler "What Is Home without Another?" was published in the magazine as if it were the work of a certain Angelica Byrd, aged seventeen years. This was, however, a decidedly modern teenage girl who knew all about jazz singers, cocktails, tennis rackets, motor cars, money, and men (since a verse on the embroidery informs us that she is dating two of the latter at the same time).[140]

It is important, in conclusion, to retrieve the reputation of George Wolfe Plank from relative obscurity and to acknowledge him as having played a key role in the development of queer visual culture during the early twentieth century. He was one of a number of queer men and women who shaped attitudes in fashionable society by finding ways to make their tastes—be they ever so eccentric or even freakish—amusing to a wider audience of consumers who wanted to stake their own claims to individual distinction. He, like Henry James before him, was an Anglophile who was attracted to the cultured queerness of aspects of British society seen in contradistinction to that of his country of birth. At the same time, his outsider's perspective as an American fostered an ironic and, on occasion, flippant stance toward hierarchy and tradition. Such attitudes came into fashion over the ensuing years. *Vogue* magazine played a particularly important role in this process, and its success meant that a range of competing publications came, to a greater or lesser extent, to promote a related set of cultural values during the 1920s.

Bright Young Things

"The old believe everything; the middle-aged suspect everything; the young know everything."

Wilde, "Phrases and Philosophies."[1]

Counterfactual history is often used to explore a range of alternative political trajectories, but it could also be put to social and cultural uses such as to speculate as to what might have happened had Wilde not lost his libel case in 1895. He might very well have avoided prison and a pauper's death in Paris in 1900. Had he lived, he would have been sixty in 1914 and could well have attended the freak parties of the 1920s as a bright old thing. But this is not what happened. His death has been received in certain quarters as a species of martyrdom that prefigured those of the many queer victims of intolerance in the twentieth century. It was only many years later that I realized why the war poetry of Wilfred Owen had had a greater emotional impact on me than any of the other literature that I studied at school. It was certainly not that, in the edgy atmosphere of the 1980s, the homoeroticism of his verse had been openly discussed in the classroom. But I nevertheless intuited a connection between same-sex desire and the literature of suffering. This was implicit in Benjamin Britten's setting of Owen's verse in the form of a requiem and was made explicit by Derek Jarman in his 1989 film adaptation of that musical work. Deaths of male youth in the First World War became linked with the contemporary extinction of gay men at the height of the AIDS epidemic.[2] For many men who fought in the war, the experience of male camaraderie was shot through with intense emotion, which was in some cases homosocial and in others also homosexual. The First World War contributed, as a result, to a greater awareness of same-sex desire.

Paul Fussell, in his pioneering book *The Great War and Modern Memory* (1975), argued that "the actuality and the recall of front-line experience [was] replete with what we can call the homoerotic. I use that term to imply a sublimated (i.e. 'chaste') form of temporary homosexuality. Of the active, unsublimated kind there was very little at the front."[3] Middle- and upper-class men in particular who had passed straight from single-sex public schools and universities to the trenches seem to have been primed to form intense emotional bonds with their comrades. Many of these men had idealized such behavior through a school curriculum that had combined study of the Greek and Roman classics with admiration of Christ and his disciples. Some women might make light of the conflict as a boys' game, but it had the very real effect of separating men from wives and girlfriends, who might resent homosocial friendships in the trenches.[4] So profound were many of the "temporary" passions of wartime that another scholar has argued that "heterosexuality in postwar England was challenged not [so much] by sexual dissidence as by memories of such relationships."[5]

Intense debates about changes in gender roles had been taking place before the war, and the experience of national service only accentuated this after 1914. Edwin Morrow in *Punch* compared the stereotype of the manly soldier of the Victorian age and his adoring little wife with the women in uniform and men dragged up for amateur theatricals on the contemporary front (Figure 4.1).[6] The American humorist Dorothy Parker claimed in a *Vogue* article, "Lovely Woman as the Honest Labouring Man," that "he who returns from the war may find that the only profession left to him is that of female impersonator."[7] Drag, of course, is a sport that people of all sexual persuasions can play. It has been argued, for instance, that it was primarily a form of "carnivalization" in the army and had little to do with homosexual desire.[8] The style of cross-dressing employed was typically, although not always, burlesque rather than glamorous.[9] Similar behavior was taking place on the German side and continued after the cessation of hostilities.[10] Groups of ex-servicemen such as "Les Rouges et Noirs" performed drag reviews in British theaters through to the 1930s. Their status as ex-servicemen appears to have reassured those who might otherwise have worried about their manliness. However, it is hard to see such spectacles as having no queer aura whatsoever.[11] The impact of the war concerned more than material appearances. Some psychologists believed that physical damage sustained by men could lead to moral weakness and degeneration. The figure of the man who had been perverted by the war began to appear in a spate of French novels in which "homosexuality re-enacts the trauma of war as the experience of spectacularly degraded manhood."[12] At first sight the party atmosphere of the postwar years appears sharply removed from this legacy of suffering, but the change of mood was partly a reaction against the austerities of wartime. This fueled the fragile gaiety of interwar Britain. The apparently superficial pleasures of the 1920s had sinister foundations.[13]

Figure 4.1 Edwin Morrow, "With Amateur Theatricals at the Front and War-Work at Home," *Punch* 150 (1916), 411. Reproduced by permission of Punch Cartoon Library/TopFoto.

"The Imitation Woman" (1923), an article published in the right-wing newspaper *John Bull*, highlighted a case in which Mr. Justice Darling sentenced a soldier who, when cross-dressed, took a compatriot into a wood with him for a sexual assignation. It was suggested that part of the blame for this lamentable situation could be attributed to the popularity of drag in military theatricals during the war. But it was furthermore revealed to the titillated reader that there were whole coteries of people who mingled sexual perversion and criminal extortion. An example of such a person was named as "Paddy." The anti-Irish implications of the name may be no coincidence, bearing in mind that the long-standing British suspicion of Catholicism as an effeminate religion is likely to have been heightened in the aftermath of the declaration of the Irish Free State on December 6, 1922.[14] "Paddy" was, we are informed,

> a very good-looking youth of a very effeminate type. He is as skillful at designing dresses and making embroideries as a West End milliner. He may be taken as a type. Crowned with a hat adorned with bird of paradise feathers, and fragrant with patchouli, he sets off for whatever fancy dress dance he has deigned to honour with his presence. After the dance Paddy usually collected a few male friends who return to his flat. A dreadful collection of people they are, with their absurd pretentions to the artistic and intellectual. That is merely a pose. They have no intelligence. They are merely degenerates.[15]

To the conservative reading public, men such as these were less a minority group with a sexualized form of identity and more a peculiarly unpleasant type of common criminal.

Scrutiny of reports published in the press over several decades shows that across the country cross-dressing was widely employed by criminals, particularly those intent on street robbery. An instance was reported in Swansea in 1899 as involving a man dressed as a woman and two women dressed as men.[16] Two years later it was reported in a newspaper article headlined "In the Twinkling of an Eye" that one Peter Roberts had been charged at Blackburn County Police Court with acts of theft from the person. Upon arrest, he was revealed to be "wearing under his clothing a woman's skirt and shawl in such a manner that he could almost instantly change his appearance from that of a man to that of a woman."[17] Disguises and deceits were prominent in interwar society.[18] To give another example, Henry Creighton Bird was apprehended in 1931 in possession of a revolver and charged with attempted theft of jewelry at the Royal Exeter Hotel, Bournemouth. He appeared in court wearing a "man's double-breasted overcoat, but with a woman's clothes, including a skirt, stockings and high-heeled shoes underneath."[19]

If cross-dressing was sometimes employed as a form of disguise during the commission of a crime, it might also be used as a means to evade capture. This was the situation with John Roberts, a twenty-five-year-old miner from Rotherham, who was accused in 1925 of sending poisoned chocolates to his wife. It was reported that he was "known as an excellent female impersonator and an adept at disguise, and because of this the police anticipated a prolonged search."[20] It had even been suggested that the infamous murder suspect Dr. Hawley Harvey Crippen might have attempted to elude capture in 1910 by cross-dressing. The idea followed a tip-off from Mrs. Adelene Harrison—who knew Crippen's family—that he might have gone further than simply dyeing his hair or attaching a stick-on beard since "on one occasion he dressed as a woman in order to amuse his friends." His slight figure, she stated, "carried out the illusion to perfection."[21] In another case, this time of a young man trying to evade military service during the First World War, it was not his dress or his demeanor that finally gave him away but his body. A waitress at the Globe Hotel in Exeter spotted that a personage presented as the niece of a middle-aged couple never removed "her" gloves and had hands that were too large for a woman.[22]

Cross-dressing was not only widespread among the criminal fraternity but was also employed by the police (Figure 6.14). It was reported in 1890 in *The Cardiff Times* that a policeman disguised as a woman had successfully obtained incriminating evidence against a man who was in the habit of exposing his person to a widow who lived next door.[23] And in a similar instance from 1913, it was reported that a man had been sent to prison for sending objectionable letters to a local woman. He was, however, completely deceived by the impersonation achieved by Constable Selwood, "a fresh-complexioned young man," and so was successfully brought to justice.[24] On another occasion, reported in the press as a case of "Policemen in Petticoats" (1908), the use of women's clothing was rather less successful. The constable had been deployed to keep watch on the Italian community in Clerkenwell in central London "without attracting suspicion." He was however recognized because, as was commented in court, the man had employed "a very bad 'make-up.'"[25]

Propensities for cross-dressing were, however, particularly associated with the crimes of sodomy and prostitution. The authorities appeared to believe that perverted individuals dressed as women in order to lure unsuspecting "normal" men to have sex with them and to provide opportunities for robbery and blackmail. Sodomitical cross-dressing featured in the Wilde trials in 1895 in which the codefendant Alfred Taylor was noted as keeping a set of lady's attire in his room.[26] Perhaps the most prominent sodomy trial of the preceding decades, that of Ernest Boulton and Frederick Park in 1871, hinged on the very question of whether male cross-dressing could be taken as evidence of sodomitical intent.[27] *The Penny Illustrated Paper* emphasized that "the mere freak of dressing in women's clothes ... might be pardoned once or twice as a piece of boyish folly," but they had gone out "not only disguised as females, but aping the manners, the affectations, and even the questionable looks and bearing of a certain class of woman." In other words, they had not simply performed the appearance of women but had specifically styled themselves after the manner of female prostitutes. It further deplored the fact that such behavior had "become so common as to have a recognized slang term attached to it," namely "going about in drag."[28]

Female prostitutes were commonly referred to in the mid-nineteenth century as "gay ladies," as can be seen from John Leech's cartoon "The Great Social Evil" (1857). Two elaborately dressed women stand miserably in the rain outside a theater showing *La Traviata* (which was about the death of a courtesan). "Ah! Fanny!" says one to the other, "How long have you been *gay*?" (Figure 4.2).[29] Any woman's outfit that was regarded as particularly excessive or outré could be identified as a "freak of fashion." In June 1897, *The Sketch* republished a mid-Victorian cartoon. This showed a woman being mistaken for a prostitute by a clergyman, who presses on her a tract. The lady replies, "'Bless me, Sir, you are mistaken! I am not a social evil; I'm only waiting for a 'bus!'" (Figure 4.3).[30] This plays on the notion that excessive dress was characteristic of prostitutes or even that some poor women sold themselves so they could afford fashionable garments.[31] This is why the clergyman has mistaken the young lady in her vast hoop skirt for a "social evil." Prostitutes were noted as wearing ostentatious clothes that would draw the eyes of men, but also for *not* in reality having the money to wear the latest fashions. The republication of this cartoon, therefore, garnered an extra element of humor, both because the clergyman's earnestness would have seemed antiquated from the standpoint of the *fin de siècle* and because the costume itself was by then spectacularly outmoded.

If it was not always clear that gay ladies were really happy, it was also not axiomatic that they were really women. The cross-dressed criminal was, in the eyes of the police, queerly suspect unless proven to have alternative motives for assuming their dubious attire. Ernest Cole, aged thirty-two years in 1901 and of German nationality, was most definitely such a queer character. *The London Daily News* reported that Cole kept "disreputable houses" in the West End where the installation of sliding panels facilitated robberies. He was described as "a thief, and associate of blackmailers, and one of the most notorious characters

Figure 4.2 John Leech, "The Great Social Evil," *Punch* 33 (1857), 114. Reproduced courtesy of Keele University Library.

in Soho." In court he was "effeminate in bearing, voice, and countenance, [and] kept his hands plunged deep into a muff." He appeared in his dress, but had removed his hat, which was a magnificent specimen of its kind "with enormous bows and feathers, a large wig of auburn hue, a veil, and such trifling things

June 23, 1897   THE SKETCH.   359

A FREAK OF FASHION.

Philanthropic Divine: May I beg of you to accept this good little book? Take it home and read it attentively—I am sure it will benefit you.
Lady: Bless me, Sir, you 're mistaken! I am not a social evil: I am only waiting for a 'bus!

Figure 4.3 Charles Culliford, "A Freak of Fashion," *Sketch,* June 23, 1897, 359. © Illustrated London News Ltd/Mary Evans.

as hat pins, silk neckerchief, brooch, etc." When arrested, he had not had "a stubbly beard and moustache" but "had rouged cheeks and painted eyebrows then, and actually carried a powder puff."[32] Cole's attire, it would seem, was not an attempt at disguise, since it was so ostentatious as to draw attention to itself.

This was deliberately performative cross-dressing and can thus be understood as "drag" (a term that may have originated in the notion of "dragging about" an extravagantly sized frock).

Laurence Senelick's *The Changing Room: Sex, Drag and Theatre* (2000) is a key study of the links between sexuality, cross-dressing, and the stage. He explains that the figure of the glamorous drag queen emerged during the mid-nineteenth century as what he terms "an offshoot of a thriving transvestite *demi-monde* that impinged on the world of popular entertainment."[33] However, the court in the case of Boulton and Park accepted that their assumption of women's dress was simply an eccentric pastime. This was of great importance because in the following decades it became very difficult to arrest individuals simply for cross-dressing in public. What the case did, however, also bring to public attention was that Boulton and Park sometimes assumed a style which, without being cross-dressed, contravened normative expectations for male attire, notably through the use of makeup.[34] In other words, they often assumed the attire of the homosexual "queen" (or, in the United States, "fairy") as opposed to full drag. In the early twentieth century, the possession by a man of a powder puff was taken by the police, and even sometimes by the courts, as evidence not merely of criminality in general but of sodomitical intent in particular.[35] The "man with the powder puff" became an object of both erotic and phobic fascination in interwar London.[36] Such men became "an integral and startling part of metropolitan modernity, embodying the nagging fear that the city offered queer men an affirmative space, where their desires were no longer abhorrent and depraved."[37]

Books such as Taylor Croft's *Cloven Hoof: A Study of Contemporary London Vices* (1932) purported to present the truth of degenerate lives. The inverted "homosexualist," the reader is informed, "rarely makes any attempt at camouflage" and dresses in bright colors with wide pants. The use of cosmetics lends "something bizarre and whorish to their faces."[38] Shortly after the publication of this exposé, the police raided a private ballroom in Holland Park, west London, and arrested sixty men, many of them in drag and others in a combination of male attire and powder. Police Constables Labbatt and Chopping had also donned makeup so as to infiltrate the crowd.[39] The event had been organized by "Lady Austin" who was in reality a twenty-four-year-old barman who lived nearby in Baron's Court. Most of those arrested were waiters, servants, chefs, and porters. This event can be seen in retrospect as representing evidence of a vibrant, queer, working-class subculture. Police records reveal that similar events had been taking place over many decades, and not just in London. One was hosted in Manchester in 1874 by a "Queen of Camp."[40] Middle-class men from the suburbs such as Quentin Crisp joined this coterie as a form of bohemian slumming. They thereby exchanged the suffocating safety of a suburban existence for—to borrow Matt Houlbrook's phrase—"perils and pleasures in the sexual metropolis."[41]

These examples notwithstanding, there is nothing inherently homosexual about cross-dressing. Before the First World War, both male-to-female and female-to-male impersonation were familiar elements of popular entertainment at the music hall, freak shows, and circuses.[42] Such acts were often comedic and might parody the latest fashions such as those worn by the New Woman.[43] An example of this can be seen in an article published in *The Sketch* entitled "Do We Need the Actress?" (1904). The overall conclusion of the piece was that, yes, indeed, the beautiful woman was needed on stage. The plates make the point by depicting a series of men in what are clearly meant to be bad impersonations of women, but their effect is not identical. "Mr. Edgar Atchison-Ely in 'Rational Dress'" is simply grotesque in his presentation of the male body as natural and the garb as bizarre (Figure 4.4).[44] The effect is to burlesque women in general and progressive specimens of their sex in particular.

"Mr. Huntly Wright at Home," by contrast, works differently (Figure 4.5).[45] Here the sex of the actor's body is not immediately apparent, nor does the dress make him appear ridiculous (unless one thinks that *any* man in the dress of the opposite sex will inherently look absurd). It is far from clear that his drag burlesques women. Indeed, the commentary accompanying the picture indicated that Wright's performance "certainly suggested certain attributes of eccentric womanhood ... overcoloured in a pleasant and by no means offensive manner."[46] It might even be said that he was making fun of the sartorial dowdiness of men in their daily lives. This self-denigration is a classic maneuver of camp. The former image reinforces traditional expectations of gender, while the latter undermines them. It is easy to see why some heterosexual women might become interested in the destabilization of the masculine norms that had insisted on female subservience. Furthermore, male-to-female cross-dressing might appeal to those of a wide range of sexual tastes, including men who "saw it as a relief from masculinity, sadomasochists who saw it as a humiliation, and adults who remembered erotic moments of childhood."[47]

We do not know the precise motivations and self-identifications of most of the cross-dressers described in most of the press reports of arrests. By the mid-twentieth century, public opinion tended only to judge homosexual cross-dressing harshly, and medical testimony started to gain legal recognition for

"DO WE NEED THE ACTRESS?"

MR. EDGAR ATCHISON-ELY IN "RATIONAL DRESS."

Photograph by Hana, Bedford Street, Strand.

Figure 4.4 Hana, *Mr. Edgar Atchison-Ely in "Rational Dress,"* in "Do We Need the Actress?" *Sketch*, June 5, 1904, supplement, 9. © Illustrated London News Ltd/ Mary Evans.

heterosexual transvestism as a successful defense in sodomy cases.[48] An example of this was reported in 1942 in the *Hartlepool Mail*—"In Woman's Clothes: He Wore Them for Pleasure."[49] There were some earlier instances in which the

4   [SUPPLEMENT.]   THE SKETCH.   JUNE 8, 1904

"DO WE NEED THE ACTRESS?"

MR. HUNTLEY WRIGHT AT HOME.
Photograph by Ellis and Walery, Baker Street, W.

Figure 4.5 Ellis and Walery, *Mr. Huntley Wright at Home*, in "Do We Need the Actress?" *Sketch,* June 5, 1904, supplement, 4. © Illustrated London News Ltd/ Mary Evans.

accused did appear to identify as a member of the opposite gender. This was the case with an army deserter who settled in Bradford where, it was explained in 1909, "he worked at the mill as a woman and went out courting with men. His manner, habits and disposition suited the role to a nicety, and he even made his own dresses."[50] But the behavior that I have been focusing on does not fit with a notion that the wearer always wished to pass as the opposite gender, whether for purposes of criminal concealment, transgender intent, or transvestite desire. Rather, what is implied in many of these cases is self-identification with visible transgression. It appears that it was this that had especially aroused the ire of the authorities in the case of Boulton and Park. The alleged "effeminacy" of Cole's bearing likewise implies that he was understood to have been not so much a criminal in disguise as a sodomite made obvious.

An important distinction in instances such as this was whether the queer freakishness of such performances was merely an occasional, if bizarre, habit or whether it reflected the underlying nature of the individual involved. It was duly argued by the prosecution in the case of Bolton and Park that their cross-dressing was "not a mere freak, but the business of their lives."[51] The failure of the prosecution meant, in practice, that it would be more of a challenge to convict men based simply on their appearance. They had been found, in essence, not to be freaks of nature but simply to have been freaking on a whim. A series of later cases, such as one reported in Edinburgh in 1892, duly followed the same logic that masquerading as a woman, even in dubious circumstances, was just a "freak" amusement.[52] The perverse—and I use that word deliberately—effect of this was to create a situation in which freakish appearance could at one and the same time stand indeterminately both for sexual transgression and for its parody. To freak, therefore, could become a mode of spectacular disguise or, to use a Wildean metaphor, a mask that told the truth.

Freak Parties

Grand public events at which the guests wore masks and costumes had been popular in many parts of Europe since the later Middle Ages. The practice was particularly associated with carnivals in Venice and became widespread in England in the eighteenth century. Events open to the general public were held at indoor venues but also in pleasure gardens such as those at Vauxhall in south London. The use of masks enabled prominent individuals to mingle incognito. Amusing confusions of identity were encouraged: commoners might ape the aristocracy and pallid Britons assume the guise of swarthy Turks. These events were often attended by women, and perhaps also men, who were interested in selling their sexual services. For such reasons the morally reformist Victorians reinvented these events to fit their evolving notions of respectability. Masks were often abandoned, and more stress was placed on "fancy dress" costumes that represented particular historical characters. Rising incomes meant that the middle classes were able to participate in such entertainments, either in public venues or at people's private homes, but costumed parties still retained a degree of association with upper-class privilege.

The "fancy" in "fancy dress" referred less to finery than to the notion that you were dressing according to your whim.[53] Victorian fancy dress balls differed from the masquerades of the eighteenth century in that they had an "emphasis on self-revelation, as opposed to antithesis."[54] A woman of progressive opinions might, therefore, choose an exaggerated form of rational dress. This enabled her to make a point about her own beliefs and yet to suggest that she found humor in their more extreme expression. Fancy clothing was also expected to reveal rather than conceal class position, and the thought of the working classes dressed in the costumes of famous aristocrats from history duly provoked mirth in *Punch*.[55] Recent research makes clear that there were social limits on what was acceptable and that the fancy dress ball at this time was typically "*not* a site for sexual experimentation."[56] While such attitudes had not vanished by the interwar period, some people were using fancy dress in a way that pushed the boundaries of revelation in gender and sexuality, as when Virginia Woolf, to take one example, assumed the character of Sappho.[57] Cross-dressing, which had long been used in single-sex schools in theater performances, became a prominent feature of the more daring fancy dress events organized by young people.[58] This can be seen as a visual and material counterpart to the literary movement that advocated for a "new decadence" involving a (homo)sexualization of that which was queer, strange, and outré.[59] Understanding how this happened involves looking at the lives and attitudes of a group of people who were referred to in the media as the "bright young things" or "bright young people."

Many of the members of this set were queer, and some of them, such as the photographer Cecil Beaton, were to play an important role in making freak chic. This was not the same as the construction of a proudly homosexual identity, since the resulting cultural work still employed the concept of freakery as a luxurious eccentricity. Their innovative fancy dress was not inspired by earnest theorizing, nor by reading pamphlets by Edward Carpenter on "the intermediate sex."[60] This had the result that homoeroticism, when it did emerge as an implication of certain freak performances, remained marginal and socially problematic. In 1930 *Punch* published a pair of cartoons titled "The Freak-Merchants" (Figure 4.6), which showed a group of young people who had developed a fad for swimming

THE FREAK-MERCHANTS; OR, THE BRIGHT YOUNG PEOPLE.

THEY USED TO THINK THAT THE DEAR OLD BOTTLE-AND-PYJAMA PARTY WAS QUITE ORIGINAL.

TILL THEY WENT ONE BETTER WITH THE BATHING SUPPER-PARTY.

Figure 4.6 Arthur Wallis Mills, "The Freak-Merchants; or, the Bright Young People," *Punch* 178 (1930), Almanack, unpaginated. Reproduced courtesy of Keele University Library.

parties in their frivolous search for new sensations.[61] By this date, the antics of a relatively small but highly visible and well-connected group of socialites had been making the headlines for several years. Masquerade parties had been wildly popular since the eighteenth century, but the association with freakishness as an aspect of society high jinks was new. In the society magazine *The Sketch*, the columnist "Mariegold" reported in 1920 that "freak parties" were enjoying a vogue among the younger set.[62] A circle of London-based individuals competed to host events where innovation was key, no matter how bizarre, or indeed queer, the results. In retrospect, it was all too easy to dismiss the phenomenon as a mere expression of social decadence, especially as the high point seems to have been reached in the months just prior to the Wall Street Crash, which began at the end of October 1929. After that, there was less money available for partying and a considerably less indulgent public mood toward the foibles and eccentricities of the economically and socially privileged few.[63]

Queer men were prominent as both guests and hosts of freak parties. What was widely acclaimed as one of the last major freak events, the Red and White party, was hosted on November 21, 1931, by the rich American Arthur Jeffress (who was a patron and partner to Francis Bacon's friend the photographer John Deakin).[64] Two years earlier, an entertainment given by the aesthetes Stephen Tennant and Brian Howard had been saluted in a headline in *The Sketch* as a "Greek 'freak party': the great urban Dionysia."[65] In June of the same year, the critic Robert Byron, who was also queer, was providing readers with commentary on "freak parties" in the pages of *Vogue* (illustrated by Cecil Beaton).[66] It is important to stress that the personal styles on display at such events were often deliberately at odds with normative constructions of gender and sexuality, involving, as they characteristically did, elements of burlesque, anachronism, and cross-dressing. This was, in other words, partying that should be taken as seriously by cultural critics as it was by the traditionalists and moralists who condemned it and who were delighted when it fell out of fashion.[67]

So, who were the "bright young things," and what did that term imply? The cartoons in Lewis Baumer's *Bright Young Things: A Book of Drawings* (1928) are full of stereotypes of fast young men, ditzy "flappers," and manly young women. Their image in the interwar media has had a huge influence on the way in which they are understood today. A representative view of this social group appears in D. J. Taylor's *Bright Young People* (2008). He adopts something of a moralizing tone toward them as snobbish youngsters who did little more than become famous for being famous. They were few and they were metropolitan. They were, however, as Taylor admits, hugely influential as a result of the media attention that they attracted.[68] A core of individuals who knew each other well thus came to influence a generation. And many of them were gay in both the earlier and the later senses of the word:

Homosexuality was as characteristic of the Bright Young People as a cloche hat or an outsize party invitation. No English youth movement, it is safe to say, has ever contained such a high proportion of homosexuals or—in an age when these activities were still illegal—been so indulgent of their behaviour.[69]

There are several reasons why this set has not been seen as central to queer history in Britain. The left-wing slant of much lesbian and gay liberation has produced a literature that tends—sometimes with good reason—to be wary of social elitism and critical of past failures to establish an agenda for law reform. In racial terms they were pale, if hardly stale. However, much cultural change has been shaped by queer members of the social elite whose creativity, even if often closeted, should not simply be dismissed. Furthermore, in comparison with mainstream attitudes of their time, they were progressive on issues of social mobility. Upstarts, so long as they were amusing, were welcomed. They focused neither on identity politics nor on establishing neat categorizations of homosexual versus heterosexual. This does not always make them easy to analyze, or indeed to like. For example, what is one to make of Evelyn Waugh? He bullied "sissies" when at school and parodied them in his bright-young-things novel *Vile Bodies* (1930). He became a husband and a father, yet same-sex desire formed the emotional core of *Brideshead Revisited* (1945), a novel in which he looked back with nostalgia at the lives of the aristocratic elite during the interwar years.[70] And what are we to make of the public reception of the group? It is no easy task to judge precisely who knew what about whom. *The People* was probably not far wrong in July 1927 when it declared that an event attended by Stephen Tennant dressed as the Queen of Sheba and by the bisexual actress Tallulah Bankhead as a male tennis star was "one of the queerest of all the 'freak' parties ever given in London."[71] But was the writer using the term "queer" to mean homosexual? And if so, was that how most contemporary readers would have interpreted it? Perhaps not.

In light of such challenges, it is tempting to set the boundary of proof high and to assert that unless there is clear testimony to the contrary, what we are seeing here is not directly an expression of same-sex desire. However, the way in which these people and their parties were interpreted was regularly suffused with suspicions of sexual nonconformity. To give an analogy from the world of art: if Henry Scott Tuke's homoeroticism had been transparently obvious, he would never have been allowed to remain as a respectable artist. His paintings of nude boys, it would seem, were primarily viewed as studies of the male form and of the play of light and color.[72] But this does not mean that everyone interpreted his work only in this way, as can been seen from Frank Reynolds's "The Academy

Brightens Cricket (after H. S. Tuke, R.A.)" (1922). In this pastiche published in *Punch*, three young men strip off and bathe together after a match. Then there is George Morrow's "The Royal Academy—Second Depressions" (1920), which was captioned "Something queer about these rocks, one of them is tickling me on the back!" (Figure 4.7).[73] The drawing implies a figure in the act of grabbing a pair of youths from behind.

Whether or not they self-identified as "homosexual," it is quite clear that many of the men and women involved in the inner or outer circles of the bright young things were well aware of the unorthodox nature of their own sexual desires. This can be seen from letters, diaries, and privately circulated texts such as Lord Berner's fantastically camp story *The Girls of Radcliff* [*sic*] *Hall*. This literary confection was supposedly written in a frenzied few hours at some point

Excited Bather. "SOMETHING QUEER ABOUT THESE ROCKS. ONE OF THEM IS TICKLING ME ON THE BACK!"

Figure 4.7 George Morrow, "*Excited Bather.* Something Queer about These Rocks," detail, "The Royal Academy—Second Depres*sio*ns," *Punch* 160 (1920), 397. Reproduced by permission of Punch Cartoon Library/TopFoto.

in the mid-1930s.[74] The "girls" in question are in fact a set of queer men, most of whom had been bright and young a few years earlier. A number of significant people are known to have possessed a copy, including the writers and critics Clive Bell, Cyril Connolly, Michael Sadleir, and Carl Van Vechten.[75] Connolly's copy is annotated with a list that identifies the main characters:

Lizzie Johnson, Peter Watson
Millie Roberts, Robert Heber-Percy
Miss Carfax, Lord Berners
Olive Mason, Oliver Messel
Madame Yoshiwara, Pavel Tchelitchew
Daisy Montgomery, David Herbert
Cecily Seymour, Cecil Beaton.[76]

The relationship between Robert Heber-Percy, who was to be Lord Berners' heir, and Peter Watson, with whom Cecil Beaton was infatuated, appears thus: "Millie was growing into a very pretty girl. She had latterly become less of a tom-boy and given up perpetually playing her silly pranks. She developed a decided talent for 'chic' and really looked very smart. Lizzie was proud of being seen about with her and was delighted at being able to show her off to her girlfriends as 'her latest conquest.'"[77]

Social life for some queer men of the time was lived figuratively, and sometimes literally, in drag. In their own writings at least, the party scene provided a whirl of activity in which one rushed from high-society parties to low-life locales in search of amusement. Upper-class pretty boys could be admired at parties and their working-class equivalents ogled on fashionable slumming trips. *Vogue* informed its readers in 1931 that "the boxing in Whitefriars on a Sunday afternoon is as fashionable as church parade under Achilles' torso used to be before the war!" (Figure 4.8).[78] Men in search of same-sex partners sometimes hung around the classical galleries of the British Museum.[79] At other times they idled near the heroic nude of Achilles by Richard Westmacott that had been erected in London's Hyde Park in 1822. Wilde hinted at this in his play *An Ideal Husband* (1895):

Mabel Chiltern [to Lady Chiltern], "... he [Mr Trafford] proposed to me in broad daylight this morning, in front of that dreadful statue of Achilles. Really, the things that go on in front of that work of art are quite appalling. The police should interfere."[80]

By the 1920s, one could also head off to the circus or the sports arena. Such places might be visited on one's own or with a sympathetic friend of either sex.

Here begins the first lap of the travels of
Cecil Beaton, the clever young Londoner
whose sketches and articles have been appearing in Vogue. As he jaunts about
this Western Hemisphere, he will continue
to send back his running fire of comment

AND NOW THEY GO TO SUNDAY BOXING-MATCHES

Figure 4.8 Cecil Beaton, "And Now They Go to Sunday Boxing-Matches," in "After
London, New York," *Vogue* (US edn) 77, no. 6, March 15, 1931, 70. Cecil Beaton,
Vogue © Condé Nast.

Yet, if there were plenty of heterosexual people who enjoyed gossiping with
queer men, there were others who did not.[81] On August 5, 1927, the highly effete
(and made-up) duo of Stephen Tennant and Cecil Beaton not only were treated

to unpleasant teasing by women at a ball given by the 5th Earl of Pembroke but also were chased by a group of hearties (i.e., jocks). Beaton was thrown into a river, and one of the assailants was heard to remark that he hoped the bugger had drowned.[82] Such (homo)phobic bullying was, it hardly needs stating, in line with popular attitudes of the time.[83] This is where class privilege played an important role. It is possible that Tennant did not suffer the same watery indignity because he was an aristocrat, whereas Beaton was merely middle class. But whereas Beaton was as obsessive about his work as he was about social climbing, Tennant was genuinely effete. He dedicated his only completed book from these years to E. M. Forster. *Leaves from a Missionary's Notebook* (1938) was a pictorial novel that Tennant had drawn in 1929. It tells the story of a priggish missionary who, complete with spinsters in tow, fails to convert the simmering mammies and hunky sailors of a tropical isle to the worship of Christ.[84] This minor level of artistic achievement notwithstanding, Tennant's true genius lay in performing himself into celebrity (Figure 4.9).[85]

The term "bright" had similar resonances to "gay" in that it could function as code for same-sex desire. "Loud" ties, it should be understood—be they tartan, or particularly red—were likely to be worn by queens.[86] The basic point about bright clothing for men was that normative male dress was—as it still is today in the case of suits—decidedly limited in terms of its color palette. The caption to J. H. Dowd's *The New River "Belle"* (1920) made it clear, in a way that the black-and-white cartoon itself could not, that it was not simply the feminine cut of the young man's attire that was being parodied but also his choice of fabric tones: "'I saw the Honourable Pamela Puntah, attended by a gorgeous creation in tangerine orange and cornflower blue, with hat and handkerchief to match.' [It was remarked that at Henley the men's river attire quite outshone the ladies.]" This cartoon deliberately confuses person and costume along the lines of Wilde's dictum that one should either "be a work of art, or wear a work of art." It also mixes up the "Puntah" who is reclining in the boat and the "gorgeous creation" who is doing the punting.[87] Some of those who were sartorially bright were indeed sexually gay. When Cecil Beaton designed a costume for himself as Apollo to take part in Olga Lynn's charity tableau *The China Shop* (1927), he conjured up an ensemble that would not have looked out of place on a particularly over-the-top chorus line, complete with three-foot-long feathers.[88]

The question that needs to be posed at this juncture is not so much what camp is, but why, as Richard Dyer has asked, "camp should be the form that male gay culture has taken."[89] For Eve Kosofsky Sedgwick, investment in camp was an instrumental process that should be viewed not merely through the lens

Figure 4.9 Cecil Beaton, *Stephen Tennant*, 1927. © The Cecil Beaton Studio Archive at Sotheby's (CM3801).

of amusement (as it was in 1920s *Vogue*) but "with more of an eye for its visceral, operatic power; the startling outcrops of overinvested erudition; the prodigal production of alternative histories; the 'over'-attachment to fragmentary, marginal, waste, lost, or leftover cultural products; the richness of affective variety; and the irrepressible, cathartic fascination with ventriloquist forms of relation."[90] The effect of the kind of effortful, time-consuming camp that I am discussing was arguably to draw attention to what had been unjustly overlooked. This included not only sexual nonconformity but also the effort that gay people had to make to survive in a hostile culture.[91] No matter if the masses, like those at a Liberace concert, misread camp—or could conveniently pretend to misread it—as mere frivolity. The function of much of this camp was, in the words of another critic, to "bring gay men together, united in pleasurable contempt."[92] Furthermore, it was a form of contempt that the relatively disempowered heterosexual women of the time could also share by reason of their own marginalization under patriarchy. They too were working hard. The new look for women might not require the elaborate layers of costume of yesteryear, but time had now to be devoted to tanning, exercising, dieting, and plucking.

The emphasis on being young was specifically about drawing a distinction between the current generation and that of its supposedly conventional and serious parents.[93] Again, as was the case with the slimline figure for women, many of these trends were well underway during the Edwardian period. A large teddy bear called Aloysius was clutched by Sebastian Flyte in Waugh's *Brideshead Revisited* (1945) as a sign that the aristocrat had not matured into a real man.[94] A cult among aesthetically inclined students for carrying teddy bears had been noted at Oxford University as early as 1911.[95] The bright young things had a habit of pretending to be still at school long after they had left and even, on occasion, pretending to be babies.[96] Many of them had, after all, known each other since childhood and had honed their skills at dandyism when taking a stroll across the playing fields of Eton. This was the school attended by many queer luminaries, including Harold Acton, Brian Howard, Oliver Messel, Robert Byron, and Robert Gathorne-Hardy. Beaton, however, went to Harrow, where he wore makeup.[97] A number of recent theorists have considered the degree to which childhood is intrinsically a queer space, in so far as adult norms of sexuality and sexual identity have yet to form there.[98] Vita Sackville-West, whose sexual desires were substantially toward other women, seems to have been alluding to something along such lines in an article on Edwardian households in which she talked of the queer ability of children to transgress between ranks and locations in the spaces of the grand family home.[99]

Much was made in the 1920s and later of the apparent androgyny of the slim "flapper" look for women, which featured cropped hair and favored those who were comparatively flat-chested. This gave rise to a paroxysm of parody of which the following, from *Punch*, is representative: "Two years ago Phyllis bobbed her hair. From a mysterious, and at times tragic, woman she changed into a boyish girl. Early this year she was shingled. She turned then from a boyish girl to an effeminate man."[100] Opportunities for gender confusion were supposedly legion, including at the Turkish baths where, as Anne Harriet Fish illustrated in *Vogue*, effeminate men might be mistaken for women with the latest haircuts: "the lady is Bertie Caraway, one of the plump youngsters whose figure and gestures are just too girlish for anything. Which proves that girls sometimes simply *will* be boys."[101]

Photographers might encourage such confusions. John Potvin has referred to a series of photographs of Noël Coward in the company of butchly dressed lesbian friends as "perverse double-portraits."[102] Olivia Wyndham, who had relationships with both men and women, evoked a similar effect in her depiction of Evelyn Waugh and Evelyn Gardiner as "A Bride and Bridegroom in Duplicate" (Figure 4.10).[103] When looking in the mirror, it is impossible to tell which of them was "He-Evelyn" and which "She-Evelyn" (as the pair were sometimes known). Nevertheless, it is important to recognize that women did not generally wish to be mistaken for men in the 1920s. As one contemporary article noted, "the very tailored suit is much harder to wear, it reveals every line of the figure and is inclined to be harsh to the woman who is not especially feminine looking."[104] Those women who did appear masculine in such dress were gradually to become coded not merely as unattractive but as potentially lesbian. This process ran parallel to the way in which the figure of the homosexual "pansy" emerged from that of the bright young man (as will be discussed in Chapter 6).[105] The message that these apparently androgynous styles aimed to give was that one was youthful and assertive. Those who took their style to extremes by "freaking" had to judge carefully when such daring became foolhardy and youth was no longer a defense against suspicions of sexual nonconformity. Cecil Beaton, as a sometime bright young thing, managed to pull off this trick and became one of the world's most successful celebrity photographers. In the second section of this chapter, I shall explore his life and work as a case study of the closeted world of freak chic.

The Uprise of Cecil Beaton

Photography was invented in the Victorian period, but it was only in the twentieth century that it came to be widely taken seriously as an artistic medium. Its ascent not merely to respectability but to glamor took place at the very time when

Figure 4.10 Olivia Wyndham, "A Bride and Bridegroom in Duplicate," *Sketch,* July 25, 1928, 165. © Reserved; © Illustrated London News Ltd/Mary Evans.

fashion was being marketed to an expanding audience of socially aspirational consumers by magazines such as *Vogue*. Although George Plank and other artists continued to work for the magazine through the 1920s, their work was gradually eclipsed by a series of celebrity photographers, many of whom were themselves also homosexual. The forerunner in this process was Baron Adolph de Meyer, who was born in Paris but educated in Dresden. He arrived in London in 1895, the year of Wilde's trials and conviction. The precise derivation of his aristocratic title has been the subject of some dispute, as has the status of his marriage to Olga Caracciolo. It seems likely that this was a *mariage blanc* that acted to conceal the homosexuality of both parties.[106] He moved to New York in 1913, where he worked for Condé Nast. Then, in 1922, he accepted an offer from William Randolph Hearst to sign up as the chief photographer of *Harper's Bazaar* in Paris.[107] De Meyer's story is, in essence, that of an arriviste who disguised his German Jewish origins by changing his name from von Meyer and who acquired or invented aristocratic credentials.[108] He aimed to imitate the effect of painted portraits in his glamor shots.[109] Many of these portraits purported to display high style, but have subsequently been regarded as high camp, such as those he produced for Elizabeth Arden cosmetics (Figure 4.11).[110] Nevertheless, he helped to transform such products from symbols of moral degeneracy to chic essentials. Why did such queer camp engage a wider audience of women? Probably because they saw it as sophisticated and wittily stylized.[111]

De Meyer's work at *Vogue* relied on an aesthetic of excess that was sold to the nouveaux riches of Britain and the United States as the height of European sophistication. De Meyer's "queer affective excess" relied on the placement of his models amid a profusion of objects, fabrics, and flowers.[112] Fairy culture at

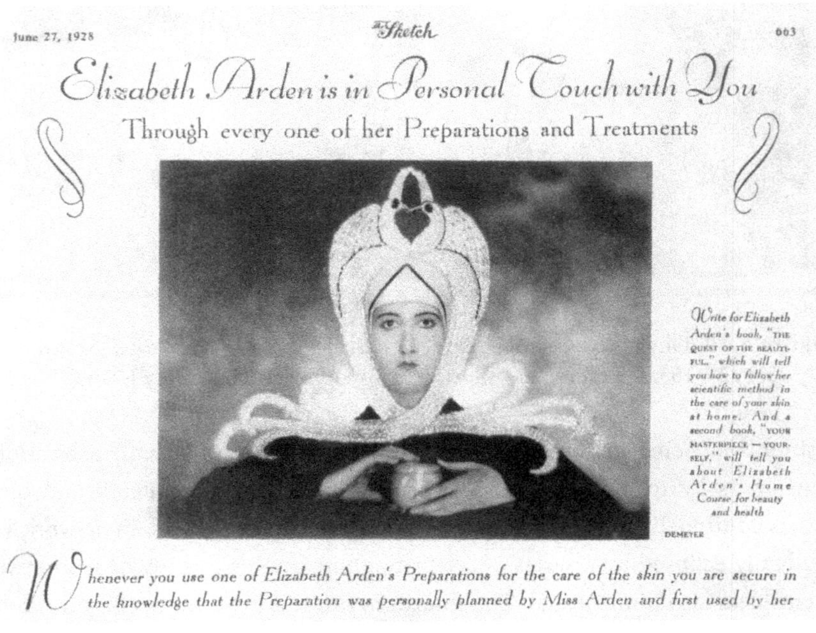

Figure 4.11 Adolph de Meyer, untitled, in detail, advertisement for Elizabeth Arden, "Elizabeth Arden Is in Personal Touch with You," *Sketch*, June 27, 1928, 663. © Illustrated London News Ltd/Mary Evans and by permission of Revlon, Inc.

this time was "signified most consistently through references to flowers" and the "adoption of faux titles."[113] De Meyer was therefore a "horticultural lad" of the kind I discuss in Chapter 6 and one noted for doing his own flower arrangements.[114] His work on *Harper's Bazaar* continued in much the same vein. When a British edition of the magazine was launched in 1929, it was clearly inspired by the amusing style of 1920s *Vogue* and featured many of the same contributors, including Hugh Walpole, Anne Harriet Fish, Robert Hichens, Oliver Messel, Virginia Woolf, Cecil Beaton, Beverley Nichols, Evelyn Waugh, and Vita Sackville-West.

Condé Nast did employ some heterosexual photographers, such as Edward Steichen (from 1923 to 1937) who was one of the leading exponents of the realist style in modern photography.[115] However, the queer tradition continued with George Hoyningen-Huene, who worked for French *Vogue* in the 1920s before moving to New York in 1935 and joining *Harper's Bazaar*.[116] He *was* born a baron. His father was from Saint Petersburg, where he had been in charge of the Tsar's stables. His mother was from Michigan and was the daughter of a diplomatic official based at the Russian court. During the Russian Revolution, he fled to Paris, where he studied drawing.[117] His work combined Steichen's modernism with a camp sense of humor and a taste for neoclassical aesthetics.[118] He was also influenced by surrealism, which during the 1930s was the height of fashion.[119] Cecil Beaton was later to comment waspishly of such compositions that "women would play a losing game as they tried to keep their dignity against huge Corinthian columns, plaster casts of Hellenic horses' heads, heads of Greek gods, or plumes of pampas grass."[120] It was Beaton himself who explicitly harked directly back to de Meyer, seeing in his work the "epitome of artificiality and luxury."[121] He also relished his predecessor's enthusiasm for a vaselined lens, saying that "whereas Steichen's pictures were taken with an uncompromising frankness of viewpoint, against a plain background, perhaps half-black, half-white, my sitters were more likely to be somewhat hazily discovered in a bower or grotto of silvery blossom or in some Hades of polka dots."[122]

In Alan Hollinghurst's celebrated novel *The Swimming Pool Library* (1988), gay men's experience both in and out of the closet is explored against the backdrop of Britain's postcolonial cultural legacy. One character in the novel, Ronald Staines, is a photographer. The narrator, William Beckwith, observes on meeting this man that "there was something about the way that he inhabited his clothes that was subversive ... His wrists were very thin and I saw that he was smaller than his authoritative suiting. He was a man in disguise, but a disguise which his gestures, his over-preserved profile and Sitwellian taste in rings drew immediate attention to."[123] Staines, like Beaton, who might well have inspired this character, displayed his closeted state as an obvious spectacle.[124] That notwithstanding, Harold Yoxall, who stepped down from the position of managing director of the magazine in London in 1956 and who had signed the photographer's first contract, attested that Beaton made "a greater contribution to the reputation of *Vogue* than any other artist."[125]

Like de Meyer, Beaton was an arriviste. He had grown up in the solidly middle-class suburbs of north London. What he called in his diaries his "uprise" concerned the achievement of social as well as commercial success.[126] As the fashion editor Diana Vreeland put it in 1980, "Cecil may have been born into the middle classes but he didn't have a middle-class bone in his body."[127] Christopher Breward, in his essay on "Couture as Queer Auto/biography," wrote that "it is surprising how many of the couturiers share memories of a common childhood, one in which the sensitive little boy inherits the practical or visionary skills of a dress-making aunt or grandmother and whiles away a lonely and persecuted school career drawing imaginary dresses and film-star portraits in his exercise books."[128] Beaton fitted neatly into this pattern. He loved getting his sisters and mother to dress up in the very best of their finery. He then photographed them as if they were grand society ladies. His genius was to understand that the space between what you want to be and what you are can be "filled with glamorous daydreams."[129]

When he arrived at Cambridge University as a student, he was noted for brightening the streets with colorful attire, the flamboyance of which was constrained more by limited funds than by notions of decorum.[130] He took to the artistic and theatrical life of the place with enthusiasm and, like his fellow student and future dress designer to the royal family Norman Hartnell, seized the opportunity to design his own frocks.[131] The Amateur Dramatic Club in Cambridge was an all-male affair and, as was the case with theater performed in single-sex public schools, men were expected to be able to act women's parts on stage. This could, after all, be justified because the classics of the repertory, such as those of Shakespeare, would originally have also been performed in this way. That does not, of course, account for the drag Beaton sported in variety revues such as *All the Vogue*, which led to him being acclaimed in *The Drama* magazine as "one of our greatest living actresses" (Figure 4.12).[132] Thus busily employed, Beaton had little time for the curriculum, and he duly left without a degree in 1925.

Dorothy Todd's replacement at British *Vogue* was Alison Settle, and it was she who invited Beaton to contribute his characteristically spidery illustrations

Figure 4.12 Dorothy Wilding, *Cecil Beaton in 'All the Vogue'*, in "'Leading Ladies' at Cambridge University," *Sphere* 101, no. 1325, June 13, 1925, 318. © Illustrated London News Ltd/Mary Evans and © William Hustler and Georgina Hustler/National Portrait Gallery, London (x36718 and CAP00528).

to the regular column "How One Lives from Day to Day." His style fitted well with the mood of the magazine in the later 1920s, which retained its delight in amusement even as it jettisoned its earlier intellectual pretentions.[133] Beaton had, however, made his photographic debut in *Vogue* a couple of years earlier when illustrating a piece about a Marlowe Dramatic Society performance of John Webster's Jacobean tragedy *The Duchess of Malfi*. The title role was played by the good-looking George "Dadie" Rylands, with whom E. F. Benson's brother Arthur had long been infatuated.[134] It was through connections made at university that Beaton began to move in high society. He brought his expertise in clothing design and cross-dressing to bright young parties.[135] Much as he relished being in *Vogue* in any capacity, Beaton kept up a steady pressure on the editors until, his complete lack of professional training notwithstanding, he was invited to contribute photographs on a regular basis. Thus, by 1929 he was supplying photographs as well as drawings to illustrate "How One Lives from Day to Day."[136]

The changing styles of the early 1930s suited the emergence of Beaton as a fashion photographer. Androgynous looks met a new interest in feminine flamboyance. By this time Beaton was working full tilt in both London and New York, and finally had the money to express his own style on a grand scale at his newly rented country residence, Ashcombe House in Wiltshire. The interior designer who most influenced him was Syrie Maugham, who had recently divorced her predominantly homosexual husband, the novelist Somerset Maugham, with whom E. F. Benson had shared a house on Capri.[137] Yet as *Harper's Bazaar* noted in "Cecil Beaton Designs for Himself," only he could have devised his "charming and witty bedroom to represent a circus" complete with a "prancing nigger" (Figure 4.13).[138] As I discussed in Chapter 2, circuses were all the rage at this time on both sides of the Atlantic, as was witnessed by Norman Hartnell's circus party in London of 1929 and its transatlantic counterpart, reported in American *Vogue* in 1932, at which the guests not only dressed up as circus characters but also put on a freak show.[139] For Stephen Calloway, the interiors of Beaton's country house were "the absolute epitome of a frothy and essentially camp baroque style."[140]

Cecil Beaton's vision for female style was inspired by the mores and snobberies of prewar Britain. Queen Alexandra, widow of Edward VII, was allotted the frontispiece in his *The Book of Beauty*—a volume that he described as "flowery"—which he published in 1930.[141] He tells us of his time as a schoolboy that "instead of doing my homework diligently, I was always thinking about Miss Lily Elsie's eyelashes and wondering what sort of picture there would be of her in the next *Sketch* or *Tatler*."[142] Just as Elsie's glory days were long past even at that date (she had been a late Victorian and Edwardian child star), so Beaton was peculiarly fascinated by aged women. He tells us that he had wanted to fill his book with those who were "pathetic little Pekinese-like hags, gallantly keeping up a pretense that they still resemble Queen Alexandra when she was young, with their rouged cheeks, marmalade wigs, and bonnets encrusted with Parma violets. But someone rather callously remarked, 'You can't fill your book with old geysers!'"[143] He fantasized about their lost youth in the Victorian period, when he supposed they would have appeared "quite unreal but divinely pretty."[144] The art of the interwar woman, he claimed, was profoundly artificial since "with a pot of paint and a brush of mascara, almost every woman can, and does, make herself look attractive."[145] Indeed it was the

Figure 4.13 George Hoyningen-Huene, *Cecil Beaton*, 1930. © George Hoyningen-Huene Estate Archives and © reserved; collection, National Portrait Gallery, London (x40421).

idea of an ugly woman—and, by implication, a man dragging up as a beautiful one—that particularly fascinated him:

> There are ladies whose natural proportions are by no means to scale, who, nevertheless, by their intelligence and sense, convert themselves into beauties. Lady Oxford, who slightingly remarks of her own face that it is but two profiles stuck together, is aesthetically one of the most striking and decorative objects of her time, with her governess-straight back, powdered hair, brittle arrogance, and witch-like delicacy.[146]

It was not merely Mary Asquith, Lady Oxford, whose freakishness Beaton admired. He declared of Lady Howe that "her poreless complexion is like icing-sugar on a birthday cake" and "her nose is like a little bleached bone."[147] In a similar fashion, the writer Edith Sitwell was declared to be both "aesthetically flawless" and "gaunt as a rock."[148] Tallulah Bankhead was admired for her "enormous snake-like eyes."[149] And Lilian Gish was acclaimed as "a divinely pretty little toy, an expensive doll made of the best-quality porcelain, with teeth of seed pearls and hair spun from a spider's web."[150] But Beaton's admiration for freakish peculiarity and eccentricity found perhaps its perfect expression in the person of the French actress and singer Gaby Deslys (Marie-Élise-Gabrielle Caire), of whom he rhapsodized:

> how well she realised the value of overdoing everything … She made herself sing, she taught herself to be an excellent dancer, she liked orchids and pearls and diamonds and emeralds and chinchilla furs, and she had more orchids than anyone, she had too much chinchilla, too many pearls, too many diamonds and emeralds, too much osprey, too many paradise plumes. (Figure 4.14)

Her house in Kensington, Beaton noted, was "glutted with crucifixes," and marble steps led the devotee up to her bed as if to an altar.[151] He positioned her as a transitional figure between the cocottes of the *fin de siècle* and the glamor-women of his own times.[152] Furthermore, he proudly declared himself to be "of the Gaby Deslys period," although of course he was not, since she had died in 1920 when he was only sixteen.[153] The extraordinary dresses that he designed for the film *My Fair Lady* (1964) were inspired by those worn by Deslys, as were many of those that he created for the freak parties of the interwar period.[154] His designs were, therefore, amusing fantasies conceptually related to those invented by George Plank for his *Vogue* covers.[155] From the time when he was a star-struck teenager, his intense fascination with female images functioned as a way to conceal his homoerotic desires since his identification with the faded diva could be taken as evidence of desire *for* her.[156]

The camp artificially of these modes of fashioning was a source of constant delight and amusement to him. Thus, it was all of a piece that his glamorous "Four Debutantes of 1928" was followed three pages later in *Vogue* by a drawing in his article "Raving Beauties" that parodied the process of taking the photograph (Figure 4.15).[157] He repeatedly drew inspiration from "freak" styles of trick photography and was duly criticized on a number of occasions by Edna Woolman Chase for having his models sniffing flowers or hanging on to hat racks "in distorted positions."[158] But he remained unrepentant, crowing in 1946 that "fashion photography grows progressively queerer and queerer."[159] His extravagant use of retouching was also celebrated as part of his style, as can be

"A FEATHER HERE, A FEATHER THERE": GABY PLUMED.

Modes à l'autruche: Mlle. Gaby Deslys in Ostrich Feathers and Diamonds.

Mlle. Gaby Deslys, once the delight of London, has been for some time in Paris. Recently she was bewailing the theft of a phonograph, worth £600, containing a record of her lines in a new production, and used by her in rehearsals. As our photo- graph shows, her taste for ostrich-feathers and colossal millinery has not diminished since her return to her native land. We are informed that the largest diamond she is wearing is valued at £20,000, the smaller necklace at £8,000. and the larger one £12,000.

Photograph by Henri Manuel.

Figure 4.14 Henri Manuel, *Gaby Deslys*, in "'A Feather Here, a Feather There': Gaby Plumed," Sketch, April 30, 1919, 129. © Illustrated London News Ltd/Mary Evans.

seen from the comment in the magazine that "our Mr. Beaton leans pensively on the camera that can never lie; however, re-touchers work lyrical transformations; hips pared wholesale, and button-eyes made starry; new debs from old."[160] D. L. Ghilchik had parodied the queer potential of a periodical's "tame

Figure 4.15 Cecil Beaton, "A Behind-the-Scene Picture of the Photograph on Page 34," in Beaton, "Raving Beauties," *Vogue* 72, no. 3, August 8, 1928, 37. Cecil Beaton/Vogue © The Condé Nast Publications Ltd.

toucher-up" who might transform girls at the beach into (very camp) rugby players, but what appeared absurd to a *Punch* cartoonist was a source of queer creative opportunity to Beaton (Figure 1.4).[161]

Blonde and brunette were conventionally terms applied only to women, but this was not so in "Blondes without, Brunettes within" from *Vogue* in 1934, in which Beaton appeared among the female models as a blonde outdoors and Stephan Tennant as an brunette indoors.[162] Mirrors provided further opportunities for images that allowed for queer play with narcissism, and Beaton took a particular interest in opportunities to create doubled images, as he did in a photographic portrait of the lesbian writer Gertrude Stein.[163] Men and women were, in Beaton's aesthetic, as potentially interchangeable as those androgynous "intelligent young persons" (himself included) whom he had shown lying in a row in a photograph published by *Vogue* in 1927.[164] Such queer aesthetics influenced the antics of the smart set and can be found informing the visual culture of fashion in the 1930s. Beaton played a key role in making freak chic. For those who were *au fait* with the private lives of their fellow socialites, this world provided myriad opportunities for gender parody, as when the masculine homosexual Tom Driberg appeared in makeup at Neil McLachlan's 1927 impersonation party as the effeminate homosexual Brian Howard. Meanwhile, Beaton himself continued to drag up, such as when he appeared in 1934 at a party at the Waldorf in the character of the lesbian actress and interior designer Elsie de Wolfe, Lady Mendl.[165]

Some of the advertisements in *Vogue* at this time appear to have picked up on aspects of queer style. An example of this is a striking Guerlain lipstick advertisement that showed a drawing by Lyse Darcy of the outline of a male face positioned in juxtaposition with a female one, but at a 45-degree angle. The image can be read either as in invitation to a heterosexual kiss or to cross-dress.[166] Beaton was able to publish some quite strikingly queer drawings of his own, such as a set of illustrations that show spinster ladies (recalling the figure of Aunt Georgie) and sailors (of the sort that Jean Cocteau liked to draw) in the act—or so it would appear—of posting Christmas cards to one another.[167] Beaton was perfectly capable of celebrating the male body, as he did in images of Johnny Weissmuller sprawling on the sand in a loincloth in 1932.[168] However, opportunities for overt homoeroticism in the pages of *Vogue* were limited. One of the earlier occasions when what might be termed a male "pinup" was featured was "Heart-Beats" in 1936, in which the reader was invited to dwell upon the high-collared charms of Anthony Eden.[169]

The easiest way to smuggle in homoerotic imagery, as Hoyningen-Huene knew very well, was to use classical statuary as props. This was prefigured in the use of classical poses by strongmen such as Eugen Sandow and reflected in the physique magazines of the 1950s and 1960s that catered to homosexual audiences.[170] It was in this mode that Beaton returned in a series of drawings to the aforementioned and massively muscled statue of Achilles in London (Figure 4.8).[171] On one level, Beaton was simply making reference to an intermittent enthusiasm for reviving the styles of the previous century, such as had surfaced in articles in *Vogue* including "The Triumph of Victorianism" (1916) and "The Victorian Age Returns" (1931).[172] But he was also practicing something that has been identified in critiques of the novels of E. M. Forster as the "reconfigured gaze." The foreground would appear heterosexual, but the gaze might be queerly redirected at strategic moments onto the male in the background.[173] The over-dressing of the women in such tableaux is thus a form of over-determination, which drains attention from their bodies to their clothes. The frocks become drag and the nudity of the statue becomes all the more startling by juxtaposition—and not only startling but also freakily excessive in terms of muscularity. The male body is thereby deflected from the world of artistic ideals into that of human performance: the artistic nude, to use Kenneth Clark's terminology, has covertly become the sexually naked.[174]

A related strategy was employed to spectacular effect in Hoyningen-Huene's 1936 depiction of a woman wearing a Hartnell frock with her arms thrown around a giant male statue (Figure 4.16).[175] So dominant is the sculpture in this visual composition that it is almost as though it has become the subject of the photograph and the woman in her frock has become the drag with which it is adorned. The accompanying article comments that "we must let the vision of glowing autumnal borders of zinnias, petunias, velvety pansies, golden marigolds, heavy snapdragons, flaming dahlias and chrysanthemums soak into our very being before we set out to choose our clothes."[176] On one level, this was a call to women to look at colors in nature before choosing their new outfits. But the passage could also be read as a call to queer men to choose the women with whom they decorated their lives, rather as they might the flowers in their buttonholes. Archives preserved by Hartnell's live-in manager, George Mitchison, who was the inheritor of the designer's estate, include a series of shots taken of Hartnell when he was at Cambridge that show him "presenting himself not as a male actor" dressed as a woman for "the sake of a theatrical performance and parody, but as a model or fashion mannequin, wearing the fashionable styles of 1921."[177] Both Beaton and Hartnell, therefore, enacted not only burlesque but also glamor drag in which they desired to inhabit the social position—if not the actual body—of a desirable woman. Flowers, frocks and women played the role of glamorized accessories in these performances.

Beaton developed another means by which to show men's bodies in images that, as I have been suggesting, are sometimes more like studies of sets of clothes than they are of the women wearing them. Significantly, this method involved the use of shadows that had the effect of implying that the ideal man was concealed behind the feminine—or indeed effeminate—exterior. In photographs illustrating an article entitled "Debutante Line-Up—This Is Their Winter" (1937), Beaton employed the visual conceit of women casting the shadows of men.[178] A more spectacular opportunity had been furnished a few years earlier by the ballet *Errante*. This was choreographed and designed

Figure 4.16 George Hoyningen-Huene, *Hartnell*, in Frances [Mrs James] Rodney, "London Laurels," *Harpers Bazaar* 15, no. 1, October, 1936, 53. Reproduced courtesy of George Hoyningen-Huene Estate Archives and Hearst Magazines UK.

by George Balanchine and Pavel Tchelitchew, respectively. The work featured a woman who dances with the shadow cast by a male dancer behind a curtain. The 1935 production was stunningly photographed by Beaton, who had been on

Figure 4.17 Cecil Beaton, *Tamara Geva in "Errante,"* 1935. © The Cecil Beaton Studio Archive at Sotheby's (KH3944).

holiday with Tchelitchew in Spain the previous year.[179] Beaton's work captures the juxtaposition between man and woman, such that he appears as a shade cast by her performance (Figure 4.17).[180] Freak parties enabled men like Beaton to enjoy social distinction as belles of the ball, but they were admired not as proud homosexuals but as amusing eccentrics. When the weekend's parties were over, the queer man in fashion went back to work arranging clothes on the women in the spotlight while his love of men remained in the shadows.

Divas

"It is only the superficial qualities that last."

Wilde, "Phrases and Philosophies."[1]

The "Modern Diana" and the "New Venus" were ideal types to which interwar women were expected to aspire.[2] The former was slim, fit, and boyish, while the latter emphasized curvaceous sexual allure and a capacity for motherhood. Cecil Beaton's preference, by contrast, was for famous but peculiar-looking women. Queer men had a tendency to bond together in shared adulation of female celebrities, particularly those who were known for their forceful personalities.[3] This was the case with Oscar Wilde when, after graduating from Oxford, he moved into a rooming house in which Frank Miles was living. John Potvin has claimed this as Wilde's "first domestic partnership."[4] The two admired flowers and the famous beauty Lillie Langtry. Later in the century Wilde, like a number of other aesthetes, was a close admirer of Sarah Bernhardt. She was another famous actress who played an important role in the creation of modern celebrity culture. Here was a woman who met your gaze straight on in her publicity photographs. She was renowned for the extreme stylization of her stage performances, which involved "hyperextension," "tempo variation," "framing," and "mobility."[5] Bernhardt was, in other words, very camp. She was also very open-minded, saying to fellow actors that "no human frailty, no ugliness, no abnormality of mind or body must repel you."[6] She had to have her right leg amputated in 1915 and became the embodiment of freak chic.[7]

Other queer men found their divas in the past rather than the present. One such was the artist Lord Ronald Gower, whose "alternative masculinity embodied a life-world in which *bric-à-brac* and idolatry, specifically the diva worship of the tragic heroine, conspicuously diverged from the social perceptions and cultural expectations of the preferred performances of masculinity premised on heroism, militarism and chivalric idealism."[8] Gower's particular object of affection was the unequivocally unattainable Marie Antoinette. Wayne Koestenbaum in *The*

Queen's Throat: Opera, Homosexuality, and the Mystery of Desire (1993) explained "the codes of diva conduct": camp, mimicry, flaunting, impersonation, and personality.[9] The diva was a fantasy figure of the stage who was both masculine in her self-assertion and feminine in her appeal to men. She might be doomed to a tragic death, but before then she would put on a spectacular and emotional show. She spoke for men who could not express their desires in public and stood as a surrogate for mothers who did not understand and women friends who knew all too well. Finally, she had a license to perform shamelessness and defiance.[10] The woman who gets what she wants, following her heart rather than her duty, struck a chord with those who wanted same-sex love rather than a conventional family.[11]

I argued in the previous chapter that Beaton's fascination with women was not what it first appeared to be—sexually normative—but was deeply queer. David Halperin has argued for the importance for many gay men during the twentieth century of various aspects of mainstream life since they seek and find "meaning and value in artifacts of heterosexual culture that were not created for them but that they can make their own and invest with a variety of queer significations."[12] Admiration of certain women, and images of those women, he further contends, has played a particularly significant role because they could provide models for identification. These ideas build on those advanced by Richard Dyer in his pioneering study *Heavenly Bodies: Film Stars and Society* (1987), in which he argued for just such a process in the construction of Judy Garland as a "gay icon."[13] I am not using an analytical framework based on trans identities, so I am not presenting evidence that the men I have been talking about saw themselves *as* women. Rather, I think they understood that their relative disempowerment and alleged effeminacy placed them, to some degree, in a comparable position *to* women. The worship of the glamorized woman, the diva, could function as an aestheticized distraction from preoccupation with men, and hence as a reinforcement for the closet. She might have the appearance of a potential lover, but the fantasized relationship might be more like that of a loving son to an ideal mother, or else the queer man might dream of standing in her stead and receiving the adulation of other men.[14]

The word "diva" literally means "goddess," and this implies that such reverent idealization could bear comparison with more conventional forms of religion. In *Visions of Queer Martyrdom* (2015), I explored aestheticized forms of Catholic revivalism in England since the mid-nineteenth century. Priests who admired beautiful statues of Jesus and the Virgin Mary were subject not only to anti-Catholic prejudice but also to suspicion of transgressions of gender and sexuality. Such thoughts lurked behind newspaper reports such as that from 1880 that stated, "as early as 4am well-known Churchmen and delicate ladies were standing outside the entrance [of Covent Garden flower market in central London] anxious to have the first bid; for so great a profit do the growers as well as the shopkeepers make of the decoration of churches that of late years they have refused to book orders in advance."[15] The word "pervert" was used to mean a convert to Roman Catholicism before it obtained its later reference to sexual deviance.[16] The unmarried priest placing flowers on an altar before a statue of the Madonna was, in effect, arranging similar elements of material culture to those employed as background in the compositions of society portraitists. There was a movement for baroque décor in Anglo-Catholic churches in interwar Britain that, like its secular equivalent, was associated with queer sexual tastes.[17] And just as many such priests came under suspicion of effeminacy, so did a number of artists and photographers who could, in some sense, be seen as their counterparts in the construction of visual-culture tableaux.

These two worlds came together at grand society weddings such as that between the Duke of Windsor and Wallis Simpson in 1937, which was photographed by Cecil Beaton. He commented:

> The conservatory floor is a mountain of imported flowers; little boys are picking the leaves from long stems; women in large picture hats, white piqué overalls, and surgical-looking rubber gloves, are trailing bundles of Madonna lilies, syringa, and laurel into the main salon.
>
> The parson is here—a genial man with a broad smile—and gives his suggestions for the placement and ornamentation of the altar.[18]

The bridal dress was one piece of spectacular couture that women of all social backgrounds were expected to dream of wearing.[19] The glamor of such occasions, centered on the visual exaltation of the bride, was not lost on the youthful Beaton, as he explained in his *Photobiography* (1951). At the age of twelve, he had taken pictures not only of his mother holding a bouquet, but also of his sisters dressed as brides.[20] Floral magnificence was a frequent aspect of Beaton's photographic compositions, and it also played a major role in his own tastes for domestic decoration. The interiors of his country home, Ashcombe, were spectacularly adorned with flowers whenever he threw a party.[21] As Jane Stevenson has commented, "excess is an important quality of the interwar use of flowers. Practically any flower can be baroque if there's enough of it."[22] The bisexual celebrity florist Constance Spry, in an article entitled "And the Church Looked Lovely," stressed that wedding flowers must not simply be chosen on the grounds of exuberant color.[23] It was widely agreed that white lilies were as suitable for brides as they were for churches because they were emblematic of purity. Nevertheless, part of the bride's glamor derived from the tacitly sexual aspect of the wedding, in that it was supposed to mark the last day of her life as a virgin.[24] In celebrity pictures such as that in *The Sketch* showing "Miss Norma Shearer's flower face," the viewer read across from the bloom, as both natural and sexual, to the woman (Figure 5.1).[25]

Figure 5.1 *Norma Shearer among the Lilies,* in "Screen Celebrities—From a New Angle: Unconventional Portraits," *Sketch*, March 12, 1930, 505. © Illustrated London News Ltd/Mary Evans.

Horst P. Horst (Horst Paul Albert Bohrmann), who was the sometime assistant and probably lover of Hoyningen-Huene, produced many images of the glamorized diva, such as in a shoot for *Vogue* in 1935 that presented women as if they were classical statues on pillars.[26] Beaton also seems to have had a preoccupation with presenting women as if they were inanimate objects. He was supposedly infatuated with Greta Garbo, but spoke of "the unutterable beauty of that strange, morbid white face" as if he were describing a statue, or indeed a corpse.[27] Another example is his depiction of the writer Edith Sitwell, who was in no sense a conventional beauty, posed as if she were a tomb effigy, with a bunch of Madonna lilies on her chest.[28]

In 1928 the homosexual artist Glyn Philpot painted *Le Jongleur de Notre-Dame* (The Juggler of Notre-Dame), which was inspired by Jules Massenet's opera that was first performed in Monte Carlo in 1902 (Figure 5.2).[29] This tells the story of a poor juggler who has abandoned his profane life and joined a monastery. As he has no other skills, he decides the only thing he can offer to the newly installed statue of the Virgin Mary is his act. He is about to be punished by the scandalized monks when he is saved by the statue, which comes to life and blesses him. Forgiven by his spiritual mother, he dies in peace.[30] The painting may owe something to the design produced by another queer artist, Charles Ricketts, for the 1924 production of George Bernard Shaw's *St Joan*. It may, in turn, have influenced Oliver Messel's designs for *The Miracle* in 1932 (originally *Das Mirakel*, which was a 1911 wordless play by Karl Vollmöller), in which a statue of the Madonna also comes to life and for which Philpot helped to model the figure of the infant Christ.[31] Playing the role of Mary brought the actress and socialite Lady Diana Cooper international fame (Figure 5.3).[32] The effect of the fabrics in Philpot's painting is to obscure the Madonna's body. As a result, the viewer becomes more intensely aware of the homoerotic potential of the young man kneeling at her feet. Jugglers worked in both circuses and freak shows, and Philpot's attraction to such performers is evident from a series of his works, such as *Acrobats Waiting to Rehearse* (1935).[33]

As Philpot was a convert to Roman Catholicism, *Le Jongleur de Notre Dame* can perhaps be thought of as a meditation on salvation from sin. However, the work was originally in the collection of Amy Gwen, Lady Melchett, whose London home, Mulberry House, also contained wall paintings by Philpot. In a photograph published in *Vogue* in 1933, she was posed such that the sinuous line of her body found its echo in the naked form of a young man painted on the wall behind her.[34] Lady Melchett was, at this time, not only one of the most glamorous figures in London society but also one of the most scandalous. She

Figure 5.2 Glyn Philpot, *Le Jongleur de Notre-Dame,* 1928, oil on canvas, private collection. Reproduced by permission of the owner.

had met her husband, the British politician, industrialist, and financier Henry Ludwig Mond, while she was living with the writer Gilbert Cannan. They formed a *ménage à trois*. Such arrangements had been a staple of Bloomsbury sexuality.[35] Mixed-gender threesomes could function in a purely heterosexual sense in that they represented an arrangement in which two men might agree to share one woman. However, such an arrangement could just as easily have accommodated

Figure 5.3 Cecil Beaton, *Lady Diana Cooper*, 1930. © The Cecil Beaton Studio Archive at Sotheby's (KH3945).

bisexual or indeed homosexual desire.[36] Such possibilities bubbled under the surface of Noël Coward's play *Design for Living* (1932), which focused on a relationship between two men and one woman and which, according to the critic Lesley Blanch writing at the end of the decade, had initially been deemed "too ambisextrous [*sic*] for London."[37] This sort of scenario was the subject of Nancy Hoyt's "Three-Cornered Love," which was serialized in *Harper's Bazaar* in the same year. This was billed as "a novel in three parts of a not-so-innocent triangular family."[38] The homosexual potential of this setup was made apparent in one of the accompanying illustrations by Floyd Davis that showed the woman toasting the two men, one of whom has his arm around the other (Figure 5.4).

Figure 5.4 Floyd Davis, untitled, in Nancy Hoyt, "Three-Cornered Love, part III," *Harper's Bazaar* 6, no. 4, July 1932, 62. Reproduced courtesy of Hearst Magazines UK and Emilie Rhys.

Figure 5.5 Cecil Beaton, "The Sitwells Are Interesting," in Sylvia Thompson, "The World Where One Amuses," *Vogue* 78, no. 3, August 5, 1931, 20. Cecil Beaton/Vogue © The Condé Nast Publications Ltd.

In 1931 Beaton drew the Sitwell brothers Osbert and Sacheverell worshipping their sister Edith as if they were supplicants and she the Madonna in a stained-glass window (Figure 5.5).[39] In the same year, he affirmed the importance he felt for the figure of the diva and her admirers—be they just two or an entire squad—in a piece recalling the theatrical good old days before the First World War. Back then, he wrote,

the male chorus was really male, and they sang lustily in their glorious uniforms, with inflated chests and outstretched arms, pointing with gloved hands to the top of the magnificently hydrangeaed staircase at which the heroine was to appear. This was the period par excellence of stagy loveliness, the colour schemes were by Comelli, actresses were really "actressy," painted dolls with arch smiles, with musical intonations to their speech, and always holding artificial roses, they were utterly mistresses of every situation.[40]

Men in this fantasized past were both virile and abundant. Glamorous women were artificial creations, "painted dolls," who need not have been played by real females at all. Since Beaton himself enjoyed dressing in drag from an early age—having begun to do so in school revues, singing numbers such as "If You Were the Only Boy in the World"—his fantasy could have been to stand in the spotlit position of the diva and be worshipped by those rows of lusty men.[41] The ability to think oneself into the subjective position of a female star was, needless to say, of immense utility in empathizing with clients and projecting their own fantasies of glamor. It was Beaton's possession of such queer expertise that fueled his uprise on both sides of the Atlantic during the interwar years. Whether they always made him gay in the sense of happy was quite another matter.

Much of the evidence for same-sex desire before the late twentieth century was written from the point of view of those hostile to it. Viewpoints that equated homosexuality with effeminacy were particularly pervasive. But, as I discussed in *Oscar Wilde Prefigured* (2016), caricature could blend into self-fashioning. If the queer dandyism of Oscar Wilde had a counterpart in interwar Britain, it might well have been that of the actor and playwright Noël Coward. They were both "self-made" men who affected a certain kind of aristocratic insouciance. Both were defined by their quips and by what they wore.[42] Coward's early life was both satirized and celebrated as a parade of bravura performances in the cheeky "Noël Coward Paper Doll" that was published in *Vogue* in 1938. The reader was invited to cut out various outfits and try them out on the celebrity in his underwear.[43] Coward offered his public risqué entertainment that was never too overtly homosexual, although works such as *Private Lives* (1930) and *Design for Living* (1932) were daring for their times.[44] Alan Sinfield has also pointed out that Coward made use of the word "gay" in song lyrics in a way that involved "tilting it just slightly more toward sexuality":

Gay to the utmost degree.
We play funny jokes
On more dignified folks
And laugh with extravagant glee.
We give lovely parties that last through the night,
I dress as a woman and scream with delight ... [45]

These lines from his song "Bright Young People" can be compared with others recalling Wilde's circle in the musical *Bittersweet* (1929):

> Pretty boys, witty boys, you may sneer
> At our disintegration.
> Haughty boys, naughty boys, dear, dear, dear!
> Swooning with affectation …
> And as we are the reason for the Nineties being gay,
> We all wear a green carnation.[46]

Gay has both an explicit and an implicit meaning in these lyrics, and it was with such mastery of innuendo that Coward was, in Sinfield's words, able to "hold homosexuality poised at the brink of public visibility."[47]

The thin, perfectly dressed man as a social ideal has conventionally been dated back to the example of George "Beau" Brummell, the sometime friend of the Prince Regent (the future George IV). This ideal had a powerful influence on British fashion in the early twentieth century, not just for men but also for women. What was a matter for parody before the First World War became an increasingly frequent sight as women took up tailored looks that recalled those of men.[48] Terry Castle in her book *Noël Coward and Radclyffe Hall: Kindred Spirits* (1996) has drawn attention to the relationships between, and the self-fashioning of, lesbians and gay men in the interwar years.[49] Coward, as I have previously noted, enjoyed being photographed with a female counterpart, often a lesbian, who was similarly dressed and posed.[50] The tendency for women to employ masculine modes of self-presentation had been critiqued since the nineteenth century as ridiculous and unnatural in terms of gender, if not yet sexuality.[51] It was held that women who wanted to do this were inherently masculine and that their search for empowerment was at the expense of men. There was, in fact, a connection between feminist thought at this time, attempts at self-empowerment, and the use of what had hitherto been seen as male attitudes and forms of dress—phenomena that Laura Doan has referred to as "gender stretching."[52] The notion that there might be a link between "uranians" (i.e., homosexuals) and suffragists had been raised as early as 1912 in *Freewoman*, although this was a publication with a limited circulation.[53]

Coward and Hall were most likely to have been read in the mid-1920s by the general public as using similar forms of self-presentation to assert their fashionable modernity.[54] The interwar years were a period when the sexes were in dialogue over self-fashioning, when certain aspects of androgyny were in fashion, and lesbians and gay men were influencing mainstream developments in style. Stars such as Marlene Dietrich defied any clear separation between masculine and feminine, heterosexual and homosexual. It was, if only for a few years, fashionable for some women to appear queerly indeterminate.[55] As Laura Doan has put it, "experimentation in clothing and gender bending was so pervasive that one could speak of an entire culture as, in a sense, cross-dressing."[56] However, as the 1920s passed into the 1930s and the general public became ever more familiar with homosexuality, dandyism in dress for both men and women became increasingly associated with same-sex desire. Freaking, in the process, also began to lose its cachet, as Anna Zinkeisen signaled in her illustrations to the "Mariegold" column in *The Sketch* in 1933: "What a bunch of Fashion's Freaks—Marlene! MUST you wear the breeks!!! [i.e., pants]."[57]

Radclyffe Hall appears to have understood her own sexuality partly in relation to notions of inversion. These supposed that lesbian desire might be produced in someone who identified as male even though they were, in reproductive terms, female. This would position Hall, in twenty-first-century terms, in relation not only to lesbian but also to trans politics. However, the way in which her self-fashioning has generally been read has been in relation to the development of lesbian identity and visibility. That notwithstanding, it is perhaps not just a question of whether Radclyffe Hall was known to be lesbian before or after a certain date, but how widely that knowledge was shared.[58] She had fallen in love with Una Troubridge after meeting her in 1915. It is possible that George Belcher knew about the true nature of their relationship. He seems to have depicted them in a *Punch* cartoon of 1925. A figure resembling Hall is shown as a "man–woman" complaining about the cost of short haircuts for women. She used to get a man's cut for 6d, but now that they have come into fashion, she has to pay ladies' prices.[59]

The stereotype of the butch lesbian appeared later in Britain than that of the effeminate sodomite, which had a tradition in visual culture dating back at least to the men known as macaronis in the 1760s and 1770s.[60] Images of same-sex desire among women before the 1930s were infrequent in the press and often associated with decadent feminity rather than with female masculinity.[61] Cross-dressing also had its own complex history. The rise in the use of hitherto masculine styles by women as a mark of fashionable self-assertion reached its height in the mid-1920s. It was in this context that Hall's novel *The Well of Loneliness* (1928) presented a portrait of Stephen as a masculine woman who desired other women.[62] The book was released in a limited print run and garnered some positive reviews. Lesbianism, therefore, could be discussed dispassionately and even, to some degree, positively at this time. This can be seen from Kenneth Bell's article on Sappho as number five in a series of "Famous Women from History." While he mentioned that there were legends that Sappho killed herself for the love of a younger man, or was a respectable wife and mother, he argued that we needed to see her on her own terms: "The Greeks had a different morality: they even allowed 'friendship' to be passionate ... it was in later ages than theirs that the limits of friendship came, no doubt for the good of the world, to be more strictly drawn."[63] He explained that "it must have been an exciting business belonging to Sappho's House of the Muses: there was a great deal of emotion about ... the little island became a centre of that cult of beauty which was somehow innate in the Greek character. If anyone had this love of beauty it was Sappho. Like Michelangelo, she was most susceptible to it when she saw it in her own sex."[64]

It was only when a court case led to the banning of Hall's novel that she became (in)famous as a lesbian and her masculine-style image began to be employed in the press to indicate same-sex desire.[65] Lilias Arkell-Smith—who was born in 1895 and married in 1918, having borne two children by another man—started to dress as a man five years later and had a series of relationships with women. But she was not at that date clearly identified as a lesbian. Contemporary observers still talked about her life in terms of practices of masquerade.[66] By the 1930s such behavior was increasingly likely to be interpreted in terms of transgressive sexuality. However, even then innuendo in the popular press concerning masculinity as an indicator of lesbianism in women was far less entrenched than it was in relation to effeminacy as a sign of homosexuality in men.[67] Overly hearty girls mostly continued to be considered aberrations of gender rather than of sexuality.[68] If homosexuality was "to some limited extent 'fashionable' between the wars," this appears to have applied more to men than women, in so far as same-sex desire was seemingly more legible in the case of the former.[69] I shall now explore how limited even that degree of fashionability was, in terms of both its overtness and its duration.

Mariegold in Society

The term "heterosexual" was, if anything, even less frequently employed in early-twentieth-century Britain than "homosexual," yet it is important to think about the attitudes of people who would be spoken of as "straight" in later decades. Those men who expressed the fear that male "effeminacy" could lead to female empowerment were not, in fact, entirely incorrect. The freak chic of the 1920s was often driven by homosexuals (both male and female) and by heterosexual women. The resulting style combined commercial awareness with sexual provocation and with stylistic and performative excess. It represented not only a phase in the history of women's fashion but also the point of origin of important elements of gay culture and sensibility. In the previous section, I looked at what queer men such as Cecil Beaton gained from their focus on the figure of the glamorous diva. It is important to emphasize, however, that the desires and objectives of queer men were not identical to those of real women with whom they were collaborating and partying. To understand the viewpoint of the latter, it is helpful to think about the female consumer as an epitome of modernity during the 1920s.[70] The cult of glamor was not just embraced by women because their queer friends liked it.[71] It offered an alternative to traditional feminine compliance.[72] As a quality, it did not depend on being pretty. What it required were confidence and personality.[73] This enabled women to compete with each other while keeping pestering male suitors at a reassuring distance.

At a time of massive divides in wealth, but also of awareness of the artificial character of the underlying class structures, status was claimed and proclaimed through spending and performance. In June 1929, *Vogue* informed its readers in "Chic: A Defence" that the Parisian woman of style was

> an artist of externals … not only in the colour harmonies (or contrasts) and lines of her clothes, but also in her walk, in the shape of her finger nails [*sic*], in the way she handles a teacup or cigarette. (Such apparently trivial actions also reveal the quantity and quality of modernity latent in this particular person's mental make-up.) This consciousness of self as part of a picture is sometimes so innate a quality of an individual's mind that it seems, paradoxically, to be an unconscious, or sub-conscious, quality.[74]

Femininity in this mode could be claimed through performative excess of the kind we now refer to as camp. The attention of *Vogue*'s readers was drawn in 1921 to a Pekinese dog that watched as "Mlle. Dorziat applied the requisite make-up to her feet: 'If she has rings on her toes, it's tea time; if there are no rings, it's morning.' These are the deductions of Peki, the canine feminist, when roused by a gentle nudge from a tiny sandal."[75] Such excess of ease and modern affectation was satirized by all manner of British cartoons. One such in *Punch* from 1928 showed a "film star" smoking a cigarette—she was using a holder that was so long that it extended out of her vast home and terminated somewhere in the garden.[76]

Abdulla Cigarettes were particularly noted for running advertisements that glamorized smoking as a fashionably decadent pleasure. One of these, "The

Bright Brigade," featured a poem by F. R. Holmes and a cartoon by Anne Harriet Fish of a model smoking in her bath and being photographed by a bright young man who was quite possibly based on Beaton (Figure 5.6).[77] The title of the poem, "Higher Photography," evokes a number of more or less flippant verbal conceits

Figure 5.6 Anne Harriet Fish, untitled, in advertisement for Abdulla Cigarettes, "The Bright Brigade" *Sketch*, September 4, 1929, 475. © Reserved; © Illustrated London News Ltd/Mary Evans.

such as "higher sodomy" that were in use in Bloomsbury circles. Fashionable women were, of course, objects of the male gaze, but they were also increasingly empowered to express their own vision of what they wanted to see in men, either as friends or as lovers. It was in this spirit that the actor Basil Rathbone, when appearing in the play "The Czarina," could be celebrated in American *Vogue* as "the darling of a queen. His part is a delightful mingling of manly firmness and petulant yielding."[78] In the final section of this chapter, I present a case study of the empowering use of strategic camp by a fictional woman that had the effect of parodying patriarchal conventions. Queer male companions appear initially as allies but morph, over the space of a few years, into embarrassments.

The gossip column by "Mariegold" was a long-running feature of the society magazine *The Sketch*. This documented events in high society and was illustrated by drawings—usually in a set of four or five narrative scenes—that featured the supposed antics of Mariegold herself. During the later twenties and early thirties, these illustrations were produced by Anna Zinkeisen (Figure 5.7).[79] She and her sister Doris were successful artists. Their family home was in Kilcreggan, Dumbartonshire, where their father was a middle-class merchant (as was Beaton's father). In 1909 the family moved to Pinner in north-west London, and the sisters were sent to Harrow School of Art, before winning scholarships to the Royal Academic Schools. They produced a very wide range of work, ranging from portraits to book illustrations and posters for major commercial clients such as the London North Eastern Railway and Imperial Chemicals Industries. They also worked on the murals of the RMS *Queen Mary*.[80] They were, as Jane Stevenson has flagged up, not merely artists but also "beauties and socialites."[81]

It was widely known in professional circles that the actor and director James Whale was homosexual, so it caused something of a stir among their friends when it was heard that he was engaged to marry Doris Zinkeisen in 1923. The two never did get married, but they remained very close friends.[82] One explanation for this was that they had decided that a *mariage blanc* was not for them. While Doris was to make a name for herself with her innovative theater designs, Whale went into the movie business and was to go on to direct a number of famous horror films, including *Frankenstein* (1931). The queerness of the freakishness and monstrosity in these works has aroused considerable critical attention.[83] Doris, who designed for a wide range of theater productions, including some by Noël Coward and others where she worked alongside Oliver Messel, was well acquainted with theatrical queer men.[84] In 1938 she published a "How to Do It" book on stage design, which included several of her costumes. For instance, the previous year she had designed a costume for Leslie Banks who had been cast as

Figure 5.7 "A Well-Known Contributor to 'The Sketch': Miss Anna K. Zinkeisen," *Sketch*, February 2, 1927, 195. © Illustrated London News Ltd/Mary Evans.

Petruchio in the New Theatre, London production of Shakespeare's *The Taming of the Shrew*.[85] Banks was known for playing gruff, intimidating characters, but Doris put him in a skintight outfit with the highest of thigh boots. The outline of his buttocks was, furthermore, picked out by a ribbon that had been tugged across them and tied up with bows. This costume had the effect of parodying conventional masculinity and turning the actor into a camp sex object (Figure 5.8). As she said in the accompanying text,

Figure 5.8 Doris Zinkeisen, *Costume for Mr. Leslie Banks as Petruchio, c.*1937, in Zinkeisen, *Designing for the Stage,* How to Do It Series 18 (London: Studio, 1938), 45. © The Estate of Doris Zinkeisen. All Rights Reserved. DACS 2020.

Furnishings—like costumes—can be submitted to fantastic treatment provided the characteristics of the period are maintained as a foundation. In such cases the materials used must be regarded as a basis from which to conjure a vivid parody, and trimmings or decorations, equally devoid of all authenticity, can nevertheless portray the essentials of the period in their own way.[86]

Her approach to costume design thus bore considerable similarity to that of Cecil Beaton or George Plank. Indeed, Doris's book contains a drawing of a "costume for a showgirl" with giant puffball sleeves that is very similar to that of the pianist dreamed up by Plank for the cover of *Vogue* in October 1919 (Figure 3.4).[87]

A similar sensibility inspired Doris's sister Anna. She replaced Gladys Peto as the illustrator of the "Mariegold" column in July 1926. Peto was particularly famous for costume designs and illustrations in children's books. Anna, however, did not merely draw cute young people but presented those youngsters as challenging their elders in, to take one example, gentlemen's clubs: "to permit the entry of the sedate wives of … elderly members was *one* thing; but that Mariegold should … [enter] the premises with her bevy of gay young friends—should sit on the arms of chairs and chatter, while drinking *cocktails*—that was something no one had bargained for, and was positively *indecent!*"[88] While the text of the Mariegold column engaged with real-life events in high society, Zinkeisen's illustrations were fantasies that parodied the older generation at the expense of the younger. Zinkeisen's Mariegold was sassy and sexually liberated. She was particularly eager to violate male spatial prerogatives when there was a chance of seeing some young flesh. On one occasion, she ventures to a lido (an outdoor swimming pool), and since the men are sunbathing topless, she does so too.[89] On another occasion she blunders into a men's shower room—"'how deliciously naughty' she thinks," before being ushered out.[90] Or she finds herself in a Turkish bath—"*Gracious!* Into what sacred male harem had she strayed?"[91]

Zinkeisen's Mariegold is a young woman who demands extremes of fashion. Her taste in fancy dress calls for excess. She is convinced on one such occasion that her frock "had to be simply enormous—bigger than any dress had ever been."[92] She is not only interested in camp clothing but also in associating with camp men. We are duly presented with her dress designer in the form of "An exclusive and charming portrait of Madame Jamais, who in private life is Mr. Pimpskin Pottle" (Figure 5.9).[93] This might be a parodic reference to the court dressmaker "Madame Desirée," who helped to give Norman Hartnell his start in London and who was really Mrs Hughes.[94] When Mariegold herself takes up costume design, the results are remarkably androgynous, as in the case of "'Plus More'! (Men such comfort should adore)." This featured knickerbockers so long

2. An exclusive and charming portrait of Madame Jamais, who in private life is Mr. Pimpskin Pottle.

Figure 5.9 Anna Zinkeisen, "An Exclusive and Charming Portrait of Madame Jamais, Who in Private Life Is Mr. Pimpskin Pottle," in "Mariegold," "Mariegold in Society," *Sketch*, January 12, 1927, 56. © Illustrated London News Ltd/Mary Evans.

that they looked like a skirt.[95] The same effect could, in real life, be seen on the legs of daring youths who wore those extraordinarily wide pants known as Oxford bags.[96]

The text in most of the Mariegold columns appears to have been composed separately from the accompanying illustrations. However, in this last example the camp of Zinkeisen's cartoon was reflected in the text, which discussed some "extraordinarily witty" verses written by Lord Berners and another queer dandy, Evan Morgan, Lord Tredegar. These could not be reprinted, however, since they were "often too personal or too direct for the public press."[97] For the most part, however, the text of the column itself (as opposed to its illustrations) focused on goings-on in high society. It specialized in describing such gatherings of the "aristocratic Intelligentsia" as one at which all the "Mayfair highbrows seemed assembled … Of course, the flowers were lovely, and the decorations included huge glass bowls filled with flowering cherry, pink azaleas, and yellow broom from Wales placed in many effective positions."[98] It was in such surroundings that the queerly amusing style flourished. Thus, on one occasion Cathleen Mann, Lady Queensberry, was duly noted for having unveiled a new painting, *Children of Lot*, which supposedly showed "a group of modern 'highbrows' clad in the gay 'woollies' and pullovers of the moment, escaping from a burning Sodom and Gomorrah."[99] *The Sketch* also called upon the talents of Anna Zinkeisen to illustrate other social events such as the Chelsea Arts Club balls that were notorious for their queer attendees and adventurous sartorial practices, including cross-dressing (Figure 5.10).[100]

Gender was highly performative in Anna's illustrations for the magazine. Mariegold was, for instance, shown as happy to help out some awfully young soldiers by fitting them with false whiskers after an edict was passed saying that the household cavalry must sport facial hair: "Willing spirits there were aplenty— / But the flesh is weak—when it's under twenty!"[101] It may just be coincidence, but the word "hair" was shown reversed as "riah" in the window of

JOHN'S NOAH AND JACK TARS! THE CHELSEA ARTS CLUB BALL.

Miss Anna K. Zinkeisen, in company with many other celebrated persons, brought in the New Year at the Chelsea Arts Club Ball, at the Albert Hall. It was "Noah's Night," with a Noah's Ark designed by Mr. Augustus John; but Miss Zinkeisen found some Jack Tars much to the fore, and has allowed them to occupy the foreground of her impression of the Ball.

SPECIALLY DRAWN FOR "THE SKETCH" BY ANNA K. ZINKEISEN.

Figure 5.10 Detail, Anna Zinkeisen, untitled, in "John's Noah and Jack Tars! The Chelsea Arts Club Ball," *Sketch*, January 8, 1930, 50. © Illustrated London News Ltd/Mary Evans.

the shop selling "Beardo" hair-growth lotion ("Riah" was used to mean "hair" in the gay argot known as Polari). On another occasion, she dressed up in uniform herself in order to drill a girls' brigade troop.[102] But there was no danger, despite her boyish figure, of Mariegold being taken for a (straight) man because she was so intent on performing feminine obsessions. It is important to note, in that context, that if Mariegold initially found effeminacy in men amusing, the same could not be said for masculinity in women.

This can be illustrated by a set of illustrations telling the story of a visit to Paris. She had bought some gossamer undies while on holiday that shocked a British customs official. "'Yer can't take these 'ere sort of things into England,'" he exclaims![103] But worse is yet to come: "Mariegold did not think that life would hold greater misery for her until she was ushered into the presence of two female officials, who eyed her coldly, maliciously, stonily, and then in silence tore the very clothes from her back" (Figure 5.11).[104] Laura Doan has argued

Figure 5.11 Anna Zinkeisen, "Mariegold Did Not Think That Life Would Hold Greater Misery," in "Mariegold," "Mariegold in Society," *Sketch,* September 21, 1927, 541. © Illustrated London News Ltd/Mary Evans.

persuasively that at this date, 1927, apparently masculine representations of women cannot usually be seen as referring to same-sex desire, but bearing in mind the sexual knowingness of the Mariegold column, this may be one of the exceptions. It is also very similar in style to later caricatures of lesbians as harridans.[105] Mariegold is very aware of her own physical charms, but is also preoccupied by thoughts of freakish deformity. In a hall of mirrors at a circus, she stares at her distorted reflection and asks herself, "were the mirrors in the corners of the room positively libellous, or did one look every inch the grotesque figure reflected?" (Figure 5.12).[106]

3. The question was, were the mirrors in the corners of the room positively libellous, or did one look every inch the grotesque figure reflected ?

Figure 5.12 Anna Zinkeisen, "The Question Was," in "Mariegold," "Mariegold in Society," *Sketch,* March 2, 1927, 393. © Illustrated London News Ltd/Mary Evans.

This camp humor is of a kind that was employed by queer men, but it was deployed here to a different purpose. During the 1920s certain women employed understandings of what we would now term gender construction and performativity to critique conventional masculinity. Some of these women, such as the Zinkeisen sisters, had queer male friends and appear to have been influenced by their styles. Men, particularly overbearingly masculine ones, were subjected to sustained mockery. Thus, when Mariegold is talent-spotted to take part in a Hollywood film, *Grubby Gump of Gory Gulch*, she falls for a model of the lead actor rather than for the man himself. It was, she thought, "unfortunate that she should mistake a dummy for the real hero; but then the dummy *looked* so much more dashing."[107] In 1927 she is found musing on whom to wed—a poet, a strong and silent type, a "sugar daddy" (should she marry gold?), or a figure embodying primitive desire:

> her thoughts wandered to the Cave Man; the brutal masterful man who would beat her when jealous, crush her in his arms when remorseful, smother her with embraces when playful, and strangle her with caresses when loving. But Mariegold soon decided that it might be *too* hectic and uncomfortable, not to say *tiring*, to live with a Cave Man.[108]

In the end, she thinks that perhaps she is better off staying single.

Mariegold even developed an overtly feminist take on contemporary politics in "Mariegold's Political Problems" (1933):

> Titans now the world remake— / Which as model should one take?
> Well! One might admit a teeny / Secret "pash" for Mussolini!
> Should one sit at Hitler's feet? / (Mr. Hitler looks so sweet!)
> Should one totter (more or less) / In the wake of "G. B. S." [George Bernard Shaw]?
> Or—while fiercer passions foam— / Be the Angel-in-the-Home? (Figures 5.13 and 5.14)[109]

Anna seems at this date to have become actively opposed not merely to patriarchy at home but also to masculinist nationalism of any kind, as can be seen from her mockery of a man waving a Union Jack: "Strange how a symbol should so inspire / The Man in the Street with a foolish fire!"[110] It was shortly after this point that she ceased to illustrate the column. Fascism was becoming identified with the reassertion of traditional gender roles, and this was sometimes extolled in fashion magazines. An example of this was Nika Dittman's peon to fascist Italy, published in *Harper's Bazaar* in 1934, as a land where "with Gertrude Stein's permission … a woman is a woman and a man is a man."[111] It was in this

2. *Well! One might admit a teeny Secret " pash " for Mussolini !*

Figure 5.13 Anna Zinkeisen, "Well! One Might Admit a Teeny Secret 'Pash' for Musolini!" in "Mariegold," "Mariegold Broadcasts," *Sketch*, May 24, 1933, 324. © Illustrated London News Ltd/Mary Evans.

land that the people were "young and active."[112] If Christopher Reed is correct in saying that "young" in 1920s *Vogue* implied "queer," that seems not have been the case by the mid-1930s.[113] Even Mariegold seems to have grown tired of her youthful camp companions:

3. *Should one sit at Hitler's feet?*
(Mr. Hitler looks so sweet!)

Figure 5.14 Anna Zinkeisen, "Should One Sit at Hitler's Feet?" in "Mariegold," "Mariegold Broadcasts," *Sketch,* May 24, 1933, 325. © Illustrated London News Ltd/Mary Evans.

Cranks find something e'er amiss— / "Do away with That or This"
We, of course, have heard for years— / "Do away with Wives' Careers!"
Now they're going to ration "spoons"— / "Do away with Honeymoons!"
Soon—it may not matter much— / "Do away with Men—as such!"
Further progress next would bring— / "Do away with EVERYTHING!!"[114]

Thus, in 1933 Anna lamented the challenges that faced contemporary women and implied that one might as well "'do away with Men—as such!'" (Figure 5.15). To illustrate this line, she depicted a flamboyant man of the type then becoming known as a homosexual "pansy." The costume is like that of the

4. Soon—*it may not matter much*—
" Do away *with Men*—*as such !* "

Figure 5.15 Anna Zinkeisen, "Soon—It May Not Matter Much—'*Do Away* with Men—as Such!'" in "Mariegold," "Mariegold Broadcasts," *Sketch*, April 26, 1933, 145. © Illustrated London News Ltd/Mary Evans.

non-crossed-dressed character, Carlo Crivelli, that Beaton had played in *All the Vogue* at Cambridge in 1925.[115] Heterosexual women played an important role as the friends and patrons of the 'gay' men who were encouraging freak chic during the 1920s. But focusing on the figure of the diva was not always empowering for such men because it implied their subordinate status and undermined claims to autonomy and individuality. Increasing public awareness of homosexuality was accompanied by a concomitant rise in mainstream disgust and media stereotyping during the 1930s. The pansy, as a type, duly came to represent not so much an amusing companion as an embarrassment and a social impediment.

The Floral Closet

"A really well-made buttonhole is the only link between Art and Nature."
Wilde, "Phrases and Philosophies."[1]

Havelock Ellis was one of the leading sexologists of his times. The English-language version of his book on sexual inversion, written with the help of John Addington Symonds, was pioneering in making available the results of German sexual science to British audiences in 1897, although it was then promptly banned.[2] In 1914 Ellis published the first of a series of diaries in which he expounded his thoughts on a wide range of topics. On April 27, 1913, his thoughts had been of flowers. "Surely it is as symbols," he wrote, "manifoldly complex symbols, that flowers appeal to us so deeply. They are, after all, the organs of sex … There is nothing so vitally intimate to himself that man has not seen it, and rightly seen it, symbolically embodied in flowers."[3] They might be sported as a fashionable gentleman's buttonhole, but a wholehearted passion for blossom was popularly held to be characteristic of women. Blooms could be associated variously with nature, purity, and religion on the one hand and artifice, sensuality, and sexuality on the other. Marigolds, being a bright orange-yellow, were not, visually, the subtlest flowers in the herbaceous border. But neither, of course, were the sunflowers that played such an important role in Victorian aesthetic taste. Flowers might, therefore, appeal to those who wished to "conceal their erotic impulses behind the innocence of petals and blooms."[4]

Flowers were widely deployed in later nineteenth-century art to refer to sexual desires that could not be depicted openly. The very act of painting flowers could be interpreted in a sexualized manner as, for instance, the male artist pollinating the canvas with his brush. The work of the eighteenth-century botanist Carl Linnaeus inspired various works that speculated on the significance of the fact that many flowers were composed of a combination of male and female reproductive organs.[5] Therefore, blooms could be employed to symbolize

androgynous or otherwise transgressive forms of gendered expression. Scenes
of children with flowers could hint at queer interests in androgynous youth.[6]
Such botanical perversity serves to remind us that decadence was not, as has
sometimes been imagined, a solely urban and artificial affair.

Queer culture of the kind that interested Oscar Wilde might involve decadent
tastes for freakish and excessive things, but it also strove insistently toward
aesthetic beauty. Thus, the sexual deviant can be seen to have been caught
between the desire to revel in his abject status and to find a way visually to redeem
it. Wilde at various times celebrated both natural and unnatural beauty and
embraced both pagan desires and Christian sentiments. Victorian religion and
aestheticism were interwoven in a myriad of complex ways. Decadent flirtations
with evil might lead us to cynicism concerning the spiritual pretensions of queer
aesthetes. Thus, the very eclecticism of the religious paintings of the homosexual
Pre-Raphaelite painter Simeon Solomon, encompassing, as they did, scenes of
Jewish as well as Christian and pagan devotion, can be held to imply a lack of
religious sincerity. Yet even Aubrey Beardsley, who filled his profane landscapes
with malevolently suggestive flowers and foliage, was to convert to Roman
Catholicism.[7] Queer male aestheticism in the early twentieth century continued
its search beyond the boundaries of Britain and of Christianity, not just in
search of decorative novelties but also of societies and their cultures that did not
discriminate against men who felt love and desire toward other men.

Blossoms could be used to display glamor and status, notably when the plants
involved were exotic and brought to perfection out of season in hothouses. They
could appear in their natural form or in artificial versions, be arranged in vases or
included in society portraits.[8] At one and the same time, they spoke to innocent
beauty and, as reproductive organs, to sexual urges. It is hardly surprising,
therefore, that Oscar Wilde made extravagant use of floral similes, such as in
his short story "The Star-Child," which appeared in *A House of Pomegranates*
(first published in 1891): "he was white and delicate as sawn ivory, and his curls
were like the rings of the daffodil. His lips, also, were like the petals of a red
flower, and his eyes were like violets by a river of pure water, and his body like
the narcissus of a field where the mower comes not."[9] In this story, the exquisite
child is well aware of his own visual charms but is wanting in moral sensibility.[10]
It was therefore with self-awareness of perilous allure that Wilde described his
lover Lord Alfred Douglas in similar terms in a letter of January 1893, which
returned to haunt its author at his libel trial two years later. "Your sonnet," wrote
Wilde to Bosie, "is quite lovely, and it is a marvel that those red rose-leaf lips
of yours should have been made no less for music of song than for madness of

kisses. Your slim gilt soul walks between passion and poetry. I know Hyacinthus, whom Apollo loved so madly, was you in Greek days."[11]

In the course of his life, Wilde positioned himself amid lilies, sunflowers, and green carnations, and also between Hellenism and Christianity.[12] It has been argued that those particular blooms with which he was associated spoke to gender confusion because they were bold rather than delicate.[13] They provided ways of evoking male beauty by means of metaphor and juxtaposition. Decadent and aesthetic verse was suffused with such sentiments, and "by the end of the century, homoerotic writing was full of flowers."[14] To give one example, when Marc-André Raffalovich published his second volume of verse, *Tuberose and Meadowsweet*, in 1885, he was making use of a set of conventions that were more usually employed by women to talk about their romantic affections.[15] Each blossom could be held to accord with particular romantic and erotic qualities, and thus a description of flowers could stand as an erotic cipher.[16] A further advantage of the language of flowers for queer purposes was that it offered the potential to mediate between the natural and the artificial worlds. Exotic blooms could stand proxy for strange loves that were rarely found in nature as elements of God's creation. Floral displays could be employed as a more or less recondite code in which to evoke a queer arcadia where same-sex desire could be both naturalized and aestheticized.[17] In the aftermath of Wilde's disgrace in 1895, the utility of what might be termed the floral closet became all the more attractive and important. Nevertheless, while gardening was held up in the twentieth century as a healthy pursuit of natural forms of beauty that was suitable for the masses, it had not entirely shrugged off its earlier associations with elite self-indulgence. Suburban gardening in particular was mocked in *Punch* in cartoons such as Tom Peddie's "Garden Suburb Amenities" (1912).[18] This showed a husband and wife at work in their garden, dressed in the aesthetic costume of the 1880s. Lilies and sunflowers in a border still evoked the poses and rhapsodies of the young Wilde, or at least the parodies on those themes that had been so immensely popular at the time.[19]

In Britain, France, and the United States, the proscribed desires of queer subcultures were "signified most consistently through references to flowers."[20] Homoerotic love in the First World War poetry was shot through with floral eroticism that drew directly on the aesthetic codes of late-Victorian verse.[21] This phenomenon was reflected in contemporary parody such as "Messrs. Hopeful and Boomage" by Jack B. Yeats (the brother of the poet William Butler Yeats).[22] In this drawing, mundane aspects of suburban life and commerce suffice to transform the manly environment of a wartime trench into a camp parody of home through products such as a "floral painting outfit that converts rifle into easel," a handy "little pet" vacuum cleaner that "removes dust from all corners," and "the Old Château exercises," which is a pulley for weight training.

A pattern of hints toward coded desires can be found in the series of gardening books by the popular writer Beverley Nichols. The first of these, *Down the Garden Path*, appeared in 1932, complete with "decorations" by Rex Whistler. Nichols graced his new country cottage with the queer spirit of Bloomsbury by installing a statue of Antinous (male lover of the emperor Hadrian):

> He once stood in the corner of an old house in Bedford Square. He was covered with grime and his limbs seemed stained eternally. I saw him after lunch on a grey day in February. After shameless hinting and ogling I persuaded my host that he was unhappy in London ... gradually the sweet country rain washed his limbs ... his perfect, lyrical shoulders began to gleam in the sunlight. Now he shines and sparkles. He is spotless. To see him when the snow is on the ground, when the snowdrops are pushing humbly at his feet, when the winter sky is silver, white blue ... ah! That is to see man as a flower, yes, as a strange white flower.[23]

In 1939 Nichols was parodied in *Punch* in the form of a clerihew, a whimsical poetic form invented by Edmund Clerihew Bentley.

"Ow!" screamed Beverley Nichols.
"Take it away! It tickles!
You *know* I simply can't bear
An earwig loose in my hair."[24]

This camp verse was illustrated by Edmund's son Nic[h]olas's drawing of Beverley bending over with his buttocks to the viewer while being watched by an amused male friend (Figure 6.1). Nichols was something of a literary lightweight, but he was, that notwithstanding, admired by other figures whose works have better stood the test of time. One such was Vita Sackville-West, whose marriage to Harold Nicholson in 1913 did not unduly impede her—or indeed his—same-sex enthusiasms.[25] It can be argued that it was not simply their marriage that was powerfully queer but also the garden they created at Sissinghurst in Kent. Hints of this can be found in a variety of their writings. For example, Vita in her poetry played with the erotic implications of English plant names, as when she compared the significance of calling colchicums Naked Boys or Naked Ladies.[26]

Gardening of the kind that I have been describing here was an aesthetic pursuit that was intimately connected with personal relationships. In the aftermath of Wilde's disgrace, the shelter of the floral closet could provide a place of aesthetic safety. But as time went by, the decadent side of these amusements came back

"Ow!" screamed Beverley Nichols.
"Take it away! It tickles!
You *know* I simply can't bear
An earwig loose in my hair."

Figure 6.1 Detail, Nic[h]olas Bentley (image), Edmund Clerihew Bentley (text), "More Clerihews," *Punch* 196 (1939), 39. Reproduced by permission of Punch Cartoon Library/TopFoto.

into prominence. Understanding this involves thinking about gardening and flower arranging as artistic practices that were associated with self-fashioning. To take one example, it has been suggested that the personal life of the celebrity florist Constance Spry—she lived with the artist Gluck (Hannah Gluckstein) between 1932 and 1936, after the failure of two relationships with men—can explain her eccentric choice of native "weeds" in some of her creations.[27] One thinks of Virginia Woolf's comment on the hero/ine of *Orlando: A Biography* (1928) that "his taste was broad; he was no lover of garden flowers only; the wild and the weeds even had always a fascination for him" (this had the implication that s/he was attracted to people of the lower class).[28] Mainstream expectations of the essentially feminine nature of floral décor could, therefore, be subtly subverted and incorporated into both rural queer lives and their chic metropolitan equivalents.[29]

Elaborate flower arrangements were an expected element in the visual adornment of upper-class houses, and they were often sourced from the gardens or hothouses of the family's country estate. There also developed an industry to supply flowers on a commercial basis, which had its London focus at Covent Garden market. Buying flowers in town would have been a task for the servants, but the mistress of the household sometimes took a personal interest, as Woolf indicated in the first line of one of her novels: "Mrs Dalloway said she would buy the flowers herself."[30] What was not expected was that men, unless they were gardeners or worked in the retail trade, should concern themselves with such matters.

The interiors of houses could be florally queered not just through arrangements but also through the adornment of walls with flowery paintings. The queer language of flowers in art developed in distinctive ways in the aftermath of the 1890s. I have been eager to stress that it was often employed as a way of subtly coding queer interests. It was therefore not in itself obviously subversive. Indeed, early twentieth-century feminists sometimes railed against the stereotype of floral femininity that acted as a sort of anti-type to the self-assertive style of the New Woman.[31] It is tempting to see the attack by the suffragette Mary Aldham (née Wood), at the opening day of the Royal Academy Summer Exhibition in May 1914, as an explosion of rage against the collusion of closeted men with mainstream misogyny. However, we cannot know if she had particular suspicions of the private life of Henry James, the subject of the painting she attacked, or of another London-based American John Singer Sargent, who had painted it.[32] The latter owed his fame to his ability to produce glamorous portraits of members of high society, notably its leading ladies. He did not marry, nor are his sexual tastes clear (which might in itself be interpreted as a queer sign).[33]

It is possible to distinguish a queer sensibility in the closeted circle of friends and associates of Henry James. Leaving aside the painter Jacques-Émile Blanche's claim, made after Sargent's death, that he had been a "frenzied bugger" in Paris and Venice, these men can be seen as "hardened bachelors" who were connected by bonds of "queer filiation."[34] In London, at least, they were discreet to the point of enigma. Nevertheless, it appears that "Sargent on occasion allowed his eye for male beauty to be reflected in his art."[35] He seems to have painted male, nude studies for personal pleasure rather than for money. A powerful sense of eroticism suffuses such works as his *Nude Study of Thomas E. McKeller* (c.1917–20).[36] This was very much a milieu of closeted desires in which "James and Sargent had [some limited] permission to express responsiveness to men in their work as long as they led 'proper' public lives."[37] The floral aspects of Sargent's work sometimes acted to distract the eye from otherwise over-evident bodily allure. Thus *Boboli* (1907), which is a painting of a statue, "is mostly devoted to capturing the atmosphere of tinted shadows and lush foliage that shrouds and encircles the tall marble creature."[38] A powerful case for Sargent as a sexually indeterminate aesthete is made by Alison Mairi Syme in her study *A Touch of Blossom: John Singer Sargent and the Queer Flora of Fin-de-Siècle Art* (2010). She argues that the painter's enthusiasm for flowers can be related to a love of sensuous beauty in all its forms, but also to floral abundance as a visual analogue for his own sexual desire.[39]

Sargent can, therefore, be seen as having been in some ways the precursor of Cecil Beaton. Both men led closeted lives and made abundant use of flowers in many of their compositions. Both thrived as a result of their genius for making glamorous images of women that focused on lavish interiors and dramatic costumes.[40] Moreover, Sargent can also be seen as having prefigured certain elements of interwar freak chic in so far as he produced, according to Fairbrother, "numerous pictures celebrating outlandish and sensual bodies ... All these images lean toward the daring, risky, unconventional, dramatic, erotically off-center, and odd. It is now obvious that they comprise a valuable subset of Sargent's oeuvre."[41] Sargent celebrated glamorous women while leaving "the door open for other audiences to pursue independent conclusions" concerning his motivations.[42] Much the same could be said of Beaton. Both men produced images that do not immediately fit into the mainstream narratives of modernism but which, at second glance, are far from simply reflections of a conservative refusal to abandon romanticism. Thus it has been argued of Sargent's *Carnation, Lily, Lily, Rose* (1885–7) that much is left unexplained if the mode of critique is merely to apply "conventional models of modernism—heroic avant-garde versus conservative reactionary academy—to late-nineteenth-century British art."[43]

It was experiments in "off-center" representation that bore particular relevance to the subsequent development of the fashion for freakery. The connection here is with floral decadence as opposed to the wider phenomenon of floral aestheticism. The classic textual reference point for decadent botany is the section in Joris-Karl Huysmans' novel *À Rebours* (1884) in which Jean des Esseintes collects and obsessively observes disgusting plants.[44] In Arcadia, too, there was death and, as such, decadents could share with botanists a fascination with carnivorous plants as vegetal counterparts of the *femme* (or *homme*) *fatal(e)*.[45] The queering of the boundary between humans and animals that suffused texts such as Bram Stoker's *Dracula* could also be brought to bear on that between humans and plants.[46] Certain types of waxy flowers such as orchids, and others that had protuberant spadices such as arums, problematized gendered distinctions between the soft and passive and the hard and active.[47] The queer effect of this can be seen in John Nash's engraving of the wild British arum lily in his *Poisonous Plants: Deadly, Dangerous and Suspect* (1927).[48]

Plants and gardens were a site of contestation between moral conservatives and radicals in the interwar period, as can be seen from an article, "Abnormalities," that appeared in the magazine *Britannia and Eve* in 1929. The author was a best-selling novelist, Warwick Deeping. He describes a confrontation between two characters, "Young Cynicus" and "Old Slyvanus." The former mocks the latter's suburban garden for its boring conformity. Sylvanus then leads Cynicus to a "to a dark corner and displayed to him a certain vile fungus that shall be nameless." "'What a nice, pornographic weed,'" cries the Cynic. "'Maybe you would like to pick it and take it home?'" asks his interlocutor. Such young cynics are, we are told, the "bright young men among the critics" who say that "what you take to be normal is only a silly transparency with which you cover reality." They "demand the unusual and the macabre." Deeping dissents: "that the abnormal should be studied and be understood is of vital importance, but that the cult of it should be allowed to take the form of a self-complacent and aggressive psychic parade is another matter. We do not want these mental mannequins to posture in public."[49] The homosexual implications of this description are made even more obvious by Deeping's subsequent invocation in this article of an earlier age of the cult of the "abnormal" in the time of Wilde.

Deeping was writing when a degree of deviance had come into fashion on both sides of the Atlantic. One of the earliest exponents of queer celebrity in the United States was the cross-dressing entertainer Bert Savoy (born Everett McKenzie). His act was heavily sexualized since the persona he adopted was that of an "outsized and blowsy dame" who evoked the life of the contemporary city with a "Rabelaisian lack of shame."[50] Savoy's sensational life ended in melodrama when he was hit by a bolt of lightning while walking along a beach on

Long Island, New York, in 1923. The queer American painter Charles Demuth produced a series of "poster portraits" in which various artists were depicted in the form of floral still lifes. One of these was completed in study form in 1923–4. It represents another homosexual painter, Marsden Hartley, through the image of a red arum (also known as a calla lily) with a prominent, and phallic, spadix.[51] Two years later Demuth exhibited a painting of a white calla lily springing from a seashell (Figure 6.2).[52] Jonathan Weinberg has cautioned against the uncritical reading of any flower picture on the part of a queer painter as necessarily being related to the expression of sexuality: "I personally do not see anything particularly evil, or, for that matter, homosexual in the majority of Demuth's watercolors of zinnias, gladiolus, daisies and iris." But, Weinberg continues, there was a different intent at play in this case since "when Demuth intended a flower to be read sexually, he was not subtle."[53] The American art critic Henry

Figure 6.2 Charles Demuth, *Calla Lilies (Bert Savoy)*, 1926, oil on board. Alfred Stieglitz Collection, Crystal Bridges Museum of American Art, co-owned by Fisk University, Nashville, Tennessee, and Crystal Bridges Museum of American Art, Bentonville, Arkansas. Photography by Edward C. Robison III.

McBride had indicated that this was intended as a portrait of an "erratic" recently deceased entertainer, and this is understood to have been Savoy, whom Demuth admired.[54] McBride commented further that "just what it is that makes the Calla so esteemed in these days, other than the fact that it was considered vulgar a generation ago, I cannot say, but possibly that in itself is sufficient reason."[55] The negative perception of the calla may have been influenced by Oscar Wilde's high estimation of it. He had suggested in January 1882, during his visit to the United States, that the "dreadful marshes" close by New York might be beautified with "great fields of callas."[56] Demuth expressed Savoy's indeterminacy of gender and sexuality by painting the beautiful, if "unnatural," emergence of a phallic flower from a vulval seashell. The consecration of such a "low" vaudeville act via the medium of high art spoke to the rise to fashionability of queer performance.

Over in Britain, Anthony Wysard made a closely related visual analogy in 1930 between a vase of calla lilies and Beaton's flowery head and curving, stem-like body (Figure 6.3). Another artist who explored the queer potential of blossom was one of Sargent's friends, the Scottish painter William Bruce Ellis Ranken. Although little known today, Ranken also developed a noted presence as a celebrity portraitist. In a number of his works, notably *The Garden Door* (1926) and *Covent Garden* (1930), he depicted attractive, young, male devotees of floral abundance. In the earlier painting it is intimated that such a youth has been picking flowers with his male friends, and in the later painting it is implied by the title that he is a seller of blooms at Covent Garden market. Bearing in mind the long associations of Covent Garden with prostitution, this also implies that the flower-seller might also be seen as part of the merchandise.[57] A few years earlier, Ranken had completed a portrait of an Indian youth that is known as *Hibiscus Flower* (c.1922) (Figure 6.4).[58] The attractive subject is naked to the waist and otherwise dressed in "exotic" fabrics. He holds a hibiscus bloom suggestively between his legs, and the viewer understands that it is he who is the sexualized exotic flower.

The closeted passion for, and pursuit of, the male body was therefore frequently figured through floral codes. When, in 1892, Jacques-Émile Blanche painted Proust wearing a white Cattleya orchid in his buttonhole, he was depicting his subject as a sophisticated dandy and aesthete.[59] By the interwar period, the cultural valences of exotic blooms meant that they could be employed ever more directly in projects of queer expression. In 1930 Cecil Beaton posed the face of the famously sexually ambivalent Marlene Dietrich as a direct visual counterpart to the spotlit Cattleya before her (Figure 6.5).[60] The flower and the face combined to imply the glamor of decadent beauty. Flowers therefore

Figure 6.3 Anthony Wysard, *Cecil Beaton*, 1930, pencil, ink and wash on board.
© Reserved; collection National Portrait Gallery, London (6438).

played a queer role in art and literature from Wilde to Proust through to the photography of Robert Mapplethorpe and beyond.[61] They could be cultivated in private as an aspect of queer domesticity, or they could be flaunted in public in acts of queer self-fashioning. They could be employed to mediate between

Figure 6.4 William Ranken, *Hibiscus Flower* (*c*.1922), oil on canvas. Reproduced by permission of Nottingham City Museums and Galleries (NCM 1946–309).

same- and opposite-sex desires and between male and female gendering. This was, of course, very often a closet art that played with tacit signaling. Yet in the interwar period, that signaling became progressively less subtle. So familiar did floral queerness become that, by the 1930s, the word "pansy" had emerged as one of the most widespread terms of contempt with which gay men were forced to contend.

Figure 6.5 Cecil Beaton, *Marlene Dietrich*, 1930. © The Cecil Beaton Studio Archive at Sotheby's (CM3293).

From Orchids to Pansies

In 1929 D. H. Lawrence published his latest volume of poems in a private edition of fifty copies. The name of the collection, *Pansies*, was, according to its author, derived from the French words *pensées* (thoughts) or *panser* (to soothe or dress a wound).[62] Not surprisingly, since he had recently completed *Lady Chatterley's*

Lover (first private edition, 1928), he was preoccupied in these verses by both sex and its repression. In "When I Went to the Circus—" he sneered at the uptight audience for not wishing to admire the bodies on show, be they "the tight-rope lady, pink and blonde and nude-looking" or "the trapeze man, slim and beautiful and like a fish in the air."[63] Lawrence has been interpreted as a man whose tastes were more or less bisexual but who was tormented by elements of self-hatred.[64] Indeed, another poem in the collection, "The Noble Englishman," had to be excised from the commercially published edition in 1930 because it dwelled on the notion of sodomitical aristocrats who used their women "unnaturally." The introduction to this expurgated edition nevertheless stressed that "flowers, to my thinking, are not merely pretty-pretty. They have in their fragrance an earthiness of the humus and the corruptive earth from which they spring. And pansies, in their streaked faces, have a look of many things besides hearts-ease."[65] It seems unlikely, given all these clues, that Lawrence was not also thinking about the recent use in both British and American slang of the word "pansy" to mean an "effeminate" homosexual.

Lawrence was not the only man of indeterminate sexuality to be preoccupied with such matters at this date. In 1930 Noël Coward humiliated Cecil Beaton by lecturing him on his self-presentation.[66] The latter was berated for being "flabby, floppy and affected, with an undulating walk, exaggerated clothes and voice both too high and too precise."[67] His style had tipped over from being a successful imitation of elite mores to an apparent parody of them.[68] Beaton had recently written slightingly of Coward, but it seems likely that it was also the latter's insecurities that led to this incident.[69] Same-sex desire had at this date become part of the appeal of stage acts in nightclubs where audiences paid to see queer entertainers. Both men feared that they would be taken for a common or garden effeminate rather than an eccentrically interesting member of high society at a time when the vogue for freak chic was waning and the fashion for staring and laughing at pansy performers was on the rise.[70]

Flowers, as has been seen, were intimately associated with sexuality and femininity, but the precise origins of an association between pansies and same-sex desire have been a matter for controversy. They were cheap and bright flowers, which had a particularly anthropomorphic quality because their markings looked like faces that had been streaked as if with smeared makeup. The pansy was also a decidedly colorful shade of purple that would only be worn by the brightest of young things in the 1920s. A possible place of origin may lie with Walter H. Butler who, in the late nineteenth century, had attempted to introduce a bill into the American House of Representatives to make the pansy the national flower and to add it to the flag. He was duly mocked in the press of his own state of Iowa as "Pansy" Butler: "what an inspiration it would have been to our soldier boys to have seen the pansy waving proudly o'er them as they charged the heights of San Juan [in the recent war with Spain] and stood as the national air of patriotism 'Only a Pansy Blossom'" was played.[71] In the course of the 1920s, the word came to be used on both sides of the Atlantic to refer, quite explicitly and more or less humorously, to the homosexual man as an alleged effeminate being. An example of this appears in the story "She Wore a Camellia" by T. W. Coghlin, which was published in an Oxford student magazine in 1925. A fashionably Eton-cropped face appears at a window with "lips from which coral had been crudely imitated."[72] "'Pansy-face,'" mutters James Skeffington as a "rich deep voice spoke into the night. 'What do you want?'" He gasps out "'I love you'" and the two arrange to meet. The mysterious other will have a camellia in their hair.[73] But when the taxi door opens, Skeffington sees it is a man, whom he calls a "'damned Æsthete.'"[74]

There suddenly seemed to be far more of such men in society, as *The Sketch* hinted in its cover of August 3, 1930, which displayed "The Origin of the Fairies! A Crowd of Pansy Faces" (Figure 6.6).[75] Innocents among the readership would have interpreted this as relating purely to the quaint notion, popular in Victorian times, that fairy elves lived at the bottom of the garden. Sophisticates would have drawn other conclusions. In New York, crowds were drawn not only to cross-dressing acts but also to observe the life of the "freak night club habitué."[76] *Variety Weekly* reported in 1930 that "reports are around that Broadway during the new season will have nite [sic] places with 'pansies' as the prime draw."[77] Two years later, one of the most prominent pansy entertainers, Gene "Jean" Malin, was recorded by a major label, Columbia, performing his hit number "I'd rather be Spanish than Mannish."[78]

This was not just an American phenomenon. Crowds were attracted to queer nightspots in Berlin and Paris where, in the case of the latter, the scenes on view were captured by the French-Hungarian photographer Brassaï (Gyula Halász).[79] This "pansy craze" was, in the main, a species of slumming, whereby audiences could pay a visit to a more or less prepackaged queer world. This enabled them to demonstrate their cosmopolitan sophistication and to return reassured of their own sexual normality.[80] *Variety Weekly* educated its readers on how to differentiate pansies from other attractive but "normal" men who were simply "good guys gone gorgeous."[81] The older figure of the working-class fairy or queen had become reimagined as a species of fashionable entertainment. But those who were explicitly known to be homosexual were still positioned

THE ORIGIN OF THE FAIRIES! A CROWD OF PANSY FACES

This photograph of a bed of pansies is quite sufficient explanation of the idea of fairies amid the flowers of the garden. The crowd of pixie faces gazing up from the border is more amusing the longer one looks at it. The variety of expressions and shape among the pansy people is endless. | *Some of them laugh; others are milky. There is an old woman with a long nose; any amount of old men, and a soldier in a helmet—just to quote a few of the outstanding personalities in the pansy—or to use the scientific modern term—the viola border.*

PHOTOGRAPH BY C.N.

Figure 6.6 "C. N.," "The Origin of the Fairies! A Crowd of Pansy Faces," *Sketch,* August 3, 1931, cover. © Illustrated London News Ltd/Mary Evans.

at the margins of society. Indeed, it seems as though the more homosexuality was openly identified as the "truth" of male effeminacy, the further the allegedly effeminate man was reduced in social status. Beautiful clothes, flowers, and accessories no longer concealed moral turpitude.

There is a sense, of course, that queer performance almost inevitably bore within it the marks of social abjection. Camp sensibilities recognized that female impersonation could not precisely reproduce the supreme glamor of the diva. Nor could the queer man ever match the masculinity of his straight male counterpart. Georges de Zayas had once drawn Jean Cocteau in full-on camp mode with hand on hip in 1924 in order to illustrate his status as a "master modernist."[82] But where male effeminacy had then been treated as terrifically modern at best or as a repellant joke at worst, it subsequently came to be regarded ever more seriously as a homosexual problem. As I argued in the previous chapter, this was essentially the trajectory traced by Mariegold's encounters with effeminate men in the pages of *The Sketch*. Caricature of camp men in fashion quickly became hostile, as can be seen by comparing Zinkeisen's amused image of "Mr. Pimpskin Pottle" from 1927 (Figure 5.9) with Alan D'Egville's "I Should be Swathing, Draping and Designing in Diaphanous Chiffons" (Figure 6.7).[83] The latter was published in the conservative periodical *Britannia* in 1929 and shows a distorted figure with a grotesquely large nose. The column that it illustrated, "A Mere Man," expatiated on what it would be like to be "a Molyneux" (i.e., Edward Henry Molyneux, who was a friend of Noël Coward and who dressed the leading ladies appearing in his shows). The popular press began running stories about unsavory men with powder puffs; one in *The Daily Mail* on blackmail—"The Crime in which Women Specialise"—was illustrated with a cartoon of a vicious young pansy.[84] Tolerating the antics of the bright young things was difficult enough for conservatives, but countenancing widespread queer imitation of them down the social spectrum was next to impossible. What was to some degree condoned in the behavior of the social elite was duly attacked when it appeared in the lower orders.

The bright young things had been intent on accommodating variations of gender and sexuality and *not* codifying behavior into tropes of normality and abnormality. Since it was the urge to classify that won out, this other tradition can seem hard to interpret and understand. Allanah Harper, who was another of the bright young things, left among her papers an undated typescript entitled "Some Memories of Brian Howard." Since he was one of the "gayest" members of the circle, it is not so surprising that Harper thought he had had about him "a rather 'Yellow Book' affectation" (she was referring to the queer culture of the decadent 1890s).[85] What might puzzle the modern reader was that she also thought seriously about marrying him. But we must remember that sexual identities were not firmly fixed in the interwar period, nor—particularly in high society—were marriages always expected to be sexually fulfilled or fulfilling.

Figure 6.7 Alan D'Egville, " … I Should be Swathing, Draping and Designing in Diaphanous Chiffons," in "A Mere Man," "This Dress Question," *Britannia* 2, no. 16, January 11, 1929, 110. © Illustrated London News Ltd/Mary Evans.

The degree to which queer men enthralled, titillated, bored, or appalled their female compatriots was of enormous importance to their social success and their acceptance within respectable society.

Many of the queer men I have been studying were, in effect, the servants of powerful women who designed new looks for them that were empowering. The hourglass figure that had been admired before the First World War was replaced by an ideal of boyish slimness, before morphing into a new ideal form that emphasized both womanliness and strength: the thirties woman was well endowed with hips and breasts, but also with shoulders.[86] From her point of view, the women of the previous decade had had a tendency to look like identical dolls.[87] The new look was allied to a sense of individualism and strong "personality." It was, in its way, androgynous but in a manner that focused on the persona. It mattered that women should be assertive and interesting as opposed to conventionally beautiful. As Beaton commented, "the young men of today are not content (as their grandfathers were) with a 'pretty face.' They would rather be amused, excited, fascinated, any day. The joys of proportion are lost on them. And a good job of grooming means far more to them than a good job of nature."[88] Lady Abdy with her "trenchant and vivid appearance" was, for Beaton, the kind of woman who was "the very opposite of that rather insipid pink and white prettiness which the word blonde too often conjures up."[89]

It must be remembered, of course, that this was the view of a queer man who could gain a receptive audience among women who were not conventionally attractive or who had reached "a certain age." This style also looked for its inspiration to a vision of prewar society characterized by forceful women and dandified men. The Edwardian era was, according to *Vogue* in 1933, "fifteen years that inspired the present mode."[90] Queer men thereby played an important role in shaping changes in style and provided inspiration for the modern woman as sophisticated consumer. Financial and social superiority could give affluent women the experience of empowerment in commercial transactions. The world of the retail trades was one in which subservience to clients, of whatever sex, on the part of male workers became associated with effeminacy and lower status. In the final section of this chapter, I shall be charting the eclipse of the high-society freaks and the blossoming of the vulgar pansies through a case study of queer men in retail.

Open for Trade

In its summer number for 1927, *Punch* introduced its readers to "The Renegade Faun." Brought up in Harrow, this suburban Nijinsky (recalling the notorious *L'Après-midi d'un faune* of 1912) had not been taken seriously by the smart set until he bought new clothes and a smart car.[91] For a modern woman such as Mariegold, pretty boys and their cars could be thought of as lifestyle accessories. The example of the motor car can be used to show how changing patterns of consumption in modernity could challenge traditional conceptions of gender. Was the car primarily an efficient machine, and therefore to be seen as masculine, or a beautiful and desirable object, and thus feminine?[92] Early cars were luxury items and often marketed to wealthy women.[93] But because it was assumed that ladies would not understand the inner workings of a vehicle, these were sold by male assistants. The latter came under the suspicion of effeminacy that adhered to men who served women. This can be seen in Arthur Wallis Mills's cartoon "Our Motor Emporiums" (1912), which shows a young dandy lounging against a car and an earnest, submissive type bending over the hood.[94] The caption reads: "No, you're wrong. The one on the left is the buyer trying to strike the right attitude of humility before the beautiful young man of the shop." The annual motor shows at London's Olympia exhibition halls became the subject of considerable controversy. The car salesman who was objectified along with his wares duly appeared in Treyer Evans's cartoon of two women out shopping in 1927:

> First Young Thing: "I think he's rather sweet, don't you?"

> Second Young Thing: "Don't be feeble. Why, can't you remember he was last year's model?"[95]

A. E. Beard's "A Brighter Olympia" (1928), published in *London Opinion,* took the parody of bright young consumables even further by presenting a fashion parade complete with a butch female mechanic and a beauty contest composed of male salesmen. Each model was labeled with the name of a car brand.[96] *Punch* had published a cartoon in 1920 that had mocked female fashion shows by suggesting that there should now be the equivalent for modes for men.[97] Five years later, the British film director Alfred Brunel produced *Typical Budget: The Only Unreliable Film Review* (1925). This was a parody of the newsreel *Topical Budget* and included the director himself modeling what was supposedly the latest in menswear (named the "The Novello" and "The Valentino"). Parody in this case only slightly predated reality since the trade magazine *Men's Wear Organiser* reported in February 1929 that "male mannequins at Olympia show artificial silk goods to the world." The reader was informed that there had been single male models before this date but never in such numbers. This was, however, a trade exhibition for the menswear industry rather than a car show open to the general public.[98] The use of the term "mannequin" rather than "model" at this date is in itself revealing. Models were, originally, working class and were not thought of as individual subjects but as interchangeable objects.[99] On the one hand this suited an aesthetic of standardization as an aspect of modernity, but fashion in the age of freak chic reacted against this in a search for individuality. Fashionable women began to play with the notion of the fashion show itself as another aspect of artificial performativity, leading eventually to a situation in which, as *Vogue* described in 1937, "people copy the mannequins, pose like them, love them."[100] Therefore, it is important to recognize that there was a struggle taking place between those who reviled and those who reveled in fashion parades.

Angus McLaren in his study of interwar "playboys" explained that "advertisements [targeted at men] implied that the larger and more expensive one's automobile, the more successful in life one would be. At an unconscious level driving was sexualized. To possess a car was the first step in possessing a woman."[101] That erotic desire could be involved in automobile transactions is made clear by Maurice Lane-Norcott's astonishingly sexist article that accompanied Beard's cartoon "This Girl-Less Olympia" (1928). This complained that "once again Olympia is a mere shop-full of young male assistants."[102] The reason why the writer objects to this state of affairs soon becomes apparent. What he wanted was a salesgirl who would agree to go for a test drive with him. One would find oneself in Brighton or at the top of Box Hill (both well-known locales for seduction) "just as the stars are coming out." One could then "take her little hand off the gear lever" and she would say you *can* have it all if you put down a £25 deposit. "Of course on the very next night she would be sitting on the top of Box Hill with another entire stranger."[103] This was, in other words, nothing more or less than a fantasy in which salesgirls were willing prostitutes. This reveals the startling degree to which economic and erotic capital were understood as aligned in an arrangement of exchange that empowered the heterosexual upper- or middle-class man. It also reveals the degree to which that traditional privilege was felt to be under threat.

All this meant that interaction with male clients in the menswear trade was freighted with an air of sexual ambiguity. That such encounters might bear an element of implicit eroticism can be seen from "Selling with the Hands," an article that appeared in *Style for Men* (the renamed *Men's Wear Organiser*) in 1932:

> The salesman, lovingly caressing a fabric with obvious deep feeling for its luxuriousness is tempting the customer; the fabric seems to be handled with such reverence for its quality that he has an irresistible desire to feel it for himself ... Touch can be, and most often is, the connecting point between interest and desire ... Ask him to hold firmly with both hands and pull open sharply ... Get your customer to the "feeling" stage, and there is only one more fence to get over. That is, the price.[104]

The male shop assistant was implicitly placed in a position of sexualized service to his customers. This may help to explain the decision of one of the attendees at the "Beau Brummell" inauguration party for Britain's "biggest ready-to-wear floor"—held at Burton's in London in 1934—to dress up as a young Oscar Wilde.[105]

The 1930s saw a rapid spread of consumerism beyond the elite. Mass marketing drove the desire for innovative, brighter styles.[106] Traditional attitudes to male attire were also coming under attack from progressive thinkers such as John Carl Flügel, a psychologist at University College, London, who was one of the founders of the Men's Dress Reform Party in 1929. This organization campaigned for "lighter and brighter clothes" that would also be more comfortable to wear.[107]

He argued that there remained but few vestiges of the natural state, paralleled in the animal kingdom, in which men were more colorful than women.[108] One such was the armed forces since "even the most gay feminine attire scarcely equals the gorgeousness of certain military uniforms."[109] It was only in the course of what he termed the "the Great Masculine Renunciation" of early modernity that "man abandoned his claim to being beautiful" and thenceforth merely aspired to be "useful."[110] These patterns of fashioning meant that the man who lived for fashion in the nineteenth century was widely held to be unmanly and one who earned his income from it was even more so. Many tailors' and drapers' assistants in Victorian and Edwardian England were badly paid and as a result could not afford to get married and start a family. Some of them lived in same-sex dormitories.[111] In a Lewis Baumer cartoon from 1915, such young men had become the butt of a patriotic joke: "'How is it you're not serving [in the army], young man?' 'Early closing to-day, sir.'"[112] The shop assistant was shown with a young woman hanging on his arm, but she would soon disappear from cartoons on similar themes as commercialized effeminacy increasingly became aligned with homosexuality.

The aforementioned *Style for Men: The Men's Wear Organiser*, founded in 1922, was a key periodical of the menswear trade.[113] It prided itself on its editorial stylishness, even acclaiming itself, in 1931, "the Beau Brummell of trade journals."[114] It aimed at a "buttoned-up" respectability, but it is perfectly possible to read between the lines of articles such as the above-mentioned paean to the delights of handling cloth or to wonder about an illustration from 1931 showing "the figures tailors dream of" (Figure 6.8).[115] One of the "Types We Know" in a drawing by Fred Gardiner from 1935 was the dance-hall "palais pansy."[116] Advertisements that appeared in this publication sometimes possessed a certain frisson, such as one for Aviator that featured a buttock-grabbing tackle.[117] Also suggestive of sexual flirtation was Courtaulds Rayon's "In All Men's Eyes," which promoted their rayon cloth with a brooding facial close-up.[118] The latter company was also responsible for an advertisement that urged shopkeepers to stock their "new-style athletic underwear" or they would lose out on sales. "Are you ever 'NOT AT HOME' to trade?" asks the advertisement, against a picture of a shadowy street (Figure 6.9).[119] Since "trade" was homosexual slang for sexual partners, particularly masculine-styled ones, this advertisement implicitly aligned commercial exchanges in the store with queer sexual encounters.

Style for Men represented the world of the high street as opposed to bespoke high fashion, but its pages reveal the degree to which the two connected, particularly via the department-store windows of London's West End. Thus,

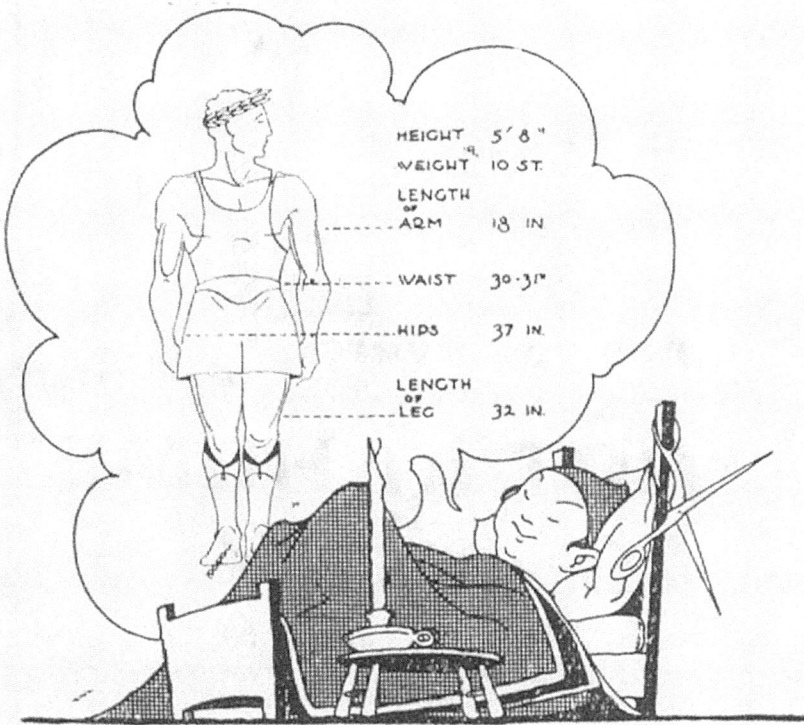

The figures tailors dream of

Figure 6.8 "The Figures Tailors Dream of," *Men's Wear Organiser* 17, no. 4 (April 1931), 241. © TI Media, Ltd., and reproduced courtesy of the British Library (LOU. LON 379 [1931]).

an article on "The Grotesque in Regent Street" described the use of freak mannequins in Nicoll's window to display underwear in 1932.[120] Male busts showing clear musculature first appeared three years later in the pages of the periodical, in a column by "The Window Man" that discussed a display of sports shirts in the windows of Harrods.[121] Rendering male mannequins attractive was problematic since the division between tailoring for men and women meant that windows were segregated by sex. Men-only tableaux had, as a result, to be constructed in ways that did not imply that the figures were flirting with each other. This was made clear in Lewis Baumer's cartoon "The Neglected Sex" of 1922 (Figure 6.10). His deadpan caption suggests, as an alternative, that "a realistic scene, say of club life, would increase the brightness of our shopping

Figure 6.9 Advertisement for Courtaulds Rayon, "Are You ever 'NOT AT HOME' to Trade?" *Style for Men* 22, no. 4, October 1933, 170. © Reserved; reproduced courtesy of Pd Courtaulds Group and of the British Library (LOU.LON 595 [1933]).

Figure 6.10 Lewis Baumer, "The Neglected Sex," *Punch* 163 (1922), 439. Reproduced by permission of Punch Cartoon Library/TopFoto.

centres" while the figures bat flirtatious glances at each other from beneath the longest of eyelashes.[122]

Early shop mannequins looked peculiar. Male versions were under-sexualized to the point of lacking bodily definition, while female ones appeared, from the point of view of later tastes at least, to be alarmingly over-sexualized. This was, in essence, the view of the *Vogue* writer who commented in 1937 that "in 1918, the mannequins were waxen, buxom, and baby doll. They held no hint of sophistication, no worldly suavity with their puffed, real hair, their lashes an inch long."[123] In 1922 *Punch* presented a drawing of what might be seen in the window of a high-end clothes store: "This is not the culminating scene from the seventeen-reel film 'The Modern Cleopatra.' It is Mr. Smith (our window-dresser) arranging his latest creation." Both figures balance balletically—in light of the Ballets Russes this is a further queer touch—in apparent admiration of each other, but while it is immediately apparent that she is not a real woman, it is likewise implied that he is not a real man.[124] Were working-class men who worked in the fashion trade all they seemed, or were they *exactly* what they seemed? Were they desiring subjects or objects of desire? How did they relate to persons of the opposite sex and to those of the same sex? And how were their lives related to the world of glamor? Image and reality threatened to blur and create all manner of queer possibilities. Men might loiter before windows of department stores and—under the cover of this subterfuge—eye the reflections of others who were doing the same.

Once the craze for being bright and young came to an end, the choice of clothes that were too young and bright for the wearer became increasingly freighted with sexual significance. This is the point behind the indignation of an old buffer in a cartoon published in the slightly risqué periodical *Men Only* in 1936. He blushes red on being told by a camp shop assistant that "Sir, I think *we're* the type who can wear a tie such as this!"[125] A number of cartoonists appear to have specialized in images of the smirking, over-dressed pansy. One such was the Hon. Patrick Bellew, an Irish commercial artist who was the half-brother of the 5th Baron Bellew. His work appeared in a number of periodicals that were predominantly aimed at a male readership such as the eponymous *Men Only*. His work showed, and assumed in its viewers, a keen awareness of queer possibility as a source of amusement. In one representative scene, he showed a burly rower breaking down in tears and declaring to the cox of the boat: "I just can't go on—you remind me of HER!" And, even more overtly, he drew a sprightly young pansy responding to a tubby policeman's cry of "'Hey! Where's the fire?'" with "'In your eyes, you gorgeous beast!'" (Figure 6.11). The volume of drawings in which these cartoons appeared also contained an iteration of the pansy shop assistant who declares to a customer who is choosing a gift, "Well, Madam, if I were a man, I'd have that one!"[126]

Of all the pansy subtypes, it is perhaps the shop assistant that has had the most durable afterlife in British popular culture, notably as a result of its embodiment

Figure 6.11 Patrick Bellew, "'Hey! Where's the Fire?' 'In Your Eyes You Gorgeous Beast!'" in Bellew, *Point of View* (London: Barker, 1935), unpaginated. © Reserved.

by John Inman in the character of Mr. Humphries in the BBC situation comedy series, *Are You Being Served?* (1972–85). That show has been the subject of considerable controversy. On the one hand it promoted a certain form of gay visibility, but on the other hand that form was one rooted in phobic stereotype.[127] However, it is worth saying that the BBC was not, to start with, comfortable with the inclusion of such an obviously gay figure, whether stereotyped or not. A senior executive asked the writer David Croft to "get rid of the poof" but he declined, saying, "if the poof goes, I go."[128] The authorities had long frowned on the humorous depiction of homosexual characters. Thus, the Lord Chancellor's department, which was in charge of the censorship of plays, had been assiduous in attempting to remove references to "pansies" in British plays until their remit to censor was rescinded in 1968.[129] This was not just about preventing queer visibility but also about protecting the upper and middle classes from "vulgar" insinuations that elite styles of male behavior were effeminate and sexually suspect.[130] Judith Walkowitz has also suggested that humorous depictions presented homosexuals in a way that did not unambiguously condemn them and so might incite the audience to laugh with them rather than at them. She points to the situation during shows at the Windmill Theatre in London's Soho that featured pansy innuendo amid its girlie burlesque acts: "these rude jokes— both heterosexual and perverse—were intended to heat up the atmosphere of sexual suggestiveness to provide more kick."[131] Thus, we may need to look again at these pansy stereotypes to ask whether they were simply the result of rising levels of disgust or can be seen as indicating a degree of amused familiarity with sexual transgression.

The stereotype of the pansy sales assistant was so well known that it made its appearance in the pages of the (by this time) most establishment of humorous magazines, *Punch*. D. L. Ghilchik thus depicted a scene in which a respectable older man asks for some underwear. The fey shopwalker beckons his even more fey young assistant and asks him to "kindly show this gentleman our new season's snuggies" (Figure 6.12).[132] The shop assistant sports the same shingled hair and stride as the various forward young men who, in a cartoon by W. K. Haselden, are described as being "so depraved as not to possess a hat!"[133] Ghilchik's cartoon therefore draws its amusement from a shared interest in tight-fitting men's underwear ("snuggies") on the part not only of men of different ages but of different classes. The older man has the demeanor of a retired army colonel, while the assistant would be assumed to have been working class. It is no accident that many of the pansies that are depicted in such cartoons are not effeminate aristocrats but (in contemporary terms) the more laughable figure of the effeminate social upstart. One such was Lewis Baumer's cockney "superior hairdresser" who asks his customer, "'Ow about 'avin' one of our permanent billows, Sir?"[134]

These cartoons from the 1930s attempted to chart a middle path between stuffy traditionalism and social radicalism. The viewer is meant to be amused by the young pansy who is trying to be up with the fashions, but they are also intended to laugh at the old buffer who, with his prewar attitudes, is so easily outraged by male effeminacy.[135] But there is more to it than that. In the fourth volume of his great novelistic cycle, published in English as *Cities of the Plain*

Figure 6.12 David Louis Ghilchik. "*Customer.* 'I Want Some Winter Underwear, Please,'" *Punch* 185 (1933), 427. Reproduced by permission of Punch Cartoon Library/TopFoto.

and *Sodom and Gomorrah*, Marcel Proust wrote of the vice of Sodom "flaunting itself, insolent and immune, where its existence is never guessed; numbering its adherents everywhere, among the people, in the army, in the church, in prison, on the throne ... speaking of the vice as of something alien to it."[136] The French writer was probably remembering a particular set of things past— namely, the Harden-Eulenburg affair that had seen the top ranks of the Prussian military establishment engulfed in homosexual scandal in the years before the First World War.[137] It is notable, therefore, that pansy cartoonists regularly discovered queer innuendo not just in supposedly effeminate professions such as haberdashery but also in the apparently ultra-masculine realms of the forces of law and order, including the police and the military. Ghilchik, for example, teased his viewers with the thought of cross-rank liaisons in the police. He drew an "absent-minded young [and pretty motor-cycle] Policeman" asking his superior officer, who is seated in the sidecar and whom he has mistaken for his wife, if he is "warm enough, darling?" (Figure 6.13).[138] Comic appearances in the operettas of Gilbert and Sullivan indicate that the police had long been a source of popular amusement, but the queerness of the innuendo concerning them was new. Some of this humor was even more subversive if one knew something of homosexual life in London. Appreciation of E. A. Shepard's "Aren't Their Statues

Absent-minded young Policeman (newly transferred to the mobile squad). "WARM ENOUGH, DARLING?"

Figure 6.13 David Louis Ghilchik, "*Absent-Minded Young Policeman*," *Punch* 184 (1933), 405. Reproduced by permission of Punch Cartoon Library/TopFoto.

Wonderful" (1937), which shows the statue of Anteros (brother of Eros) at Piccadilly replaced by a policeman in a balletic pose, was helped if one knew that this was the central homosexual pick-up point in the city. In a similar vein, Anne Harriet Fish's "Preparing for a Raid. The Green Room at Scotland Yard" (1932) documented the contemporary practice of cross-dressing by policemen to infiltrate queer parties (Figure 6.14).[139]

Pansy cartoons were particularly abundant in the aforementioned *Men Only*, which was a pocket-sized publication introduced by the Pearson Group in December 1935. This, together with *Lilliput*, which was launched in 1937, sold substantial print runs of between 50,000 and 200,000 copies. The target readership was considerably different from that of *Vogue* in that it was predominantly male and of middling social and economic status. A "poem" published in *The Bystander*, but reprinted in *Men Only*, indicates that the publication was self-consciously—perhaps a little *too* self-consciously—intended as sexually normative and homosocial:

> For its prose and pictures are
> (using the vernacular)
> Far from "sissy" or "just too-too," but full
> Of honest and full-blooded meat,
> That suits the manly man a treat.[140]

PREPARING FOR A RAID.
THE GREEN ROOM AT SCOTLAND YARD.

Figure 6.14 Anne Harriet Fish, "Preparing for a Raid. The Green Room at Scotland Yard," *Punch* 182 (1932), 613. Reproduced by permission of Punch Cartoon Library/ TopFoto.

The magazine thus explicitly rejected the effeminate "sissy" (another term for pansy) and the "too-too" mode associated with Oscar Wilde's circle of the previous century. Yet the repeated inclusion of pansy cartoons in *Men Only* indicates a lively awareness of queer possibilities within the homosocial realm, from which the "manly man" had constantly to assert his distance.[141] A number of these cartoons did indeed veer toward a more obviously phobic mode when they showed brightly painted pansies attempting to solicit other men. An example of this was Edward Hynes's "Oh, Sir, Spare a Copper" (1936), in which a pansy wearing makeup asks an outraged police sergeant either for money (a copper coin) or a police constable (a "copper").[142] The image of the fashionable young eccentric disappeared from cartoons and was replaced by that of the painted urban poof. The pansy stereotype functioned as a way not just of classifying but also of down-classing homosexuals, and it both drove and evidenced the fall from fashion of the queer freak.

To some extent, this was a rerun of what had happened from the fall of Oscar Wilde to the First World War, when dandyism had been associated with unpatriotic behavior and extravagant bad taste. As has been seen in this chapter, such sentiments never entirely vanished during the interwar period.[143] In 1927 Christopher Millard sent his "Iconography of Oscar Wilde," which was a sort of biography constructed through images, to William Andrews Clark, to whom he would sell his collection. Millard was a pioneering scholar of Wilde, and this "Iconography" displayed an astonishing variety of images of its subject: aesthetic Wildes, charlatan Wildes, tragic Wildes, disgusting Wildes, and more or less homosexual Wildes.[144] Interwar literary responses to Oscar Wilde tended to focus on the image of genius brought low, as in the case of the critic James Agate, who referred to Wilde in *Lilliput* (another men's magazine) as "the most tragic literary figure" of his times.[145] Those who were more hostile tended to pay attention to his appearance, as was the case with Edgar Jepson's article "The Man with the Green Carnation," which was published in *Men Only* in 1936. Jepson described Wilde's "fine grey eyes and forehead and a shocking bad mouth, the lips thick, loose, self-indulgent to the limit, and a heavy, almost brutal jaw— obviously Jekyll, obviously Hyde."[146] Wilde most often appeared in contemporary cartoons as a man of affectation and physical excess, as was the case in Alan Odle's 1925 drawing of him at the first night of *The Importance of Being Earnest*. Odle's caption explained that the object that Wilde was holding was not a powder puff but a green carnation.[147] It is not surprising that the playwright was often depicted as a pansy, because his life and style had been important in shaping the formation of that very stereotype.

Rhonda Garlick has pointed out that Wilde fused "French [and British] dandyism with typically American or Americanized skill in merchandising and promotion."[148] He therefore prefigured Beaton and others of his set in the interwar period. It is perhaps not surprising that many such men became fascinated with late Victoriana. Yet they were also careful to focus on being bright and amusing as a way of establishing conceptual distance between their own performances and those of the decadents of the *fin de siècle* who were tainted with the aura of failure.[149] In his own lifetime, Oscar Wilde had been drawn either as a

Figure 6.15 Anthony Wysard, untitled, in Evelyn Waugh, "Let Us Return to the Nineties, but Not to Oscar Wilde," *Harper's Bazaar* 3, no. 2, November 1930, 51. © Reserved; reproduced courtesy of Hearst Magazines UK.

wasp-waisted aesthete or as a bloated profligate (Figure 2.5).[150] In the interwar period, he was often shown as a camp young thing, as he was by Anthony Wysard in association with a caustic essay by Evelyn Waugh entitled "Let Us Return to the Nineties but Not to Oscar Wilde" (Figure 6.15).[151] Waugh was not alone in vacillating between homage, nostalgia, and derision.[152] Unflattering comparisons were indeed being made between Wilde and the interwar dandies. An Etonian balletomane recalled seeing Harold Acton and Brian Howard (over) dressed at the ballet and "looking perhaps like a couple of Oscar Wildes."[153] The Irishman's legacy was, therefore, important but problematic for queer men during the interwar period.

This chapter has shown that the emergence to popular visibility of homosexuality as the open secret of a good deal of eccentric freakery had the effect of stripping fashionability from such displays and marginalizing the queer freak as a déclassé figure. He became popularly associated with lower-class young men who were attempting to act above their station. Gone were the hothouse flowers of the *fin de siècle*, and in their place sprouted the common or garden pansies who, in the form of working-class queens, had been there all along. But if the attempt to brighten the lives of the aspiring classes had wilted, it had not been for nothing, nor, needless to say, was vibrantly queer life at an end. The advent of the Second World War reinforced the values of duty and sobriety but also offered new opportunities for cross-class and indeed cross-nationality experimentation. Thus, Quentin Crisp, who employed a most queenly style of self-presentation, recalled that the bodies of US soldiers stationed in London "bulged through every straining khaki fibre toward our feverish hands … Never in the history of sex was so much offered to so many by so few."[154] Camp dandyism became a countercultural stance and was employed as such by self-identified bohemians in London, whether queer such as Crisp or straight such as the novelist Julian Maclaren-Ross.[155] By contrast, as can be seen from postwar novels such as *The Heart in Exile* (1953) by Adam de Hegedus (writing as "Rodney Garland"), closeted homosexuals who were seeking respectability were very much at pains to distance themselves from the pansy as "a freak of nature to be variously pitied or condemned."[156] Masculine queers who might be bought as trade informed the figure of the postwar spiv, but it was the image of the effeminate male that was to blossom into the most widespread and oppressive stereotype of gay men in the later twentieth century.[157]

7

Conclusions

No crime is vulgar, but vulgarity is crime. Vulgarity is the conduct of others.
Wilde, "Phrases and Philosophies."[1]

The married Anglo-American socialite Freda Dudley Ward was "typical of the beauty that excited our admiration" in 1928 (Figure 7.1).[2] She was also widely known in elite circles as the lover of Edward, Princes of Wales, before he fell for Wallis Simpson. Cecil Beaton not only recognized that Ward's beauty was of a different kind from that of the legendary Helen of Troy but drew her as the epitome of a freak who was chic. *Freak to Chic* has explained why and how this was possible. A crucial role was played by queer understandings of style and subversion. This was a time when openly homosexual expression was scandalous, but coded visual rhetoric was able to operate within the context of a system of otherwise closeted desires. The world of glamor, fashion, and art provided rich opportunities for the construction of queer spectacle, such that the interwar period saw the appearance of startlingly new fashions for androgynous self-presentation.

This book has focused on a range of forms of visual and material culture—from glamor photography to flower appreciation, interior design, and women's fashion—which were not obviously homoerotic but which developed as modes for queer men's self-expression. *Fin-de-siècle* aestheticism adopted flowery camouflage in response to a world in which there was increasing knowledge of, and often concomitant hostility toward, male homosexuality. Chapter 2 examined the persons and lives of those who, rather than hiding their difference, were displayed in freak shows that were often attached to traveling circuses. It was seen that certain characteristic types of freaks, such as bearded ladies and exaggeratedly muscled strongmen, had particular relevance to histories of gender transgression and queer performance. The term "freak" was also used to refer to an amusement, whimsy, or fancy. The apparently perverse act of dressing androgynously or cross-dressing could be claimed to be freakish in this

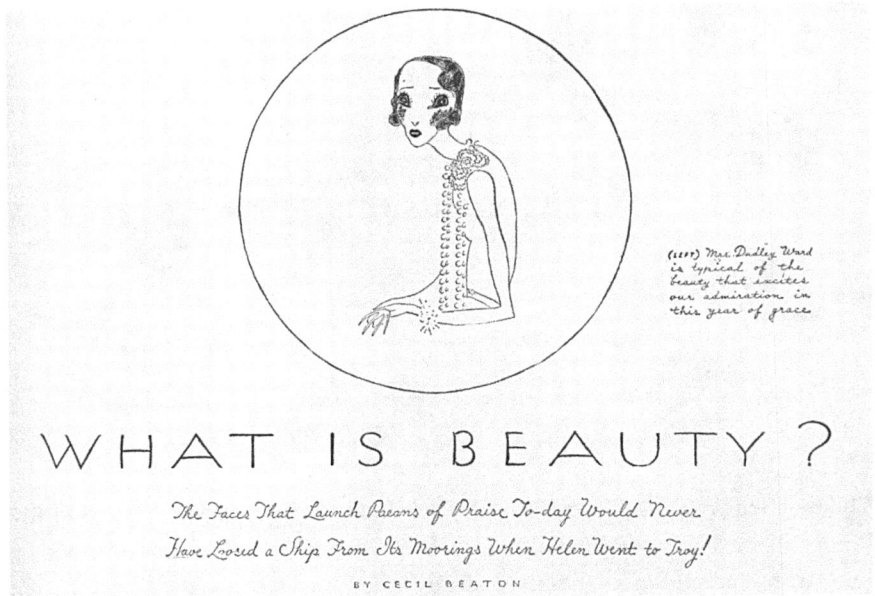

Figure 7.1 Cecil Beaton, "Mrs. Dudley Ward," in Beaton, "What Is Beauty?" *Vogue* (US edn) 72, no. 11, November 24, 1928, 47. Cecil Beaton, Vogue © Condé Nast.

less alarming sense. This provided the pretext from which the interwar cult of freak chic reimagined high society itself as an amusing freak show.

Vogue was one of the most influential fashion magazines of the twentieth century. In the 1920s its British edition in particular became a focus for various forms of queer visual and cultural expression that can be referred to as the "amusing style." Chapter 3 argued that one of the points of origin of that style that delighted in camp display can be traced to the personal and artistic collaboration between the American artist George Wolfe Plank and the British writer E. F. Benson during the First World War. The illustrations that Plank produced for Benson's book of satirical sketches of life in London's high society *The Freaks of Mayfair* (1916) directly prefigured the camp images that Plank designed for the covers of both the American and the British editions of the magazine. Therefore, Plank can be understood to have played a key role in the development of queer visual culture during the early twentieth century. He can be positioned as one of a number of queer American Anglophiles who settled in Britain; another was Henry James, whose house in the town of Rye was subsequently Benson's home. It was in such works as this that the low world of the circus and freak show was fused with the fashionable eccentricities of high society.

Changing social mores in the wake of the First World War produced a context in which there was a market among younger sophisticated consumers for daring forms of expression that could function as signs of individuality. Fancy dress parties and balls had been widespread in respectable society in the later nineteenth century. These typically involved the wearing of historical costumes and might involve the impersonation of famous people. Sexualized cross-dressing and other forms of gender subversion were not usual elements of these events before 1918, but were associated with working-class entertainments such as the music hall and with criminal practices. Chapter 4 focused on the postwar lives and attitudes of a group of people who were referred to in the media as the "bright young things." Many of the members of this set were queer, and some of them, notably the photographer Cecil Beaton, were to play an important role in the construction of images that made freak chic. Some of them had money, but others did not. The fancy dress they wore was valued, therefore, more for its novelty than its costliness. Experimentation in costume had been taking place among artists, in France and in Russia among other places, who regarded themselves as part of the modernist avant-garde.[3] British equivalents have not been taken seriously, in contrast, perhaps because they did not take themselves seriously. Daring displays of peculiarity attracted social attention in this social set. However, wearing freak costumes at freak parties was projected as desirable not primarily because it was sexually queer but because it represented amusing eccentricity. This had the result that homosexual desire remained a marginalized element in these social performances since it was sidelined as camp.

At first sight, the world of the freak show and that of the high-society "freak party" would seem to be quite different. The first relied on the objectification of freaks for a paying audience while the latter centered upon the self-expression of a privileged elite. However, freak performers can also be understood as a type of celebrity whose images were disseminated across a range of visual media, from postcards to newspapers and magazines. The prewar use of the term "freaks of fashion" implied a degree of fascination with those whose looks stood out in a spectacular fashion. The social conditions of the 1920s led to a widespread questioning of convention on the part of younger generations. Some of them found inspiration in marginalized communities including those of the freak shows and circuses. The reinterpretation of freaking as an act of personal creativity and privilege duly came to influence images of desirable youth as depicted in society and fashion magazines.

Chapters 5 and 6 explored the queer uses of flowers in the aftermath of the *fin de siècle* and the ambiguous role of women as divas and customers. As the twenties ended and the thirties began, queer floweriness became a vulgar stereotype, and male androgyny ceased to be an amusing aspect of youthful freakishness. The emergence into widespread visibility of homosexuality as the open secret of much high-society freakery had the effect of stripping fashionability from such displays. The hothouse flower in the Establishment closet and the queer young thing became conflated with the figure of the working-class queen. To appear androgynous was no longer to be associated with youthful modernity, and the "pansy" blossomed as a déclassé figure. This had the effect of dissociating the upper and middle classes from homosexuality as a public scandal and connecting it with the supposedly vulgar world of the masses. Evidence for this process can be found in the illustrations provided by Anna Zinkeisen for the "Mariegold in Society" gossip column in *The Sketch* (a magazine aimed at fashionable women) and in pansy cartoons that were published in a range of men's publications.

The move from high-society eccentric to the declassé figure of the "pansy" needs to be seen in the context of the waning power of aristocratic mores in the face of an increasingly populist press. The pansy, poof, or sissy was a popular stereotypical representation of the homosexual man as contemptible because he was an "effeminate" creature whose economic existence often depended on the whims of rich women, be they mothers or clients. This belief was derived from the misogynistic idea that to be like a woman was to be both physically and intellectually weak. It was no accident that one of the pansy's most frequent manifestations was as a worker in the fashion and clothing industries. Such queer men were depicted as bad imitators, rather than talented innovators, of style. They were derided as imposters in terms of both social class and gender.

The alignment of queer indeterminacy with fashion was, therefore, not to be sustained. Nevertheless, the bricolage culture of freak chic, which involved the construction of seemingly bizarre images that juxtaposed lilies and ladies with freaks and athletes, can be seen to have influenced post-Second World War developments such as Pop Art.[4] Glamor and the abject informed the camp sensibility of many homosexuals after 1945 and found outlets in creative traditions of drag and other forms of queer personal self-expression. Established traditions of freak-show entertainment and working-class drag had provided inspiration for interwar radicals. This helps to explain why the apparently exclusive culture of the bright young things possessed the potential to cross between classes. It thereby contained a degree of radical social potential that saved it from being the prerogative of a privileged elite. The mixture of overt nonconformity and closet complicity in the practices of freakery meant that it became a highly contested element in sexual politics with the rise of lesbian and gay liberation. Yet we can now, at this distance, appreciate the queer work done by freak chic in an age when open sexual avowal was not a widely available option and desire was characteristically mingled with disgust.

Oscar Wilde Revamped

A key theme of this book has been the afterlife of various signs—the alleged peculiarities of his body, flowers, and fashion—by which Oscar Wilde was visually stereotyped in the first decades of the twentieth century. At certain times there was a stronger element of floral aestheticism that attempted to disguise the abject aspects of same-sex desire and at other times an element of decadence that toyed with revelation. I argued in *Oscar Wilde Prefigured* (2016) that the association of Wilde's image with same-sex desire was rooted in traditions that dated from the eighteenth century. It was not so much that these signs came to mean "homosexual" as a result of his trials in 1895 but that media coverage of those events led to public knowledge concerning such matters becoming much more widespread. The term "freak" was used to negotiate understandings of men who were similarly stereotyped in early-twentieth-century Britain because it had two major referents: to whimsy and to monstrosity. Transgressive behavior could be excused under the alibi that it was just a matter of eccentricity and humorous play. However, as the homosexual content of this freaking became more obvious, it was increasingly depicted by critics as a modern freak show. Many of those who had once embraced freak styles as a way of seeming fashionably daring ceased to do so—as when, to take one example, very short hair for women *did* begin to signify lesbianism. Freak chic therefore represented a particular phase that enabled only partial legibility of same-sex desire.

These processes involved reimagining the past. Lytton Strachey's *Eminent Victorians* (1918) provided a series of biographical readings that relied on intimations of irregularities of gender and sexuality.[5] In an age of high modernism, a fascination with obsolescent styles and modes of life assumed almost countercultural significance.[6] The result was that, in certain quarters, the modes of the nineteenth century came back into fashion precisely in so far as they were imagined as perverse, a process that Helen Davies, in her book *Neo-Victorian Freakery: The Cultural Afterlife of the Victorian Freak Show* (2015), has referred to as the "enfreakment" of the Victorians.[7] This had begun even before the end of the First World War. *Vogue* commented in 1916 that Victorianism seems to be the latest fashion, though few men will want to go "the full freak of Victorian dress" daily.[8]

In 1922 W. K. Haseldon drew three dining scenes in order to illustrate a contrast between what he termed the "chop and steak" age of the early Victorian period, the "age of luxury" before 1914, and the modernist "freak age."[9] However, as I argued in *Oscar Wilde Prefigured* (2016), such caricature should be seen as a medium not only of criticism but also of the construction of queerness. It was not simply the queer freaks who contributed to the cultural construction of queer freakery but also those who observed and mocked them. A couple of years later, apparently androgynous modes for women were so commonplace that it was the styles of the nineteenth century that had started to appear bizarre. This can be seen from David Low's "Are Our Women Degenerating?" which was published in *The Star* on December 30, 1924. It shows the woman of the near future with her radical bobbed hair being eyed askance by a "Chorus of departed modes." "What a freak!" they exclaim. "'Oh, the same to you, old fruit'" is the response of "Miss 1925" (Figure 7.2).[10] Much the same point was made

THE STAR, TUESDAY, DECEMBER 30, 1924.

CHORUS OF DEPARTED MODES : "WHAT A FREAK!"
MISS 1925 : "OH, THE SAME TO YOU, OLD FRUIT."

Are Our Women Degenerating ?

Figure 7.2 David Low, "Are Our Women Degenerating?" *The Star,* December 30, 1924, 3. © David Low/Solo Syndication, and reproduced courtesy of the British Cartoon Archive, University of Kent.

in the caption to J. T. Grein's "Criticisms in Cameo" (1930), which pointed out that "modern young people may not believe that their parents ever appeared in such comically elaborate garments—but they did!"[11] The viewer knew that these were the usual garments of the day, not ones put on in a moment of whimsy. The implication was that the women of the older generation would see their younger counterparts as looking like something from a freak show. The latter, of course, would take the same attitude to the former. To freak, in a liberatory sense, was to transcend the stylistic—or indeed the misogynistic or homophobic—attitudes of the moment.

The idea that both past and present fashions were freakish was a distinctive aspect of the 1920s, and it showed a degree of ironic appreciation of the rapidity of cultural change at this time. It is no coincidence that, as Quentin Crisp put it, "'Camp' is set in the twenties."[12] Writing in 1968, he argued that "the whole set of stylizations that are known as 'camp' (a word that I was hearing then for the first time) was, in 1926, self-explanatory. Women moved and gesticulated in this way. Homosexuals wished, for obvious reasons, to copy them."[13] This book has argued that queer men played an important role in inspiring women to behave in this way in the first place. I have drawn attention to a period when a number of queer men had embarked on a project of what George Chauncey has called cultural "bricolage."[14] Women, both straight and lesbian, were also involved in this project, although for my current purposes I have been focusing on their role in relation to male practices of queer image construction. Another account of the period could have been written that privileged gender over sexuality and that centered on trans issues. Mine is one of a range of possible engagements with the material I have been presenting since my aim has been to explore male same-sex desire.

Working-class queens in London—as their fairy counterparts in New York had done for decades, if not centuries—picked and chose between imagery, styles, and cultural signifiers that were normatively applied to women and made them their own, without in many cases rejecting their own identity as male. The resulting culture was based on a sense of gender as an artificial performance and of sexual desire as being insecurely connected to gender. Oscar Wilde became infamous not merely for being homosexual but also for mingling with lower-class men. Having lived life between what could be presented as the gutter and the stars, Wilde became exemplary of associations between fashionable society and abject sodomy. He was thus sufficiently controversial that his person was rarely *openly* referenced as an inspiration in the following decades. His example and image hovered in the background as an enticement and a warning to imitators.

What was new about freak chic in the early twentieth century was that it was employed not just by a celebrity playwright and his coterie but by a range of socially prominent middle- and upper-class men who were having a wide impact on contemporary fashions. This seems to have happened first in London, in the context of *Vogue*, but rapidly became a transatlantic development. It is thus only fitting that part of the critical inspiration for my thought on such queer self-fashioning has come from those working on the American experience, such as Michael Bronski. His classic account of the "making of gay sensibility" from 1984 began: "There was a full moon. Judy Garland had just been buried that afternoon. And the queers of Christopher Street had had enough."[15] While the significance of the Stonewall Riot has been increasingly critiqued in recent years, the importance of Judy Garland has continued to receive endorsement, notably in the wake of Richard Dyer's essay on her importance for gay men. He argued that Garland provided a combination of strength and vulnerability, ordinariness and individuality, that spoke to those living as gay people in a homophobic society.[16] What Dyer says of Garland helps us to understand why some men who desired sex with other men fixed their attention on women.

Richard Dyer has argued that camp can be applauded and should not be dismissed simply as a misogynist practice on the part of "licensed decorators on the edges of society" that involves little more than the objectification of women.[17] Camp, as I have been eager to stress, was also deployed by women such as Anna Zinkeisen. David Halperin has argued that to work with femininity is potentially to contest the assumption that masculinity is inherently superior.[18] He argues that there is a need for advocacy on this subject because, as he put it, many men of his generation believed that "to be gay ... was to have *a sexuality, not a culture*."[19] This he rejects, saying, controversially, that "gay liberation has actually not been all that successful in its efforts to remake the subjective lives of gay men" and that "gay men have not stopped finding gay meaning in female icons."[20]

Freak chic can, therefore, be defended from charges of inherent misogyny. It can also be understood as not inherently elitist. One of its roots was working-class queening, and its effect was to relativize class distinctions. Furthermore, it is worth considering that the homosexual use of the term "queen" implies some degree of subversion of the British social order. Men such as Cecil Beaton can, therefore, be understood as having been involved in creative practices that, to a greater or a lesser degree, had the effect of prizing form from content and, in the process, problematizing the boundary between the freak as whimsy and the freak as monster—and hence between "masks" and "essences."[21] The fact that queer freaking blurred the boundaries not only of gender but also of class may even provide some inspiration for contemporary political struggles, bearing in mind that levels of income inequality in Britain and the United States are currently back to where they were in the 1920s.

To what extent was interwar freak chic the result of a struggle for liberation? It is a difficult question to answer. The production of queer imagery provided a means to hint at personal desires without making them explicit. In some cases it is possible to gain access to personal thoughts by reading materials such as letters and private diaries, but often the study of closeted desires has to proceed via the interpretation of carefully coded forms of self-expression. This means that it is often hard to assess directly the degree to which the behavior in question was self-conscious and premeditated. The focus on knowledge in Eve Sedgwick's *Epistemology of the Closet* (1990) was based on the figure of the author and on the extent to which authors' intentions could be read from their texts. For example, in Proust's *In Search of Lost Time*, the reader was explicitly given queer knowledge about the Baron de Charlus.[22] This is done in such a way that Proust himself was placed at a distance from the queer spectacle of the closet provided by the Baron, and it takes an interpretative leap on the part of the reader to intuit that the novel itself is part of the spectacle of the author's own closet. I have returned in several sections of this book to Cecil Beaton since he has provided me with a key case study of the workings of freak chic as it operated within the realms of visual and material culture. Beaton, as "author," generated imagery that suggested that a generalized and unspecified queerness was not simply part of the social scene but was the epitome of stylishness. His was, however, an *implicit* message, and his was still an art of the closet in which the queer man was both revealed and camouflaged by his performance.

The ability of freak chic to advance queer freedom was predicated on the particular balance of public knowledge at the time. This lay in a shifting position between complete ignorance of the possibilities of same-sex love and full apprehension. As male same-sex desire came to be increasingly legible as a central meaning of effeminate camp, so phobic stereotyping eroded the liberatory potential of freak chic. That phenomenon duly began to collapse in the 1930s when its (homo)sexual aspects began to be widely recognized. No longer could homosexuals safely express themselves through androgyny understood as fashionable, artistic, or eccentric, since those very qualities were becoming increasingly infused with sexual significance. However, those who took part at the time might well have hoped that things would turn out otherwise. After all, it might have been thought that diversity in personal performance and sexual tastes would become accepted by the mass of the population as part of everyday experience. In the event, such attitudes did not spread out beyond restricted social groups. Most homosexual men and women were, of necessity, in a position of deep insecurity throughout the period covered by this book. On a day-to-day basis, degrees of queer self-expression were often a matter not so much of grand strategy but of immediate tactics. In other words, it was a question of what one could, day by day and social encounter by social encounter, get away with.

Cecil Beaton suffered from intense anxiety about the degree to which he was, or was thought to be, a fairy. In January 1926, for example, he wrote nervously in his diary about his time at Harrow School when he had openly played the "tart" without, in fact, having many homosexual encounters:[23]

> I wondered why I had painted my face [at school]. I always used to powder and put red stuff on my lips. It's so idiotic to think that people don't notice it … Now I squirm to see a man powdered. I must have been rather awful at Harrow and I used to think I was so marvelous, so witty and bright and subtle and interesting.[24]

In *Father Figure* (1972), Beverley Nichols told a story of the older generation's misrecognition of queer signs. His father showed no dismay at the presence of a rouged effeminate friend who had taken an interest in his son and had sent a "letter which contained copious quotations from almost every homosexual author who has ever set pen to paper, from Shakespeare to Walt Whitman."[25] One style of dealing with homosexuality that was falling out of favor by this point was to pretend that it simply was not there. His father was only horrified when he caught the young Beverley reading a copy of Wilde's *The Picture of Dorian Gray* (1890) because that author undeniably represented the reality of sodomy. He could not bring himself to say what the problem was. In the end he left a note to say Wilde had been guilty of "*illum crimen horribile quod non nominandum est*" (that horrible crime which is not to be named).[26]

To patronize the antics of bright young things in the 1920s as merely the result of childlike absurdity was to shelve awkward questions concerning sexual desire. By the 1930s homosexuality as a widespread phenomenon was, for the first time, being openly recognized (and derided). This book has documented a wide range of critical and satirical responses to gender transgression, but there were still many people who wanted to be reassured that there was nothing to be worried about after all. Jacob Bloomfield has documented the media reception of the "Splinters" troupe of cross-dressed ex-servicemen. The fact that they were former squaddies reassured the audience of their normality, and the shows were reviewed by *The Daily Telegraph* as "jolly, honest fun" in 1919.[27] In the same year *The London Mail* noted: "how they have managed to eliminate all trace of that subtle unpleasantness so often associated with this type of thing I know not, but it has been done."[28] This stance became much more difficult to sustain by the latter part of the interwar period.[29] News of the bright young things in the mass media brought deviant performance to public attention. Intimations of homosexuality were, as a result, more difficult to ignore than they had been hitherto. The queer aristocratic eccentric who amused society women had, with the notable exception of Wilde, been allowed to remain in the closet. That style of life was now both protected and threatened by the popular conflation of floweriness, freakiness, and the figure of the urban queen—protected because the pansy was associated with the working classes, and threatened because the working classes now increasingly read many of their social superiors as queens. Ordinary people began to distinguish more between those who were termed normal heterosexuals and those who were not. Homosexual men were, as a result, not seen in the period after 1945 as freaks of fancy that shaped a glamorous (because unspecified) queerness through their talent to amuse. They were popularly regarded as freaks of nature to be variously pitied, medicalized, laughed at, or exhibited.

Beaton had been protected by a culture at Harrow that at that date allowed for camp deviance as an expression of elite style. Many other schoolboys were not so lucky. Later in 1926, newspapers reported the tragic death on Wimbledon Common in south London of a certain Michael Holland. He was a boy who was preparing at Lancing School in Sussex to take the examination for a scholarship to Oxford University. James Holland of the Brompton Oratory, who was the uncle and guardian of the boy, said that his school reports had always been top class but the last one had mentioned effeminacy. "He was the most brilliant boy I have ever seen," attested Fr. Holland, "and he had taken up poetry and music. I laughed at him and told him he should take up games. The Housemaster told me there must be a 'kink' in the boy's brain, but that he had no vice." The authorities simply did not understand what was wrong with the youth, bearing in mind that even though he was apparently a superb specimen of boyhood—"his muscles and limbs were perfect"—he was found to have been using face powder, and yet was not apparently guilty of sex with other boys.[30]

This was the same line of thinking as that employed by the doctor in E. M. Forster's novel *Maurice* (which was first published in 1971 but which was first drafted in the months immediately before World War One). The medic thought Maurice could not be homosexual—"an unspeakable of the Oscar Wilde sort"—because he was a sportsman with a good physique.[31] The doctor who performed the autopsy on Holland's corpse mentioned that he had never seen such "deep grey matter in anyone's brain before" and that this showed extraordinary brilliance. "I am astonished," added the doctor, "that he was not a games player, because I never saw a better developed boy in my life."[32] The Coroner recorded an open verdict of "found dead" in order to spare his family the scandal of the conclusion of suicide. But the facts were that the boy had run away from school. He had gone to his uncle who had insisted that he had to change his behavior and go back. In the boy's pocket was found a scrap of paper that read, "forgive me, I am going to kill myself."[33]

It had been understood during the nineteenth century that boys at single-sex public schools had a tendency to have sex with each other. Traditionally, this was discouraged but also accepted as one of the unpleasant realities of adolescence. Intense friendships between boys, understood on Christian spiritual principles, were encouraged as an alternative to same-sex "vice."[34] However, toward the end of the century, boys were encouraged to focus on team sports as school authorities increasingly began to see romantic friendships as the essence of, rather than a distraction from, homosexual activity. At the same time the idolization of the healthy male body presented further challenges to attempts to displace homoeroticism from the educational experience.[35] Great attention was paid to the occasional effeminate deviant who was understood to attract the attention of his peers in the absence of girls.[36] Such individuals, it was thought, were both mentally and physically somewhat akin to women and thus inferior in attributes to other boys. To be excellent in both mind and body but at the same time to show effeminate interests in arts and cosmetics could only be conceived as being the result of an incomprehensible "kink." This interpretative system did not operate everywhere and at all times with the same intensity. Beaton seems to have been spared at Harrow, but Michael Holland at Lancing was not.

Those boys who made it to university found themselves in an environment where they had far more stylistic autonomy. The subsequent behavior of many of the bright young things, Beaton included, was influenced by their experience of the greater freedoms available at college. Terence Greenidge's *Degenerate Oxford? A Critical Study of Modern University Life* (1930) provides a contemporary take on the culture of undergraduate aesthetes ("arties") and sportsmen ("hearties"). Greenidge makes it clear that Oxbridge student culture was an extension of that found at the public schools.[37] Athletes partook of same-sex affairs on an occasional basis, while aesthetes frequently professed homosexual desire to be an essential element of their lives.[38] He argues that "the object of the Aesthete's admiration is frequently the Athlete, and often the Athlete feels a counter-admiration for the Aesthete, or—if that does not happen—at least indulges in friendship with him."[39] The ongoing story of those who have finished their degrees and are "down from University" is taken up in Greenidge's later novel *The Magnificent* (1933), in which the mutual object of adulation of the male narrator and a female friend is a blond ex-Oxford man who has become a film star:

> "And what do you make of him?" I inquired.
> "I love him," she said.
> "And so do I," I said—with equal frankness.[40]

What we might now term the media and creative industries provided a powerful draw for middle-class aesthetes without the income that allowed for genteel leisure. Beaton was simply one of the most high-profile of the former Oxbridge men who made their careers by self-fashioning, networking, and gossiping in London.[41]

If the culture produced in London had many distinctively British attributes, it was, as I have been arguing, shaped by influences from other cities, notably Paris and New York. My approach could, therefore, be extended to explore the cultures of cities other than London in more detail and to examine lesbian identities and cultural practices. Robin Blyn has identified linkages between glamor, aestheticism, capitalism, and queer performance in the transatlantic world described in *Nightwood* (1936). That classic lesbian novel by Djuna Barnes features Nikka, who used to fight bears at the Cirque de Paris. Blyn argues that "as embodied in Nikka, the freak show performer becomes the heir to the decadent aesthetics of the *fin de siècle* ... the dandy has become a freak."[42] The surviving scrapbooks of the American homosexual photographer George Platt Lynes are pasted with a mixture of imagery in which opera divas are juxtaposed with naked "savages," and freaks with portraits of European aristocracy.[43] It is a heady mixture that aligns the marginality of the abject, as seen in the freak show, with its elite counterpart.[44] Lynes's scrapbooks bear strong similarities to those kept by Beaton that range back and forth between high and low social contexts and between pre- and postwar society.[45]

Other literary counterparts to these expressions of queer visual culture include such novels as *The Scarlet Pansy* (1933) by "Robert Scully" (which was possibly the pseudonym of Robert McAlmon). This explored a world of "drag," "dykes," and camp but was set in the years before 1914.[46] Charles Henri Ford and Parker Tyler's *The Young and Evil* (1933), which was written between New York and Paris, gave a very similar picture of urban, queer life.[47] Beaton was a good friend of Ford and his artist partner Pavel Tchelitchew, whom the novelist had met in Paris for the first time in 1931.[48] The latter's art also provides examples of queer and freakish bricolage such as "Phenomena," which was reproduced in *Vogue* in 1938. This featured "circus rings, an *auto da fe* [*sic*], freaks, celebrities, triple perspectives and macabre *double entendres*."[49] Beaton was considerably more socially uptight than these American friends, and it is no accident that he chose to photograph Charles Henri Ford in the mid-1930s sprawled on a bed covered with tabloid newspapers.[50]

Ford's interwar diaries show that he was involved not only in Beaton's high life in New York but also in introducing him to low-life alternatives. In the first months of 1935, for instance, he and "Cecil" had cocktails on January 9 and 24, and lunch and cocktails on January 27; they partied at Cecil's hotel on March 1 and had dinner at the Waldorf on March 20. They enjoyed more cocktails on March 28 and yet more on April 4, 10, and 17. Other entries suggest more varied entertainments. On May 24 they went to the "flying trapeze." On March 8 the following year, there is the teasing and cryptic comment, "no luck for Cecil (or me)." On March 13 they saw "Fidelio" at the Metropolitan Opera, and on March 17 they went "slumming."[51] The clear implication is that they alternated between the enjoyment of elite culture and the pursuit of men in dive bars. This represents the performative equivalent of the imagery in Platt Lynes and Cecil Beaton's scrapbooks that juxtaposed the "gutter" and the "stars."

For queer men there was more at stake than for those who just wanted to flirt with transgression before settling down to a fulfilling marriage and a sensible career. The danger of freakishness as a basis for the self emerges starkly from the manuscript of Charles Henri Ford's unpublished novel *Confessions of a Freak*, which dates from the mid-1930s.[52] The protagonist of this story has an unspecified monstrosity, as is explained in the synopsis:

> I cannot bear to hide my true state any longer. I must find someone to whom I can tell everything. How my deformity had only developed during adolescence, and how I have always hidden it. Unconscious disclosures of the effect of my "freakishness" on my behaviour as a youth and an adult. *No friends, incapability of falling in love. ...* My unsuccessful search for someone to whom I could reveal myself. Visit to freak museum, description of freaks and their effect on me. My meeting on going out of a deformed man staring at the posters of the *living wonders*, freaks of nature.[53]

The deformed beggar he meets is Emil, who has a maiming sexually transmitted disease. He had once worked as a "seal boy" since he had a flipper-like hand attached directly to his shoulder.[54] The narrative explores the implicitly sexual relationship between the two men, which includes elements of attraction and repulsion. After betrayal and blackmail, the antihero is himself offered a job as an exhibit in the museum.[55] What we are seeing here is a vision of homosexuality as the monstrosity within.

It is possible to argue that Ford's interest in freakishness was not simply capitulation to a negative stereotype but represented a degree of strategic embrace.[56] However, negative associations of queer freakishness were widely present in mid-twentieth-century culture. British seaside resorts continued to entertain holidaymakers with freak-show displays of height, girth, and mutation.[57] The bawdiness of the seaside postcard was firmly heterosexual and presented queer men, when they were noticed at all, as bizarre spectacles.[58] This can be seen from a postcard by "Tony" which implicitly compared a young homosexual man with a "half-woman half-man" on display at the "World's Greatest Freak Show" (Figure 7.3).[59]

Just as Noël Coward's precious dandyism has been read as concealing gay shame, so queer freaking was built on foundations of fear and sorrow.[60] Yet engaging with painful aspects of the past can be a challenging but significant aspect of shaping the self, and even failure can be reframed as a queer alternative to what society normally thinks of as "success."[61] Quentin Crisp has said that "if at first you don't succeed, failure may be your style," and Jack Halberstam has argued that "failure presents an opportunity rather than a dead end; in true camp fashion, the queer artist works with rather than against failure and inhabits the darkness. Indeed, the darkness becomes a crucial part of a queer aesthetic."[62] Oscar Wilde's downfall had been part of the shame of social aspirants such as Cecil Beaton. By attempting to fuse freakery with youth, brightness, and success, they sought to reimagine the image of the predatory, overweight sodomite that was established in the course of the trials of 1895.

The concept of glamor was first mentioned in *Vogue* in 1927.[63] Its closest predecessor was perhaps the term "vamp," which could be used as both a noun and a verb. If the image of Oscar Wilde had been prefigured in the earlier nineteenth century, it was revamped in the twentieth. This was a Wilde who was intent on being amusing and was at home in the increasingly commercialized culture of transatlantic high society with its admiration for sexually adventurous women. But vamping was not simply associated with glamor and erotic forwardness but also with sickness and monstrosity, built as it was on the sexual ambiguity of the figure of the vampire as popularized in Bram Stoker's novel of 1897.[64] Wilde as a homosexual remained in many ways a tabooed figure, and his "sexual life remained largely unspoken in Britain until after 1945."[65] It was not

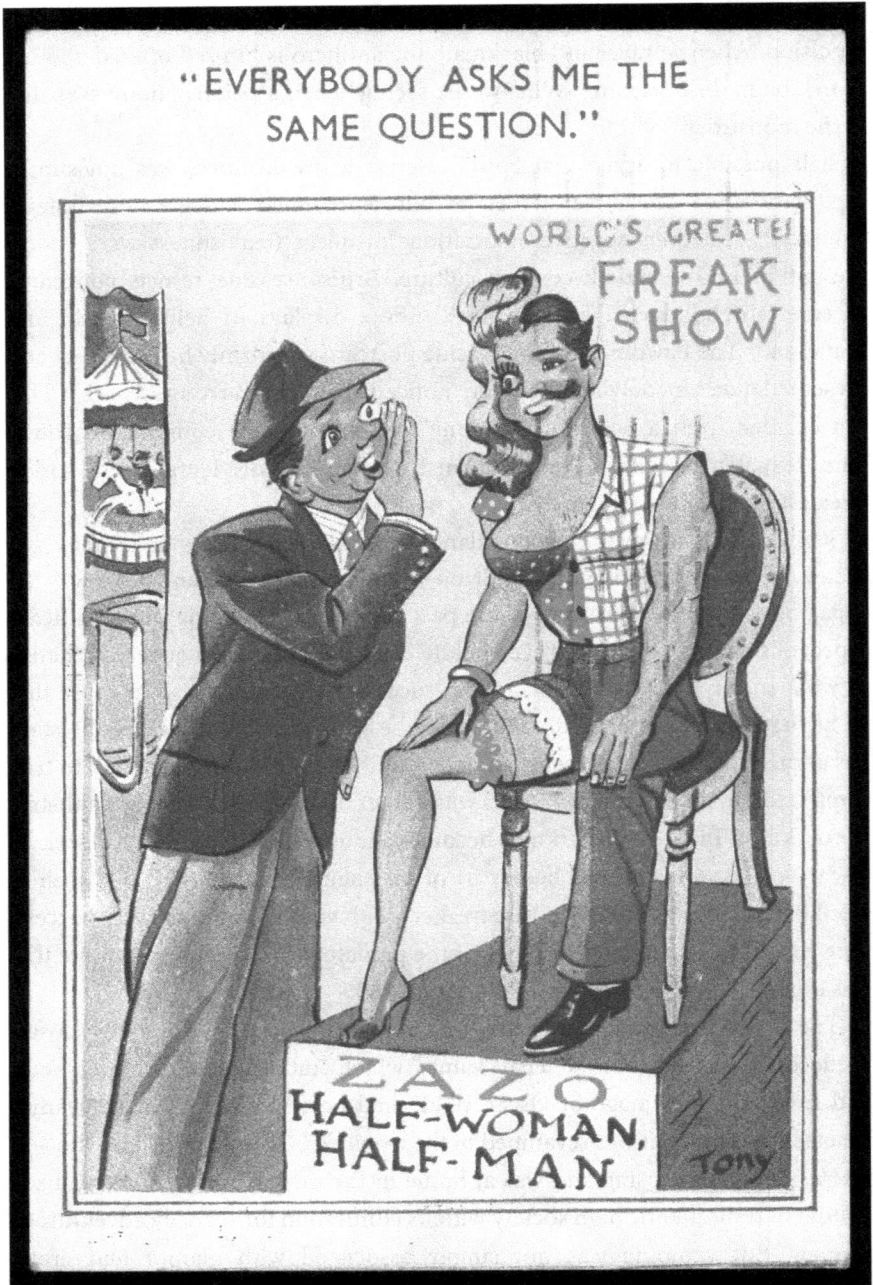

Figure 7.3 "Tony," "'Everybody Asks Me the Same Question'" (London: E. Marks, c.1953), postcard. James Gardiner Collection, photograph album labelled "Drag." © Reserved; reproduced courtesy of Wellcome Library (2045346i).

until late in the twentieth century, in the context of lesbian and gay liberation, queer activism, and the AIDS crisis, that Wilde could be acclaimed as both saint and sodomite. The hero of Neil Bartlett's *Who Was That Man? A Present for Mr Oscar Wilde* (1988) was a figure of both *fins de siècle* who could be addressed at his grave in the Père Lachaise cemetery, Paris, as "Dear Oscar" and between the sheets as "*Oscar, you fat bitch.*"[66]

Carl Van Vechten hailed the creativity of his own times as being rooted in attempts both to reference and to transcend the past by saying that "to be 1890 in 1890 might be considered almost normal. To be 1890 in 1920 might be considered almost queer. There is a difference, however. The colour is magenta. Oscar's hue was green. The fun is warmer; the vice more léger."[67] The lightness of the amusing style was a key reason for its not being taken too seriously. But that was precisely the point: it was important not to be earnest so as to keep the abject implications of freakery at bay. The florally decorative aspects of the amusing style were remembered by homosexuals in postwar Britain such as Jocelyn Brooke. In his novel *The Military Orchid* (1948), he recounted the plant-hunting enthusiasms of a certain "botanophil" who had a fascination with orchidaceous "floral aristocrats."[68] Brooke had left school in 1927, and he recalled the voice of that decade as "half revealing (like the voice of M. de Charlus) behind its ill-assumed masculinity a whole bevy of *jeunes filles en fleurs.*"[69]

Many aspects of the homosexual cultures of the post-1945 world were derived from the milieus of interwar freak chic. The queer creativity of that earlier age has lived on to shape sexual dissidence from the 1960s to our own day. By the time I went to university and came out in 1989, the AIDS epidemic was at its height. Dying men, including celebrities such as Rock Hudson, had been photographed in all their visceral horror and ugliness. Once more, and with ever greater tragic effect, the melodrama of glamorized fantasy and abject reality was played out in the full glare of the media. One of the major queer artists who died that year was Robert Mapplethorpe. His overtly sexual photographs were enormously controversial at the time, but it was his images of flowers that were, to me, just as significant.[70] I had been a floral child, spending time in the garden rather than running out to play ball with the other boys. Perhaps I already intuited that natural loveliness could conceal and yet somehow express my desires. However, the aesthetic closet with its conventional ideas of beauty was a poor defense against attacks that posited personal allure as an essentially feminine quality. Certain lesbian, gay, and trans identities align better than others with normative notions of masculinity and femininity. Some male aesthetes could argue that they were inverts whose desires were essentially those of women. But there were others for whom existing categories did not provide a home. Today I honor attempts by a previous generation of queer men, working for and alongside women, to reinvent the marginal as the ideal.

Notes

Chapter 1

1   Oscar Wilde, "Phrases and Philosophies for the Use of the Young," in *Epigrams; Phrases and Philosophies for the Use of the Young* (London: Keller, 1907), 144.

2   Cecil Beaton, *Cecil Beaton's Fair Lady* (London: Weidenfeld and Nicolson, 1964), 45.

3   Claudette Sartiliot, *Herbarium/Verbarium: The Discourse of Flowers* (Lincoln, NB: University of Nebraska Press, 1993), 34.

4   Neal Oxenhandler, "Jean Cocteau: Theatre as Parade," *Yale French Studies* 14 (1954), 72.

5   Jean Genet, *Notre-Dame-des-Fleurs* (Monte Carlo: [Denoël and Morihien], 1943); Jean Genet, *Miracle de la rose* (Lyon: Barbezat, 1946).

6   Tennessee Williams, *Garden District: Two Plays* (London: Secker and Warburg, 1959), 29.

7   Tennessee Williams, *Garden District*, 72, emphasis in original.

8   Oscar Wilde, *An Ideal Husband: A Play* (London: Methuen, [1895] 1909), 88–9. On the alleged or actual queerness of the Church at this date, see Dominic Janes, *Visions of Queer Martyrdom from John Henry Newman to Derek Jarman* (Chicago: University of Chicago Press, 2015).

9   There is a vast literature on gender and performativity, but classic works on camp and queer performativity include Judith Butler, "Critically Queer," *GLQ: A Journal of Lesbian and Gay Studies* 1, no. 1 (1993): 17–32; Eve Kosofsky Sedgwick, "Queer Performativity: Henry James's 'The Art of the Novel,'" *GLQ: A Journal of Lesbian and Gay Studies* 1, no. 1 (1993): 1–16; Moe Meyer, ed., *The Politics and Poetics of Camp* (London: Routledge, 1994); Fabio Cleto, ed., *Camp: Queer Aesthetics and the Performing Subject: A Reader* (Edinburgh: Edinburgh University Press, 1999).

10 Oscar Wilde, *Oscar Wilde in America: The Interviews*, ed. Matthew Hofer and Gary Scharnhorst (Urbana: University of Illinois Press, 2010), 37, 143, 164.

11 Discussed in Dominic Janes, *Oscar Wilde Prefigured: Queer Fashioning and British Caricature, 1750–1900* (Chicago: University of Chicago Press, 2016), 199–200.

12 Regina Kunzel, "The Power of Queer History," *American Historical Review* 123, no. 5 (2018): 1575.

13 Valerie Steele, "A Queer History of Fashion: From the Closet to the Catwalk," in *A Queer History of Fashion: From the Closet to the Catwalk*, ed. Valerie Steele (New Haven: Yale University Press, 2013).

14 John Potvin, *Bachelors of a Different Sort: Queer Aesthetics, Material Culture and the Modern Interior in Britain* (Manchester: Manchester University Press, 2014), 29.

15 Molly McGarry and Fred Wasserman, *Becoming Visible: An Illustrated History of Lesbian and Gay Life in Twentieth-Century America* (New York: Penguin, 1998), 66–70; Martin Aston, *Breaking Down the Walls of Heartache: How Music Came Out* (London: Constable, 2016), 22; Jim Elledge, *The Boys of Fairy Town: Sodomites, Female Impersonators, Third-Sexers, Pansies, Queers, and Sex Morons in Chicago's First Century* (Chicago: Chicago Review Press, 2018), 99.

16 Leslie Fiedler, *Freaks: Myths and Images of the Secret Self* (New York: Simon and Schuster, 1978), 300–19. See also Daniel P. Mannix, *Freaks: We Who Are Not as Others* (San Francisco: Research Publications, 1976).

17 Colin McDowell, "Le Freak C'est Chic," *The Sunday Times Supplement*, October 23, 2005, 23.

18 Clark's O.N.T. Spool Cotton, *Jumbo Aesthetic* (New York: Buek and Lindner, c.1882); John Strachan and Claire Nally, *Advertising, Literature and Print Culture in Ireland, 1891–1922* (Basingstoke: Palgrave Macmillan, 2012), 172–3; Roy Morris, *Declaring His Genius: Oscar Wilde in America* (Cambridge, MA: Harvard University Press, 2013), 64.

19 Michael Pickering, *Blackface Minstrelsy in Britain* (London: Routledge, 2017).

20 Michèle Mendelssohn, *Making Oscar Wilde* (Oxford: Oxford University Press, 2018), 91; Sharon Marcus, *The Drama of Celebrity* (Princeton: Princeton University Press, 2019), 163–4.

21 Monica L. Miller, *Slaves to Fashion: Black Dandyism and the Styling of Black Diasporic Identity* (Durham, NC: Duke University Press, 2009), 58–9.

22 Elspeth H. Brown, *Work! A Queer History of Modeling* (Durham, NC: Duke University Press, 2019), 10.

23 Ellen Crowell, "Queer," *Victorian Literature and Culture* 46, no. 3–4 (2018): 817.

24 Michael S. Foldy, *The Trials of Oscar Wilde: Deviance, Morality, and Late Victorian Society* (New Haven: Yale University Press, 1997), 22.

25 Matt Houlbrook, "Thinking Queer: The Social and the Sexual in Interwar Britain," in *British Queer History: New Approaches and Perspectives*, ed. Brian Lewis (Manchester: Manchester University Press, 2013), 135.

26 For the role played by lesbians in queer modernist style, see Jane Stevenson, *Baroque between the Wars: Alternative Style in the Arts, 1918–1939* (Oxford: Oxford University Press, 2018), 41–65. For lesbian landscapes and flowers, see Lisa L. Moore, *Sister Arts: The Erotics of Lesbian Landscapes* (Minneapolis: University of Minnesota Press, 2011).

27 Laura Doan, *Fashioning Sapphism: The Origins of a Modern Lesbian Culture* (New York: Columbia University Press, 2001); Doan, *Disturbing Practices: History, Sexuality, and Women's Experience of Modern War* (Chicago: University of Chicago Press, 2013).

28 Doan, *Disturbing Practices,* 133, 192.

29 Elsa Richardson, "New Queer Histories: Laura Doan's *Disturbing Practices* and the Constance Maynard Archive," *Women's History Review* 25, no. 1 (2016): 167.

30 For example, Brian Lewis, ed., *British Queer History: New Approaches and Perspectives*, Manchester: Manchester University Press, 2013.

31 There is increasing interest in studies of culture that attempt to bridge what has been termed the "Victorian/modernist divide," on which see Anne Besnault-Levita and Anne Florence Gillard Estrada, ed., *Beyond the Victorian/Modernist Divide: Remapping the Turn-of-the-Century Break in Literature, Culture and the Visual Arts* (New York: Routledge, 2018).

32 "A.S.," "Paris: Uniformed and Beflagged," *Vogue* 50, no. 3, early August 1917, 11.

33 Patricia McDonnell, "'Essentially Masculine': Marsden Hartley, Gay Identity, and the Wilhelmine German Military," *Art Journal* 56, no. 2 (1997): 62–8.

34 Harry Hervey, *The Gay Sarong* (London: Thornton Butterworth, 1926), 336. Discussed in Harlan M. Greene, "The Multi-Talented Harry Hervey," *Gay and Lesbian Review Worldwide* 24, no. 3 (2017): 25. Compare with Lucy Laing, *David and Jonathan; or, the Mystery of the Farmer's Boy* (London: Pickering and Inglis, 1936), 94–5, discussed in Janes, *Visions of Queer Martyrdom,* 169; it is a story of the intense friendship of two young Englishmen that ends with them sailing away to New Zealand.

35 G. Legman, "The Language of Homosexuality: An American Glossary," in *Sex Variants: A Study of Homosexual Patterns*, volume 1 (of 2), ed. George William Henry (New York: Hoeber, 1941), 1167. See also Ronald D. Butters, "Gary Grant and the Emergence of Gay 'Homosexual,'" *Dictionaries* 19, no. 1 (1998): 192–3.

36 *Vogue* 82, no. 10, "London and Paris: Recent Events Seen by a Visitor," November 15, 1933, 63.

37 Virginia Postrel, *The Power of Glamour: Longing and the Art of Visual Persuasion* (London: Simon and Schuster, 2013), 11.

38 Potvin, *Bachelors of a Different Sort,* 200.

39 Florence Tamagne, *A History of Homosexuality in Europe: Berlin, London, Paris, 1919–1939* (New York: Algora, 2006), 9.

40 Tamagne, *A History of Homosexuality in Europe,* 16.

41 Tamagne, *A History of Homosexuality in Europe,* 89.

42 Potvin, *Bachelors of a Different Sort,* 200.

43 Christine Bard, *Les Garçonnes: modes et fantasmes des années folles* (Paris: Flammarion, 1998).

44 Carolyn J. Dean, *The Frail Social Body: Pornography, Homosexuality, and Other Fantasies in Interwar France*, Studies in the History of Science and Culture 36 (Berkeley: University of California Press, 2000), 130–72.

45 Lenard R. Berlanstein, "Breeches and Breaches: Cross-Dress Theater and the Culture of Gender Ambiguity in Modern France," *Comparative Studies in Society and History* 38, no. 2 (1996): 368.

46 Brooke L. Blower, *Becoming Americans in Paris: Transatlantic Politics and Culture between the World Wars* (Oxford: Oxford University Press, 2011), 139. Compare Vincent Bouvet and Gérard Durozol, *Paris between the Wars: Art, Style and Glamour in the Crazy Years*, trans. Ruth Sharman (London: Thames and Hudson, 2010), 398–405.

47 Laurie Marhoefer, *Sex and the Weimar Republic: German Homosexual Emancipation and the Rise of the Nazis* (Toronto: University of Toronto Press, 2015), 144–5.

48 Tamagne, *A History of Homosexuality in Europe*, 105.

49 Noel Annan, "The Cult of Homosexuality in England 1850–1950," *Biography* 13, no. 3 (1990): 189.

50 Tamagne, *A History of Homosexuality in Europe*, 405.

51 Tamagne, *A History of Homosexuality in Europe*, 407.

52 Tamagne, *A History of Homosexuality in Europe*, 239.

53 Matt Houlbrook, *Queer London: Perils and Pleasures in the Sexual Metropolis, 1918–1957*, paperback edn (Chicago: University of Chicago Press, 2006), 265, emphasis in original.

54 Houlbrook, *Queer London*, 7, 163, 168, and 171.

55 Houlbrook, *Queer London*, 27 and 226.

56 Houlbrook, *Queer London*, 222.

57 George Chauncey, *Gay New York: Gender, Urban Culture, and the Making of the Gay Male World, 1890–1940* (New York: Basic Books, 1994), 48.

58 Chauncey, *Gay New York*, 16–18.

59 Chauncey, *Gay New York*, 32, Figure 1.1; Brent Shannon, *The Cut of His Coat: Men, Dress, and Consumer Culture in Britain, 1860–1914* (Athens, OH: Ohio University Press, 2006), 141.

60 Chauncey, *Gay New York*, 235.

61 Chauncey, *Gay New York*, 8 and 356.

62 Herbert Farjeon, "Seen on the Stage," *Vogue* 72, no.1, July 11, 1928, 48. This references Jacques-Louis David, *Portrait of Madame Récamier* (1800), which shows the socialite reclining on a chaise longue.

63 Claude A. Shepperton, "If We Ordered Our Lives after the Manner of the Russian Ballet," *Punch* 160, *Almanack* (1920): unpaginated.

64 Lynn Garafola, "Reconfiguring the Sexes," in *The Ballets Russes and Its World*, ed. Lynn Garafola and Nancy Van Norman Baer (New Haven: Yale University Press, 1999), 246–7.

65 Lynn Garafola, *Diaghilev's Ballets Russes* (Oxford: Oxford University Press, 1989), 323.

66 Tirza True Latimer, "Balletomania: A Sexual Disorder?" *GLQ: A Journal of Lesbian and Gay Studies* 5, no. 2 (1999): 192.

67 Martin Green, *Children of the Sun: A Narrative of Decadence in England after 1918* (London: Pimlico, 1992) 334; see also Kristin Bluemel, *George Orwell and*

the Radical Eccentrics: Intermodernism in Literary London (Basingstoke: Palgrave Macmillan, 2004).

68 Doan, *Disturbing Practices*, 133.

69 Janes, *Oscar Wilde Prefigured*.

70 Richard Pine, *The Dandy and the Herald: Manners, Mind and Morals from Brummell to Durrell* (New York: St. Martin's Press, 1988), 137; George Lachmann Mosse, *The Image of Man: The Creation of Modern Masculinity* (Oxford: Oxford University Press, 1996), 98; Richard Dellamora, "Productive Decadence: 'The Queer Comradeship of Outlawed Thought': Vernon Lee, Max Nordau, and Oscar Wilde," *New Literary History* 35, no. 4 (2004): 529.

71 Benjamin Kahan, "Queer Modernism," in *A Handbook of Modernism Studies*, ed. Jean-Michel Rabaté (Chichester: Wiley-Blackwell, 2013), 348 and 353–6.

72 Kate Hext and Alex Murray, "Introduction," in *Decadence in the Age of Modernism*, ed. Kate Hext and Alex Murray (Baltimore: Johns Hopkins University Press, 2019), 5.

73 Dellamora, "Productive Decadence," 529; Vincent Sherry, *Modernism and the Reinvention of Decadence* (Cambridge: Cambridge University Press, 2015), 23–9.

74 James E. Miller, "T. S. Eliot's 'Uranian Muse': The Verdenal Letters," *ANQ: A Quarterly Journal of Short Articles, Notes and Reviews* 11, no. 4 (1998): 5; Ronald Bush, "In Pursuit of Wilde Possum: Reflections on Eliot, Modernism, and the Nineties," *Modernism/Modernity* 11, no. 3 (2004): 469–70; Suzanne Wintsch Churchill, "Outing T. S. Eliot," *Criticism* 47, no. 1 (2005): 8; Christopher Reed, *Art and Homosexuality: A History of Ideas* (Oxford: Oxford University Press, 2011), 106.

75 Kristin Mahoney, *Literature and Politics of Post-Victorian Decadence* (Cambridge: Cambridge University Press, 2015), 9–11.

76 Ryan Linkof, *Public Images: Celebrity, Photojournalism, and the Making of the Tabloid Press* (London: Bloomsbury, 2018).

77 Frank Mort, "Accessible Sovereignty: Popular Attitudes to the British Monarchy during the Great War," *Social History* 45, no. 3 (2020): 328–59; Mort, "On Tour with the Prince: Monarchy, Imperial Politics and Publicity in the Prince of Wales's Dominion Tours, 1919–20," *Twentieth Century British History* 29, no. 1 (2018): 25–37; Mort, "Safe for Democracy: Constitutional Politics, Popular Spectacle, and the British Monarchy, 1910–1914," *Journal of British Studies* 58, no. 1 (2019): 109–41.

78 Michael Camille, "Editor's Introduction," *Art History* 24, no. 2 (2001): 164.

79 George Stampa, "'This Is Great. You're Just the Type I've Been Looking for for Years,'" *Punch* 178 (1930): 144, italics in original.

80 Lewis Baumer, "'Well, What Do You Think of My New Flat, Uncle John?'" *Punch* 178 (1930): 216.

81 Vanessa Bell quoted in Darren Clarke, "Duncan Grant and Charleston's Queer Arcadia," in *Queer Bloomsbury*, ed. Brenda Helt and Madelyn Detloff (Edinburgh: Edinburgh University Press, 2016), 163.

82   Susan P. Casteras, "Pre-Raphaelite Challenges to Victorian Canons of Beauty," *Huntington Library Quarterly* 55, no. 1 (1992): 13–35; J. B. Bullen, *The Pre-Raphaelite Body: Fear and Desire in Painting, Poetry, and Criticism* (Oxford: Oxford University Press, 1998), 186; Peter McNeil, "Everything Degenerates: The Queer Buttonhole," in *The Languages of Flowers: Media of Floral Communication*, ed. Isabel Kranz, Alexander Schwan, and Elke Wittrock (Berlin: Wilhelm Fink, 2016), 415.

83   Carolyn Conroy, "Mingling with the Ungodly: Simeon Solomon in Queer Victorian London," in *Sex, Time and Place: Queer Histories of London, c. 1850 to the Present*, ed. Simon Avery and Katherine M. Graham (London: Bloomsbury, 2016), 189.

84   Guy Willoughby, *Art and Christhood: The Aesthetics of Oscar Wilde* (Cranbury: Associated University Presses, 1993), 27 and 53.

85   Jamie Horrocks, "Asses and Aesthetes: Ritualism and Aestheticism in Victorian Periodical Illustration," *Victorian Periodicals Review* 6, no. 1 (2013): 1–36.

86   Jerusha Hull McCormack, *John Gray: Poet, Dandy, and Priest* (Hanover, NH: Brandeis University Press, 1991). See also David Hilliard, "UnEnglish and Unmanly: Anglo-Catholicism and Homosexuality," *Victorian Studies* 25, no. 2 (1982): 181–210; Timothy Willem Jones, *Sexual Politics in the Church of England, 1857–1957* (Oxford: Oxford University Press, 2013); Janes, *Visions of Queer Martyrdom*.

87   Andrew Elfenbein, "Byronism and the Work of Homosexual Performance in Early Victorian England," *Modern Language Quarterly* 54, no. 4 (1993): 535–67.

88   Dennis Denisoff, "'Men of My Own Sex': Genius, Sexuality, and George Du Maurier's Artists," in *Victorian Sexual Dissidence*, ed. Richard Dellamora (Chicago: University of Chicago Press, 1999) 155; Dennis Denisoff, *Aestheticism and Sexual Parody, 1840–1940*, Cambridge Studies in Nineteenth-Century Literature and Culture 31 (Cambridge: Cambridge University Press, 2001), 71–96.

89   Susan Fillin-Yeh, "Dandies, Marginality and Modernism: Georgia O'Keeffe, Marcel Duchamp and Other Cross-Dressers," *Oxford Art Journal* 18, no. 2 (1995): 33–44; Paul B. Franklin, "Object Choice: Marcel Duchamp's *Fountain* and the Art of Queer Art History," *Oxford Art Journal* 23, no. 1 (2000): 25–50; Robert Harvey, "Where's Duchamp? Out Queering the Field," *Yale French Studies* 109 (2006): 82–97.

90   Dennis Denisoff, *Sexual Visibility from Literature to Film, 1850–1950* (Basingstoke: Palgrave Macmillan, 2004), 79.

91   Michael Mitchell, *Monsters of the Gilded Age: The Photographs of Charles Eisenmann* (Toronto: Gage Publishing, 1979), 66, plate 31.

92   Claire Weissman Wilks, *The Magic Box: The Eccentric Genius of Hannah Maynard* (Toronto: Exile Editions, 1980), 11; Petra Rigby Watson, "Hannah Maynard's Multiple Exposures," *History of Photography* 20, no. 2 (1996): 155–7.

93   David Louis Ghilchik, "This Charming Photograph, Which Was to Have Been Called 'Joie de Vivre on the Beach at Brighton,'" *Punch* 173 (1927): 431. Compare

Lewis Baumer, "Society in the Sun," *Punch* 144 (1913): 221; "Pretty Play at Putney," *Punch* 157 (1919): 253.

94 Mia Fineman, *Faking It: Manipulated Photography before Photoshop* (New York: Metropolitan Museum of Art, 2012), 19, 31 and 117.

95 Fineman, *Faking It*, 124.

96 Fineman, *Faking It*, 34.

97 Mehemed F. Agha, "Whistler's Hippopotamus," *Vogue* (US edn) 89, no. 6, 1937, 138.

98 Theodore Dreiser, *Dreiser Looks at Russia* (London: Constable, 1928), 190.

99 Elizabeth Wilson, "A Note on Glamour," *Fashion Theory* 11, no. 1 (2007): 98.

100 Stevenson, *Baroque between the Wars*, 1. Stephen Calloway, *Baroque Baroque: The Culture of Excess* (London: Phaidon, 1994), 15, explored a "curious, hybrid, referential, highly-strung and self-conscious baroque—this 'Baroque Baroque.'"

101 Deena Weinstein and Michael Weinstein, "Celebrity Worship as Weak Religion," *Word and World* 23, no. 3 (2003): 298. See also Brett Farmer, "The Fabulous Sublimity of Gay Diva Worship," *Camera Obscura* 20, no. 2 (59) (2005): 165–95.

102 Postrel, *The Power of Glamour*, 6.

103 Stephen Gundle and Clino T. Castelli, *The Glamour System* (Basingstoke: Palgrave Macmillan, 2006), 11.

104 Katie Sutton, "Sexology's Photographic Turn: Visualizing Trans Identity in Interwar Germany," *Journal of the History of Sexuality* 27, no. 3 (2018): 471–2. See also Katie Sutton, *The Masculine Woman in Weimar Germany*, Monographs in German History 32 (New York: Berghahn, 2011); Katie Sutton, "'We Too Deserve a Place in the Sun': The Politics of Transvestite Identity in Weimar Germany," *German Studies Review* 35, no. 2 (2012): 335–54.

105 Katie Sutton, "Sexological Cases and the Prehistory of Transgender Identity Politics in Interwar Germany," in *Case Studies and the Dissemination of Knowledge*, ed. Joy Damousi, Birgit Lang, and Katie Sutton (New York: Routledge, 2015), 86.

106 Robert Mills, *Seeing Sodomy in the Middle Ages* (Chicago: University of Chicago Press, 2015), 84 and 86.

107 See Susan Stryker, "General Editor's Introduction," *Transgender Studies Quarterly* 5, no. 4 (2018): 515–17; Leah DeVun and Zeb Tortorici, "Trans, Time and History," *Transgender Studies Quarterly* 5, no. 4 (2018): 518–39.

108 For key studies on transgendering, see Alison Oram, "Cross-Dressing and Transgender," in *The Modern History of Sexuality*, ed. H. G. Cocks and Matt Houlbrook (Basingstoke: Palgrave Macmillan, 2006); Alison Oram, *Her Husband Was a Woman! Women's Gender-Crossing in Modern British Popular Culture* (London: Routledge, 2007); Elizabeth Reis, *Bodies in Doubt: An American History of Intersex* (Baltimore: Johns Hopkins University Press, 2009); Sutton, "Sexological Cases and the Prehistory of Transgender Identity Politics."

109 Quentin Crisp, *The Last Word: An Autobiography*, ed. Philip Ward and Laurence Watts (Place of publication not identified: MB Books, 2017), 5–6.

110 Robert Heylmun, "Letter to the Editor: 'How I Rescued Quentin Crisp's Memoir,'" *Gay and Lesbian Review Worldwide*, 25, no. 5 (2018), 7–8.

111 Rita Felski, "The Counterdiscourse of the Feminine in Three Texts by Wilde, Huysmans, and Sacher-Masoch," *PMLA* 106, no. 5 (1991): 1103.

112 Abby Coykendall, "Queer Counterhistory and the Spectre of Effeminacy," in *Heteronormativity in Eighteenth-Century Literature and Culture*, ed. Ana de Freitas Boe and Abby Coykendall (Farnham: Ashgate Publishing, 2015), 111–29.

113 D. J. Taylor, *Bright Young People: The Rise and Fall of a Generation, 1918–1940* (London: Chatto and Windus, 2007), 53 and 59.

114 Jack Butler Yeats [pseud. "W. Bird"], "Hints to Artists and Writers Who Need to Advertise Themselves by Some Eccentricity of Costume," *Punch* 146 (1914): 295.

115 *Vogue* 60, no. 9, "Public Opinion and Personal Liberty," early November 1922, 69.

116 Oram, "Cross-Dressing and Transgender," 272.

117 Miranda Gill, *Eccentricity and the Cultural Imagination in Nineteenth-Century Paris* (Oxford: Oxford University Press, 2009), 2.

118 Gill, *Eccentricity and the Cultural Imagination*, 283.

119 Jack Halberstam [Judith Halberstam], *In a Queer Time and Place: Transgender Bodies, Subcultural Lives* (New York: New York University Press, 2005), 1.

120 Janes, *Oscar Wilde Prefigured*, 104–5. I argued that the *lack* of sexual scandal concerning Brummell can, in the light of Regency mores, be read as a queer sign.

121 John Timbs, *English Eccentrics and Eccentricities*, volume 1 (London: Richard Bentley, 1866), v–viii.

122 Timbs, *English Eccentrics*, volume 1, iii–iv.

123 John Woolf, *The Wonders: Lifting the Curtain on the Freak Show, Circus and Victorian Age* (London: Michael O'Mara, 2019), 58.

124 Clive Bell quoted in Mark Hussey, "Clive Bell. 'A Fathead and Voluptuary': Conscientious Objection and British Masculinity," in *Queer Bloomsbury*, 254.

125 Dominic Janes, *Picturing the Closet: Male Secrecy and Homosexual Visibility in Britain* (Oxford: Oxford University Press, 2015), 53–67.

126 Charlotte Ross, *Eccentricity and Sameness: Discourses on Lesbianism and Desire between Women in Italy, 1860s–1930s* (Oxford: Peter Lang, 2015).

127 Henry Degras [pseud. Mark Benney], *What Rough Beast: A Biographical Fantasia on the Life of Professor J. R. Neave otherwise Known as Ironfoot Jack* (London: Peter Davis, 1939), 319. See also Jack Neave, *The Surrender of Silence: The Memoirs of Ironfoot Jack, King of the Bohemians*, ed. Colin Stanley (London: Strange Attractor, 2018), 114–24; Raymond M. Lee, "'The Man Who Committed a Hundred Burglaries': Mark Benney's Strange and Eventful Sociological Career," *Journal of the History of the Behavioral Sciences* 51, no. 4 (2015): 409–33.

128 Judith R. Walkowitz, *Nights Out: Life in Cosmopolitan London* (New Haven: Yale University Press, 2012), 203.

129 Virginia Nicholson, *Among the Bohemians: Experiments in Living, 1900–1939* (London: Penguin Books, 2002), 112 and 153.

130 Seth Koven, *Slumming: Sexual and Social Politics in Victorian London* (Princeton, NJ: Princeton University Press, 2004), 269.

131 George Orwell, *Down and Out in Paris and London* (London: Gollancz, 1933); Koven, *Slumming*, 83–4.

132 Kevin J. Mumford, *Interzones: Black/White Sex Districts in Chicago and New York in the Early Twentieth Century* (New York: Columbia University Press, 1997), 145.

133 Alistair O'Neill, *London: After a Fashion* (London: Reaktion, 2007), 125; Paul Deslandes, "Exposing, Adorning and Dressing the Body in the Modern Era," in *The Routledge History of Sex and the Body: 1500 to the Present*, ed. Sarah Toulalan and Kate Fisher (London: Routledge, 2013), 179–203.

134 Simon Szreter and Kate Fisher, *Sex before the Sexual Revolution: Intimate Life in England 1918–1963* (Cambridge: Cambridge University Press, 2010), 293.

135 "How," "The Well Dressed Man," *Vogue* (US edn) 30, no. 11, September 12, 1907, 292.

136 Robert Byron, "The Perfect Party," *Vogue* 73, no. 12, June 12, 1929, 43, illustrated by Cecil Beaton.

137 Celia Marshik, *At the Mercy of Their Clothes: Modernism, the Middlebrow, and British Garment Culture* (New York: Columbia University Press, 2017), 107.

138 Anca L. Lasc, "Angels and Rebels: The Obsessions and Transgressions of the Modern Interior," in *Designing the French Interior: The Modern Home and Mass Media*, ed. Anca L. Lasc, Georgina Downey, and Mark Taylor (London: Bloomsbury, 2015), 49.

139 Quoted in Hugo Vickers, *Cecil Beaton: The Authorised Biography* (London: Weidenfeld and Nicolson, 1985), 134.

140 Hugo Vickers, *Loving Garbo: The Story of Greta Garbo, Cecil Beaton and Mercedes de Acosta* (London: Random House, 2012), 36.

141 Quoted and discussed in Sofka Zinovieff, *The Mad Boy, Lord Berners, My Grandmother and Me* (London: Jonathan Cape, 2014), 111, and Robin Muir, *Cecil Beaton's Bright Young Things* (London: National Portrait Gallery, 2020), 228.

142 On gay shame, see Sally Munt, *Queer Attachments: The Cultural Politics of Shame* (Aldershot: Ashgate, 2008); David M. Halperin and Valerie Traub, ed., *Gay Shame* (Chicago: Chicago University Press, 2009).

143 Vickers, *Loving Garbo*.

144 *Sunday Dispatch*, "Greta Garbo's One Ambition—She Wants to Play a Man's Rôle on the Stage," April 21, 1935, 3, emphasis in original.

145 On Oscar Wilde in the twentieth century, see Uwe Böker, Richard Corballis and Julie Hibbard, ed., *The Importance of Reinventing Oscar: Versions of Wilde during the Last 100 Years* (Amsterdam: Rodopi, 2002); Angela Kingston, *Oscar Wilde as a Character in Victorian Fiction* (Basingstoke: Palgrave Macmillan, 2007), 234–46;

Joseph Bristow, ed., *Oscar Wilde and Modern Culture: The Making of a Legend* (Athens, OH: Ohio University Press, 2008); Stefano Evangelista, ed., *The Reception of Oscar Wilde in Europe* (London: Continuum, 2010).

146 Lisa Duggan, *The Twilight of Equality? Neoliberalism, Cultural Politics, and the Attack on Democracy* (Boston: Beacon Press, 2003), 50.

147 Nishant Shahani, *Queer Retrosexualities: The Politics of Reparative Return* (Bethlehem, PA: Lehigh University Press, 2012).

148 Alan Downs, *The Velvet Rage: Overcoming the Pain of Growing up Gay in a Straight Man's World* (Cambridge, MA: Da Capo, 2005).

149 Shahani, *Queer Retrosexualities*, 20; Janes, *Oscar Wilde Prefigured*, 100–16.

150 Timothy Brittain-Catlin, *Bleak Houses: Disappointment and Failure in Architecture* (Cambridge, MA: MIT Press, 2014), 91.

151 Amy Gluckman and Betsy Reed, ed., *Homo Economics: Capitalism, Community, and Lesbian and Gay Life* (Routledge: New York, 1997), 6.

152 Anne Emmanuelle Berger, *The Queer Turn in Feminism: Identities, Sexualities, and the Theater of Gender*, trans. Catherine Porter (New York: Fordham University Press, 2014), 92.

153 Victoria Pitts, "Visibly Queer: Body Technologies and Sexual Politics," *Sociological Quarterly* 41, no. 3 (2000): 460.

Chapter 2

1   Wilde, "Phrases and Philosophies," 143.

2   Quoted in Richard Altick, *The Shows of London* (Cambridge, MA: Harvard University Press, 1978), 36.

3   Andrew N. Sharpe, *Foucault's Monsters and the Challenge of Law* (Abingdon: Routledge, 2010), 23.

4   Nadja Durbach, *Spectacle of Deformity: Freak Shows and Modern British Culture* (Berkeley: University of California Press, 2009), 1.

5   Rachel Adams, *Sideshow USA: Freaks and the American Cultural Imagination* (Chicago: University of Chicago Press, 2001), 11; John Woolf, *The Wonders*, 169; Jeffrey Weeks, "Inverts, Perverts, and Mary-Annes: Male Prostitution and the Regulation of Homosexuality in England in the Nineteenth and Early Twentieth Centuries," *Journal of Homosexuality* 6, no. 1–2 (1981): 113–34.

6   Bluford Adams, "'A Stupendous Mirror of Departed Empires': The Barnum Hippodromes and Circuses, 1874–1891," *American Literary History* 8, no. 1 (1996): 35–8.

7   Victoria and Albert Museum, London, Gabrielle Enthoven Collection, S.1–2009, *Fairground Showman at a "Freak Show" Booth*, nineteenth century, probably from London, print on paper. See also Alvin Goldfarb, "Gigantic and Miniscule Actors

on the Nineteenth-Century American Stage," *Journal of Popular Culture* 10, no. 2 (1976): 267–79.

8 Robert Bogdan, *Freak Show: Presenting Human Oddities for Amusement and Profit* (Chicago: University of Chicago Press, 1988), 208.

9 Matthew Sweet, *Inventing the Victorians* (London: Faber and Faber, 2001), 141.

10 Joan Hawkins, "'One of Us': Tod Browning's *Freaks*," in *Freakery: Cultural Spectacles of the Extraordinary Body*, ed. Rosemarie Garland Thomson (New York: New York University Press, 1996), 274.

11 Robert Bogdan, Martin Elks, and James A. Knoll, *Picturing Disability: Beggar, Freak, Citizen, and Other Photographic Rhetoric* (Syracuse: Syracuse University Press, 2012), 9.

12 Bogdan, Elks and Knoll, *Picturing Disability*, 11.

13 Marlene Tromp and Karyn Valerius, "Towards Situating the Victorian Freak," in *Victorian Freaks: The Social Context of Freakery in Britain*, ed. Marlene Tromp (Columbus: Ohio State University Press, 2008), 7–9.

14 Rosemarie Garland Thomson, *Extraordinary Bodies: Figuring Physical Disability in American Culture and Literature* (New York: Columbia University Press, 1996), 62.

15 James W. Cook, *The Arts of Deception: Playing with Fraud in the Age of Barnum* (Cambridge, MA: Harvard University Press, 2001), 225; Sweet, *Inventing the Victorians*, 137–40.

16 Michael M. Chemers, *Staging Stigma: A Critical Examination of the American Freak Show* (New York: Palgrave Macmillan, 2008), 25.

17 Clare Sears, "Electric Brilliance: Cross-Dressing Law and Freak Show Displays in Nineteenth-Century San Francisco," in *The Transgender Studies Reader 2*, ed. Susan Stryker and Aren Z. Aizura (New York: Routledge, 2013), 555 and 560; Clare Sears, *Arresting Dress: Cross-Dressing, Law, and Fascination in Nineteenth-Century San Francisco* (Durham, NC: Duke University Press, 2015), 103–5.

18 *The Times*, "None Will Grudge Mr. Barnum," November 11, 1889, 9.

19 Stanley Rogers, *Freak Ships* (London: John Lane, 1936), ix.

20 Peter Cryle and Elizabeth Stephens, *Normality: A Critical Genealogy* (Chicago: University of Chicago Press, 2017), 270.

21 Cryle and Stephens, *Normality*, 289.

22 *Daily Mirror*, "Today's Gossip," February 15, 1918, 6–7, emphasis in original.

23 Fiedler, *Freaks*, 180–1; Sears, *Arresting Dress*, 103.

24 Wilkie Collins, quoted in Martha Stoddard Holmes, "Queering the Marriage Plot: Wilkie Collins's *The Law and the Lady*," in *Victorian Freaks*, 237.

25 Margrit Shildrick, *Embodying the Monster: Encounters with the Vulnerable Self* (London: Sage, 2001), 25.

26 Jennifer Tyburczy, *Sex Museums: The Politics and Performance of Display* (Chicago: University of Chicago Press, 2016), 21, on the "sexual architecture" of the freak show.

27 Marc Hartzman, *American Sideshow: An Encyclopedia of History's Most Wondrous and Curiously Strange Performers* (New York: Jeremy P. Tarcher/Penguin, 2006), 113–14.

28 William Livingston Alden, *Among the Freaks* (London: Longmans, Green, 1896), 184.

29 George Ives Papers, gen. mss. 426, Clippings Album 3, 102, Beinecke Rare Book and Manuscript Library, Yale University; the photograph is dated 1903.

30 George Ives, *Man Bites Man: The Scrapbook of an Edward Eccentric*, ed. Paul Sieveking (London: Jay Landesmann, 1980); Matt Cook, "Families of Choice? George Ives, Queer Lives and the Family," *Gender and History* 22, no. 1 (2010): 1–21.

31 Bogdan, *Freak Show*, 224.

32 Arthur Goddard, "'Even as You and I': At Home with the Barnum Freaks," *English Illustrated Magazine* 173 (February 1898): 495.

33 *Tenby Observer Weekly List of Visitors and Directory*, "Death of the 'Bearded Lady,'" October 11, 1883, 6.

34 Hartzman, *American Sideshow*, 109–10.

35 *The Times*, "Pygmies in Piccadilly," November 19, 1880, 8. Compare with National Fairground and Circus Archive, University of Sheffield, John Bramwell Taylor Collection, Ref: 178T1.25, "Frank Uffner's Royal American Midgets."

36 *Funny Folks* 15, no. 782, "Oh, Limp Here!" November 16, 1889, 364–5.

37 Thomas Carlyle, *Sartor Resartus: The Life and Opinions of Herr Teufelsdröckh in Three Books* (London: Chapman and Hall, 1869), 189.

38 Kevin P. Murphy, *Political Manhood: Red Bloods, Mollycoddles, and the Politics of Progressive Era Reform* (New York: Columbia University Press, 2008), 16.

39 Goddard, "'Even as You and I,'" 493–4; Hartzman, *American Sideshow*, 30–1.

40 Janes, *Oscar Wilde Prefigured*, 8–9.

41 Arthur Hopkins, "Cut Short," *Punch* 111 (1896): 234.

42 Lewis Baumer, "The Sex Question (a Study in Bond Street)," *Punch* 140 (1911): 235; Christopher Breward, *The Culture of Fashion: A New History of Fashionable Dress* (Manchester: Manchester University Press, 1995), 185.

43 Janes, *Picturing the Closet*, 33.

44 N. John Hall, *Max Beerbohm: A Kind of a Life* (New Haven: Yale University Press, 2002), 38.

45 Lewis R. Farnell, *An Oxonian Looks Back* (London: Martin Hopkinson), 57.

46 Dellamora, "Productive Decadence."

47 Edgar C. Beall, *The Life Sexual: A Study of the Philosophy, Physiology, Science, Art, and Hygiene of Love* (New York: Vim Publishing Company, 1905), 173–5.

48 See the comments in relation to the commercial production of post-1945 muscle magazines for homosexual men by James Kirchick, "Pictorial Physiques: James Kirchick on the Links between Bodybuilding, Capitalism and Gay Rights," *The Times Literary Supplement*, August 7, 2019, 28, reviewing David K. Johnson, *Buying*

Gay: How Physique Entrepreneurs Sparked a Movement (New York: Columbia University Press, 2019).

49 Matthew Tinkom, *Working Like a Homosexual: Camp, Capital, Cinema* (Durham, NC: Duke University Press, 2002), 26.

50 Stephanie Green, "Oscar Wilde's *The Woman's World*," *Victorian Periodicals Review* 30, no. 2 (1997): 102–20; Anya Clayworth, "*The Woman's World*: Oscar Wilde as Editor," *Victorian Periodicals Review* 30, no. 2 (1997): 97; Catharine Ksinan, "Wilde as Editor of *Woman's World*: Fighting a Dull Slumber in Stale Certitudes," *English Literature in Transition, 1880–1920* 41, no. 4 (1998): 408–26; Margaret Diane Stetz, "The Bi-Social Oscar Wilde and 'Modern' Women," *Nineteenth-Century Literature* 55, no. 4 (2001): 528; Sally Ledger, "Wilde Women and *The Yellow Book*: The Sexual Politics of Aestheticism and Decadence," *English Literature in Transition, 1880–1920* 50, no. 1 (2007): 5–26.

51 Petra Clark, "'Cleverly Drawn': Oscar Wilde, Charles Ricketts, and the Art of *The Woman's World*," *Journal of Victorian Culture* 20, no. 3 (2015): 383.

52 Kate Hext, "Just Oscar," *The Times Literary Supplement*, November 23, 2018, 4.

53 Princeton University Library, TC040, scrapbook 2, box 18, contains press cuttings associated with the flotation, lists of share values, and copies of sale documents for shares.

54 Leonard Raven Hill, "The Tug of Peace," *Punch* 149 (1915): 483.

55 Walkowitz, *Nights Out*, 63.

56 Janes, *Picturing the Closet*, 122.

57 Eve Kosofsky Sedgwick, *Epistemology of the Closet*, reissued edn (New York: Columbia University Press, 2008), 231.

58 Barry Spurr, "Camp Mandarin: The Prose Style of Lytton Strachey," *English Literature in Transition 1880–1920* 33, no. 1 (1990): 31; Barry Spurr, *A Literary-Critical Analysis of the Complete Prose Works of Lytton Strachey (1880–1932): A Reassessment of His Work and Career*, Studies in British Literature 19 (New York, Edwin Mellen Press, 1995), 226–7; David A. J. Richards, *The Rise of Gay Rights and the Fall of the British Empire: Liberal Resistance and the Bloomsbury Group* (Cambridge: Cambridge University Press, 2013), 118; Janes, *Picturing the Closet*, 114–25.

59 Edward Irenaeus Prime-Stevenson [pseud. Xavier Mane], *The Intersexes: A History of Similisexualism as a Problem in Social Life* (Rome: Privately printed, 1908), 83.

60 Prime-Stevenson, *The Intersexes* (1908), 188.

61 Bassano Ltd., *Edward Dudley ["Fruity"] Metcalfe*, 1919. Bromide print. National Portrait Gallery, London, x83717.

62 Alfred Bryan, "Eclipsed: A Regent Street Study in the Slack Season," *Punch* 133 (1907): 161.

63 Jane Tynan, *British Army Uniform and the First World War: Men in Khaki* (Basingstoke: Palgrave Macmillan, 2013), 107.

64 George Ives Papers, gen. mss. 426, Clippings Album 15, 43, Beinecke Rare Book and Manuscript Library, Yale University.

65 Photopress and "E. P.," "Strange—but True. The Bogeymen and the Beauty Spider," *Sketch*, January 9, 1929, 47; Peta Tait, *Circus Bodies: Cultural Identity in Aerial Performance* (London: Routledge, 2005), 138.

66 Richard Viner, "Ladies Love a Fight." *Vogue* 90, no. 16, February 2, 1938, 44–5 and 70.

67 Green, *Children of the Sun*, 44–7.

68 Oscar Wilde, "London Models," *English Illustrated Magazine* 64 (January 1889): 318.

69 Wilde, "London Models," 319.

70 O'Neill, *London: After a Fashion*, 69.

71 Hugh David, *On Queer Street: A Social History of British Homosexuality, 1895–1995* (London: HarperCollins, 1997), 200.

72 Mae West, *Babe Gordon* (New York: Macaulay, 1930), 160.

73 *London Pavilion, Piccadilly, W.: Every Evening at 10.45: The Tallest Man in the World: Herr Winkelmeier* (c. 1887). Poster, Wellcome Library, London, General Collection, EPH ++53.

74 Hartzman, *American Sideshow*, 114.

75 Matt Houlbrook, "Soldier Heroes and Rent Boys: Homosex, Masculinities, and Britishness in the Brigade of Guards, circa 1900–1960," *Journal of British Studies* 42, no. 3 (2003): 351–88.

76 Alden, *Among the Freaks*, 184.

77 Max Beerbohm, "The Incomparable Beauty of Modern Dress," *Spirit Lamp* 4, no. 2, June 6, 1893, 94.

78 David L. Chapman, *Sandow the Magnificent: Eugen Sandow and the Beginnings of Bodybuilding*, paperback edn (Urbana: University of Illinois Press, 2006), 51; Fae Brauer, "Virilizing and Valorizing Homoeroticism: Eugen Sandow's Queering of Body Cultures before and after the Wilde Trials," *Visual Culture in Britain* 18, no. 1 (2017): 46 and 49.

79 Alden, *Among the Freaks*, 181.

80 Maurizia Boscagli, *Eye on the Flesh: Fashions of Masculinity in the Early Twentieth Century* (Boulder: Westview Press, 1996), 108.

81 Charles Harrison, "Awful Prophetic Picture of How M. Paderewski Will Appear Next Season," *Punch* 115 (1898): 97. See also Ignacy Jan Paderewski, "Piano Playing and Muscle," *Physical Culture* 1, no. 3 (1898): 189–1.

82 Edward Tennyson Reed, "Celebrities Out of Their Element.—II. Mr. Sandow in the Throes of Light Verse—Which We Understand He Varies with a Little Needlework or Delicate Embroidery," *Punch* 140 (1911): 13.

83 James Henry Dowd, "Portrait—When Composing Elusive Answer to Challenge," *Punch* 136 (1909): 32.

84 Leslie Wilson, "The Regeneration of the Johnny," *Physical Culture* 1, no. 1 (1898): 31.

85 Rupert Hart-Davis, *A Catalogue of the Caricatures of Max Beerbohm* (Cambridge, MA: Harvard University Press, 1972), 144, fig. 100.

86 Arthur Wallis Mills, "Visitor (Who Has Been Asked to Criticize the Latest Masterpiece)," *Punch* 170 (1926): 461.

87 Ina Zweiniger-Bargielowska, "Building a British Superman: Physical Culture in Interwar Britain," *Journal of Contemporary History* 41, no. 4 (2006): 600.

88 Ana Carden-Coyne, *Reconstructing the Body: Classicism, Modernism, and the First World War* (Oxford: Oxford University Press, 2009), 204; Joan Tumblety, *Remaking the Male Body: Masculinity and the Uses of Physical Culture in Interwar and Vichy France* (Oxford: Oxford University Press, 2012), 43.

89 Cecile Lindsay, "Bodybuilding: A Postmodern Freak Show," in *Freakery*, 356–67.

90 Lewis Baumer, "'Looks a Bit Affected, Don't 'E?'" *Punch* 190 (1936): 98.

91 Durbach, *Spectacle of Deformity*, 174.

92 Durbach, *Spectacle of Deformity*, 176.

93 Thomson, *Extraordinary Bodies*, 79.

94 Julie Peakman, *The Pleasure's All Mine: A History of Perverse Sex* (London: Reaktion, 2013), 7.

95 Alden, *Among the Freaks*, 190.

96 Quoted and discussed in Durbach, *Spectacle of Deformity*, 181.

97 Chemers, *Staging Stigma*, 62.

98 Chemers, *Staging Stigma*, 93.

99 Adams, *Sideshow USA*, 114.

100 Reis, *Bodies in Doubt*, 61–2.

101 Eugene Solomon Talbot, *Degeneracy: Its Causes, Signs and Results*, ed. Havelock Ellis, Contemporary Science Series 35 (London: Walter Scott, 1898).

102 Dana Seitler, "Queer Physiognomies; or, How Many Ways Can We Do the History of Sexuality?" *Criticism* 46, no. 1 (2004): 79.

103 Chris Waters, "Havelock Ellis, Sigmund Freud and the State: Discourses of Homosexual Identity in Interwar Britain," in *Sexology in Culture: Labelling Bodies and Desire*, ed. Lucy Bland and Laura Doan (London: University of Chicago Press, 1998), 166.

104 Quoted in Adams, *Sideshow USA*, 93.

105 Adams, *Sideshow USA*, 93, emphasis in original.

106 Robert McRuer, "Compulsory Able-bodiedness and Queer/Disabled Existence," in *The Disability Studies Reader*, 2nd edn, ed. Lennard J. David (New York: Routledge, 2006), 301–2.

107 Anna Mollow and Robert McRuer, "Introduction," in *Sex and Disability*, ed. Anna Mollow and Robert McRuer (Durham, NC: Duke University Press, 2012), 1.

108 Elizabeth Stephens, "Geeks and Gaffs: The Queer Legacy of the 1950s American Freak Show," in *Queer 1950s: Rethinking Sexuality in the Postwar Years*, ed. Heike Bauer and Matt Cook (Basingstoke: Palgrave, 2012), 183–95.

109 Alison Kafer, *Feminist Crip Queer* (Bloomington: Indiana University Press, 2013), 15.

110 Suzannah Biernoff, *Portraits of Violence: War and the Aesthetics of Disfigurement* (Ann Arbor: University of Michigan Press, 2017), 56.

111 Joanna Bourke, *Dismembering the Male: Men's Bodies, Britain and the Great War* (London: Reaktion, 1996), 75. See also Joanna Bourke, "Fragmentation, Fetishization and Men's Bodies in Britain, 1890–1939," *Women: A Cultural Review* 7, no. 3 (1996): 240–9.

112 Matt Franks, "Crip/Queer Aesthetics in the Great War," *MFS Modern Fiction Studies* 65, no. 1 (2019): 64.

113 Franks, "Crip/Queer Aesthetics," 76.

114 Dominic Janes, "Eminently Queer Victorians and the Bloomsbury Group's Critique of British Leadership," in *The Palgrave Handbook of Masculinity and Political Culture in Europe: From Antiquity to the Contemporary World*, ed. Sean Brady, Christopher Fletcher, Rachel Moss, and Lucy Riall (Basingstoke: Palgrave, 2018), 360–3.

115 Richard Meyer, "Threesomes: Lincoln Kirstein's Queer Arithmetic," in *Lincoln Kirstein's Modern*, ed. Samantha Friedman and Jodi Hauptman (New York: Museum of Modern Art, 2019), 102. See also Elspeth H. Brown, "Queering Glamour in Interwar Fashion Photography: The 'Amorous Regard' of George Platt Lynes," *GLQ: A Journal of Lesbian and Gay Studies* 23, no. 3 (2017): 289–326.

116 Ina Zweiniger-Bargielowska, *Managing the Body: Beauty, Health, and Fitness in Britain, 1880–1939* (Oxford: Oxford University Press, 2010), 19.

117 Carden-Coyne, *Reconstructing the Body*, 176.

118 Carden-Coyne, *Reconstructing the Body*, 204–5.

119 Bourke, *Dismembering the Male*, 180.

120 Philip Mann, *The Dandy at Dusk: Taste and Melancholy in the Twentieth Century* (London: Head of Zeus, 2017), 113.

121 Steven Bruhm and Natasha Hurley, ed., *Curiouser: On the Queerness of Children* (Minneapolis: University of Minnesota Press, 2004); Kathryn Bond Stockton, *The Queer Child, or Growing Sideways in the Twentieth Century* (Durham, NC: Duke University Press, 2009).

Chapter 3

1 Wilde, "Phrases and Philosophies," 143.

2 Aileen Ribeiro, *Clothing Art: The Visual Culture of Fashion, 1600–1914* (New Haven: Yale University Press, 2017), 1.

3   Nancy J. Troy, *Couture Culture: A Study in Modern Art and Fashion* (Cambridge, MA: MIT Press, 2003), 295–8.

4   Quoted in Matthew Gelbart, "Persona and Voice in the Kinks' Songs of the Late 1960s," *Journal of the Royal Musical Association* 128, no. 2 (2003): 226.

5   Janes, *Oscar Wilde Prefigured*.

6   *Vogue* (US edn) 34, no. 8, "Curious Coincidences of Hat Styles," August 19, 1909, 206.

7   *Vogue* (US edn) 41, no. 2, "*Vogue* Patterns: French Lingerie Patterns," January 15, 1913, 59.

8   *Vogue* (US edn) 34, no. 6, "Paris," August 5, 1909, 152.

9   Leigh Gordon Giltner, "A Butterfly Fancy: Part II," *Vogue* (US edn) 30, no. 9, 1907, 241.

10 Elizabeth Wilson, *Adorned in Dreams: Fashion and Modernity*, new edn (London: I.B. Tauris, 2003), 130–2.

11 Lewis Baumer [and "Violetta"], "The Distressing Decadence," *Punch* 143 (1912): 369.

12 Arthur Norris, "What a Large Dolly That Gentleman's Got!" *Punch* 136 (1909): 161.

13 *Dundee Evening Telegraph*, "The Woman Who Did," October 30, 1895, 2. See also Linda Dowling, "The Decadent and the New Woman in the 1890's," *Nineteenth-Century Fiction* 33, no. 4 (1979): 434–53.

14 *Liverpool Echo*, "The New Fashions," March 24, 1914, 4.

15 *Daily Mirror*, "Inventive Dress Designer Provides Skirt Alternative to the Handbag," March 17, 1914, 17.

16 *Daily Mirror*, "Freak Telephones Becoming Popular," January 31, 1914, 9.

17 Abigail Joseph, "'A Wizard of Silks and Tulle': Charles Worth and the Queer Origins of Couture," *Victorian Studies* 56, no. 2 (2014): 251.

18 Joseph, "'A Wizard of Silks and Tulle,'" 275.

19 Abigail Joseph, "Queer Things: Victorian Objects and the Fashioning of Homosexuality" (PhD diss., Columbia University, USA, 2012), 60.

20 Joseph, "Queer Things," 58.

21 Joel H. Kaplan and Sheila Stowell, *Theatre and Fashion: Oscar Wilde to the Suffragettes* (Cambridge: Cambridge University Press, 1994), 117.

22 Mary Lynn Stewart, *Dressing Modern Frenchwomen; Marketing Haute Couture, 1919–1939* (Baltimore: Johns Hopkins University Press, 2008), 36.

23 Ribeiro, *Clothing Art*, 512.

24 Erté, quoted in Nancy J. Troy, "The Theatre of Fashion: Staging Haute Couture in Early 20th Century France," *Theatre Journal* 53, no. 1 (2001): 2.

25 *Vogue* 71, no. 3, "The Frock of the Future: Dresses Designed by Cecil Beaton for a Ball at Claridge's," February 8, 1928, 26–7.

26 Lewis Baumer, "Le Mot Juste," *Punch* 149 (1915): 390, emphasis in original.

27 Howard Cox and Simon Mowatt, "*Vogue* in Britain: Authenticity and the Creation of Competitive Advantage in the UK Magazine Industry," *Business History* 54, no. 1 (2012): 73.

28 Mary E. Davis, *Classic Chic: Music, Fashion, and Modernism* (Berkeley: University of California Press, 2006), 181.

29 Davis, *Classic Chic*, 49.

30 Stewart, *Dressing Modern Frenchwomen*, 37–9.

31 Caroline Seebohm, *The Man Who Was "Vogue": The Life and Times of Condé Nast* (New York: Viking, 1982), 140.

32 Cox and Mowatt, "*Vogue* in Britain," 71.

33 Seebohm, *The Man Who Was "Vogue,"* 134.

34 Adam Geczy and Vicki Karaminas, *Fashion's Double: Representations of Fashion in Painting, Photography and Film* (London: Bloomsbury, 2016), 22.

35 Adam Geczy, *Fashion and Orientalism: Dress, Textiles and Culture from the 17th to the 21st Century* (London: Bloomsbury, 2013), 136–53.

36 Seebohm, *The Man Who Was "Vogue,"* 128 and 131.

37 Aurelea Mahood, "Fashioning Readers: The Avant Garde and British *Vogue*, 1920–9," *Women: A Cultural Review* 13, no. 1 (2002): 37–47.

38 Rohan McWilliam, "Elsa Lanchester and Bohemian London in the Early Twentieth Century," *Women's History Review* 23, no. 2 (2014): 178.

39 Mahood, "Fashioning Readers," 42; Christopher Reed, "Bloomsbury Bashing: Homophobia and the Politics of Criticism in the Eighties," in *Queer Bloomsbury*, 39. See also Nicola Luckhurst, *Bloomsbury in "Vogue,"* Bloomsbury Heritage Series 19 (London: Cecil Woolf, 1998).

40 Mass Observation Archive, University of Sussex, file report 108, *Fashion: Opinion-Forming and the Creative Artist,* May 15, 1940. Reproduced with permission of Curtis Brown Group Ltd, London, on behalf of The Trustees of the Mass Observation Archive. © The Trustees of the Mass Observation Archive.

41 Matt Cook, *Queer Domesticities: Homosexuality and Home Life in Twentieth-Century London* (Basingstoke: Palgrave Macmillan, 2014), 61.

42 Peter McNeil, "Designing Women: Gender, Sexuality and the Interior Decorator, *c.* 1890–1940." *Art History* 17, no. 4 (1994): 635–9; Jasmine Rault, "Designing Sapphic Modernity: 1926," in *Networks of Design: Proceedings of the 2008 Annual International Conference of the Design History Society (UK)*, ed. Jonathan Glynne, Fiona Hackney, and Viv Minton (Boca Raton: Universal-Publishers, 2009), 472–6.

43 Christopher Reed, *Bloomsbury Rooms: Modernism, Subculture and Domesticity* (New Haven: Yale University Press, 2004).

44 Christopher Reed, "Design for (Queer) Living: Sexual Identity, Performance, and Décor in British *Vogue*, 1922–1926," *GLQ: A Journal of Lesbian and Gay Studies* 12, no. 3 (2006): 377.

45 Reed, "Design for (Queer) Living," 377.

46 Reed, "Design for (Queer) Living," 396.

47 Reed, "Design for (Queer) Living," 397.

48 Jane Garrity, "Selling Culture to the 'Civilized': Bloomsbury, British *Vogue*, and the Marketing of National Identity," *Modernism/Modernity* 6, no. 2 (1999): 35.

49 Garrity, "Selling Culture to the 'Civilized,'" 35. See also Barbara Fassler, "Theories of Homosexuality as Sources of Bloomsbury's Androgyny," *Signs* 5, no. 2 (1979): 237–51.

50 Reed, "Design for (Queer) Living," 379 and 385.

51 Christopher Reed, "A *Vogue* That Dare Not Speak Its Name: Sexual Subculture during the Editorship of Dorothy Todd, 1922–26," *Fashion Theory: The Journal of Dress, Body and Culture* 10, no. 1–2 (2006): 39–72. See also Amanda Juliet Carrod, "'A Plea for a Renaissance': Dorothy Todd's Modernist Experiment in British *Vogue*, 1922–1926," (PhD diss., Keele University, UK, 2015).

52 Reed, "A *Vogue* That Dare Not Speak Its Name," 59.

53 Edna Woolman Chase and Ilka Chase, *Always in Vogue* (London: Gollancz, 1954), 130.

54 Anne Pender, "'Modernist Madonnas': Dorothy Todd, Madge Garland and Virginia Woolf," *Women's History Review* 16, no. 4 (2007): 520.

55 Julie Kavanagh, *Secret Muses: The Life of Frederick Ashton* (London: Faber and Faber, 1996), 77; Pender, "'Modernist Madonnas,'" 520; Stevenson, *Baroque between the Wars*, 293.

56 Stevenson, *Baroque between the Wars*, 52.

57 Una Troubridge, *The Life and Death of Radclyffe Hall* (London: Hammond, 1961), 82.

58 Julie Anne Taddeo, "Plato's Apostles: Edwardian Cambridge and the 'New Style of Love,'" *Journal of the History of Sexuality* 8, no. 2 (1997): 227.

59 *Vogue* 65, no. 5, "An Economist and Modern Art: The Cambridge Rooms of Mr. Keynes," early March 1925, 46–7; Robert Skidelsky, *John Maynard Keynes, 1883–1946: Economist, Philosopher, Statesman* (London: Penguin, 2003), 254; Reed, *Bloomsbury Rooms*, 220–1.

60 Quoted in Jane Garrity, "Virginia Woolf, Intellectual Harlotry, and 1920s British *Vogue*," in *Virginia Woolf in the Age of Mechanical Reproduction*, ed. Pamela L. Caughie (New York: Garland, 2000), 198. See also Luckhurst, *Bloomsbury in "Vogue"*, 6; Lisa Cohen, "Virginia Woolf, Fashion and British *Vogue*," *Charleston Magazine* 18 (1998), 5; Lisa Cohen, "'Frock Consciousness': Virginia Woolf, the Open Secret, and the Language of Fashion," *Fashion Theory* 3, no. 2 (1999): 162.

61 Garrity, "Virginia Woolf, Intellectual Harlotry, and 1920s British *Vogue*," 213.

62 Allen J. Frantzen, *Bloody Good: Chivalry, Sacrifice, and the Great War* (Chicago: University of Chicago Press, 2004), 146.

63 Tamagne, *A History of Homosexuality in Europe*, 184; Brenda S. Helt, "Passionate Debates on 'Odious Subjects': Bisexuality and Woolf's Opposition to Theories of Androgyny and Sexual Identity," *Twentieth Century Literature* 56, no. 2 (2010): 131–67.

64 Cohen, "'Frock Consciousness'"; Richards, *The Rise of Gay Rights*.

65 *Vogue* 64, no. 6, "Why the Wedding Ceremony Ought to Be Revised," late September 1924, 48.

66 Susan Sontag, "Notes on 'Camp,'" *Partisan Review* 31, no. 4 (1964): 515–30. For studies that take camp seriously, and often positively, as a creative cultural form see David Bergman, ed., *Camp Grounds: Style and Homosexuality* (Amherst: University of Massachusetts Press,1993); Meyer, *The Politics and Poetics of Camp*; Daniel Harris, "The Death of Camp: Gay Men and Hollywood Diva Worship, from Reverence to Ridicule," *Salmagundi* 112 (1996): 166–91; Cleto, *Camp*.

67 Terry Castle, "Some Notes on 'Notes on Camp,'" in *The Scandal of Susan Sontag*, ed. Barbara Ching and Jennifer A. Wagner-Lawlor (New York: Columbia University Press, 2009), 25.

68 Ann Pellegrini, "After Sontag: Future Notes on Camp," in *A Companion to Lesbian, Gay, Bisexual, Transgender and Queer Studies*, ed. George E. Haggerty and Molly McGarry (Oxford: Blackwell, 2007), 184.

69 Reed, *Bloomsbury Rooms*, 242.

70 Reed, *Bloomsbury Rooms*, 251.

71 Cook, *Queer Domesticities*, 84.

72 *Vogue* 61, no. 8, "Wedding Rings, Cakes and Favours," late April 1923, 50.

73 Claude Lepape and Thierry Defert, *The Art of Georges Lepape: From the Ballets Russes to "Vogue,"* trans. Jane Brenton (London: Thames and Hudson, 1984), 66–77.

74 William Packer, *Fashion Drawing in "Vogue"* (London: Thames and Hudson, 1983), 44.

75 Erté, *Things I Remember: An Autobiography* (London: Peter Owen, 1975), 37; Stella Blum, ed., *Fashion Drawings and Illustrations from "Harper's Bazaar"* (New York: Dover, 1976); Charles Spencer, *Erté* (London: Studio Vista, 1970), 24.

76 Reed, "A *Vogue* That Dare Not Speak Its Name," 45 and 47, fig. 2.

77 Vivien Whelpton, *Richard Aldington: Poet, Soldier and Lover, 1911–1929* (Cambridge: Lutterworth Press, 2014), 256–8.

78 Carolyn A. Kelley, "Aubrey Beardsley and H. D.'s *Astrid*: The Ghost and Mrs. Pugh of Decadent Aestheticism and Modernity." *Modernism/Modernity* 15, no. 3 (2008): 452; Diana Collecott, *H. D. and Sapphic Modernism, 1910–1950* (Cambridge: Cambridge University Press, 1999).

79 Cassandra Laity, *H.D. and the Victorian Fin de Siècle: Gender, Modernism, Decadence*, Cambridge Studies in American Literature and Culture 104 (Cambridge: Cambridge University Press, 2009).

80 William Packer, *The Art of "Vogue" Covers* (London: Octopus, 1980), 16–17.

81 John Potvin, "Housing the New Dandy, 1920–1924," *Designing the French Interior*, 195, fig. 15.1.

82 Clark, "Cleverly Drawn."

83 Cook, *Queer Domesticities*, 33 and 38.

84 Potvin, *Bachelors of a Different Sort*, 87.

85 See Stevenson, *Baroque between the Wars*, 23–38, on the role of social climbing.

86 E. F. Benson, *The Freaks of Mayfair* (London: T. N. Foulis, 1916), 167.

87 George Wolfe Plank, untitled cover illustration, *Vogue* (US edn) 55, no. 8, October 15, 1919, cover.

88 W. and D. Downey, "A Favourite of the Lyric Stage: Miss Marie Dainton—'Resting,'" *Sketch,* August 3, 1904, supplement, 6.

89 Benson, *The Freaks of Mayfair*, 202.

90 Benson, *The Freaks of Mayfair*, 210.

91 Benson, *The Freaks of Mayfair*, 33.

92 Benson, *The Freaks of Mayfair*, 34. Compare Janes, *Oscar Wilde Prefigured*, on the tradition of British caricature of male effeminates prior to 1900.

93 George Plank Papers, MSS 28. Series 1, box 1, folder 5, Yale Collection of American Literature, Beinecke Rare Book and Manuscript Library, Yale University.

94 Pearsall Smith quoted in John Russell, ed., *A Portrait of Logan Pearsall Smith Drawn from His Letters and Diaries* (London: Dropmore, 1950), 91.

95 Michael H. Whitworth, "Logan Pearsall Smith and *Orlando*," *Review of English Studies* 55, no. 221 (2004): 599.

96 Allan Downend, "Benson, E. F.,1867–1940," in *The 1890s: An Encyclopedia of British Literature, Art, and Culture*, ed. G. A. Cevasco (New York: Garland, 1993), 54.

97 Sayoni Basu, "Benson, Edward Frederic (1867–1940)," *Oxford Dictionary of National Biography* (Oxford: Oxford University Press, May 2005), unpaginated.

98 Simon Goldhill, *A Very Queer Family Indeed: Sex, Religion, and the Bensons in Victorian Britain* (Chicago: University of Chicago Press, 2016), 287.

99 Hugo Vickers, "Introduction," in E. F. Benson, *Final Edition* (London: Hogarth Press, 1988), unpaginated.

100 Robert F. Kiernan, *Frivolity Unbound: Six Masters of the Camp Novel* (New York: Continuum, 1990), 86.

101 Kiernan, *Frivolity Unbound*, 78–80.

102 E. F. Benson, *As We Were: A Victorian Peep Show* (London: Longmans, Green and Co., 1930), 210.

103 Benson, *As We Were*, 294.

104 Howard J. Booth, "Experience and Homosexuality in the Writing of Compton Mackenzie," *English Studies* 88, no. 3 (2007): 321.

105 Gregory Woods, *Homintern: How Gay Culture Liberated the Modern World* (New Haven: Yale University Press, 2016), 215; Brooks and Maugham had previously been in a relationship.

106 Benson, *As We Were*, 294.

107 Brian Masters, *The Life of E. F. Benson* (London: Chatto and Windus, 1991), 287.

108 Benson, *As We Were*, 295.

109 Masters, *The Life of E. F. Benson*, 251.

110 Masters, *The Life of E. F. Benson*, 251.

111 George Plank Papers, Yale Collection of American Literature, Beinecke Rare Book and Manuscript Library, Yale University.

112 George Plank Papers, MSS 28, series 2, box 8, folder 127, Yale Collection of American Literature, Beinecke Rare Book and Manuscript Library, Yale University. See also John Blatchley, *The Bookplates of George Wolfe Plank and a Selection of His Book Illustrations* (London: Bookplate Society, 2002).

113 George Plank Papers, series 1, box 1, folder 13.

114 George Plank Papers, series 1, box 1, folder 6.

115 George Plank Papers, series 1, box 1, folder 14.

116 George Plank Papers, series 1, box 1, folder 15.

117 E. F. Benson, *Final Edition* (London: Hogarth Press, 1988), 142.

118 George Plank Papers, series 1, box 1, folder 15.

119 George Plank Papers, series 1, box 1, folder 15.

120 George Plank Papers, series 1, box 1, folder 6.

121 George Plank Papers, series 1, box 1, folder 16.

122 George Plank Papers, series 1, box 1, folder 16.

123 George Plank Papers, series 1, box 1, folder 16.

124 George Plank Papers, series 1, box 1, folder 6.

125 George Plank Papers, series 1, box 1, folder 5.

126 George Plank Papers, series 1, box 1, folder 17.

127 George Plank Papers, series 1, box 1, folder 6.

128 George Plank Papers, series 1, box 1, folder 17.

129 George Plank Papers, series 1, box 1, folder 5.

130 George Plank Papers, series 1, box 2, folder 19.

131 George Plank Papers, series 1, box 2, folder 19.

132 George Plank Papers, series 1, box 2, folder 23.

133 George Plank Papers, series 1, box 1, folder 16.

134 Janes, *Picturing the Closet*, 5.

135 Benson, *The Freaks of Mayfair*, 39.

136 *Vogue* (US edn) 51, no. 1, "What They Read," 1918, 74.

137 Allan Downend, "E. F. Benson's 'Originals' no. 2: George Plank," *Dodo: The E. F. Benson Society Journal* 24 (2010): 18 and 20–1.

138 Jack Adrian, "Introduction," in E. F. Benson, *Desirable Residences* (Oxford: Oxford University Press, 1991), xiii.

139 *Vogue* (US edn) 61, no. 1, "Our American Artists in Paris and London," January 1, 1923, 79, emphasis in original.

140 George Wolfe Plank, "What Is Home without Another?" reproduced in *Vogue* (US edn) 72, no. 5, "Dear Me! These Modern Samplers!" September 1, 1928, 64. See also Joseph McBrinn, "'Nothing Is More Terrifying to Me than to See Ernest Thesiger Sitting under the Lamplight Doing His Embroidery': Ernest Thesiger

(1879–1961). 'Expert Embroiderer,'" *Text: For the Study of Textile Art, Design and History* 43 (2015–16): 20–6. Joseph McBrinn, "Queer Hobbies: Ernest Thesiger and Interwar Embroidery," *Textile: Journal of Cloth and Culture* 15, no. 3 (2017): 312 suggests that the camp actor Ernest Thesiger, who was known for his embroidery skills, was an inspiration for the figure of Georgie.

Chapter 4

1   Wilde, "Phrases and Philosophies," 144.
2   Martin Taylor, ed., *Lads: Love Poetry of the Trenches* (London: Constable, 1989).
3   Paul Fussell, *The Great War and Modern Memory* (Oxford: Oxford University Press, 1975), 272. See also Bourke, *Dismembering the Male*, 124–70; John Ibson, "Masculinity under Fire: *Life's* Presentation of Camaraderie and Homoeroticism before, during, and after the Second World War," in *Looking at "Life" Magazine*, ed. Erika Doss (Washington, DC: Smithsonian Institution Press, 2001), 192; Leonard V. Smith, "Paul Fussell's *The Great War and Modern Memory*: Twenty-Five Years Later," *History and Theory* 40, no. 2 (2001): 241–60.
4   Dorothy Parker, "The Bride He Left behind Him," *Vogue* 51, no. 10, late May 1918, 53. Compare *Vogue* 52, no. 4, "The High Cost of Dressing," late August 1918, 42–3; Nancy Christie and Michael Gauvreau, *Bodies, Love, and Faith in the First World War: Dardanella and Peter* (Basingstoke: Palgrave Macmillan, 2018), 196, on the trenches as a locale that threatened to undermine normative heterosexuality.
5   Santanu Das, "'Kiss Me, Hardy': Intimacy, Gender, and Gesture in First World War Trench Literature," *Modernism/Modernity* 9, no. 1 (2002): 69.
6   Edwin Morrow, "With Amateur Theatricals at the Front and War-Work at Home," *Punch* 150 (1916): 411.
7   Dorothy Parker, "Lovely Woman as the Honest Labouring Man," *Vogue* 54, no. 3 (early August 1919): 31.
8   David A. Boxwell, "The Follies of War: Cross-Dressing and Popular Theatre on the British Front Lines, 1914–18," *Modernism/Modernity* 9, no. 1 (2002): 17.
9   Laurence Senelick, *The Changing Room: Sex, Drag and Theatre* (London: Routledge, 2000), 295 and 302; Boxwell, "The Follies of War," 6.
10 Jason Crouthamel, "Cross-Dressing for the Fatherland: Sexual Humour, Masculinity and German Soldiers in the First World War," *First World War Studies* 2, no. 2 (2011): 208.
11 David Haldane Lawrence, "Chorus Boys: Words, Music and Queerness (*c.* 1900–*c.* 1936)," *Studies in Musical Theatre* 3, no. 2 (2009): 167; Jacob Bloomfield, "Male Cross-Dressing Performance in Britain, 1918–1970" (PhD diss., The University of Manchester, UK, 2017), 49.
12 Dean, *The Frail Social Body*, 144.

13 Adrian Caesar, *Taking It Like a Man: Suffering, Sexuality, and the War Poets: Brooke, Sassoon, Owen, Graves* (Manchester: Manchester University Press, 1993).

14 Janes, *Victorian Reformation: The Fight over Idolatry in the Church of England, 1840–1860* (Oxford: Oxford University Press, 2009), 46–50; Janes, *Visions of Queer Martyrdom*, 18–25.

15 *John Bull*, "The Imitation Woman," July 21, 1923, 16.

16 *Evening Express*, "Street Robberies at Swansea," extra special edn, January 3, 1899, 1.

17 *Manchester Courier and Lancashire General Advertiser*, "In the Twinkling of an Eye," August 29, 1901, 8.

18 Matt Houlbrook, *Prince of Tricksters: The Incredible True Story of Netley Lucas, Gentleman Crook* (Chicago: University of Chicago Press, 2016). See also Angus McLaren, "Smoke and Mirrors: Willy Clarkson and the Role of Disguises in Inter-War England," *Journal of Social History* 40, no. 3 (2007): 597–618.

19 *Dundee Evening Telegraph*, "Alleged Theft of Jewellery," December 28, 1931, 5.

20 *Sunday Post*, "Poison among Chocolates," September 27, 1925, 4.

21 *Weekly Mail*, "Father's Appeal," July 23, 1910, 7.

22 *Evening Dispatch*, "The Hidden Hands," August 20, 1917, 4.

23 *Cardiff Times*, "Serious Charge against a Contractor," January 11, 1890, 7.

24 *Ballymena Observer*, "Policeman Dressed as a Woman," April 4, 1913, 10.

25 *Evening Express*, 2nd edn, "Policemen in Petticoats," June 24, 1908, 3.

26 Foldy, *The Trials of Oscar Wilde*, 15.

27 There is a burgeoning literature on Boulton and Park. See Weeks, "Inverts, Perverts, and Mary-Annes"; Charles Upchurch, "Forgetting the Unthinkable: Cross-Dressers and British Society in the Case of the Queen vs. Boulton and Others," *Gender and History* 12, no. 1 (2000): 127–57; Michelle Liu Carriger, "'The Unnatural History and Petticoat Mystery of Boulton and Park': A Victorian Sex Scandal and the Theatre Defense," *TDR/The Drama Review* 57, no. 4 (2013): 135–56; Neil McKenna, *Fanny and Stella: The Young Men Who Shocked Victorian England* (London: Faber and Faber, 2013).

28 *Penny Illustrated Paper*, "The Last Vile Fashion," June 4, 1870, 354. See also *Morning Post*, "Charge of Personating Women," May 14, 1870, 6.

29 John Leech, "The Great Social Evil," *Punch* 33 (September 12, 1857): 114, emphasis in original. See also Henry J. Miller, "John Leech and the Shaping of the Victorian Cartoon: The Context of Respectability," *Victorian Periodicals Review* 42, no. 3 (2009): 267–91.

30 *Sketch*, "A Freak of Fashion," June 23, 1897, 359. Discussed in Lynda Nead, *Victorian Babylon: People, Streets and Images in Nineteenth-Century London* (New Haven: Yale University Press, 2000), 63–4, fig. 32.

31 Mariana Valverde, "The Love of Finery: Fashion and the Fallen Woman in Nineteenth-Century Social Discourse," *Victorian Studies* 32, no. 3 (1989): 169–88.

32 *London Daily News*, "A Rogue and a Vagabond," January 16, 1901, 9.

33 Senelick, *The Changing Room*, 295 and 302; Laurence Senelick, "Boys and Girls Together: Subcultural Origins of Glamour Drag and Male Impersonation on the Nineteenth-Century Stage," in *Crossing the Stage: Controversies on Cross-Dressing*, ed. Lesley Ferris (London: Routledge, 1993), 80–95.

34 Senelick, *The Changing Room*, 306.

35 Matt Houlbrook, "'The Man with the Powder Puff' in Interwar London," *Historical Journal* 50, no. 1 (2007): 145–71.

36 Houlbrook, "'The Man with the Powder Puff,'" 170. See also Matt Houlbrook, "Queer Things: Men and Make-Up between the Wars," in *Gender and Material Culture in Britain since 1600*, ed. Hannah Greig, Jane Hamlett, and Leonie Hannan (London: Palgrave, 2016).

37 Matt Houlbrook, "'Lady Austin's Camp Boys': Constituting the Queer Subject in 1930s London," *Gender and History* 14, no. 1 (2002): 39.

38 Taylor Croft, *Cloven Hoof: A Study of Contemporary London Vices* (London: Denis Archer, 1932), 63.

39 Houlbrook, "Lady Austin's Camp Boys," 45.

40 Rictor Norton, ed., "Queen of Camp, 1874," *Homosexuality in Nineteenth-Century England: A Sourcebook*, December 4, 2018, expanded October 30, 2019.

41 The quoted phrase is the subtitle of Houlbrook, *Queer London*. See also Houlbrook, "Lady Austin's Camp Boys," 40.

42 Vern L. Bullough and Bonnie Bullough, *Cross Dressing, Sex, and Gender* (Philadelphia: University of Pennsylvania Press, 1993), 236–7; Senelick, *The Changing Room*, 296–97.

43 Roger Baker, *Drag: A History of Female Impersonation in the Performing Arts* (London: Cassell, 1994), 178.

44 *Sketch*, "Do We Need the Actress?" June 8, 1904, supplement, 9.

45 *Sketch*, "Do We Need the Actress?" supplement, 4.

46 *Sketch*, "Do We Need the Actress?" 272.

47 Lisa Z. Sigel, *Making Modern Love: Sexual Narratives and Identities in Interwar Britain* (Philadelphia: Temple University Press, 2012), 150.

48 Angus McLaren, *The Trials of Masculinity: Policing Sexual Boundaries* (Chicago: University of Chicago Press, 1997), 218.

49 *Hartlepool Mail*, "In Woman's Clothes: He Wore Them for Pleasure," November 23, 1942, 8.

50 *Hull Daily Mail*, "Man Dressed as a Woman," October 6, 1909, 3.

51 *London Evening Standard*, "The Trial of Boulton and Park," May 10, 1871, 6.

52 *Edinburgh Evening News*, "Masquerading as a Woman," August 31, 1892, 3.

53 Marshik, *At the Mercy of Their Clothes*, 103.

54 Rebecca Mitchell, "The Victorian Fancy Dress Ball, 1870–1900," *Fashion Theory* 21, no. 3 (2017): 311.

55 Marshik, *At the Mercy of Their Clothes*, 118.

56 Mitchell, "The Victorian Fancy Dress Ball," 310, emphasis in original.

57 Marshik, *At the Mercy of Their Clothes*, 136.

58 Senelick, *The Changing Room*, 353.

59 Kirsten MacLeod, "The Queerness of Being 1890 in 1922: Carl van Vechten and the New Decadence," in *Decadence in the Age of Modernism*, 230.

60 Edward Carpenter, *The Intermediate Sex: A Study of Some Transitional Types of Men and Women* (London: George Allen and Unwin: 1912). See also Chris Waters, "Havelock Ellis, Sigmund Freud and the State"; Sheila Rowbotham, *Edward Carpenter: A Life of Liberty and Love* (London: Verso, 2008).

61 Arthur Wallis Mills, "The Freak-Merchants; or, the Bright Young People," *Punch* 178, *Almanack* (1930): unpaginated.

62 "Mariegold," "Mariegold in Society," *Sketch*, March 13, 1920, 482.

63 Geczy and Karaminas, *Fashion's Double*, 80.

64 Gill Headley, *Arthur Jeffress: A Life in Art* (London: Bloomsbury Academic, 2020).

65 *Sketch*, "Society's Greek 'Freak Party': The Great Urban Dionysia," April 17, 1929, 126.

66 Byron, "The Perfect Party," 43–5 and 86.

67 Green, *Children of the Sun*, 485.

68 Taylor, *Bright Young People*, 47 and 190.

69 Taylor, *Bright Young People*, 203.

70 David Leon Higdon, "Gay Sebastian and Cheerful Charles: Homoeroticism in Waugh's *Brideshead* Revisited," *ARIEL: A Review of International English Literature* 25, no. 4 (1994): 77–89.

71 Quoted and discussed in Oram, *Her Husband Was a Woman!* 80.

72 Julia F. Saville, "The Romance of Boys Bathing: Poetic Precedents and Respondents to the Paintings of Henry Scott Tuke," in *Victorian Sexual Dissidence*, ed. Richard Dellamora (Chicago: University of Chicago Press, 1999), 253–77.

73 George Morrow, "The Royal Academy—Second Depressions," *Punch* 160 (1920): 397.

74 Vickers, *Cecil Beaton*, 171; Adrian Clark and Jeremy Dronfield, *Queer Saint: The Cultured Life of Peter Watson, Who Shook Twentieth-Century Art and Shocked High Society* (London: John Blake, 2015), 101–3.

75 Gerald Berners, *The Girls of Radcliff Hall*, ed. John Byrne (London: Montcalm and the Cygnet Press, 2000), vii.

76 Berners, *The Girls of Radcliff Hall*, 95–6.

77 Berners, *The Girls of Radcliff Hall*, 69.

78 *Vogue* 77, no. 9, "A *Vogue*'s Eye View of the Season," April 29, 1931, 54.

79 Matt Cook, *London and the Culture of Homosexuality, 1885–1914* (Cambridge: Cambridge University Press, 2003), 33–5.

80 Wilde, *An Ideal Husband*, 110.

81 Jane Garrity, "Mary Butt's 'Fanatical Pédérastie': Queer Urban Life in 1920s London and Paris," in *Sapphic Modernities: Sexuality, Women and National Culture*, ed. Laura Doan and Jane Garrity (Basingstoke: Palgrave Macmillan, 2006), 233–51; Woods, *Homintern*, 170.

82 Philip Hoare, *Serious Pleasures: The Life of Stephen Tennant* (London: Hamish Hamilton, 1990), 85.

83 Potvin, *Bachelors of a Different Sort*, 261.

84 Stephen Tennant, *Leaves from a Missionary's Notebook* (London: Secker and Warburg, 1937).

85 Robin Muir, *Cecil Beaton's*, 76–81.

86 Arthur Wallis Mills, "*The Girl*. 'But, Darling, You've Chosen a Reddish Tie,'" *Punch* 177 (1929): 341.

87 James Henry Dowd, "The New River 'Belle,'" *Punch* 159 (1920): 28; Wilde, "Phrases and Philosophies," 143.

88 *Vogue* (US edn) 71, no. 4, "More News of the Sophisticates of Mayfair," February 15, 1928, 140.

89 Richard Dyer, *The Culture of Queers* (London: Routledge, 2002), 52.

90 Eve Kosofsky Sedgwick, *The Weather in Proust*, ed. Jonathan Goldberg (Durham, NC: Duke University Press, 2011), 66.

91 Tinkom, *Working Like a Homosexual*, 12.

92 Steven M. Kates, "Camp as Cultural Capital: Further Elaboration of a Consumption Taste," *Advances in Consumer Research* 28 (2001): 339.

93 Green, *Children of the Sun*, 27.

94 Evelyn Waugh, *Brideshead Revisited* (London: Chapman and Hall, 1945), 26.

95 Paul Deslandes, *Oxbridge Men: British Masculinity and the Undergraduate Experience, 1850–1920* (Bloomington: Indiana University Press, 2005), 52.

96 Abdulla Cigarettes, "The Babies' Ball," *Sketch*, October 16, 1929, 126.

97 Green, *Children of the Sun*, 92; Vickers, *Cecil Beaton*, 23.

98 Bruhm and Hurley, *Curiouser*; Stockton, *The Queer Child*.

99 Vita Sackville-West, "The Edwardians below Stairs," *Vogue* 78, no. 11, November 25, 1931, 55–7.

100 *Punch* 167, "The New Coiffure," (1924): 433.

101 *Vogue* 66, no. 8, "Baring the Secrets of the Turkish Bath," late October 1925, 67.

102 Potvin, *Bachelors of a Different Sort*, 215.

103 *Sketch*, "A Bride and Bridegroom in Duplicate," July 25, 1928, 165.

104 *Vogue* 69, no. 5, "The Fur Scarf and the Tailored Suit," early March 1927, 70.

105 Anne Witchard, "Sink Street: The Sapphic World of Pre-Chinatown Soho," in *Sex, Time and Place*, 227.

106 Seebohm, *The Man Who Was "Vogue,"* 194; Elspeth H. Brown, "De Meyer at *Vogue*: Commercializing Queer Affect in First World War-Era Fashion Photography," *Photography and Culture* 2, no. 3 (2009): 256.

107 Norberto Angeletti and Alberto Oliva, *In "Vogue": The Illustrated History of the World's Most Famous Fashion Magazine* (New York: Rizzoli, 2006), 60–3.

108 Brown, *Work!* 34–5.

109 Brown, *Work!* 46.

110 Elizabeth Arden, "Elizabeth Arden Is in Personal Touch with You," *Sketch*, June 27, 1928, 663. See also Geczy and Karaminas, *Fashion's Double*, 27.

111 Matthew Tinkom, "Working Like a Homosexual: Camp Visual Codes and the Labor of Gay Subjects in the MGM Freed Unit," *Cinema Journal* 35, no. 2 (1996): 30.

112 Brown, "De Meyer at *Vogue*," 261.

113 Brown, "De Meyer at *Vogue*," 263.

114 Brown, "De Meyer at *Vogue*," 263.

115 Angeletti and Oliva, *In "Vogue*," 64–7.

116 William A. Ewing, *The Photographic Art of Hoyningen-Huene* (London: Thames and Hudson, 1986).

117 Angeletti and Oliva, *In "Vogue*," 68–71.

118 Brown, *Work!* 120 and 122.

119 Richard Martin, *Fashion and Surrealism* (London: Thames and Hudson, 1988), 217. See also Robyn Gibson, "Schiaparelli, Surrealism and the Desk Suit," *Dress* 30, no. 1 (2003): 48–58. For an interwar example, see *Harper's Bazaar* 14, no. 5, "Sur-realisation," August 1936, 57.

120 Cecil Beaton, *Photobiography* (London: Odhams, 1951), 38.

121 Beaton, *Photobiography*, 26.

122 Beaton, *Photobiography*, 53.

123 Alan Hollinghurst, *The Swimming Pool Library* (London: Chatto and Windus, 1988), 42. Discussed in Thomas Dukes, "'Mappings of Secrecy and Disclosure': *The Swimming Pool Library*, the Closet, and the Empire," *Journal of Homosexuality* 31, no. 3 (1996): 98.

124 Sedgwick, *Epistemology of the Closet*, 231; Janes, *Picturing the Closet*, 5.

125 Harold W. Yoxall, *A Fashion for Life* (London: Heinemann, 1966), 105.

126 Taylor, *Bright Young People*, 53 and 59.

127 Quoted in Vickers, *Cecil Beaton*, 41.

128 Christopher Breward, "Couture as Queer Auto/Biography," in *A Queer History of Fashion*, 121.

129 John Berger, *Ways of Seeing* (London: Penguin, 1972), 148.

130 Shaun Cole, "Don We Now Our Gay Apparel": *Gay Men's Dress in the Twentieth Century* (Oxford: Berg, 2000), 17; Benjamin Wild, *A Life in Fashion: The Wardrobe of Cecil Beaton* (London: Thames and Hudson, 2016), 32.

131 Michael Pick, *Norman Hartnell: The Biography* (London: Zuleika, 2019), 39.

132 Quoted in Andrew Ginger, *Cecil Beaton at Home: An Interior Life* (New York: Rizzoli, 2016), 18. See also *Sphere* 101, "Leading Ladies at Cambridge University," June 13, 1925, 318; Terence Pepper, *Dorothy Wilding: The Pursuit of Perfection* (London: National Portrait Gallery Publications, 1991), 13–14, discusses the photographs that were taken by Wilding in her studio in London.

133 Cindy Richards, ed., *Society in "Vogue"* (London: Condé Nast, 1992), 11.

134 *Vogue* 63, no. 7, "Undergraduates in Tragedy," early April 1924, 55.

135 Vickers, *Cecil Beaton*, 97.

136 *Vogue* 73, no. 10, "How One Lives from Day to Day," May 15, 1929, 72–3 and 108.

137 Ginger, *Cecil Beaton at Home*, 61.

138 Derek Patmore, "Cecil Beaton Designs for Himself," *Harper's Bazaar* 6, no. 6, September 1932, 57; Ginger, *Cecil Beaton at Home*, 68–76. *Prancing Nigger* was the title given to the American edition of *Sorrow in Sunlight* (1924), a novel by the decadent, homosexual novelist Ronald Firbank.

139 *Vogue* (US edn) 80, no. 6, "A Circus Party and Dutch Treat Dinner," September 15, 1932, 52–3.

140 Calloway, *Baroque Baroque*, 90. See also Stevenson, *Baroque between the Wars*, 189 and 256.

141 Cecil Beaton, *The Book of Beauty* (London: Duckworth), 9. The volume was inspired, perhaps, by fellow photographer Hugh Cecil [Saunders]'s *A Book of Beauty* (1926).

142 Beaton, *The Book of Beauty*, 1.

143 Beaton, *The Book of Beauty*, 4.

144 Beaton, *The Book of Beauty*, 4.

145 Beaton, *The Book of Beauty*, 5.

146 Beaton, *The Book of Beauty*, 8.

147 Beaton, *The Book of Beauty*, 27.

148 Beaton, *The Book of Beauty*, 36.

149 Beaton, *The Book of Beauty*, 41.

150 Beaton, *The Book of Beauty*, 43.

151 Beaton, *The Book of Beauty*, 23.

152 Beaton, *The Book of Beauty*, 38.

153 Cecil Beaton quoted in James Gardiner, *Gaby Deslys: A Fatal Attraction* (London: Sidgwick and Jackson, 1986), 189–90. See also Carol Dyhouse, *Glamour: Women, History, Feminism* (London: Zed Books, 2010), 12–13.

154 Vickers, *Cecil Beaton*, 463.

155 *Vogue* (US edn) 87, no. 8, "The Incomparable Mr. Cochran's Stage Revue of 1936. 'Follow the Sun,'" April 15, 1936, 72–3.

156 Diana Fuss, "Fashion and the Homospectatorial Look," *Critical Inquiry* 18, no. 4 (1992): 716.

157 Cecil Beaton, "Four Debutantes of 1928," *Vogue* 72, no. 3, August 8, 1928, 34; Cecil Beaton, "Raving Beauties," *Vogue* 72, no. 3, August 8, 1928, 37.

158 Chase quoted in Josephine Ross, *Beaton in "Vogue"* (London: Thames and Hudson, 1986), 11.

159 Cecil Beaton, *Time Exposure*, 2nd edn (London: B. T. Batsford), 38–9.

160 *Vogue* 90, no. 5, "The Works," September 1, 1937, 38.

161 Ghilchik, "This Charming Photograph," 431.

162 *Vogue* 83, no. 5, "Blondes without, Brunettes within," March 7, 1934, 90–1.

163 Steven Bruhm, *Reflecting Narcissus: A Queer Aesthetic* (Minneapolis: University of Minnesota Press, 2001); Jack Halberstam, *The Queer Art of Failure* (Durham, NC: Duke University Press, 2011), 101–2. Compare Gen Doy, *Claude Cahun: A Sensual Politics of Photography* (London: I.B. Tauris, 2007), 56–9, on the early twentieth-century lesbian photographer Claude Cahun and her interest in mirror photographs.

164 *Vogue* 70, no. 9, "Our Lives from Day to Day," November 2, 1927, 57.

165 *Vogue* (US edn) 83, no. 9, "Our Best Families: Party at the Waldorf," May 1, 1934, 55. On Elsie de Wolfe see Stevenson, *Baroque between the Wars*, 61–5.

166 Guerlain, "Advertisement," *Vogue* 87, no. 4, February 19, 1936, 49.

167 Cecil Beaton, "Merry Christmas," *Vogue* 82, no. 1, November 29, 1933, 65. See also Andrew Stephenson, "'Our Jolly Marin Wear': The Queer Fashionability of the Sailor Uniform in Interwar France and Britain," *Fashion, Style and Popular Culture* 3, no. 2 (2016): 157–72.

168 Thomas Waugh, *Hard to Imagine: Gay Male Eroticism in Photography and Film from Their Beginnings to Stonewall* (New York: Columbia University Press, 1996), 104, fig. 2.30

169 *Vogue* 87, no. 9, "Heart-Beats," April 29, 1936, 68.

170 K. Mitchell Snow, "Does This Fig Leaf Make Me Look Gay? Strongmen, Statue Posing and Physique Photography," *Early Popular Visual Culture* 17, no. 2 (2019): 135–55; Amy Richlin, "Eros Underground: Greece and Rome in Gay Print Culture, 1953–65," *Journal of Homosexuality* 49, no. 3–4 (2005): 421–61.

171 For example, Cecil Beaton, "The London Season," *Vogue* 73, no. 9, early May 1929, 40; *Vogue*, "A Vogue's Eye View," 54.

172 *Vogue* 48, no. 1, "The Triumph of Victorianism," July 1, 1916, 50–1 and 96; *Vogue* 77, no. 1, "The Victorian Age Returns," January 7, 1931, 56–7.

173 A. A. Markley, "E. M. Forster's Reconfigured Gaze and the Creation of a Homoerotic Subjectivity," *Twentieth Century Literature* 47, no. 2 (2001): 268.

174 Kenneth Clark, *The Nude: A Study of Ideal Art* (London: John Murray, 1956), 1–25.

175 Frances Rodney [Mrs. James Rodney], "London Laurels," *Harper's Bazaar* 15, no. 1, October 1936, 53.

176 Rodney, "London Laurels," 52.

177 Jane Hattrick, "An 'Unexpected Pearl': Gender and Performativity in the Public and Private Lives of London Couturier Norman Hartnell," in *Dress History: New Directions in Theory and Practice*, ed. Charlotte Nicklas and Annebella Pollen (London: Bloomsbury, 2015), 150. See also Jane Hattrick, "Collecting and Displaying Identity, Intimacy and Memory in the Staged Interiors of the Royal Couturier Norman Hartnell," in *Narrating Objects, Collecting Stories: Essays in Honour of Professor Susan M. Pearce*, ed. Sandra H. Dudley, Amy Jane Barnes, Jennifer Binnie, Julia Petrov, and Jennifer Walklate (London: Routledge, 2012).

178 *Vogue* (US edn) 90, no. 10, "Debutante Line-Up—This Is Their Winter," November 15, 1937, 68.

179 On queer networks of friendship see Brown, *Work!* 158.

180 Cecil Beaton, *Tamara Geva in "Errante,"* 1935. Photograph. Sotheby's, Cecil Beaton Studio Archive.

Chapter 5

1 Wilde, "Phrases and Philosophies," 143.

2 Carden-Coyne, *Reconstructing the Body*, 230.

3 Rhonda Garelick, *Rising Star: Dandyism, Gender, and Performance in the Fin de Siècle* (Princeton: Princeton University Press, 1998), 43 and 128–53.

4 Potvin, *Bachelors of a Different Sort*, 60.

5 Marcus, *The Drama of Celebrity*, 60.

6 Quoted in Marcus, *The Drama of Celebrity*, 117.

7 Ignacio Ramos-Gay, "'Partly American!': Sarah Bernhardt's Transnational Disability in the American Press (1915–1918)," *Atlantis: Journal of the Spanish Association for Anglo-American Studies* 40, no. 2 (2018): 63–80.

8 Potvin, *Bachelors of a Different Sort*, 44.

9 Wayne Koestenbaum, *The Queen's Throat: Opera, Homosexuality, and the Mystery of Desire* (London: GMP, 1993), 84.

10 Koestenbaum, *The Queen's Throat*, 84–133. See also Marcus, *The Drama of Celebrity*, 24.

11 Paul Ward, *Britishness since 1870* (London: Routledge, 2004), 48.

12 David M. Halperin, *How to Be Gay* (Cambridge, MA: Harvard University Press, 2012), 123.

13 Richard Dyer, *Heavenly Bodies: Film Stars and Society* (Basingstoke: Macmillan 1987), 193. See also David Lugowski, "Ginger Rogers and Gay Men? Queer Film Studies, Richard Dyer, and Diva Worship," in *Screening Genders*, ed. Krin Gabbard and William Luhr (New Brunswick, NJ: Rutgers University Press, 2008), 95–110.

14 Halperin, *How to Be Gay*, 241.

15 Quoted and discussed in Agnes Lambert, "The Ceremonial Use of Flowers: A Sequel," *Nineteenth Century* 7, 1880, 813–14.

16 Dominic Janes, "When 'Perverts' Were Religious: The Protestant Sexualisation of Asceticism in Nineteenth-Century Britain, India and Ireland," *Cultural and Social History* 11, no. 3 (2014): 425–39; Monika Mazurek, "Perverts to Rome: Protestant Gender Roles and the Abjection of Catholicism," *Victorian Literature and Culture* 44, no. 3 (2016): 687–723.

17 Stevenson, *Baroque between the Wars*, 208–12. See also Martin Stringer, "Of Gin and Lace: Sexuality, Liturgy and Identity Among Anglo-Catholics in the Mid-Twentieth Century," *Theology and Sexuality* 7, no. 13 (2000): 35–54.

18 Cecil Beaton, "Wedding of the Duke and Duchess of Windsor," *Vogue* (US edn) 90, no. 1, July 1, 1937, 33.

19 Marnie Fogg, *Vintage Weddings: One Hundred Years of Bridal Fashion and Style* (London: Carlton, 2011), 27–59.

20 Beaton, *Photobiography*, after 24.

21 Potvin, *Bachelors of a Different Sort*, 275.

22 Stevenson, *Baroque between the Wars*, 267.

23 Constance Spry, "And the Church Looked Lovely," *Vogue* 90, no. 23, May 11, 1938, 70–1 and 132. See also Sue Shephard, *The Surprising Life of Constance Spry* (London: Pan Macmillan, 2010).

24 Timothy Willem Jones, "'Unduly Conscious of Her Sex': Priesthood, Female Bodies, and Sacred Space in the Church of England." *Women's History Review* 21, no. 4 (2012): 651.

25 *Sketch*, "Screen Celebrities—From a New Angle: Unconventional Portraits," March 12, 1930, 505. Compare Dyhouse, Glamour, 54, on Joan Crawford montaged into a gardenia.

26 Horst P. Horst, "Schiaparelli's Dress of Black Satin," *Vogue* 85, no. 9, May 1, 1935, 118–19.

27 Beaton, *The Book of Beauty*, 47.

28 Victoria Glendinning, *Edith Sitwell: A Unicorn among Lions* (London: Weidenfeld and Nicolson, 1981), 109–11; Joanna Skipwith, ed., *The Sitwells and the Arts of the 1920s and 1930s* (London: National Portrait Gallery, 1994), 114–15, fig. 3.43; Richard Greene, *Edith Sitwell: Avant-Garde Poet, English Genius* (London: Virago, 2011), 185; Andrew Ginger, *Cecil Beaton at Home: An Interior Life* (New York: Rizzoli, 2016), 24; Muir, *Cecil Beaton's*, 56–7.

29 Glyn Philpot, *Le Jongleur de Notre Dame* (1928), discussed by Jan M. Ziolkowski, *The Juggler of Notre Dame and the Medievalizing of Modernity*, volume 4, *Picture That: Making a Show of the Jongleur* (Cambridge: Open Book Publishers, 2018), 325–27 and fig. 7.29.

30 Robin Gibson, *Glyn Philpot, 1884–1937: Edwardian Aesthete to Thirties Modernist* (London: National Portrait Gallery, 1984), 69, fig. 41.

31 Charles Castle, *Oliver Messel: A Biography* (London: Thames and Hudson, 1986), 73; J. G. P. Delaney, *Glyn Philpot: His Life and Work* (Aldershot: Ashgate, 1999), 85; Muir, *Cecil Beaton's*, 179.

32 Muir, *Cecil Beaton's*, 61.

33 Alden, *Among the Freaks*, 162–77.

34 *Vogue* 81, no. 11, "Lady Melchett," May 31, 1933, 60.

35 Regina Marler, "The Bloomsbury Love Triangle," in *Queer Bloomsbury*, 135–51.

36 Eve Kosofsky Sedgwick, *Between Men: English Literature and Male Homosocial Desire* (New York: Columbia University Press, 1985), 21.

37 Lesley Blanch, "Vogue's Spotlight," *Vogue* 90, no. 41 (January 25, 1939): 35; Potvin, *Bachelors of a Different Sort*, 234.

38 Nancy Hoyt, "*Three-Cornered Love: Part III*," *Harper's Bazaar* 6, no. 4, July 1932, 62.

39 Sylvia Thompson, "The World Where One Amuses," *Vogue* 78, no. 3, August 5, 1931, 20; Hugo Vickers, ed., *Cecil Beaton: Portraits and Profiles* (London: Frances Lincoln, 2014), 40–1.

40 Cecil Beaton, "Four Stars in Waltz Time," *Vogue* (US edn) 77, no. 10, May 15, 1931, 79.

41 Green, *Children of the Sun*, 157.

42 Philip Hoare, *Noël Coward: A Biography* (London: Sinclair-Stevenson, 1995), 140; Stephen Gundle, *Glamour: A History* (Oxford: Oxford University Press, 2008), 167; Martin Pugh, *We Danced All Night: A Social History of Britain between the Wars* (London: Bodley Head, 2008), 345.

43 *Vogue* 90, no. 18, "The Noël Coward Paper Doll," March 2, 1938, 68. Paper dolls of various celebrities had been a regular feature of *Vanity Fair* before this date.

44 Nicholas De Jongh, *Not in Front of the Audience: Homosexuality on Stage* (London: Routledge, 1992), 20 and 25; Penny Farfan, *Performing Queer Modernism* (Oxford: Oxford University Press, 2017), 68.

45 Coward quoted in Alan Sinfield, "Private Lives/Public Theater: Noël Coward and the Politics of Homosexual Representation," *Representations* 36 (Autumn 1991): 55.

46 Coward quoted in Sinfield, "Private Lives/Public Theater," 53–4.

47 Sinfield, "Private Lives/Public Theater," 58; Potvin, *Bachelors of a Different Sort*, 240.

48 Lewis Baumer, "The Sex Question," 235.

49 Terry Castle, *Noël Coward and Radclyffe Hall: Kindred Spirits* (New York: Columbia University Press, 1996), 107–9.

50 Castle, *Noël Coward and Radclyffe Hall*, 26–7.

51 Deborah Cohler, *Citizen, Invert, Queer: Lesbianism and War in Early Twentieth-Century Britain* (Minneapolis: University of Minnesota Press, 2010), 31.

52 Cohler, *Citizen, Invert, Queer*, xiii; Laura Doan, *Disturbing Practices*, 111.

53 Cohler, *Citizen, Invert, Queer*, 88.

54 Marjorie Garber, *Vested Interests: Cross-Dressing and Cultural Anxiety* (New York: Routledge, 1992), 152; Penny Farfan, "Noël Coward and Sexual Modernism: Private Lives as Queer Comedy," *Modern Drama* 48, no. 4 (2005): 678.

55 Rebecca Kennison, "Clothes Make the (Wo)man: Marlene Dietrich and 'Double Drag,'" *Journal of Lesbian Studies* 6, no. 2 (2002): 150. See also Jack Halberstam [Judith Halberstam], *Female Masculinity* (Durham, NC: Duke University Press, 1998), 46; Laura Doan, "Sex Education and the Great War Soldier: A Queer Analysis of the Practice of 'Hetero' Sex," *Journal of British Studies* 51, no. 3 (2012): 663.

56 Laura Doan, *Fashioning Sapphism*, xxii.

57　Anna Zinkeisen, "Models on Marlene!" in "Mariegold," "Mariegold at a Very Ducal Affair," *Sketch*, March 8, 1933, 408, emphasis in original.

58　Doan, *Fashioning Sapphism*, xiii.

59　George Belcher, "Man-Woman. 'In the Old Days I Never Paid More Than Sixpence for a Haircut,'" *Punch* 189 (1925): 9.

60　Janes, *Oscar Wilde Prefigured*, 25–54.

61　Oram, *Her Husband*, 56.

62　Quote from Elisa Glick, *Materializing Queer Desire: Oscar Wilde to Andy Warhol* (Albany: State University of New York Press, 2009), 72. See also Esther Newton, "The Mythic Mannish Lesbian: Radclyffe Hall and the New Woman," *Signs* 9, no. 2 (1984): 557–75; Doan, *Fashioning Sapphism*, 141.

63　Kenneth Bell, "Famous Women from History, No. 5: Sappho," *Britannia and Eve* 1, no. 5 (September 1929): 46.

64　Bell, "Famous Women from History," 47.

65　Doan, *Fashioning Sapphism*, xii.

66　James Vernon, "'For Some Queer Reason': The Trials and Tribulations of Colonel Barker's Masquerade in Interwar Britain," *Signs* 26, no. 1 (2000): 58.

67　Oram, *Her Husband Was a Woman!* 83. See also Rebecca Jennings, "From 'Woman-Loving Woman' to 'Queer': Historiographical Perspectives on Twentieth-Century British Lesbian History," *History Compass* 5, no. 6 (2007): 1901–20; Cohler, Citizen, Invert, Queer, 109.

68　Arthur Wallis Mills, "An Inducement," *Punch* 130 (1906): 261; Clare Tebbutt, "The Spectre of the 'Man-Woman Athlete': Mark Weston, Zdenek Koubek, the 1936 Olympics and the Uncertainty of Sex," *Women's History Review* 24, no. 5 (2015): 724 and 732.

69　Gregory Woods, "British Homosexuality, 1920–1939," in *W. H. Auden in Context*, ed. Tony Sharpe (Cambridge: Cambridge University Press, 2013), 90.

70　Anna Clark, *Desire: A History of European Sexuality* (New York: Routledge, 2008), 168; Christopher Breward, *Fashioning London: Clothing and the Modern Metropolis* (Oxford: Berg, 2004), 102.

71　For a study of relations between women and gay men later in the twentieth century see John Portmann, *Women and Gay Men in the Postwar Period* (London: Bloomsbury Academic, 2016).

72　Dyhouse, *Glamour*, 3–4.

73　Susan Fillin-Yeh, "Introduction: New Strategies for a Theory of Dandies," in *Fashion and Finesse in Art and Culture*, ed. Susan Fillin-Yeh (New York: New York University Press, 2001), 20; Dyhouse, Glamour, 56.

74　*Vogue* 73, no. 12, "Chic: A Defence," June 12, 1929, 61.

75　*Vogue* 57, no. 9, "In Paris This Season," early May 1921, 44, illustrated by Eduardo Benito.

76 "Fitz," "Study of a Film Star—Smoking—a Cigarette," *Punch* 154 (1928): 63. On smoking and the modern woman, see Ellen Moers, *The Dandy: Brummell to Beerbohm* (London: Secker and Warburg, 1960), 309; Penny Tinkler, *Smoke Signals: Women, Smoking and Visual Culture in Britain* (Oxford: Berg, 2006), 81–92; Penny Tinkler and Cheryl Krasnick Warsh, "Feminine Modernity in Interwar Britain and North America: Corsets, Cars, and Cigarettes," *Journal of Women's History* 20, no. 3 (2008): 113–43; Julia Skelly, *Addiction and British Visual Culture, 1751–1919* (Farnham: Ashgate, 2014), 150.

77 Abdulla Cigarettes, "The Bright Brigade," *Sketch*, September 4, 1929, 475; Julie Anne Taddeo, *Lytton Strachey and the Search for Modern Sexual Identity: The Last Eminent Victorian* (London: Routledge, 2012), 23.

78 Kenneth MacGowan, "Seen on the Stage," *Vogue* (US edn) 59, no. 9, May 1, 1922, 62.

79 *Sketch*, "The Artist Side of Our A.P.H.Orisms," February 2, 1927, 195.

80 Philip Kelleway, *Highly Desirable: The Zinkeisen Sisters and Their Legacy* (Leiston: Leiston Press, 2008), 101; Ruth Artmonskey, *Designing Women: Women Working in Advertising and Publicity from the 1920s to the 1960s* (London: Artmonskey Arts, 2012), 107–8.

81 Stevenson, *Baroque between the Wars*, 229.

82 James Curtis, *James Whale: A New World of Gods and Monsters* (London: Faber and Faber, 1998).

83 Harry M. Benshoff, *Monsters in the Closet: Homosexuality and the Horror Film* (Manchester: Manchester University Press, 1997), 40–51.

84 Rosamond Harcourt-Smith, "Oliver Messel's Costume Ball," *Vogue* 89, no. 9, April 28, 1937): 120–1 and 171; Sarah Woodcock, "Messel on Stage," in *Oliver Messel in the Theatre of Design*, ed. Thomas Messel (New York: Rizzoli, 2011), 54–83.

85 Doris Zinkeisen, *Designing for the Stage*, How to Do It Series 18 (London: Studio, 1938), 45, fig. 22; J. P. Wearing, *The London Stage 1930–1939: A Calendar of Productions, Performers, and Personnel*, 2nd edn (Lanham: Rowman and Littlefield, 2014), 591.

86 Zinkeisen, *Designing for the Stage*, 46.

87 Zinkeisen, *Designing for the Stage*, 59, fig. 33.

88 "Mariegold," "Mariegold in Society," *Sketch*, January 15, 1930a, 88, caption to fig. 2, emphases in original.

89 "Mariegold," "Mariegold in Society," *Sketch*, August 17, 1927e, 296, fig. 4.

90 "Mariegold," "Mariegold in Society," *Sketch*, November 10, 1926, 281.

91 "Mariegold," "Mariegold in Society," *Sketch*, March 28, 1928, 585, emphasis in original. Compare Fish's illustrations to *Vogue* 66, no. 8, "Baring the Secrets of the Turkish Bath," 66–7.

92 "Mariegold," "Mariegold in Society," *Sketch*, December 4, 1929b, 482.

93 "Mariegold," "Mariegold in Society," *Sketch*, January 12, 1927a, 56.

94 Pick, *Norman Hartnell*, 50.

95 "Mariegold," "Mariegold Is Amused," *Sketch*, March 1, 1933, 364. The supposed similarity between men's knickerbockers and shorter skirts had been noted in J.H. Thorpe, "Diehard (Stroking His Beard) 'My Dear Girl It's Our Only Chance Left,'" *Punch* 168 (1925): 163.

96 Mann, *The Dandy at Dusk*, 120.

97 "Mariegold," "Mariegold Is Amused," *Sketch*, March 1, 1933, 364.

98 "Mariegold," "Mariegold in Society," *Sketch*, 14 May1930b, 310.

99 "Mariegold," "Mariegold in Society," *Sketch*, January 16, 1929a, 89.

100 *Sketch*, "John's Noah and Jack Tars! The Chelsea Arts Club Ball," January 8, 1930, 50. See also *Sketch*, "The Chelsea Arts Club Ball: Anna Zinkeisen Impressions," January 9, 1929, 48; Matt Cook, "Queer Conflicts: Love, Sex and War, 1914–1967," in *A Gay History of Britain: Love and Sex between Men since the Middle Ages*, ed. Matt Cook (Oxford: Greenwood, 2007), 152.

101 "Mariegold," "Mariegold Broadcasts," *Sketch*, May 3, 1933b, 189.

102 "Mariegold," "Mariegold in Society," *Sketch*, August 24, 1927f, 344–45.

103 "Mariegold," "Mariegold in Society," *Sketch*, September 21, 1927g, 540.

104 "Mariegold," "Mariegold in Society," 1927g, 541.

105 Such as "Palmer," "'Frankly Speaking, I Think a Lot of Women Join Up with a View to Matrimony—Present Company Excepted of Course,'" *Men Only* 25, no. 101, April 1944, 42.

106 "Mariegold," "Mariegold in Society," *Sketch*, March 2, 1927b, 393.

107 "Mariegold," "Mariegold in Society," *Sketch*, April 13, 1927c, 68.

108 "Mariegold," "Mariegold in Society," *Sketch*, June 8, 1927d, 477.

109 Captions to figs. 1 to 5 in "Mariegold," "Mariegold Broadcasts," *Sketch*, May 24, 1933c, 324–25.

110 "Mariegold," "Mariegold Broadcasts," *Sketch*, June 28, 1933d, 553.

111 Nika Dittman, "Italy," *Harper's Bazaar* 11, no. 3, December 1934, 60.

112 Dittman, "Italy," 82.

113 Reed, "Design for (Queer) Living," 379 and 385.

114 Captions to figs. 1 to 5 in "Mariegold," "Mariegold Broadcasts," *Sketch*, April 26, 1933a, 144–5, emphasis in original.

115 Muir, *Cecil Beaton's*, 41.

Chapter 6

1 Wilde, "Phrases and Philosophies," 141.

2 Havelock Ellis and John Addington Symonds, *Studies in the Psychology of Sex*, volume 1, *Sexual Inversion* (London: Wilson and Macmillan, 1897); Havelock Ellis

and John Addington Symonds, *Sexual Inversion: A Critical Edition* (Basingstoke: Palgrave Macmillan, 2008).

3   Havelock Ellis, *Impressions and Comments* (London: Constable, 1914), 138.

4   Ann Elias, "Flowers and Manliness: The Flower Paintings of George Lambert, Hans Heysen, and Arthur Streeton," *Journal of Interdisciplinary Gender Studies* 10, no. 2 (2008): 25.

5   Robert Deam Tobin, *Peripheral Desires: The German Discovery of Sex* (Philadelphia: University of Pennsylvania Press, 2015), 38.

6   Alison Mairi Syme, *A Touch of Blossom: John Singer Sargent and the Queer Flora of Fin-de-Siècle Art* (University Park: Pennsylvania State Press, 2010), 166.

7   Frances Knight, *Victorian Christianity at the Fin de Siècle: The Culture of English Religion in a Decadent Age* (London: I.B. Tauris, 2016), 48.

8   Peter McNeil and Georgio Riello, *Luxury: A Rich History* (Oxford: Oxford University Press, 2016), 172–5.

9   Oscar Wilde, *A House of Pomegranates* (London: Methuen, 1911), 155.

10   Jarlath Killeen, *The Fairy Tales of Oscar Wilde* (Aldershot: Ashgate, 2007), 159.

11   Oscar Wilde, *The Complete Letters of Oscar Wilde*, ed. Merlin Holland and Rupert Hart-Davis (London: Fourth Estate, 2000), 544. Discussed in David Schulz, "Redressing Oscar: Performance and the Trials of Oscar Wilde," *TDR/The Drama Review* 40, no. 2 (1996): 43.

12   Joseph Bristow, "Picturing His Exact Decadence: The British Reception of Oscar Wilde," *The Reception of Oscar Wilde in Europe*, 21: 20–50.

13   Talia Schaffer, "Fashioning Aestheticism by Aestheticizing Fashion: Wilde, Beerbohm, and the Male Aesthetes' Sartorial Codes," *Victorian Literature and Culture* 28, no. 1 (2000): 44.

14   Ed Madden, "Say It with Flowers: The Poetry of Marc-Andre Raffalovich," *College Literature* 24, no. 1 (1997): 14.

15   Madden, "Say It with Flowers," 13. On women and the language of flowers see Amy M. King, *Bloom: The Botanical Vernacular in the English Novel* (Oxford: Oxford University Press, 2003); Beverley Seaton, *The Language of Flowers: A History* (Charlottesville: University Press of Virginia, 1995); Judith Page and Elise L. Smith, *Women, Literature, and the Domestic Landscape: England's Disciples of Flora, 1780–1870* (Cambridge: Cambridge University Press, 2014).

16   Laura Valentine, *The Language and Sentiment of Flowers and the Classical Floral Legends* (London: Warne, *c.* 1860).

17   Byrne R. S. Fone, "This Other Eden: Arcadia and the Homosexual Imagination," *Journal of Homosexuality* 8, no. 3–4 (1983): 20; David Bell, "Farm Boys and Wild Men: Rurality, Masculinity, and Homosexuality," *Rural Sociology* 65, no. 4 (2000): 553; David Bell and Ruth Holliday, "Naked as Nature Intended," *Body and Society* 6, no. 3–4 (2000): 127–40.

18   Tom Peddie, "Garden Suburb Amenities," *Punch* 143 (1912): 35.

19 Ann Heilmann, "Wilde's New Women: The New Woman on Wilde," in *The Importance of Reinventing Oscar*, 135: 135–45.

20 Brown, "De Meyer at *Vogue*," 263.

21 Fussell, *The Great War and Modern Memory*, 248.

22 Jack Butler Yeats, "Messrs. Hopeful and Boomage," *Punch* 149 (1915): 257.

23 Beverley Nichols, *Down the Garden Path* (London: Jonathan Cape, 1932), 42. See also Joshua Adair, "Wilde Nostalgia: Queer Tradition in Beverley Nichols's Garden Trilogies," *Sic* 13 (2016): unpaginated.

24 Edmund Clerihew Bentley, "More Clerihews," *Punch* 196 (1939): 39, emphasis in original.

25 Bryan Connon, *Beverley Nichols: A Life* (London: Constable, 1991), 161.

26 Rebecca Nagel, "Naming Plants in *The Garden* by Vita Sackville-West," *Interdisciplinary Studies in Literature and Environment* 22, no. 2 (2015): 256–8.

27 Alexandra Harris, *Romantic Moderns: English Writers, Artists and the Imagination from Virginia Woolf to John Piper* (London: Thames and Hudson, 2010), 140; Shephard, *The Surprising Life of Constance Spry*, 153; Clare Barlow, ed., *Queer British Art, 1861–1967* (London: Tate Publishing, 2017), 117; Stevenson, *Baroque between the Wars*, 270–4. See also Joe Crowdy, "Queer Undergrowth: Weeds and Sexuality in the Architecture of the Garden," *Architecture and Culture* 5, no. 3 (2017): 423–33, on the queerness of garden weeds.

28 Virginia Woolf, *Orlando: A Biography* (London: L. and V. Woolf, 1933), 28.

29 Constance Spry, *Flower Decoration* (London: Dent, 1934), 5; Diana Souhami, *Gluck, 1895–1978: Her Biography*, revised edn (London: Weidenfeld and Nicolson, 2000), 98.

30 Quoted and discussed in Jennifer Wicke, "'Mrs. Dalloway' Goes to Market: Woolf, Keynes, and Modern Markets," *Novel: A Forum on Fiction*, 28, no. 1 (1994): 13.

31 Annette Stott, "Floral Femininity: A Pictorial Definition," *American Art* 6, no. 2 (1992): 61.

32 Rowena Fowler, "Why Did Suffragettes Attack Works of Art?" *Journal of Women's History* 2, no. 3 (1991): 117. See also Miranda El-Rayess, "The Violence of Representation: James, Sargent and the Suffragette," *Critical Quarterly* 53, no. 2 (2011): 30–45.

33 Diana Maltz, "'Baffling Arrangements': Vernon Lee and John Singer Sargent in Queer Tangier," in *Rethinking the Interior, c. 1867–1896: Aestheticism and Arts and Crafts*, ed. Jason Edwards and Imogen Hart (Farnham: Ashgate, 2010), 200.

34 Michael Anesko, *Henry James and Queer Filiation: Hardened Bachelors of the Edwardian Era* (London: Palgrave, 2018), 126. See also Howard P. Chudacoff, *The Age of the Bachelor: Creating an American Subculture* (Princeton: Princeton University Press, 1999); Potvin, *Bachelors of a Different Sort*.

35 Trevor J. Fairbrother, *John Singer Sargent: The Sensualist* (New Haven: Yale University Press, 2000), 165.

36 Santanu Das, *Touch and Intimacy in First World War Literature* (Cambridge: Cambridge University Press, 2005), 4.

37 Fairbrother, *John Singer Sargent*, 97.

38 Fairbrother, *John Singer Sargent*, 132.

39 Syme, *A Touch of Blossom*, 166.

40 Fairbrother, *John Singer Sargent*, 104.

41 Fairbrother, *John Singer Sargent*, 97.

42 Fairbrother, *John Singer Sargent*, 97.

43 Anne Helmreich, "John Singer Sargent. 'Carnation, Lily, Lily, Rose,' and the Condition of Modernism in England, 1887," *Victorian Studies* 45, no. 3 (2003): 451.

44 McNeil, "Everything Degenerates," 412.

45 Mark De Cicco, "The Queer God Pan: Terror and Apocalypse, Reimagined," in *Monsters and Monstrosity from the Fin de Siècle to the Millennium*, ed. Hutchison Sharla and Rebecca A. Brown (Jefferson: McFarland, 2015), 60; Alison Mairi Syme, "Bohemians of the Vegetable World," in *Queer Difficulty in Art and Poetry: Rethinking the Sexed Body in Verse and Visual Culture*, ed. Jongwoo Jeremy Kim and Christopher Reed (New York: Routledge, 2017), 10–23.

46 Robert Azzarello, "Unnatural Predators: Queer Theory Meets Environmental Studies in Bram Stoker's *Dracula*," in *Queering the Non/Human*, ed. Noreen Giffney and Myra J. Hird (Aldershot: Ashgate, 2008), 137–58. See also the other essays in Giffney and Hird, ed., *Queering the Non/Human*.

47 Stott, "Floral Femininity," 70.

48 John Nash, *Poisonous Plants: Deadly, Dangerous and Suspect* (London: Frederick Etchells and Hugh MacDonald, 1927), 11–13.

49 Warwick Deeping, "Abnormalities," *Britannia and Eve* 1, no. 2 (June 1929): 57.

50 Senelick, *The Changing Room*, 314.

51 Barbara Haskell, *Charles Demuth* (New York: Whitney Museum of American Art, 1988), 178; Robin Jaffee Frank, *Charles Demuth: Poster Portraits, 1923–1929* (New Haven: Yale University Art Gallery, 1994), 15–22. See also Tyrus Miller, "Ridiculously Modern Marsden: Tragicomic Form and Queer Modernity," *Modernist Cultures* 2, no. 2 (2006): 87–101.

52 Charles Demuth, *Calla Lilies (Bert Savoy)*, 1926. Oil on board. Alfred Stieglitz Collection, Crystal Bridges Museum of American Art, co-owned by Fisk University, Nashville, Tennessee, and Crystal Bridges Museum of American Art, Inc., Bentonville, Arkansas. See also Frank, *Charles Demuth*, 54–62.

53 Jonathan Weinberg, *Speaking for Vice: Homosexuality in the Art of Charles Demuth, Marsden Hartley, and the First American Avant-Garde* (New Haven: Yale University Press, 1995), 51.

54 Haskell, *Charles Demuth*, 180–8; Charles H. Eldredge, "Calla Moderna: 'Such a Strange Flower,'" in *Georgia O'Keefe and the Calla Lily in American Art, 1860–1940*, ed. Barbara Buhler Lynes (New Haven: Yale University Press, 2002), 22–3.

55 McBride, quoted in Betsy Fahlman, *Pennsylvania Modern: Charles Demuth of Lancaster* (Philadelphia: University of Pennsylvania Press, 1983), 61.

56 Wilde, *Oscar Wilde in America*, 27.

57 The current whereabouts of Ranken, *Covent Garden* is unknown. It was exhibited at the Royal Academy in 1931 and was last sold at auction by Bonhams in London on November 5, 1992 by a now deceased member of the extended Ranken family.

58 William Ranken, *Hibiscus Flower, c.* 1922. Oil on canvas. Nottingham Castle Museum and Art Gallery.

59 Janes, *Picturing the Closet*, 4 and 8.

60 Cecil Beaton, *Marlene Dietrich*, 1930. Sotheby's, Cecil Beaton Studio Archive.

61 Christopher Looby, "Flowers of Manhood: Race, Sex and Floriculture from Thomas Wentworth Higginson to Robert Mapplethorpe," *Criticism* 37, no. 1 (1995): 109–56; Herbert Muschamp, *Mapplethorpe: The Complete Flowers* (Düsseldorf: teNeues, 2006).

62 D. H. Lawrence, "Introduction," in *Pansies* (London: Stephenson, 1929), unpaginated.

63 Lawrence, *Pansies*, 18–19.

64 Jeffrey Meyers, "D. H. Lawrence, Comedian," *Salmagundi* 152 (Fall 2006): 217. See also Emile Delavenay, *D. H. Lawrence and Edward Carpenter: A Study in Edwardian Transition* (London: Heinemann, 1971), and Howard J. Booth, "D. H. Lawrence and Male Homosexual Desire," *Review of English Studies* 53, no. 209 (2002): 86–107.

65 D. H. Lawrence, *Pansies: Poems* (London: Martin Secker, 1930), 3.

66 Potvin, *Bachelors of a Different Sort*, 257.

67 Noël Coward, *The Noël Coward Diaries*, ed. Graham Payn and Sheridan Morley (London: Weidenfeld and Nicolson, 1982), 38 note 2.

68 Stevenson, *Baroque between the Wars*, 33.

69 Hoare, *Noël Coward*, 201.

70 Scott Herring, *Queering the Underworld: Slumming, Literature, and the Undoing of Lesbian and Gay History* (Chicago: Chicago University Press, 2007), 3.

71 *Denison Review* 34, no. 84, "Pansy Butler," October 27, 1899, 1.

72 T. W. Coghlin, "She Wore a Camellia," *Cherwell* 17, no. 1 (new series) (April 29, 1925): 9.

73 Coghlin, "She Wore a Camellia," 9.

74 Coghlin, "She Wore a Camellia," 11.

75 "C. N.," "The Origin of the Fairies! A Crowd of Pansy Faces," *Sketch*, August 3, 1931, cover.

76 *Variety Weekly*, "*Femme de Minuit (Midnight Lady)*", January 7, 1931, 70.

77 *Variety Weekly*, "'Pansy' Palaces on Broadway," September 10, 1930, 1.

78 Aston, *Breaking Down the Walls of Heartache*, 29.

79 Brassaï, *The Secret Paris of the 30s*, trans. Richard Miller (London: Thames and Hudson, 1976); Frances E. Hutchins, "The Pleasures of Discovery: Representations

of Queer Space by Brassaï and Colette," in *Lesbian Inscriptions in Francophone Society and Culture*, ed. Renate Günther and Wendy Michallat (Durham: University of Durham, 2007), 198; Reed, *Art and Homosexuality*, 111.

80   Chad Heap, *Slumming: Sexual and Racial Encounters in American Nightlife, 1885–1940* (Chicago: University of Chicago Press, 2009), 232 and 237.

81   *Variety Weekly*, "Hollywood's Male Magnolias," October 4, 1930, 1.

82   Georges de Zayas in Clive Bell, "Jean Cocteau: A Master Modernist," *Vanity Fair* (US edn) 21, no. 5, 1925, 52.

83   "Mariegold," "Mariegold in Society," 1927a, 56; Alan D'Egville in "A Mere Man," "This Dress Question," *Britannia* 2, no. 16, January 11, 1929, 110. See also Hoare, *Noël Coward*, 111.

84   Edgar Wallace, "The Crime in Which Women Specialise," *Daily Mail*, June 13, 1929, 87; Houlbrook, "Queer Things."

85   Allanah Harper Papers, series 1, subseries B, box 3, folder 8, 1, Harry Ransom Center, University of Texas at Austin.

86   Ina Zweiniger-Bargielowska, "The Making of a Modern Female Body: Beauty, Health and Fitness in Interwar Britain," *Women's History Review* 20, no. 2 (2011): 300.

87   *Vogue*, "A *Vogue*'s Eye View," 51.

88   *Vogue* 85, no. 9, "There Are No Beauties," May 1, 1935, 111. The article is unsigned but is probably by Beaton.

89   *Vogue* 84, no. 4, "We Hand It to Beauty," August 22, 1934, 22. The article is also unsigned and again probably by Beaton.

90   *Vogue* 82, no. 9, "Weight and What to Do about It," November 1, 1933, 65.

91   Edmund Knox [pseud. "Evoe"], text, and Ernest H. Shepard, images, "The Renegade Faun," *Punch* 172, summer number (May 23, 1927): unpaginated. *L'Après-midi d'un faune* is not overtly homosexual but is open to queer readings, on which see Farfan, *Performing Queer Modernism*, 48.

92   David Jeremiah, *Representations of British Motoring* (Manchester: Manchester University Press, 2007), 84–94.

93   See, for example, *Vogue* 55, no. 8, "An Ideal Tour of Motor Row," late April 1920, 72–3 and 102; *Vogue* 55, no. 2, "Colour Schemes for the Car," late January 1920, 82.

94   Arthur Wallis Mills, "Our Motor Emporiums," *Punch* 143 (1912): 167.

95   Trevor Evans, "'I Think He's Rather Sweet, Don't You?'" *London Opinion*, week ending October 20, 1928, 8.

96   A. B. Beard, "A Brighter Olympia," *London Opinion*, week ending October 20, 1928, 13.

97   Shepperton, "If We Ordered Our Lives," 347.

98   *Men's Wear Organiser* 12, no. 2, "Male Mannequins at Olympia Show Artificial Silk Goods to the World," February 1929, 74–5.

99 O'Neill, *London: After a Fashion*, 56. For the origins of female fashion parades see Caroline Evans, "Multiple, Movement, Model, Mode: The Mannequin Parade, 1900–1929," in *Fashion and Modernity*, ed. Christopher Breward and Caroline Evans (Oxford: Berg, 2005), 125–46; Caroline Evans, "Jean Patou's American Mannequins: Early Fashion Shows and Modernism," *Modernism/Modernity* 15, no. 2 (2008): 243–63; Caroline Evans, *The Mechanical Smile: Modernism and the First Fashion Shows in France and America, 1900–1929* (New Haven: Yale University Press, 2013).

100 *Vogue* 90, no. 8, "Wire, Wax and Plaster of Paris," October 13, 1937, 76.

101 Angus McLaren, *Playboys and Mayfair Men: Crime, Class, Masculinity and Fascism in 1930s London* (Baltimore: Johns Hopkins University Press, 2017), 146.

102 Maurice Lane-Norcott, "This Girl-Less Olympia," *London Opinion*, week ending October 20, 1928, 13.

103 Lane-Norcott, "This Girl-Less Olympia," 14.

104 *Style for Men* 20, no. 6, "Selling with the Hands," December 1932, 326.

105 *One of the Episodes at Beau Brummell's Party Which Inaugurated the New Floor* [photograph], in *Style for Men* 24, no. 5, "Britain's Biggest Ready-to-Wear Floor" (November 1934): 301.

106 Deslandes, "Exposing, Adorning and Dressing the Body in the Modern Era."

107 Barbara Burman, "Better and Brighter Clothes: The Men's Dress Reform Party, 1929–1940," *Journal of Design History* 8, no. 4 (1995): 275–90; Joanna Bourke, "The Great Male Renunciation: Men's Dress Reform in Inter-War Britain," *Journal of Design History* 9, no. 1 (1996): 23–33; Ina Zweiniger-Bargielowska, "'Healthier and Better Clothes for Men': Men's Dress Reform in Interwar Britain," in *Consuming Behaviours: Identity, Politics and Pleasure in Twentieth-Century Britain*, ed. Erika Rappaport, Mark J. Crowley, and Sandra Trudgen Dawson (London: Bloomsbury, 2015), 42.

108 J. C. Flügel, "Sex Difference in Dress," in *Women and Cross-Dressing 1800–1939*, volume 1, ed. Heike Bauer (London: Routledge, 2006), 60. Facsimile of 1930 edition.

109 J. C. Flügel, "The Psychology of Clothes," *Women and Cross-Dressing 1800–1939*, volume 1, 41. Facsimile of 1930 edition.

110 Flügel, "The Psychology of Clothes," 48.

111 Laura Ugolini, *Men and Menswear: Sartorial Consumption in Britain 1880–1939* (Aldershot: Ashgate Publishing, 2007), 127–54; Deborah Wynne, "The 'Despised Trade' in Textiles: H. G. Wells, William Paine, Charles Cavers and the Male Draper's Life, 1870–1914," *Textile History* 46, no. 1 (2015): 102.

112 Lewis Baumer, "'How Is It You're Not Serving, Young Man?'" *Punch* 148 (1915): 310.

113 It was originally *The Men's Wear Organiser* but changed its name in 1931.

114 *Style for Men* 17, no. 5, "The Beau Brummell of Trade Journals," May 1931, 312.

115 *Men's Wear Organiser* 17, no. 4, "The Figures Tailors Dream Of," April 1931, 241.

116 Gardiner in *Style for Men* 25, no. 3, "At the BIF Exhibition," March 1935, 217.

117 Aviator, "International Popularity," *Style for Men* 25, no. 1, January 1935, 57.

118 Courtaulds Rayon, "In All Men's Eyes," *Style for Men* 5, no. 20, November 1932, 234–5. See also Paul Jobling, *Man Appeal: Advertising, Modernism and Menswear* (Berg: Oxford, 2005), 130.

119 Courtaulds, "Are You Ever 'Not at Home' to Trade?" *Style for Men* 22, no. 4, October 1933, 170, emphasis in original.

120 *Style for Men* 20, no. 5, "The Grotesque in Regent Street," November 1932, 248.

121 "The Window Man," "Display of Sports Shirts," *Style for Men* 25, no. 5, May 1935, 369.

122 Lewis Baumer, "The Neglected Sex," *Punch* 163 (1922): 439.

123 *Vogue*, "Wire, Wax and Plaster of Paris," 76.

124 Ernest H. Shepard, "This Is Not the Culminating Scene from the Seventeen-Reel Film 'The Modern Cleopatra,'" *Punch* 162 (1922): 213.

125 "Well, Sir, I Think *We're* the Type Who Can Wear a Tie Such as This!" *Men Only* 3, no. 11, October 1936, 77, emphasis in original. See also Mills, "*The Girl*," 341; Anne Herrmann, *Queering the Moderns: Poses/Portraits/Performances* (Basingstoke: Palgrave, 2000), 158. Tobin, *Peripheral Desires*, 197, notes that red ties were associated with homosexuality in Germany in the early twentieth century.

126 Patrick Bellew, *Point of View* (London: Arthur Barker, 1935), unpaginated. See also Justin Bengry, "Courting the Pink Pound: *Men Only* and the Queer Consumer, 1935–39," *History Workshop Journal* 68 (Autumn 2009): 143, fig. 6.

127 Murray Healy, "Were We Being Served? Homosexual Representation in Popular British Comedy," *Screen* 36, no. 3 (1995): 243.

128 Anthony Slide, *Some Joe You Don't Know: An American Biographical Guide to 100 British Television Personalities* (Westport, CT: Greenwood, 1996), 122.

129 Geoffrey Wansell, *Terence Rattigan* (London: Fourth Estate, 1995), 61.

130 McLaren, *Playboys and Mayfair Men*, 117.

131 Walkowitz, *Nights Out*, 267.

132 David Lewis Ghilchik, "*Customer.* 'I Want Some Winter Underwear, Please,'" *Punch* 185 (1933): 427.

133 William Kerridge Haselden, "Oh, My Hat!" *Daily Mirror*, November 30, 1934, 13.

134 Lewis Baumer, "Superior Hairdresser: ''Ow about 'Avin' One of Our Permanent Billows, Sir?'" *Punch* 179 (1930): 326.

135 Samuel Hynes, *The Auden Generation: Literature and Politics in England in the 1930s* (London: Bodley Head, 1976), 19.

136 Proust quoted and discussed in Sedgwick, *Epistemology of the Closet*, 218.

137 James D. Steakley, "Iconography of a Scandal: Political Cartoons and the Eulenburg Affair," in *History of Homosexuality in Europe and America*, volume 5, ed. Wayne R. Dynes and Stephen Donaldson (New York: Garland, 1992), 349–61; Jean Findlay,

Chasing Lost Time: The Life of C. K. Moncrieff: Soldier, Spy and Translator (London: Chatto and Windus, 2014), 283.

138 David Lewis Ghilchik, "Absent-Minded Young Policeman," *Punch* 184 (1933): 405.

139 Ernest H. Shepard, "Aren't Their Statues Wonderful," *Punch* 192 (1937): 339; Anne Harriet Fish, "Preparing for a Raid. The Green Room at Scotland Yard," *Punch* 182 (1932): 613.

140 "B. W.," "Men Only," *Men Only* 2, no. 1, April 1936, 13.

141 Jill Greenfield, Sen O'Connell, and Chris Reid, "Fashioning Masculinity: *Men Only*, Consumption and the Development of Marketing in the 1930s," *Twentieth Century British History* 10, no. 4 (1999): 461 and 465, fig. 1.

142 Edward Hynes, "'Oh, Sir, Spare a Copper,'" *Men Only* 3, no. 12, November 1936, 95. See also Bengry, "Courting the Pink Pound," 133, fig. 3.

143 Philip Hoare, *Wilde's Last Stand: Decadence, Conspiracy, and the First World War* (London: Duckworth, 1997), 11 and 188.

144 Daniel A. Novak, "Picturing Wilde: Christopher Millard's 'Iconography of Oscar Wilde,'" *Nineteenth-Century Contexts* 32, no. 4 (2010): 328.

145 James Agate, "Writers of the Reign," *Lilliput* 6 (December 1936): 76.

146 Edgar Jepson, "The Man with the Green Carnation," *Men Only* 1, no. 2, January 1936, 90. See also Julia Skelly, "The Paradox of Excess: Oscar Wilde, Caricature, and Consumption," in *The Uses of Excess in Visual and Material Culture, 1600–2010*, ed. Julia Skelly (Farnham: Ashgate, 2014), 137–60.

147 Alan Odle, "Theatrical First Nights down the Ages," *Vogue* 65, no. 5 (early March 1925): 73. See also Martin Steenson, *The Life and Work of Alan Odle* (Stroud: Books and Things, 2012).

148 Garelick, *Rising Star*, 154.

149 Green, *Children of the Sun*, 189.

150 Max Beerbohm, "Oscar Wilde," *Pick-Me-Up*, September 22, 1894, 390; Janes, *Oscar Wilde Prefigured*, 220–4.

151 Evelyn Waugh, "Let Us Return to the Nineties but Not to Oscar Wilde," *Harper's Bazaar* 3, no. 2, November 1930, 51.

152 Alex Murray, "Decadence Revisited: Evelyn Waugh and the Afterlife of the 1890s," *Modernism/Modernity* 22, no. 3 (2015): 593–607.

153 Latimer, "Balletomania," 189.

154 Quentin Crisp, *The Naked Civil Servant* (London: Jonathan Cape, 1968), 156–7.

155 Charlotte Charteris, "Inside Julian Maclaren-Ross's Closet: Clothing as Communication in Wartime Britain," *Journal of War and Culture Studies* 7, no. 4 (2014): 521.

156 Matt Houlbrook and Chris Waters, "*The Heart in Exile*: Detachment and Desire in 1950s London," *History Workshop Journal* 62 (2006): 160.

157 David, *On Queer Street*, 154; Richard Hornsey, *The Spiv and the Architect: Unruly Life in Postwar London* (Minneapolis, MN: University of Minnesota Press, 2010), 26–8.

Chapter 7

1   Wilde, "Phrases and Philosophies," 142.

2   Cecil Beaton, "What Is Beauty?" *Vogue* (US edn) 72, no. 1, November 24, 1928, 47.

3   Colleen McQuillen, "From The Fairground Booth to Futurism: The Sartorial and Material Estrangement of Masquerade," *Russian Review* 71, no. 3 (2012): 413–35.

4   Dominic Janes, "Cecil Beaton, Richard Hamilton and the Queer, Transatlantic Origins of Pop Art," *Visual Culture in Britain* 16, no. 3 (2015): 308–30. See also Lawrence Alloway, "The Development of British Pop," in *Pop Art*, ed. Lucy R. Lippard (London: Thames and Hudson, 1966), 27–68; Hal Foster, "Notes on the First Pop Age (2003)," in *Richard Hamilton*, ed. Hal Foster and Alex Bacon (Cambridge, MA: MIT Press, 2010), 45–64; Martin Hammer, "The Independent Group take on Francis Bacon," *Visual Culture in Britain* 15, no. 1 (2014): 69–89.

5   Dominic Janes, "Eminent Victorians, Bloomsbury Queerness and John Maynard Keynes' The Economic Consequences of the Peace (1919)," *Literature and History* 23, no. 1 (2014): 19–32; Max Jones, "'National Hero and Very Queer Fish': Empire, Sexuality and the British Remembrance of General Gordon, 1918–72," *Twentieth Century British History* 26, no. 2 (2014): 175–202.

6   Daniel M. Abramson, *Obsolescence: An Architectural History* (Chicago: University of Chicago Press, 2016).

7   Helen Davies, *Neo-Victorian Freakery: The Cultural Afterlife of the Victorian Freak Show* (Basingstoke: Palgrave Macmillan, 2015).

8   *Vogue* (US edn) 48, no. 8, "As Seen by Him," October 15, 1916, 57.

9   William Kerridge Haselden, "Our Restaurants at Several Periods," *Daily Mirror*, October 20, 1922, 7.

10 David Low, "Are Our Women Degenerating?" *Star*, December 30, 1924, 3.

11 J. T. Grein, "Criticisms in Cameo," *Sketch*, March 5, 1930, 454.

12 Crisp, *The Naked Civil Servant*, 26.

13 Crisp, *The Naked Civil Servant*, 25.

14 Chauncey, *Gay New York*, 25.

15 Michael Bronski, *Culture Clash: The Making of Gay Sensibility* (Boston: South End Press, 1984), 2.

16 Dyer, *Heavenly Bodies*, 153.

17 Dyer, *The Culture of Queers*, 59.

18 Halperin, *How to Be Gay*, 375.

19 Halperin, *How to Be Gay*, 46, emphasis in original.

20 Halperin, *How to Be Gay*, 349.

21 Dyer, *The Culture of Queers*, 52.

22 Marcel Proust, *Cities of the Plain*, volume 1, trans. C. K. Scott Moncrieff, 20.

23 Quoted in Vickers, *Cecil Beaton*, 23.

24 Cecil Beaton quoted in Vickers, *Cecil Beaton*, 23.

25   Beverley Nichols, *Father Figure* (London: Heinemann, 1972), 92.

26   Sedgwick, *Between Men*, 95; Nichols, *Father Figure*, 89–99, quote at 99. See also
     Oscar Wilde, *The Picture of Dorian Gray: An Annotated, Uncensored Edition*, ed.
     Nicholas Frankel (Cambridge, MA: Harvard University Press. 2011).

27   Jacob Bloomfield, "Splinters: Cross-Dressing Ex-Servicemen on the Interwar Stage,"
     Twentieth Century British History 30, no. 1 (2019): 12.

28   Bloomfield, "Splinters," 22.

29   Bloomfield, "Splinters," 25.

30   *Taunton Courier and Western Advertiser*, "Boy's Death Mystery," July 7, 1926, 2;
     Sunday Post (Glasgow), "Boy's Body Found in Shrubbery," June 27, 1926, 2.

31   E. M. Forster, *Maurice*, ed. P. N. Furbank (London: Penguin, 2005), 138.

32   *Taunton Courier and Western Advertiser*, "Boy's Death Mystery," 2.

33   *Taunton Courier and Western Advertiser*, "Boy's Death Mystery," 2.

34   Janes, *Picturing the Closet*, 119–35.

35   Sarah Cole, *Modernism, Male Friendship, and the First World War* (Cambridge:
     Cambridge University Press, 2003), 32–4.

36   Janes, *Picturing the Closet*, 124.

37   See also Deslandes, *Oxbridge Men*, 111–12.

38   Terence Greenidge, *Degenerate Oxford? A Critical Study of Modern University Life*
     (London: Chapman and Hall, 1930), 91.

39   Greenidge, *Degenerate Oxford?* 98.

40   Greenidge, *Degenerate Oxford?* 202.

41   Ryan Linkof, "'Those Young Men Who Come Down from Oxford and Write
     Gossip': Society Gossip, Homosexuality and the Logic of Revelation in the Interwar
     Popular Press," in *British Queer History*, 109–33.

42   Robin Blyn, "Nightwood's Freak Dandies: Decadence in the 1930s," *Modernism/
     Modernity* 15, no. 3 (2008): 503 and 505. See also, for wider context, Blower,
     Becoming Americans in Paris.

43   Yale Collection of American Literature mss 139, box 3, folder 23, Beinecke Library,
     Yale University.

44   Stephens, "Geeks and Gaffs," 185; Donald Albrecht and Stephen Vider, *Gay Gotham:
     Art and Underground Culture in New York* (New York: Skira Rizzoli, 2016), 130.

45   James Danziger, *Beaton: The Art of the Scrapbook* (New York: Assouline, 2010).

46   Robert Scully, *A Scarlet Pansy* (New York: William Faro, 1933). Discussed in Jay A.
     Gertzman, "A Scarlet Pansy Goes to War: Subversion, Schlock, and an Early Gay
     Classic," *Journal of American Culture* 33, no. 3 (2010): 230–9.

47   Albrecht and Vider, *Gay Gotham*, 118–19; Sam See, "Making Modernism New:
     Queer Mythology in *The Young and Evil*," *ELH* 76, no. 4 (2009): 1073–105.

48   Parker Tyler, *The Divine Comedy of Pavel Tchelitchew: A Biography* (New York:
     Fleet, 1967), 371.

49 Pavel Tchelitchew, "Phenomena," *Vogue* 90, no. 29, August 3, 1938, 27.

50 Ryan Linkof, "Shooting Charles Henri Ford: Cecil Beaton and the Erotics of the 'Low' in the New York Tabloids," *Études Photographiques* 29 (2012): unpaginated.

51 Ford's diaries quoted here are in the Charles Henri Ford Papers, 1928–81, box 20, folder 2, Harry Ransom Center, University of Texas at Austin.

52 For unpublished material from Ford, "Confessions of a Freak" see the Charles Henri Ford Papers, MSS 32, box 14, Yale Collection of American Literature, Beinecke Rare Book and Manuscript Library; and Charles Henri Ford Papers (afterward given as CHF), box 1, folder 6, Harry Ransom Center, University of Texas at Austin. For the date see Charles Henri Ford and Allen Frame, "Interview," *Journal of Contemporary Art, Interviews*, n.d., unpaginated.

53 Charles Henri Ford, "Confessions of a Freak," 1, typed annotations in pen shown in italics, CHF, box 1, folder 6, emphases in original.

54 Ford, "Confessions of a Freak," 55, CHF, box 1, folder 6; compare Hartzman, *American Sideshow*, 211–12, on Stanley Berent (1903–80) who performed as "Sealo the Seal Boy."

55 Ellen Jean Samuels, "My Body, My Closet: Invisible Disability and the Limits of Coming-Out Discourse," *GLQ: A Journal of Lesbian and Gay Studies* 9, no. 1–2 (2003): 249.

56 Tirza True Latimer, *Eccentric Modernisms: Making Differences in the History of American Art* (Berkeley: University of California Press, 2017), 91–2.

57 Emma Purce, "Scales of Normality: Displays of Extreme Weight and Weight Loss in Blackpool 1920–1940," *Cultural and Social History* 14, no. 5 (2017): 669–89.

58 See, for example, Elfreda Buckland, *The World of Donald McGill* (Poole: Blandford Press, 1984).

59 Hartzman, *American Sideshow*, 111–12.

60 Potvin, *Bachelors of a Different Sort*, 240.

61 Heather Love, *Feeling Backward: Loss and the Politics of Queer History* (Cambridge, MA: Harvard University Press, 2007), 160.

62 Crisp, *The Naked Civil Servant*, 196; Halberstam, *The Queer Art of Failure*, 96.

63 Brown, *Work!* 106.

64 Bram Stoker, *Dracula* (London: Constable, 1897); Christopher Craft, "'Kiss Me with Those Red Lips': Gender and Inversion in Bram Stoker's Dracula," *Representations* 8 (Autumn 1984): 107–33; Talia Schaffer, "'A Wilde Desire Took Me': The Homoerotic History of Dracula," *ELH* 61, no. 2 (1994): 381–425.

65 Chris Waters, "Wilde in the Fifties," in *Sex, Knowledge, and Receptions of the Past*, ed. Kate Fisher and Rebecca Langlands (Oxford: Oxford University Press, 2015), 269 and 289.

66 Neil Bartlett, *Who Was That Man? A Present for Mr. Oscar Wilde* (London: Serpent's Tail, 1988), 211–12, emphasis in original.

67 Carl Van Vechten, *Excavations* (New York: Knopf, 1926), 172. Discussed in Mahoney, *Literature and Politics of Post-Victorian Decadence*, 11; MacLeod, "The Queerness of Being 1890 in 1922," 230.

68 Jocelyn Brooke, *The Military Orchid* (London: Bodley Head, 1948), 22.

69 Brooke, *The Military Orchid*, 67, emphasis in original.

70 Robert Mapplethorpe, *Flora: The Complete Flowers*, ed. Mark Holborn and Dimitri Levas (London: Phaidon, 2016).

Bibliography

This bibliography lists primary and secondary textual and visual sources in printed documents but not manuscripts from archives, which are referenced in the notes. References are given directly to a cartoon or photograph where it appears on its own, or to the article that contains it. Periodicals which were published in more than one location are referenced as follows: *Vogue* refers to the London edition of this magazine, and *Vogue* (US edn) to the New York version.

Abdulla Cigarettes. "The Babies' Ball." *Sketch*, October 16, 1929, 126.

Abdulla Cigarettes. "The Bright Brigade." *Sketch*, September 4, 1929, 475.

Abramson, Daniel M. *Obsolescence: An Architectural History*. Chicago: University of Chicago Press, 2016.

Adair, Joshua. "Wilde Nostalgia: Queer Tradition in Beverley Nichols's Garden Trilogies." *Sic* 13 (2016): unpaginated.

Adams, Bluford. "'A Stupendous Mirror of Departed Empires': The Barnum Hippodromes and Circuses, 1874–1891." *American Literary History* 8, no. 1 (1996): 34–56.

Adams, Rachel. *Sideshow USA: Freaks and the American Cultural Imagination*. Chicago: University of Chicago Press, 2001.

Adrian, Jack. "Introduction." In E. F. Benson, *Desirable Residences*, ix–xiv. Oxford: Oxford University Press, 1991.

Agate, James. "Writers of the Reign." *Lilliput* 6 (December 1936): 71–9.

Agha, Mehemed F. "Whistler's Hippopotamus." *Vogue* (US edn) 89, no. 6, 1937, 74–5, 138–9, and 144.

Albrecht, Donald, and Stephen Vider. *Gay Gotham: Art and Underground Culture in New York*. New York: Skira Rizzoli, 2016.

Alden, William Livingston. *Among the Freaks*. London: Longmans, Green, 1896.

Alloway, Lawrence. "The Development of British Pop." In *Pop Art*, edited by Lucy R. Lippard, 27–68. London: Thames and Hudson, 1966.

Altick, Richard. *The Shows of London*. Cambridge, MA: Harvard University Press, 1978.

Anesko, Michael. *Henry James and Queer Filiation: Hardened Bachelors of the Edwardian Era*. London: Palgrave, 2018.

Angeletti, Norberto, and Alberto Oliva. *In "Vogue": The Illustrated History of the World's Most Famous Fashion Magazine*. New York: Rizzoli, 2006.

Annan, Noel. "The Cult of Homosexuality in England 1850–1950." *Biography* 13, no. 3 (1990): 189–202.

Artmonskey. Ruth. *Designing Women: Women Working in Advertising and Publicity from the 1920s to the 1960s*. London: Artmonskey Arts, 2012.

"A. S." "Paris: Uniformed and Beflagged." *Vogue* 50, no. 3, early August 1917, 11–15.

Aston, Martin. *Breaking Down the Walls of Heartache: How Music Came Out*. London: Constable, 2016.

Aviator. "International Popularity." *Style for Men* 25, no. 1, January 1935, 57.

Azzarello, Robert. "Unnatural Predators: Queer Theory Meets Environmental Studies in Bram Stoker's *Dracula*." In *Queering the Non/Human*, edited by Noreen Giffney and Myra J. Hird, 137–58. Aldershot: Ashgate, 2008.

Baker, Roger. *Drag: A History of Female Impersonation in the Performing Arts*. London: Cassell, 1994.

Ballymena Observer. "Policeman Dressed as a Woman." April 4, 1913, 10.

Bard, Christine. *Les Garçonnes: modes et fantasmes des années folles*. Paris: Flammarion 1998.

Baring Gould, Sabine. *Freaks of Fanaticism and Other Strange Events*. London: Methuen, 1891.

Barlow, Clare, ed. *Queer British Art, 1861–1967*. London: Tate Publishing, 2017.

Bartlett, Neil. *Who Was That Man? A Present for Mr. Oscar Wilde*. London: Serpent's Tail, 1988.

Basu, Sayoni. "Benson, Edward Frederic (1867–1940)." *Oxford Dictionary of National Biography*. Oxford: Oxford University Press, May 2005. Available online: http://www.oxforddnb.com/view/article/30713 (accessed June 16, 2016).

Baumer, Lewis. *The Bright Young Things: A Book of Drawings*. London: Methuen, 1928.

Baumer, Lewis. "'How Is It You're Not Serving, Young Man?'" *Punch* 148 (1915): 310.

Baumer, Lewis. "Le Mot Juste." *Punch* 149 (1915): 390.

Baumer, Lewis. "'Looks a Bit Affected, Don't 'E?'" *Punch* 190 (1936): 98.

Baumer, Lewis. "The Neglected Sex." *Punch* 163 (1922): 439.

Baumer, Lewis. "The Sex Question (a Study in Bond Street)." *Punch* 140 (1911): 235.

Baumer, Lewis. "Society in the Sun." *Punch* 144 (1913): 221.

Baumer, Lewis. "Superior Hairdresser: ''Ow about 'Avin' One of Our Permanent Billows, Sir?'" *Punch* 179 (1930): 326.

Baumer, Lewis. "'Well, What Do You Think of My New Flat, Uncle John?'" *Punch* 178 (1930): 216.

Baumer, Lewis, and "Violetta." "The Distressing Decadence of the Fashion-Plate Young Lady." *Punch* 143 (1912): 369.

Beall, Edgar C. *The Life Sexual: A Study of the Philosophy, Physiology, Science, Art, and Hygiene of Love*. New York: Vim Publishing Company, 1905.

Beard, A. B. "A Brighter Olympia." *London Opinion*, week ending October 20, 1928, 13.

Beaton, Cecil. *The Book of Beauty*. London: Duckworth, 1930.

Beaton, Cecil. *Cecil Beaton's Fair Lady*. London: Weidenfeld and Nicolson, 1964.

Beaton, Cecil. "Four Debutantes of 1928." *Vogue* 72, no. 3, August 8, 1928, 34.

Beaton, Cecil. "Four Stars in Waltz Time." *Vogue* (US edn) 77, no. 10, May 15, 1931, 78–9, 128, 130, and 132.

Beaton, Cecil. *The Glass of Fashion*. London: Weidenfeld and Nicolson, 1954.

Beaton, Cecil. "The London Season." *Vogue* 73, no. 9, early May 1929, 39–41.

Beaton, Cecil. "Merry Christmas." *Vogue* 82, no. 11, November 29, 1933, 63–5 and 104.

Beaton, Cecil. *Photobiography*. London: Odhams, 1951.

Beaton, Cecil. "Raving Beauties." *Vogue* 72, no. 3, August 8, 1928, 36–7 and 62.

Beaton, Cecil. *Time Exposure*. 2nd edn. London: B. T. Batsford, 1946.

Beaton, Cecil. "Wedding of the Duke and Duchess of Windsor." *Vogue* (US edn) 90, no. 1, July 1, 1937, 32–5.

Beaton, Cecil. "What Is Beauty?" *Vogue* (US edn) 72, no. 11, November 24, 1928, 47–9 and 120.

Beerbohm, Max. "The Incomparable Beauty of Modern Dress." *Spirit Lamp* 4, no. 2 (June 6, 1893): 90–8.

Beerbohm, Max. "Oscar Wilde." *Pick-Me-Up*, September 22, 1894, 392.

Belcher, George. "*Man-Woman.* 'In the Old Days I Never Paid More Than Sixpence for a Haircut.'" *Punch* 189 (1925): 9.

Bell, Clive. "Jean Cocteau: A Master Modernist." *Vanity Fair* (US edn) 21, no. 5, 1925, 52 and 82.

Bell, David. "Farm Boys and Wild Men: Rurality, Masculinity, and Homosexuality." *Rural Sociology* 65, no. 4 (2000): 547–61.

Bell, David, and Ruth Holliday. "Naked as Nature Intended." *Body and Society* 6, no. 3–4 (2000): 127–40.

Bell, Kenneth. "Famous Women from History, No. 5: Sappho." *Britannia and Eve* 1, no. 5 (September 1929): 44–7 and 162.

Bellew, Patrick. *Point of View*. London: Arthur Barker, 1935.

Bengry, Justin. "Courting the Pink Pound: *Men Only* and the Queer Consumer, 1935–39." *History Workshop Journal* 68 (Autumn 2009): 122–48.

Benshoff, Harry M. *Monsters in the Closet: Homosexuality and the Horror Film*. Manchester: Manchester University Press, 1997.

Benson, E. F. *As We Were: A Victorian Peep Show*. London: Longmans, Green and Co., 1930.

Benson, E. F. *Final Edition*. London: Hogarth Press, 1988.

Benson, E. F. *The Freaks of Mayfair*. London: T. N. Foulis, 1916.

Bentley, Edmund Clerihew. "More Clerihews." *Punch* 196 (1939): 39.

Berger, Anne Emmanuelle. *The Queer Turn in Feminism: Identities, Sexualities, and the Theater of Gender*, trans. Catherine Porter. New York: Fordham University Press, 2014.

Berger, John. *Ways of Seeing*. London: Penguin, 1972.

Bergman, David, ed. *Camp Grounds: Style and Homosexuality*. Amherst: University of Massachusetts Press, 1993.

Berlanstein, Lenard R. "Breeches and Breaches: Cross-Dress Theater and the Culture of Gender Ambiguity in Modern France." *Comparative Studies in Society and History* 38, no. 2 (1996): 338–69.

Berners, Gerald. *The Girls of Radcliff Hall*, edited by John Byrne. London: Montcalm and the Cygnet Press, 2000.

Besnault-Levita, Anne, and Anne Florence Gillard Estrada, ed. *Beyond the Victorian/ Modernist Divide: Remapping the Turn-of-the-Century Break in Literature, Culture and the Visual Arts*. New York: Routledge, 2018.

Biernoff, Suzannah. *Portraits of Violence: War and the Aesthetics of Disfigurement*. Ann Arbor: University of Michigan Press, 2017.

Blanch, Lesley. "Vogue's Spotlight." *Vogue* 90, no. 41 (January 25, 1939): 34–5 and 65.

Blatchley, John. *The Bookplates of George Wolfe Plank and a Selection of His Book Illustrations*. London: Bookplate Society, 2002.

Bloomfield, Jacob. "Male Cross-Dressing Performance in Britain, 1918–1970." PhD Dissertation, The University of Manchester, UK, 2017.

Bloomfield, Jacob. "*Splinters*: Cross-Dressing Ex-Servicemen on the Interwar Stage." *Twentieth Century British History* 30, no. 1 (2019): 1–28.

Blower, Brooke L. *Becoming Americans in Paris: Transatlantic Politics and Culture between the World Wars*. Oxford: Oxford University Press, 2011.

Bluemel, Kristin. *George Orwell and the Radical Eccentrics: Intermodernism in Literary London*. Basingstoke: Palgrave Macmillan, 2004.

Blum, Stella, ed. *Fashion Drawings and Illustrations from "Harper's Bazaar."* New York: Dover, 1976.

Blyn, Robin. "*Nightwood's* Freak Dandies: Decadence in the 1930s." *Modernism/ Modernity* 15, no. 3 (2008): 503–26.

Bogdan, Robert. *Freak Show: Presenting Human Oddities for Amusement and Profit*. Chicago: University of Chicago Press, 1988.

Bogdan, Robert, Martin Elks, and James A. Knoll. *Picturing Disability: Beggar, Freak, Citizen, and Other Photographic Rhetoric*. Syracuse: Syracuse University Press, 2012.

Böker, Uwe, Richard Corballis, and Julie Hibbard, ed. *The Importance of Reinventing Oscar: Versions of Wilde during the Last 100 Years*. Amsterdam: Rodopi, 2002.

Booth, Howard J. "D. H. Lawrence and Male Homosexual Desire." *Review of English Studies* 53, no. 209 (2002): 86–107.

Booth, Howard J. "Experience and Homosexuality in the Writing of Compton Mackenzie." *English Studies* 88, no. 3 (2007): 320–31.

Boscagli, Maurizia. *Eye on the Flesh: Fashions of Masculinity in the Early Twentieth Century*. Boulder: Westview Press, 1996.

Bourke, Joanna. *Dismembering the Male: Men's Bodies, Britain, and the Great War*. London: Reaktion, 1996.

Bourke, Joanna. "Fragmentation, Fetishization and Men's Bodies in Britain, 1890–1939." *Women: A Cultural Review* 7, no. 3 (1996): 240–9.

Bourke, Joanna. "The Great Male Renunciation: Men's Dress Reform in Inter-War Britain." *Journal of Design History* 9, no. 1 (1996): 23–33.

Bouvet, Vincent, and Gérard Durozol. *Paris between the Wars: Art, Style and Glamour in the Crazy Years*, trans. Ruth Sharman. London: Thames and Hudson, 2010.

Boxwell, David A. "The Follies of War: Cross-Dressing and Popular Theatre on the British Front Lines, 1914–18." *Modernism/Modernity* 9, no. 1 (2002): 1–20.

Brassaï. *The Secret Paris of the 30s*, trans. Richard Miller. London: Thames and Hudson, 1976.

Brauer, Fae. "Virilizing and Valorizing Homoeroticism: Eugen Sandow's Queering of Body Cultures before and after the Wilde Trials." *Visual Culture in Britain* 18, no. 1 (2017): 35–67.

Breward, Christopher. "Couture as Queer Auto/Biography." In *A Queer History of Fashion: From the Closet to the Catwalk*, edited by Valerie Steele, 117–33. New Haven: Yale University Press, 2013.

Breward, Christopher. *The Culture of Fashion: A New History of Fashionable Dress*. Manchester: Manchester University Press, 1995.

Breward, Christopher. *Fashioning London: Clothing and the Modern Metropolis*. Oxford: Berg, 2004.

Bristow, Joseph, ed. *Oscar Wilde and Modern Culture: The Making of a Legend*. Athens, OH: Ohio University Press, 2008.

Bristow, Joseph. "Picturing His Exact Decadence: The British Reception of Oscar Wilde." In *The Reception of Oscar Wilde in Europe*, edited by Stefano Evangelista, 20–50. London: Continuum, 2010.

Brittain-Catlin, Timothy. *Bleak Houses: Disappointment and Failure in Architecture*. Cambridge, MA: MIT Press, 2014.

Bronski, Michael. *Culture Clash: The Making of Gay Sensibility*. Boston: South End Press, 1984.

Brooke, Jocelyn. *The Military Orchid*. London: Bodley Head, 1948.

Brown, Elspeth H. "De Meyer at *Vogue*: Commercializing Queer Affect in First World War-Era Fashion Photography." *Photography and Culture* 2, no. 3 (2009): 253–73.

Brown, Elspeth H. "Queering Glamour in Interwar Fashion Photography: The 'Amorous Regard' of George Platt Lynes." *GLQ: A Journal of Lesbian and Gay Studies* 23, no. 3 (2017): 289–326.

Brown, Elspeth H. *Work! A Queer History of Modeling*. Durham, NC: Duke University Press, 2019.

Bruhm, Steven. *Reflecting Narcissus: A Queer Aesthetic*. Minneapolis: University of Minnesota Press, 2001.

Bruhm, Steven, and Natasha Hurley, ed. *Curiouser: On the Queerness of Children*. Minneapolis: University of Minnesota Press, 2004.

Bryan, Alfred. "Eclipsed: A Regent Street Study in the Slack Season." *Punch* 133 (1907): 161.

Buckland, Elfreda. *The World of Donald McGill*. Poole: Blandford Press, 1984.

Bullen, J. B. *The Pre-Raphaelite Body: Fear and Desire in Painting, Poetry, and Criticism*. Oxford: Oxford University Press, 1998.

Bullough, Vern L., and Bonnie Bullough. *Cross Dressing, Sex, and Gender*. Philadelphia: University of Pennsylvania Press, 1993.

Burman, Barbara. "Better and Brighter Clothes: The Men's Dress Reform Party, 1929–1940." *Journal of Design History* 8, no. 4 (1995): 275–90.

Bush, Ronald. "In Pursuit of Wilde Possum: Reflections on Eliot, Modernism, and the Nineties." *Modernism/Modernity* 11, no. 3 (2004): 469–85.

Butler, Judith. "Critically Queer." *GLQ: A Journal of Lesbian and Gay Studies* 1, no. 1 (1993): 17–32.

Butters, Ronald D. "Gary Grant and the Emergence of *Gay* 'Homosexual.'" *Dictionaries* 19, no. 1 (1998): 188–204.

"B. W." "Men Only." *Men Only* 2, no. 1, April 1936, 13.

Byron, Robert. "The Perfect Party." *Vogue* 73, no. 12 (June 12, 1929): 43–5 and 86.

Caesar, Adrian. *Taking It Like a Man: Suffering, Sexuality, and the War Poets: Brooke, Sassoon, Owen, Graves*. Manchester: Manchester University Press, 1993.

Calloway, Stephen. *Baroque Baroque: The Culture of Excess*. London: Phaidon, 1994.

Camille, Michael. "Editor's Introduction." *Art History* 24, no. 2 (2001): 163–8.

Carden-Coyne, Ana. *Reconstructing the Body: Classicism, Modernism, and the First World War*. Oxford: Oxford University Press, 2009.

Cardiff Times. "Serious Charge against a Contractor." January 11, 1890, 7.

Carlyle, Thomas. *Sartor Resartus: The Life and Opinions of Herr Teufelsdröckh in Three Books*. London: Chapman and Hall, 1869.

Carpenter, Edward. *The Intermediate Sex: A Study of Some Transitional Types of Men and Women*. London: George Allen and Unwin, 1912.

Carriger, Michelle Liu. "'The Unnatural History and Petticoat Mystery of Boulton and Park': A Victorian Sex Scandal and the Theatre Defense." *TDR/The Drama Review* 57, no. 4 (2013): 135–56.

Carrod, Amanda Juliet. "'A Plea for a Renaissance': Dorothy Todd's Modernist Experiment in British *Vogue*, 1922–1926." PhD dissertation, Keele University, UK, 2015.

Casteras, Susan P. "Pre-Raphaelite Challenges to Victorian Canons of Beauty." *Huntington Library Quarterly* 55, no. 1 (1992): 13–35.

Castle, Charles. *Oliver Messel: A Biography*. London: Thames and Hudson, 1986.

Castle, Terry. *Noël Coward and Radclyffe Hall: Kindred Spirits*. New York: Columbia University Press, 1996.

Castle, Terry. "Some Notes on 'Notes on Camp.'" In *The Scandal of Susan Sontag*, edited by Barbara Ching and Jennifer A. Wagner-Lawlor, 21–31. New York: Columbia University Press, 2009.

Cecil, Hugh. *A Book of Beauty*. London: P. Allan, 1926.

Chapman, David L. *Sandow the Magnificent: Eugen Sandow and the Beginnings of Bodybuilding*. Paperback edn. Urbana: University of Illinois Press, 2006.

Charteris, Charlotte. "Inside Julian Maclaren-Ross's Closet: Clothing as Communication in Wartime Britain." *Journal of War and Culture Studies* 7, no. 4 (2014): 320–35.

Chase, Edna Woolman, and Ilka Chase. *Always in Vogue*. London: Gollancz, 1954.

Chauncey, George. *Gay New York: Gender, Urban Culture, and the Making of the Gay Male World, 1890–1940*. New York: Basic Books, 1994.

Chemers, Michael M. *Staging Stigma: A Critical Examination of the American Freak Show*. New York: Palgrave Macmillan, 2008.

Christie, Nancy, and Michael Gauvreau. *Bodies, Love, and Faith in the First World War: Dardanella and Peter*. Basingstoke: Palgrave Macmillan, 2018.

Chudacoff, Howard P. *The Age of the Bachelor: Creating an American Subculture*. Princeton: Princeton University Press, 1999.

Churchill, Suzanne Wintsch. "Outing T. S. Eliot." *Criticism* 47, no. 1 (2005): 7–30.

Clark, Adrian, and Jeremy Dronfield. *Queer Saint: The Cultured Life of Peter Watson, Who Shook Twentieth-Century Art and Shocked High Society*. London: John Blake, 2015.

Clark, Anna. *Desire: A History of European Sexuality*. New York: Routledge, 2008.

Clark, Kenneth. *The Nude: A Study of Ideal Art*. London: John Murray, 1956.

Clark, Petra. "'Cleverly Drawn': Oscar Wilde, Charles Ricketts, and the Art of *The Woman's World*." *Journal of Victorian Culture* 20, no. 3 (2015): 375–400.

Clarke, Darren. "Duncan Grant and Charleston's Queer Arcadia." In *Queer Bloomsbury*, edited by Brenda Helt and Madelyn Detloff, 152–71. Edinburgh: Edinburgh University Press, 2016.

Clayworth, Anya. "*The Woman's World*: Oscar Wilde as Editor." *Victorian Periodicals Review* 30, no. 2 (1997): 84–101.

Cleto, Fabio, ed. *Camp: Queer Aesthetics and the Performing Subject: A Reader*. Edinburgh: Edinburgh University Press, 1999.

"C. N." "The Origin of the Fairies! A Crowd of Pansy Faces." *Sketch*, August 3, 1931, cover.

Coghlin, T. W. "She Wore a Camellia." *Cherwell* 17, no. 1 (new series) (April 29, 1925): 9 and 11.

Cohen, Lisa. "'Frock Consciousness': Virginia Woolf, the Open Secret, and the Language of Fashion." *Fashion Theory* 3, no. 2 (1999): 149–74.

Cohen, Lisa. "Virginia Woolf, Fashion and British *Vogue*." *Charleston Magazine* 18 (1998), 5–12.

Cohler, Deborah. *Citizen, Invert, Queer: Lesbianism and War in Early Twentieth-Century Britain*. Minneapolis: University of Minnesota Press, 2010.

Cole, Sarah. *Modernism, Male Friendship, and the First World War*. Cambridge: Cambridge University Press, 2003.

Cole, Shaun. "*Don We Now Our Gay Apparel*": Gay Men's Dress in the Twentieth Century*. Oxford: Berg, 2000.

Collecott, Diana. *H. D. and Sapphic Modernism, 1910–1950*. Cambridge: Cambridge University Press, 1999.

Connon, Bryan. *Beverley Nichols: A Life*. London: Constable, 1991.

Conroy, Carolyn. "Mingling with the Ungodly: Simeon Solomon in Queer Victorian London." In *Sex, Time and Place: Queer Histories of London, c. 1850 to the Present*, edited by Simon Avery and Katherine M. Graham, 185–201. London: Bloomsbury, 2016.

Cook, James W. *The Arts of Deception: Playing with Fraud in the Age of Barnum* Cambridge, MA: Harvard University Press, 2001.

Cook, Matt. "Families of Choice? George Ives, Queer Lives and the Family." *Gender and History* 22, no. 1 (2010): 1–21.

Cook, Matt. *London and the Culture of Homosexuality, 1885–1914*. Cambridge: Cambridge University Press, 2003.

Cook, Matt. "Queer Conflicts: Love, Sex and War, 1914–1967." In *A Gay History of Britain: Love and Sex between Men since the Middle Ages*, edited by Matt Cook, 145–77. Oxford: Greenwood, 2007.

Cook, Matt. *Queer Domesticities: Homosexuality and Home Life in Twentieth-Century London*. Basingstoke: Palgrave Macmillan, 2014.

Courtaulds Rayon. "Are You Ever 'Not at Home' to Trade?" *Style for Men* 22, no. 4, October 1933, 170.

Courtaulds Rayon. "In All Men's Eyes." *Style for Men* 5, no. 20, November 1932, 234–5.

Coward, Noël. *The Noël Coward Diaries*, edited by Graham Payn and Sheridan Morley. London: Weidenfeld and Nicolson, 1982.

Cox, Howard, and Simon Mowatt. "*Vogue* in Britain: Authenticity and the Creation of Competitive Advantage in the UK Magazine Industry." *Business History* 54, no. 1 (2012): 67–87.

Coykendall, Abby. "Queer Counterhistory and the Spectre of Effeminacy." In *Heteronormativity in Eighteenth-Century Literature and Culture*, edited by Ana de Freitas Boe and Abby Coykendall, 111–29. Farnham: Ashgate Publishing, 2015.

Craft, Christopher. "'Kiss Me with Those Red Lips': Gender and Inversion in Bram Stoker's *Dracula*." *Representations* 8 (Autumn 1984): 107–33.

Crisp, Quentin. *The Last Word: An Autobiography*, edited by Philip Ward and Laurence Watts. Place of publication not identified: MB Books, 2017.

Crisp, Quentin. *The Naked Civil Servant*. London: Jonathan Cape, 1968.

Croft, Taylor. *Cloven Hoof: A Study of Contemporary London Vices*. London: Denis Archer, 1932.

Crouthamel, Jason. "Cross-Dressing for the Fatherland: Sexual Humour, Masculinity and German Soldiers in the First World War." *First World War Studies* 2, no. 2 (2011): 195–215.

Crowdy, Joe. "Queer Undergrowth: Weeds and Sexuality in the Architecture of the Garden." *Architecture and Culture* 5, no. 3 (2017): 423–33.

Crowell, Ellen. "Queer." *Victorian Literature and Culture* 46, no. 3–4 (2018): 816–20.

Cryle, Peter, and Elizabeth Stephens. *Normality: A Critical Genealogy*. Chicago: University of Chicago Press, 2017.

Curtis, James. *James Whale: A New World of Gods and Monsters*. London: Faber and Faber, 1998.

Daily Mirror. "Freak Telephones Becoming Popular." January 31, 1914, 9.

Daily Mirror. "Inventive Dress Designer Provides Skirt Alternative to the Handbag." March 17, 1914, 17.

Daily Mirror. "Today's Gossip." February 15, 1918, 6–7.

Danziger, James. *Beaton: The Art of the Scrapbook*. New York: Assouline, 2010.

Das, Santanu. "'Kiss Me, Hardy': Intimacy, Gender, and Gesture in First World War Trench Literature." *Modernism/Modernity* 9, no. 1 (2002): 51–74.

Das, Santanu. *Touch and Intimacy in First World War Literature*. Cambridge: Cambridge University Press, 2005.

David, Hugh. *On Queer Street: A Social History of British Homosexuality, 1895–1995*. London: HarperCollins, 1997.

Davies, Helen. *Neo-Victorian Freakery: The Cultural Afterlife of the Victorian Freak Show*. Basingstoke: Palgrave Macmillan, 2015.

Davis, Mary E. *Classic Chic: Music, Fashion, and Modernism*. Berkeley: University of California Press, 2006.

De Cicco, Mark. "The Queer God Pan: Terror and Apocalypse, Reimagined." In *Monsters and Monstrosity from the Fin de Siècle to the Millennium*, edited by Hutchison Sharla and Rebecca A. Brown, 49–68. Jefferson: McFarland, 2015.

De Hegedus, Adam [pseud. Rodney Garland]. *The Heart in Exile*. London: W. H. Allen, 1953.

De Jongh, Nicholas. *Not in Front of the Audience: Homosexuality on Stage*. London: Routledge, 1992.

Dean, Carolyn J. *The Frail Social Body: Pornography, Homosexuality, and Other Fantasies in Interwar France*, Studies in the History of Science and Culture 36. Berkeley: University of California Press, 2000.

Deeping, Warwick. "Abnormalities." *Britannia and Eve* 1, no. 2 (June 1929): 57 and 204.

Degras, Henry [pseud. Mark Benney]. *What Rough Beast: A Biographical Fantasia on the Life of Professor J. R. Neave otherwise Known as Ironfoot Jack*. London: Peter Davis, 1939.

Delaney, J. G. P. *Glyn Philpot: His Life and Work*. Aldershot: Ashgate, 1999.

Delavenay, Emile. *D. H. Lawrence and Edward Carpenter: A Study in EdwardianTransition*. London: Heinemann, 1971.

Dellamora, Richard. "Productive Decadence: 'The Queer Comradeship of Outlawed Thought': Vernon Lee, Max Nordau, and Oscar Wilde." *New Literary History* 35, no. 4 (2004): 529–46.

Denisoff, Dennis. *Aestheticism and Sexual Parody, 1840–1940*, Cambridge Studies in Nineteenth-Century Literature and Culture 31. Cambridge: Cambridge University Press, 2001.

Denisoff, Dennis. "The Dissipating Nature of Decadent Paganism from Pater to Yeats." *Modernism/Modernity* 15, no. 3 (2008): 431–46.

Denisoff, Dennis. "'Men of My Own Sex': Genius, Sexuality, and George Du Maurier's Artists." In *Victorian Sexual Dissidence*, edited by Richard Dellamora, 147–69. Chicago: University of Chicago Press, 1999.

Denisoff, Dennis. *Sexual Visibility from Literature to Film, 1850–1950*. Basingstoke: Palgrave Macmillan, 2004.

Denison Review 34, no. 84. "Pansy Butler." October 27, 1899, 1.

Deslandes, Paul. "Exposing, Adorning and Dressing the Body in the Modern Era." In *The Routledge History of Sex and the Body: 1500 to the Present*, edited by Sarah Toulalan and Kate Fisher. 179–203. London: Routledge, 2013.

Deslandes, Paul. *Oxbridge Men: British Masculinity and the Undergraduate Experience, 1850–1920*. Bloomington: Indiana University Press, 2005.

DeVun, Leah, and Zeb Tortorici. "Trans, Time and History." *Transgender Studies Quarterly* 5, no. 4 (2018): 518–39.

Dittman, Nika. "Italy." *Harper's Bazaar* 11, no. 3, December 1934, 60–3 and 82.

Doan, Laura. *Disturbing Practices: History, Sexuality, and Women's Experience of Modern War*. Chicago: University of Chicago Press, 2013.

Doan, Laura. *Fashioning Sapphism: The Origins of a Modern Lesbian Culture*. New York: Columbia University Press, 2001.

Doan, Laura. "Portrait—When Composing Elusive Answer to Challenge." *Punch* 136 (1909): 32.

Dowd, James Henry. "The New River 'Belle.'" *Punch* 159 (1920): 28.

Dowd, James Henry. "Sex Education and the Great War Soldier: A Queer Analysis of the Practice of 'Hetero' Sex." *Journal of British Studies* 51, no. 3 (2012): 641–63.

Dowling, Linda. "The Decadent and the New Woman in the 1890's." *Nineteenth-Century Fiction* 33, no. 4 (1979): 434–53.

Downend, Allan. "Benson, E. F., 1867–1940." In *The 1890s: An Encyclopedia of British Literature, Art, and Culture*, edited by G. A. Cevasco, 53–4. New York: Garland, 1993.

Downend, Allan. "E. F. Benson's 'Originals' no. 2: George Plank." *Dodo: The E. F. Benson Society Journal* 24 (2010): 12–22.

Downey, W. and D. "A Favourite of the Lyric Stage: Miss Marie Dainton—'Resting.'" *Sketch*, August 3, 1904, Supplement, 6.

Downs, Alan. *The Velvet Rage: Overcoming the Pain of Growing up Gay in a Straight Man's World*. Cambridge, MA: Da Capo, 2005.

Doy, Gen. *Claude Cahun: A Sensual Politics of Photography*. London: I.B. Tauris, 2007.

Dreiser, Theodore. *Dreiser Looks at Russia*. London: Constable, 1928.

Duggan, Lisa. *The Twilight of Equality? Neoliberalism, Cultural Politics, and the Attack on Democracy*. Boston: Beacon Press, 2003.

Dukes, Thomas. "'Mappings of Secrecy and Disclosure': *The Swimming Pool Library*, the Closet, and the Empire." *Journal of Homosexuality* 31, no. 3 (1996): 95–107.

Dundee Evening Telegraph. "Alleged Theft of Jewellery." December 28, 1931, 5.

Dundee Evening Telegraph. "The Woman Who Did." October 30, 1895, 2.

Durbach, Nadja. *Spectacle of Deformity: Freak Shows and Modern British Culture*. Berkeley: University of California Press, 2009.

Dyer, Richard. *The Culture of Queers*. London: Routledge, 2002.

Dyer, Richard. *Heavenly Bodies: Film Stars and Society*. Basingstoke: Macmillan 1987.

Dyhouse, Carol. *Glamour: Women, History, Feminism*. London: Zed Books, 2010.

Edinburgh Evening News. "Masquerading as a Woman." August 31, 1892, 3.

Eldredge, Charles H. "Calla Moderna: 'Such a Strange Flower.'" In *Georgia O'Keefe and the Calla Lily in American Art, 1860–1940*, edited by Barbara Buhler Lynes, 4–37. New Haven: Yale University Press, 2002.

Elfenbein, Andrew. "Byronism and the Work of Homosexual Performance in Early Victorian England." *Modern Language Quarterly* 54, no. 4 (1993): 535–67.

Elias, Ann. "Flowers and Manliness: The Flower Paintings of George Lambert, Hans Heysen, and Arthur Streeton." *Journal of Interdisciplinary Gender Studies* 10, no. 2 (2008): 14–29.

Elizabeth Arden. "Elizabeth Arden Is in Personal Touch with You." *Sketch*, June 27, 1928, 663.

Elledge, Jim. *The Boys of Fairy Town: Sodomites, Female Impersonators, Third-Sexers, Pansies, Queers, and Sex Morons in Chicago's First Century.* Chicago: Chicago Review Press, 2018.

Ellis, Havelock. *Impressions and Comments.* London: Constable, 1914.

Ellis, Havelock, and John Addington Symonds. *Sexual Inversion: A Critical Edition.* Basingstoke: Palgrave Macmillan, 2008.

Ellis, Havelock, and John Addington Symonds. *Studies in the Psychology of Sex,* volume 1, *Sexual Inversion.* London: Wilson and Macmillan, 1897.

El-Rayess, Miranda. "The Violence of Representation: James, Sargent and the Suffragette." *Critical Quarterly* 53, no. 2 (2011): 30–45.

Erté [Roman Petrovich Tyrtov]. *Things I Remember: An Autobiography.* London: Peter Owen, 1975.

Evangelista, Stefano, ed. *The Reception of Oscar Wilde in Europe.* London: Continuum, 2010.

Evans, Caroline. "Jean Patou's American Mannequins: Early Fashion Shows and Modernism." *Modernism/Modernity* 15, no. 2 (2008): 243–63.

Evans, Caroline. *The Mechanical Smile: Modernism and the First Fashion Shows in France and America, 1900–1929.* New Haven: Yale University Press, 2013.

Evans, Caroline. "Multiple, Movement, Model, Mode: The Mannequin Parade, 1900–1929." In *Fashion and Modernity,* edited by Christopher Breward and Caroline Evans, 125–46. Oxford: Berg, 2005.

Evans, Treyer. "'I Think He's Rather Sweet, Don't You?'" *London Opinion,* week ending October 20, 1928, 8.

Evening Dispatch. "The Hidden Hands." August 20, 1917, 4.

Evening Express. 2nd edn. "Policemen in Petticoats." June 24, 1908, 3.

Evening Express. Extra special. "Street Robberies at Swansea." January 3, 1899, 1.

Ewing, William A. *The Photographic Art of Hoyningen-Huene* (London: Thames and Hudson, 1986).

Fahlman, Betsy. *Pennsylvania Modern: Charles Demuth of Lancaster.* Philadelphia: University of Pennsylvania Press, 1983.

Fairbrother, Trevor J. *John Singer Sargent: The Sensualist.* New Haven: Yale University Press, 2000.

Farfan, Penny. "Noël Coward and Sexual Modernism: *Private Lives* as Queer Comedy." *Modern Drama* 48, no. 4 (2005): 677–88.

Farfan, Penny. *Performing Queer Modernism.* Oxford: Oxford University Press, 2017.

Farjeon, Herbert. "Seen on the Stage." *Vogue* 72, no.1, July 11, 1928, 48–9 and 80.

Farmer, Brett. "The Fabulous Sublimity of Gay Diva Worship." *Camera Obscura* 20, no. 2 (59) (2005): 165–95.

Farnell, Lewis R. *An Oxonian Looks Back*. London: Martin Hopkinson, 1934.

Fassler, Barbara. "Theories of Homosexuality as Sources of Bloomsbury's Androgyny." *Signs* 5, no. 2 (1979): 237–51.

Felski, Rita. "The Counterdiscourse of the Feminine in Three Texts by Wilde, Huysmans, and Sacher-Masoch." *PMLA* 106, no. 5 (1991): 1094–105.

Fiedler, Leslie, *Freaks: Myths and Images of the Secret Self*. New York: Simon and Schuster, 1978.

Fillin-Yeh, Susan. "Dandies, Marginality and Modernism: Georgia O'Keeffe, Marcel Duchamp and Other Cross-Dressers." *Oxford Art Journal* 18, no. 2 (1995): 33–44.

Fillin-Yeh, Susan. "Introduction: New Strategies for a Theory of Dandies." In Susan Fillin-Yeh, *Dandies: Fashion and Finesse in Art and Culture*, 1–34. New York: New York University Press, 2001.

Findlay, Jean. *Chasing Lost Time: The Life of C. K. Moncrieff: Soldier, Spy and Translator*. *London*: Chatto and Windus, 2014.

Fineman, Mia, *Faking It: Manipulated Photography before Photoshop*. New York: Metropolitan Museum of Art, 2012.

Firbank, Ronald, *Sorrow in Sunlight*. London: Brentano, *c*. 1924.

Fish, Anne Harriet. "Preparing for a Raid. The Green Room at Scotland Yard." *Punch* 182 (1932): 613.

"Fitz." "Study of a Film Star—Smoking—a Cigarette." *Punch* 154 (1928): 63.

Flügel, J. C. "The Psychology of Clothes." In *Women and Cross-Dressing 1800–1939*, volume 1 (of 3), edited by Heike Bauer, 39–59. London: Routledge, 2006 [facsimile of 1930 edition].

Flügel, J. C. "Sex Difference in Dress." In *Women and Cross-Dressing 1800–1939*, volume 1 (of 3), edited by Heike Bauer, 60–6. London: Routledge, 2006 [facsimile of 1930 edition].

Fogg, Marnie. *Vintage Weddings: One Hundred Years of Bridal Fashion and Style*. London: Carlton, 2011.

Foldy, Michael S. *The Trials of Oscar Wilde: Deviance, Morality, and Late Victorian Society*. New Haven: Yale University Press, 1997.

Fone, Byrne R. S. "This Other Eden: Arcadia and the Homosexual Imagination." *Journal of Homosexuality* 8, no. 3–4 (1983): 13–34.

Ford, Charles Henri, and Allen Frame. "Interview." *Journal of Contemporary Art, Interviews* (n.d.): unpaginated. Available online: http://www.jca-online.com/ford.html (accessed June 10, 2017).

Ford, Charles Henri, and Parker Tyler. *The Young and Evil*. Paris: Obelisk Press, 1933.

Forster, E. M. *Maurice*, edited by P. N. Furbank. London: Penguin, 2005.

Foster, Hal. "Notes on the First Pop Age (2003)." In *Richard Hamilton*, edited by Hal Foster and Alex Bacon, 45–64. Cambridge, MA: MIT Press, 2010.

Fowler, Rowena. "Why Did Suffragettes Attack Works of Art?" *Journal of Women's History* 2, no. 3 (1991): 109–25.

Frank, Robin Jaffee. *Charles Demuth: Poster Portraits, 1923–1929*. New Haven: Yale University Art Gallery, 1994.

Franklin, Paul B. "Object Choice: Marcel Duchamp's *Fountain* and the Art of Queer Art History." *Oxford Art Journal* 23, no. 1 (2000): 25–50.

Franks, Matt. "Crip/Queer Aesthetics in the Great War." *MFS Modern Fiction Studies* 65, no. 1 (2019): 60–88.

Frantzen, Allen J. *Bloody Good: Chivalry, Sacrifice, and the Great War*. Chicago: University of Chicago Press, 2004.

Funny Folks 15, no. 782. "Oh, Limp Here!" November 16, 1889, 364–5.

Fuss, Diana. "Fashion and the Homospectatorial Look." *Critical Inquiry* 18, no. 4 (1992): 713–37.

Fussell, Paul. *The Great War and Modern Memory*. Oxford: Oxford University Press, 1975.

Garafola, Lynn. *Diaghilev's Ballets Russes*. Oxford: Oxford University Press, 1989.

Garafola, Lynn. "Reconfiguring the Sexes." In *The Ballets Russes and Its World*, edited by Lynn Garafola and Nancy Van Norman Baer, 245–68. New Haven: Yale University Press, 1999.

Garber, Marjorie. *Vested Interests: Cross-Dressing and Cultural Anxiety*. New York: Routledge, 1992.

Gardiner, James. *Gaby Deslys: A Fatal Attraction*. London: Sidgwick and Jackson, 1986.

Garelick, Rhonda. *Rising Star: Dandyism, Gender, and Performance in the Fin de Siècle* Princeton: Princeton University Press, 1998.

Garrity, Jane. "Mary Butt's 'Fanatical Pédérastie': Queer Urban Life in 1920s London and Paris." In *Sapphic Modernities: Sexuality, Women and National Culture*, edited by Laura Doan and Jane Garrity, 233–51. Basingstoke: Palgrave Macmillan, 2006.

Garrity, Jane. "Selling Culture to the 'Civilized': Bloomsbury, British *Vogue*, and the Marketing of National Identity." *Modernism/Modernity* 6, no. 2 (1999): 29–58.

Garrity, Jane. "Virginia Woolf, Intellectual Harlotry, and 1920s British *Vogue*." In *Virginia Woolf in the Age of Mechanical Reproduction*, edited by Pamela L. Caughie, 185–218. New York: Garland, 2000.

Geczy, Adam. *Fashion and Orientalism: Dress, Textiles and Culture from the 17th to the 21st Century*. London: Bloomsbury, 2013.

Geczy, Adam, and Vicki Karaminas, *Fashion's Double: Representations of Fashion in Painting, Photography and Film*. London: Bloomsbury, 2016.

Gelbart, Matthew. "Persona and Voice in the Kinks' Songs of the Late 1960s." *Journal of the Royal Musical Association* 128, no. 2 (2003): 200–41.

Genet, Jean. *Miracle de la rose*. Lyon: Barbezat, 1946.

Genet, Jean. *Notre-Dame-des-Fleurs*. Monte Carlo: [Denoël and Morihien], 1943.

Gertzman, Jay A. "A Scarlet Pansy Goes to War: Subversion, Schlock, and an Early Gay Classic." *Journal of American Culture* 33, no. 3 (2010): 230–9.

Ghilchik, David Louis. "Absent-Minded Young Policeman." *Punch* 184 (1933): 405.

Ghilchik, David Louis. "*Customer.* 'I Want Some New Underwear, Please.'" *Punch* 185 (1933): 427.

Ghilchik, David Louis. "This Charming Photograph, Which Was to Have Been Called 'Joie de Vivre on the Beach at Brighton.'" *Punch* 173 (1927): 431.

Gibson, Robin. *Glyn Philpot, 1884–1937: Edwardian Aesthete to Thirties Modernist.* London: National Portrait Gallery, 1984.

Gibson, Robyn. "Schiaparelli, Surrealism and the Desk Suit." *Dress* 30, no. 1 (2003): 48–58.

Giffney, Noreen, and Myra J. Hird. *Queering the Non/Human.* Aldershot: Ashgate, 2008.

Gill, Miranda. *Eccentricity and the Cultural Imagination in Nineteenth-Century Paris.* Oxford University Press: Oxford, 2009.

Giltner, Leigh Gordon. "A Butterfly Fancy: Part II." *Vogue* (US edn) 30, no. 9, 1907, 228 and 241.

Ginger, Andrew. *Cecil Beaton at Home: An Interior Life.* New York: Rizzoli, 2016.

Glendinning, Victoria. *Edith Sitwell: A Unicorn among Lions.* London: Weidenfeld and Nicolson, 1981.

Glick, Elisa. *Materializing Queer Desire: Oscar Wilde to Andy Warhol.* Albany: State University of New York Press, 2009.

Gluckman, Amy, and Betsy Reed, ed. *Homo Economics: Capitalism, Community, and Lesbian and Gay Life.* Routledge: New York, 1997.

Goddard, Arthur. "'Even as You and I': At Home with the Barnum Freaks." *English Illustrated Magazine* 173 (February 1898): 493–6.

Goldfarb, Alvin. "Gigantic and Miniscule Actors on the Nineteenth-Century American Stage." *Journal of Popular Culture* 10, no. 2 (1976): 267–79.

Goldhill, Simon. *A Very Queer Family Indeed: Sex, Religion, and the Bensons in Victorian Britain.* Chicago: University of Chicago Press, 2016.

Green, Martin. *Children of the Sun: A Narrative of Decadence in England after 1918.* London: Pimlico, 1992.

Green, Stephanie. "Oscar Wilde's *The Woman's World.*" *Victorian Periodicals Review* 30, no. 2 (1997): 102–20.

Greene, Harlan M. "The Multi-Talented Harry Hervey." *Gay and Lesbian Review Worldwide* 24, no. 3 (2017): 24–7.

Greene, Richard. *Edith Sitwell: Avant-Garde Poet, English Genius.* London: Virago, 2011.

Greenfield, Jill, Sean O'Connell, and Chris Reid. "Fashioning Masculinity: *Men Only*, Consumption and the Development of Marketing in the 1930s." *Twentieth Century British History* 10, no. 4 (1999): 457–76.

Greenidge, Terence. *Degenerate Oxford? A Critical Study of Modern University Life.* London: Chapman and Hall, 1930.

Greenidge, Terence. *The Magnificent.* London: Fortune Press, 1933.

Grein, J. T. "Criticisms in Cameo." *Sketch*, March 5, 1930, 454.

Guerlain. "Advertisement." *Vogue* 87, no. 4, February 19, 1936, 49.

Gundle, Stephen. *Glamour: A History*. Oxford: Oxford University Press, 2008.

Gundle, Stephen, and Clino T. Castelli. *The Glamour System*. Basingstoke: Palgrave Macmillan, 2006.

Halberstam, Jack [Judith Halberstam]. *Female Masculinity*. Durham, NC: Duke University Press, 1998.

Halberstam, Jack. *In a Queer Time and Place: Transgender Bodies, Subcultural Lives*. New York: New York University Press, 2005.

Halberstam, Jack. *The Queer Art of Failure*. Durham, NC: Duke University Press, 2011.

Hall, N. John. *Max Beerbohm: A Kind of a Life*. New Haven: Yale University Press, 2002.

Halperin, David M. *How to Be Gay*. Cambridge, MA: Harvard University Press, 2012.

Halperin, David M., and Valerie Traub, ed. *Gay Shame*. Chicago: Chicago University Press, 2009.

Hammer, Martin. "The Independent Group Take on Francis Bacon." *Visual Culture in Britain* 15, no. 1 (2014): 69–89.

Harcourt-Smith, Rosamond. "Oliver Messel's Costume Ball." *Vogue* 89, no. 9, April 28, 1937, 120–1 and 171.

Harper's Bazaar 14, no. 5. "Sur-realisation." August 1936, 57.

Harris, Alexandra. *Romantic Moderns: English Writers, Artists and the Imagination from Virginia Woolf to John Piper*. London: Thames and Hudson, 2010.

Harris, Daniel. "The Death of Camp: Gay Men and Hollywood Diva Worship, from Reverence to Ridicule." *Salmagundi* 112 (1996): 166–91.

Harrison, Charles. "Awful Prophetic Picture of How M. Paderewski Will Appear Next Season." *Punch* 115 (1898): 97.

Hart-Davis, Rupert. *A Catalogue of the Caricatures of Max Beerbohm*. Cambridge, MA: Harvard University Press, 1972.

Hartlepool Mail. "In Woman's Clothes: He Wore Them for Pleasure." November 23, 1942, 8.

Hartzman, Marc. *American Sideshow: An Encyclopedia of History's Most Wondrous and Curiously Strange Performers*. New York: Jeremy P. Tarcher/Penguin, 2006.

Harvey, Robert. "Where's Duchamp? Out Queering the Field." *Yale French Studies* 109 (2006): 82–97.

Haseldon, William Kerridge. "Oh, My Hat!" *Daily Mirror*, November 30, 1934, 13.

Haseldon, William Kerridge. "Our Restaurants at Several Periods." *Daily Mirror*, October 20, 1922, 7.

Haskell, Barbara. *Charles Demuth*. New York: Whitney Museum of American Art, 1988.

Hattrick, Jane. "Collecting and Displaying Identity, Intimacy and Memory in the Staged Interiors of the Royal Couturier Norman Hartnell." In *Narrating Objects, Collecting Stories: Essays in Honour of Professor Susan M. Pearce*, edited by Sandra H. Dudley, Amy Jane Barnes, Jennifer Binnie, Julia Petrov, and Jennifer Walklate, 136–52. London: Routledge, 2012.

Hattrick, Jane. "'An 'Unexpected Pearl': Gender and Performativity in the Public and Private Lives of London Couturier Norman Hartnell." In *Dress History: New

Directions in Theory and Practice, edited by Charlotte Nicklas and Annebella Pollen, 145–60. London: Bloomsbury, 2015.

Hawkins, Joan. "'One of Us': Tod Browning's *Freaks*." In *Freakery: Cultural Spectacles of the Extraordinary Body*, edited by Rosemarie Garland Thomson, 265–76. New York: New York University Press, 1996.

Headley, Gill. *Arthur Jeffress: A Life in Art*. London: Bloomsbury Academic, 2020.

Healy, Murray. "Were We Being Served? Homosexual Representation in Popular British Comedy." *Screen* 36, no. 3 (1995): 243–56.

Heap, Chad. *Slumming: Sexual and Racial Encounters in American Nightlife, 1885–1940*. Chicago: University of Chicago Press, 2009.

Heilmann, Ann. "Wilde's New Women: The New Woman on Wilde." In *The Importance of Reinventing Oscar: Versions of Wilde during the Last 100 Years*, edited by Uwe Böker, Richard Corballis and Julie Hibbard, 135–45. Rodopi: Amsterdam, 2002.

Helmreich, Anne. "John Singer Sargent. 'Carnation, Lily, Lily, Rose,' and the Condition of Modernism in England, 1887." *Victorian Studies* 45, no. 3 (2003): 433–55.

Helt, Brenda S. "Passionate Debates on 'Odious Subjects': Bisexuality and Woolf's Opposition to Theories of Androgyny and Sexual Identity." *Twentieth Century Literature* 56, no. 2 (2010): 131–67.

Herring, Scott. *Queering the Underworld: Slumming, Literature, and the Undoing of Lesbian and Gay History*. Chicago: Chicago University Press, 2007.

Herrmann, Anne. *Queering the Moderns: Poses/Portraits/Performances*. Basingstoke: Palgrave, 2000.

Hervey, Harry. *The Gay Sarong*. London: Thornton Butterworth, 1926.

Hext, Kate. "Just Oscar." *The Times Literary Supplement*, November 23, 2018, 3–4.

Hext, Kate, and Alex Murray. "Introduction." In *Decadence in the Age of Modernism*, edited by Kate Hext and Alex Murray, 1–26. Baltimore: Johns Hopkins University Press, 2019.

Heylmun, Robert. "Letter to the Editor: 'How I Rescued Quentin Crisp's Memoir.'" *Gay and Lesbian Review Worldwide*, 25, no. 5 (2018): 7–8.

Higdon, David Leon. "Gay Sebastian and Cheerful Charles: Homoeroticism in Waugh's *Brideshead* Revisited." *ARIEL: A Review of International English Literature* 25, no. 4 (1994): 77–89.

Hill, Leonard Raven. "The Tug of Peace." *Punch* 149 (1915): 483.

Hilliard, David. "UnEnglish and Unmanly: Anglo-Catholicism and Homosexuality." *Victorian Studies* 25, no. 2 (1982): 181–210.

Hoare, Philip. *Noël Coward: A Biography*. London: Sinclair-Stevenson, 1995.

Hoare, Philip. *Serious Pleasures: The Life of Stephen Tennant*. London: Hamish Hamilton, 1990.

Hoare, Philip. *Wilde's Last Stand: Decadence, Conspiracy and the First World War*. London: Duckworth, 1997.

Hollinghurst, Alan. *The Swimming Pool Library*. London: Chatto and Windus, 1988.

Holmes, Martha Stoddard. "Queering the Marriage Plot: Wilkie Collins's *The Law and the Lady*." In *Victorian Freaks: The Social Context of Freakery in Britain*, edited by Marlene Tromp, 237–58. Columbus: Ohio State University Press, 2008.

Hopkins, Arthur. "Cut Short." *Punch* 111 (1896): 234.

Hornsey, Richard. *The Spiv and the Architect: Unruly Life in Postwar London*. Minneapolis, MN: University of Minnesota Press, 2010.

Horrocks, Jamie. "Asses and Aesthetes: Ritualism and Aestheticism in Victorian Periodical Illustration." *Victorian Periodicals Review* 6, no. 1 (2013): 1–36.

Horst, Horst P. "Schiaparelli's Dress of Black Satin." *Vogue* 85, no. 9, May 1, 1935, 118–19.

Houlbrook, Matt. "'Lady Austin's Camp Boys': Constituting the Queer Subject in 1930s London." *Gender and History* 14, no. 1 (2002): 31–61.

Houlbrook, Matt. "'The Man with the Powder Puff' in Interwar London." *Historical Journal* 50, no. 1 (2007): 145–71.

Houlbrook, Matt. *Prince of Tricksters: The Incredible True Story of Netley Lucas, Gentleman Crook*. Chicago: University of Chicago Press, 2016.

Houlbrook, Matt. *Queer London: Perils and Pleasures in the Sexual* Metropolis, *1918–1957*. Chicago: University of Chicago Press, 2006.

Houlbrook, Matt. "Queer Things: Men and Make-Up between the Wars." In *Gender and Material Culture in Britain since 1600*, edited by Hannah Greig, Jane Hamlett, and Leonie Hannan, 120–37. London: Palgrave, 2016.

Houlbrook, Matt. "Soldier Heroes and Rent Boys: Homosex, Masculinities, and Britishness in the Brigade of Guards, circa 1900–1960." *Journal of British Studies* 42, no. 3 (2003): 351–88.

Houlbrook, Matt. "Thinking Queer: The Social and the Sexual in Interwar Britain." In *British Queer History: New Approaches and Perspectives*, edited by Brian Lewis, 134–64. Manchester: Manchester University Press, 2013.

Houlbrook, Matt, and Chris Waters. "*The Heart in Exile*: Detachment and Desire in 1950s London." *History Workshop Journal* 62 (2006): 142–65.

"How." "The Well Dressed Man." *Vogue* (US edn) 30, no. 11, September 12, 1907, 292.

Hoyt, Nancy. "Three-Cornered Love: Part III." *Harper's Bazaar* 6, no. 4, July 1932, 62, 88, and 90–1.

Hull Daily Mail. "Man Dressed as a Woman." October 6, 1909, 3.

Hussey, Mark. "Clive Bell. 'A Fathead and Voluptuary': Conscientious Objection and British Masculinity." In *Queer Bloomsbury*, edited by Brenda Helt and Madelyn Detloff, 240–57. Edinburgh: Edinburgh University Press, 2016.

Hutchins, Frances E. "The Pleasures of Discovery: Representations of Queer Space by Brassaï and Colette." In *Lesbian Inscriptions in Francophone Society and Culture*, edited by Renate Günther and Wendy Michallat, 189–203. Durham: University of Durham, 2007.

Hynes, Edward. "'Oh, Sir, Spare a Copper.'" *Men Only* 3, no. 12, November 1936, 95.

Hynes, Samuel. *The Auden Generation: Literature and Politics in England in the 1930s*. London: Bodley Head, 1976.

Ibson, John. "Masculinity under Fire: *Life's* Presentation of Camaraderie and Homoeroticism before, during, and after the Second World War." In *Looking at "Life" Magazine*, edited by Erika Doss, 178–99. Washington, DC: Smithsonian Institution Press, 2001.

Ives, George. *Man Bites Man: The Scrapbook of an Edward Eccentric*, edited by Paul Sieveking. London: Jay Landesmann, 1980.

Janes, Dominic. "'The Catholic Florist': Flowers and Deviance in the Mid-Nineteenth-Century Church of England." *Visual Culture in Britain* 12, no. 1 (2011): 77–96.

Janes, Dominic. "Cecil Beaton, Richard Hamilton and the Queer, Transatlantic Origins of Pop Art." *Visual Culture in Britain* 16, no. 3 (2015): 308–30.

Janes, Dominic. "Eminent Victorians, Bloomsbury Queerness and John Maynard Keynes' *The Economic Consequences of the Peace* (1919)." *Literature and History* 23, no. 1 (2014): 19–32.

Janes, Dominic. "Eminently Queer Victorians and the Bloomsbury Group's Critique of British Leadership." In *The Palgrave Handbook of Masculinity and Political Culture in Europe: From Antiquity to the Contemporary World*, edited by Sean Brady, Christopher Fletcher, Rachel Moss, and Lucy Riall, 359–78. Basingstoke: Palgrave, 2018.

Janes, Dominic. *Oscar Wilde Prefigured: Queer Fashioning and British Caricature, 1750–1900*. Chicago: University of Chicago Press, 2016.

Janes, Dominic. *Picturing the Closet: Male Secrecy and Homosexual Visibility in Britain*. Oxford: Oxford University Press, 2015.

Janes, Dominic. *Victorian Reformation: The Fight over Idolatry in the Church of England, 1840–1860*. Oxford: Oxford University Press, 2009.

Janes, Dominic. *Visions of Queer Martyrdom from John Henry Newman to Derek Jarman*. Chicago: University of Chicago Press, 2015.

Janes, Dominic. "When 'Perverts' Were Religious: The Protestant Sexualisation of Asceticism in Nineteenth-Century Britain, India and Ireland." *Cultural and Social History* 11, no. 3 (2014): 425–39.

Jennings, Rebecca. "From 'Woman-Loving Woman' to 'Queer': Historiographical Perspectives on Twentieth-Century British Lesbian History." *History Compass* 5, no. 6 (2007): 1901–20.

Jepson, Edgar. "The Man with the Green Carnation." *Men Only* 1, no. 2, January 1936, 90–3.

Jeremiah, David. *Representations of British Motoring*. Manchester: Manchester University Press, 2007.

Jobling, Paul. *Man Appeal: Advertising, Modernism and Menswear*. Berg: Oxford, 2005.

John Bull. "The Imitation Woman." July 21, 1923, 16.

Johnson, David K. *Buying Gay: How Physique Entrepreneurs Sparked a Movement*. New York: Columbia University Press, 2019.

Jones, Max. "'National Hero and Very Queer Fish': Empire, Sexuality and the British Remembrance of General Gordon, 1918–72." *Twentieth Century British History* 26, no. 2 (2014): 175–202.

Jones, Timothy Willem. *Sexual Politics in the Church of England, 1857–1957*. Oxford: Oxford University Press, 2013.

Jones, Timothy Willem. "'Unduly Conscious of Her Sex': Priesthood, Female Bodies, and Sacred Space in the Church of England." *Women's History Review* 21, no. 4 (2012): 639–55.

Joseph, Abigail. "Queer Things: Victorian Objects and the Fashioning of Homosexuality." PhD Dissertation, Columbia University, USA, 2012.

Joseph, Abigail. "'A Wizard of Silks and Tulle': Charles Worth and the Queer Origins of Couture." *Victorian Studies* 56, no. 2 (2014): 251–79.

Kafer, Alison. *Feminist Crip Queer*. Bloomington: Indiana University Press, 2013.

Kahan, Benjamin. "Queer Modernism." In *A Handbook of Modernism Studies*, edited by Jean-Michel Rabaté, 347–62. Chichester: Wiley-Blackwell, 2013.

Kaplan, Joel H., and Sheila Stowell. *Theatre and Fashion: Oscar Wilde to the Suffragettes*. Cambridge: Cambridge University Press, 1994.

Kates, Steven M. "Camp as Cultural Capital: Further Elaboration of a Consumption Taste." *Advances in Consumer Research* 28 (2001): 334–9.

Kavanagh, Julie. *Secret Muses: The Life of Frederick Ashton*. London: Faber and Faber, 1996.

Kelleway, Philip. *Highly Desirable: The Zinkeisen Sisters and Their Legacy*. Leiston: Leiston Press, 2008.

Kelley, Carolyn A. "Aubrey Beardsley and H. D.'s *Astrid*: The Ghost and Mrs. Pugh of Decadent Aestheticism and Modernity." *Modernism/Modernity* 15, no. 3 (2008): 447–75.

Kennison, Rebecca. "Clothes Make the (Wo)man: Marlene Dietrich and 'Double Drag.'" *Journal of Lesbian Studies* 6, no. 2 (2002): 147–56.

Kiernan, Robert F. *Frivolity Unbound: Six Masters of the Camp Novel*. New York: Continuum, 1990.

Killeen, Jarlath. *The Fairy Tales of Oscar Wilde*. Aldershot: Ashgate, 2007.

King, Amy M. *Bloom: The Botanical Vernacular in the English Novel*. Oxford: Oxford University Press, 2003.

Kingston, Angela. *Oscar Wilde as a Character in Victorian Fiction*. Basingstoke: Palgrave Macmillan, 2007.

Kirchick, James. "Pictorial Physiques: James Kirchick on the Links between Bodybuilding, Capitalism and Gay Rights." *The Times Literary Supplement*, no. 6071, August 7, 2019, 28.

Knight, Frances. *Victorian Christianity at the Fin de Siècle: The Culture of English Religion in a Decadent Age*. London: I.B. Tauris, 2016.

Knox, Edmund [pseud. "Evoe"], text, and Ernest H. Shepard, images. "The Renegade Faun." *Punch* 172, Summer number (May 23, 1927): unpaginated.

Koestenbaum, Wayne. *The Queen's Throat: Opera, Homosexuality, and the Mystery of Desire*. London: GMP, 1993.

Koven, Seth. *Slumming: Sexual and Social Politics in Victorian London*. Princeton: Princeton University Press, 2004.

Ksinan, Catharine. "Wilde as Editor of *Woman's World*: Fighting a Dull Slumber in Stale Certitudes." *English Literature in Transition, 1880–1920* 41, no. 4 (1998): 408–26.

Kunzel, Regina. "The Power of Queer History." *American Historical Review* 123, no. 5 (2018): 1560–82.

Laing, Lucy. *David and Jonathan; or, the Mystery of the Farmer's Boy*. London: Pickering and Inglis, 1936.

Laity, Cassandra. *H.D. and the Victorian Fin de Siècle: Gender, Modernism, Decadence*, Cambridge Studies in American Literature and Culture 104. Cambridge: Cambridge University Press, 2009.

Lambert, Agnes. "The Ceremonial Use of Flowers: A Sequel." *Nineteenth Century* 7, 1880, 808–27.

Lane-Norcott, Maurice. "This Girl-Less Olympia." *London Opinion*, week ending October 20, 1928, 13–14.

Lasc, Anca L. "Angels and Rebels: The Obsessions and Transgressions of the Modern Interior." In *Designing the French Interior: The Modern Home and Mass Media*, edited by Anca L. Lasc, Georgina Downey, and Mark Taylor, 47–58. London: Bloomsbury, 2015.

Latimer, Tirza True. "Balletomania: A Sexual Disorder?" *GLQ: A Journal of Lesbian and Gay Studies* 5, no. 2 (1999): 173–97.

Latimer, Tirza True. *Eccentric Modernisms: Making Differences in the History of American Art*. Berkeley: University of California Press, 2017.

Lawrence, D. H. *Pansies*. London: Stephenson, 1929.

Lawrence, D. H. *Pansies: Poems*. London: Martin Secker, 1930.

Lawrence, David Haldane. "Chorus Boys: Words, Music and Queerness (*c.* 1900–*c.* 1936)." *Studies in Musical Theatre* 3, no. 2 (2009): 157–69.

Ledger, Sally. "Wilde Women and *The Yellow Book*: The Sexual Politics of Aestheticism and Decadence." *English Literature in Transition, 1880–1920* 50, no. 1 (2007): 5–26.

Lee, Raymond M. "'The Man Who Committed a Hundred Burglaries': Mark Benney's Strange and Eventful Sociological Career." *Journal of the History of the Behavioral Sciences* 51, no. 4 (2015): 409–33.

Leech, John. "The Great Social Evil." *Punch* 33, September 12, 1857: 114.

Legman, G. "The Language of Homosexuality: An American Glossary." In George William Henry, *Sex Variants: A Study of Homosexual Patterns*, volume 1 (of 2), 1149–79. New York: Hoeber, 1941.

Lepape, Claude, and Thierry Defert. *The Art of Georges Lepape: From the Ballets Russes to "Vogue,"* trans. Jane Brenton. London: Thames and Hudson, 1984.

Lewis, Brian, ed. *British Queer History: New Approaches and Perspectives*. Manchester: Manchester University Press, 2013.

Lindsay, Cecile. "Bodybuilding: A Postmodern Freak Show." In *Freakery: Cultural Spectacles of the Extraordinary Body*, edited by Rosemarie Garland Thomson, 356–67. New York: New York University Press, 1996.

Linkof, Ryan. *Public Images: Celebrity, Photojournalism, and the Making of the Tabloid Press*. London: Bloomsbury, 2018.

Linkof, Ryan. "Shooting Charles Henri Ford: Cecil Beaton and the Erotics of the 'Low' in the New York Tabloids." *Études Photographiques* 29 (2012): unpaginated. Available online: http://etudesphotographiques.revues.org/3478 (accessed July 8, 2015).

Linkof, Ryan. "'Those Young Men Who Come Down from Oxford and Write Gossip': Society Gossip, Homosexuality and the Logic of Revelation in the Interwar Popular Press." In *British Queer History: New Approaches and Perspectives*, edited by Brian Lewis, 109–33. Manchester: Manchester University Press, 2013.

London Daily News. "A Rogue and a Vagabond." January 16, 1901, 9.

London Evening Standard. "The Trial of Boulton and Park." May 10, 1871, 6–7.

Looby, Christopher. "Flowers of Manhood: Race, Sex and Floriculture from Thomas Wentworth Higginson to Robert Mapplethorpe." *Criticism* 37, no. 1 (1995): 109–56.

Lord, William Barry [pseud. "W. B. L."]. *Freaks of Fashion, with Illustrations of the Changes in the Corset and the Crinoline from Remote Periods to the Present Time*. London: Ward, Lock and Tyler, 1870.

Love, Heather. *Feeling Backward: Loss and the Politics of Queer History*. Cambridge, MA: Harvard University Press, 2007.

Low, David. "Are Our Women Degenerating?" *Star*, December 30, 1924, 3.

Luckhurst, Nicola. *Bloomsbury in "Vogue,"* Bloomsbury Heritage Series 19. London: Cecil Woolf, 1998.

Lugowski, David. "Ginger Rogers and Gay Men? Queer Film Studies, Richard Dyer, and Diva Worship." In *Screening Genders*, edited by Krin Gabbard and William Luhr, 95–110. New Brunswick, NJ: Rutgers University Press, 2008.

MacGowan, Kenneth. "Seen on the Stage." *Vogue* (US edn) 59, no. 9, May 1, 1922, 62–3, 108, 110, 112, and 114.

MacLeod, Kirsten. "The Queerness of Being 1890 in 1922: Carl van Vechten and the New Decadence." In *Decadence in the Age of Modernism*, edited by Kate Hext and Alex Murray, 229–50. Baltimore: Johns Hopkins University Press, 2019.

Madden, Ed. "Say It with Flowers: The Poetry of Marc-Andre Raffalovich." *College Literature* 24, no. 1 (1997): 11–27.

Mahoney, Kristin. *Literature and Politics of Post-Victorian Decadence*. Cambridge: Cambridge University Press, 2015.

Mahood, Aurelea. "Fashioning Readers: The Avant Garde and British *Vogue*, 1920–9." *Women: A Cultural Review* 13, no. 1 (2002): 37–47.

Maltz, Diana. "'Baffling Arrangements': Vernon Lee and John Singer Sargent in Queer Tangier." In *Rethinking the Interior, c. 1867–1896: Aestheticism and Arts and Crafts*, edited by Jason Edwards and Imogen Hart, 185–210. Farnham: Ashgate, 2010.

Manchester Courier and Lancashire General Advertiser. "In the Twinkling of an Eye." August 29, 1901, 8.

Mann, Philip. *The Dandy at Dusk: Taste and Melancholy in the Twentieth Century*. London: Head of Zeus, 2017.

Mannix, Daniel P. *Freaks: We Who Are Not as Others*. San Francisco: Research Publications, 1976.

Mapplethorpe, Robert. *Flora: The Complete Flowers*, edited by Mark Holborn and Dimitri Levas. London: Phaidon, 2016.

Marcus, Sharon, *The Drama of Celebrity*. Princeton: Princeton University Press, 2019.

Marhoefer, Laurie. *Sex and the Weimar Republic: German Homosexual Emancipation and the Rise of the Nazis*. Toronto: University of Toronto Press, 2015.

"Mariegold." "Mariegold at a Very Ducal Affair." *Sketch*, March 8, 1933, 408–9.

"Mariegold." "Mariegold Broadcasts." *Sketch*, April 26, 1933a, 144–5.

"Mariegold." "Mariegold Broadcasts." *Sketch*, May 3, 1933b, 188–9.

"Mariegold." "Mariegold Broadcasts." *Sketch*, May 24, 1933c, 324–5.

"Mariegold." "Mariegold Broadcasts." *Sketch*, June 28, 1933d, 552–3.

"Mariegold." "Mariegold in Society." *Sketch*, March 13, 1920, 482–3.

"Mariegold." "Mariegold in Society." *Sketch*, November 10, 1926, 281.

"Mariegold." "Mariegold in Society." *Sketch*, January 12, 1927a, 56–7.

"Mariegold." "Mariegold in Society." *Sketch*, March 2, 1927b, 392–3.

"Mariegold." "Mariegold in Society." *Sketch*, April 13, 1927c, 68–9.

"Mariegold." "Mariegold in Society." *Sketch*, June 8, 1927d, 476–7.

"Mariegold." "Mariegold in Society." *Sketch*, August 17, 1927e, 296.

"Mariegold." "Mariegold in Society." *Sketch*, August 24, 1927f, 344–5.

"Mariegold." "Mariegold in Society." *Sketch*, September 21, 1927g, 540–1.

"Mariegold." "Mariegold in Society." *Sketch*, March 28, 1928, 585.

"Mariegold." "Mariegold in Society." *Sketch*, January 16, 1929a, 88–9.

"Mariegold." "Mariegold in Society." *Sketch*, December 4, 1929b, 482–3.

"Mariegold." "Mariegold in Society." *Sketch*, January 15, 1930a, 88.

"Mariegold." "Mariegold in Society." *Sketch*, May 14, 1930b, 310–11.

"Mariegold." "Mariegold is Amused." *Sketch*, March 1, 1933, 364.

Markley, A. A. "E. M. Forster's Reconfigured Gaze and the Creation of a Homoerotic Subjectivity." *Twentieth Century Literature* 47, no. 2 (2001): 268–92.

Marler, Regina. "The Bloomsbury Love Triangle." In *Queer Bloomsbury*, edited by Brenda Helt and Madelyn Detloff, 135–51. Edinburgh: Edinburgh University Press, 2016.

Marshik, Celia. *At the Mercy of Their Clothes: Modernism, the Middlebrow, and British Garment Culture*. New York: Columbia University Press, 2017.

Martin, Richard. *Fashion and Surrealism*. London: Thames and Hudson, 1988.

Masters, Brian. *The Life of E. F. Benson*. London: Chatto and Windus, 1991.

Mazurek, Monika. "Perverts to Rome: Protestant Gender Roles and the Abjection of Catholicism." *Victorian Literature and Culture* 44, no. 3 (2016): 687–723.

McBrinn, Joseph. "'Nothing Is More Terrifying to Me than to See Ernest Thesiger Sitting under the Lamplight Doing His Embroidery': Ernest Thesiger (1879–1961). 'Expert Embroiderer.'" *Text: For the Study of Textile Art, Design and History* 43 (2015–16): 20–6.

McBrinn, Joseph. "Queer Hobbies: Ernest Thesiger and Interwar Embroidery." *Textile: Journal of Cloth and Culture* 15, no. 3 (2017): 1–31.

McCormack, Jerusha Hull. *John Gray: Poet, Dandy, and Priest.* Hanover, NH: Brandeis University Press, 1991.

McDonnell, Patricia. "'Essentially Masculine:' Marsden Hartley, Gay Identity, and the Wilhelmine German Military." *Art Journal* 56, no. 2 (1997): 62–8.

McDowell, Colin. "Le Freak C'est Chic." *The Sunday Times Supplement*, October 23, 2005, 23.

McGarry, Molly, and Fred Wasserman. *Becoming Visible: An Illustrated History of Lesbian and Gay Life in Twentieth-Century America.* New York: Penguin, 1998.

McKenna, Neil. *Fanny and Stella: The Young Men Who Shocked Victorian England.* London: Faber and Faber, 2013.

McLaren, Angus. *Playboys and Mayfair Men: Crime, Class, Masculinity and Fascism in 1930s London.* Baltimore: Johns Hopkins University Press, 2017.

McLaren, Angus. "Smoke and Mirrors: Willy Clarkson and the Role of Disguises in Inter-War England." *Journal of Social History* 40, no. 3 (2007): 597–618.

McLaren, Angus. *The Trials of Masculinity: Policing Sexual Boundaries.* Chicago: University of Chicago Press, 1997.

McLaren, Angus. "Everything Degenerates: The Queer Buttonhole." In *The Languages of Flowers: Media of Floral Communication*, edited by Isabel Kranz, Alexander Schwan, and Elke Wittrock, 401–20. Berlin: Wilhelm Fink, 2016.

McLaren, Angus, and Georgio Riello. *Luxury: A Rich History.* Oxford: Oxford University Press, 2016.

McNeil, Peter. "Designing Women: Gender, Sexuality and the Interior Decorator, *c.* 1890–1940." *Art History* 17, no. 4 (1994): 631–57.

McQuillen, Colleen. "From *The Fairground Booth* to Futurism: The Sartorial and Material Estrangement of Masquerade." *Russian Review* 71, no. 3 (2012): 413–35.

McRuer, Robert. "Compulsory Able-bodiedness and Queer/Disabled Existence." In *The Disability Studies Reader*, 2nd edn, edited by Lennard J. David, 301–8. New York: Routledge, 2006.

McWilliam, Rohan. "Elsa Lanchester and Bohemian London in the Early Twentieth Century." *Women's History Review* 23, no. 2 (2014): 171–87.

Mendelssohn, Michèle. *Making Oscar Wilde.* Oxford: Oxford University Press, 2018.

Men Only 3, no. 11. "'Well, Sir, I Think We're the Type Who Can Wear a Tie Such as This!'" October 1936, 77.

Men's Wear Organiser 12, no. 2. "Male Mannequins at Olympia Show Artificial Silk Goods to the World." February 1929, 74–5.

Men's Wear Organiser 17, no. 4. "The Figures Tailors Dream Of." April 1931, 241.

"A Mere Man." "This Dress Question." *Britannia* 2, no, 16, January 11, 1929, 110.

Meyer, Moe, ed. *The Politics and Poetics of Camp*. London: Routledge, 1994.

Meyer, Richard. "Threesomes: Lincoln Kirstein's Queer Arithmetic." In *Lincoln Kirstein's Modern*, edited by Samantha Friedman and Jodi Hauptman, 98–105. New York: Museum of Modern Art, 2019.

Meyers, Jeffrey. "D. H. Lawrence, Comedian." *Salmagundi* 152 (Fall 2006): 205–22.

Miller, Henry J. "John Leech and the Shaping of the Victorian Cartoon: The Context of Respectability." *Victorian Periodicals Review* 42, no. 3 (2009): 267–91.

Miller, James E. "T. S. Eliot's 'Uranian Muse': The Verdenal Letters." *ANQ: A Quarterly Journal of Short Articles, Notes and Reviews* 11, no. 4 (1998): 4–20.

Miller, Monica L. *Slaves to Fashion: Black Dandyism and the Styling of Black Diasporic Identity*. Durham, NC: Duke University Press, 2009.

Miller, Tyrus. "Ridiculously Modern Marsden: Tragicomic Form and Queer Modernity." *Modernist Cultures* 2, no. 2 (2006): 87–101.

Mills, Arthur Wallis. "The Freak-Merchants; or, the Bright Young People." *Punch* 178, *Almanack* (1930): unpaginated.

Mills, Arthur Wallis. "*The Girl*. 'But, Darling, You've Chosen a Reddish Tie.'" *Punch* 177 (1929): 341.

Mills, Arthur Wallis. "An Inducement." *Punch* 130 (1906): 261.

Mills, Arthur Wallis. "Our Motor Emporiums." *Punch* 143 (1912): 167.

Mills, Arthur Wallis. "*Visitor (Who Has Been Asked to Criticize the Latest Masterpiece)*." *Punch* 170 (1926): 461.

Mills, Robert. *Seeing Sodomy in the Middle Ages*. Chicago: University of Chicago Press, 2015.

Mitchell, Michael. *Monsters of the Gilded Age: The Photographs of Charles Eisenmann*. Toronto: Gage Publishing, 1979.

Mitchell, Rebecca N. "The Victorian Fancy Dress Ball, 1870–1900," *Fashion Theory* 21, no. 3 (2017): 291–315.

Moers, Ellen. *The Dandy: Brummell to Beerbohm*. London: Secker and Warburg, 1960.

Mollow, Anna, and McRuer, Robert. "Introduction." In *Sex and Disability*, edited by Robert Mollow and Anna McRuer, 1–34. Durham, NC: Duke University Press, 2012.

Moore, Lisa L. *Sister Arts: The Erotics of Lesbian Landscapes*. Minneapolis: University of Minnesota Press, 2011.

Morning Post. "Charge of Personating Women." May 14, 1870, 6.

Morris, Roy. *Declaring His Genius: Oscar Wilde in America*. Cambridge, MA: Harvard University Press, 2013.

Morrow, Edwin. "With Amateur Theatricals at the Front and War-Work at Home." *Punch* 150 (1916): 411.

Morrow, George. "The Royal Academy—Second Depressions." *Punch* 160 (1920): 397.

Mort, Frank. "Accessible Sovereignty: Popular Attitudes to the British Monarchy during the Great War." *Social History* 45, no. 3 (2020): 328–59.

Mort, Frank. "On Tour with the Prince: Monarchy, Imperial Politics and Publicity in the Prince of Wales's Dominion Tours, 1919–20." *Twentieth Century British History* 29, no. 1 (2018): 25–37.

Mort, Frank. "Safe for Democracy: Constitutional Politics, Popular Spectacle, and the British Monarchy, 1910–1914." *Journal of British Studies* 58, no. 1 (2019):109–41.

Mosse, George Lachmann. *The Image of Man: The Creation of Modern Masculinity.* Oxford: Oxford University Press, 1996.

Muir, Robin. *Cecil Beaton's Bright Young Things.* London: National Portrait Gallery, 2020.

Mumford, Kevin J. *Interzones: Black/White Sex Districts in Chicago and New York in the Early Twentieth Century.* New York: Columbia University Press, 1997.

Munt, Sally. *Queer Attachments: The Cultural Politics of Shame.* Aldershot: Ashgate, 2008.

Murphy, Kevin P. *Political Manhood: Red Bloods, Mollycoddles, and the Politics of Progressive Era Reform.* New York: Columbia University Press, 2008.

Murray, Alex. "Decadence Revisited: Evelyn Waugh and the Afterlife of the 1890s." *Modernism/Modernity* 22, no. 3 (2015): 593–607.

Muschamp, Herbert. *Mapplethorpe: The Complete Flowers.* Düsseldorf: teNeues, 2006.

Nagel, Rebecca. "Naming Plants in *The Garden* by Vita Sackville-West." *Interdisciplinary Studies in Literature and Environment* 22, no. 2 (2015): 241–63.

Nash, John. *Poisonous Plants: Deadly, Dangerous and Suspect.* London: Frederick Etchells and Hugh MacDonald, 1927.

Nead, Lynda. *Victorian Babylon: People, Streets and Images in Nineteenth-Century London.* New Haven: Yale University Press, 2000.

Neave, Jack. *The Surrender of Silence: The Memoirs of Ironfoot Jack, King of the Bohemians,* edited by Colin Stanley. London: Strange Attractor, 2018.

Newton, Esther. "The Mythic Mannish Lesbian: Radclyffe Hall and the New Woman." *Signs* 9, no. 2 (1984): 557–75.

Nichols, Beverley. *Down the Garden Path.* London: Jonathan Cape, 1932.

Nichols, Beverley. *Father Figure.* London: Heinemann, 1972.

Nicholson, Virginia. *Among the Bohemians: Experiments in Living, 1900–1939.* London: Penguin Books, 2002.

Norris, Arthur. "What a Large Dolly That Gentleman's Got!" *Punch* 136 (1909): 161.

Norton, Rictor, ed. "Queen of Camp, 1874." In *Homosexuality in Nineteenth-Century England: A Sourcebook* (December 4, 2018; expanded October 30, 2019): unpaginated. Available online: http://rictornorton.co.uk/eighteen/1874camp.htm.

Novak, Daniel A. "Picturing Wilde: Christopher Millard's 'Iconography of Oscar Wilde.'" *Nineteenth-Century Contexts* 32, no. 4 (2010): 305–55.

Odle, Alan. "Theatrical First Nights down the Ages." *Vogue* 65, no. 5, early March 1925, 73.

O'Neill, Alistair. *London: After a Fashion.* London: Reaktion, 2007.

Oram, Alison. "Cross-Dressing and Transgender." In *The Modern History of Sexuality*, edited by H. G. Cocks and Matt Houlbrook, 256–85. Basingstoke: Palgrave Macmillan, 2006.

Oram, Alison. *Her Husband Was a Woman! Women's Gender-Crossing in Modern British Popular Culture*. London: Routledge, 2007.

Orwell, George. *Down and Out in Paris and London*. London: Gollancz, 1933.

Oxenhandler, Neal. "Jean Cocteau: Theatre as Parade." *Yale French Studies* 14 (1954): 71–5.

Packer, William. *The Art of "Vogue" Covers*. London: Octopus, 1980.

Packer, William. *Fashion Drawing in "Vogue."* London: Thames and Hudson, 1983.

Paderewski, Ignacy Jan. "Piano Playing and Muscle." *Physical Culture* 1, no. 3 (1898): 189–91.

Page, Judith, and Elise L. Smith. *Women, Literature, and the Domestic Landscape: England's Disciples of Flora, 1780–1870*. Cambridge: Cambridge University Press, 2014.

"Palmer." "'Frankly Speaking, I Think a Lot of Women Join Up with a View to Matrimony—Present Company Excepted of Course.'" *Men Only* 25, no. 101, April 1944, 42.

Paoletti, Jo B. *Sex and Unisex: Fashion, Feminism, and the Sexual Revolution*. Bloomington: Indiana University Press, 2015.

Parker, Dorothy. "The Bride He Left behind Him." *Vogue* 51, no. 10, late May 1918, 53 and 74.

Parker, Dorothy. "Lovely Woman as the Honest Labouring Man." *Vogue* 54, no. 3, early August 1919, 31 and 78.

Patmore, Derek. "Cecil Beaton Designs for Himself." *Harper's Bazaar* 6, no. 6, September 1932, 57.

Peakman, Julie. *The Pleasure's All Mine: A History of Perverse Sex*. London: Reaktion, 2013.

Peddie, Tom. "Garden Suburb Amenities." *Punch* 143 (1912): 35.

Pellegrini, Ann. "After Sontag: Future Notes on Camp." In *A Companion to Lesbian, Gay, Bisexual, Transgender and Queer Studies*, edited by George E. Haggerty and Molly McGarry, 168–93. Oxford: Blackwell, 2007.

Pender, Anne. "'Modernist Madonnas': Dorothy Todd, Madge Garland and Virginia Woolf." *Women's History Review* 16, no. 4 (2007): 519–33.

Penny Illustrated Paper. "The Last Vile Fashion." June 4, 1870, 354.

Pepper, Terence. *Dorothy Wilding: The Pursuit of Perfection*. London: National Portrait Gallery Publications, 1991.

Photopress and "E. P." "Strange—but True. The Bogeymen and the Beauty Spider." *Sketch*, January 9, 1929, 47.

Pick, Michael. *Norman Hartnell: The Biography*. London: Zuleika, 2019.

Pickering, Michael, *Blackface Minstrelsy in Britain*. London: Routledge, 2017.

Pine, Richard. *The Dandy and the Herald: Manners, Mind and Morals from Brummell to Durrell*. New York: St. Martin's Press, 1988.

Pitts, Victoria. "Visibly Queer: Body Technologies and Sexual Politics." *Sociological Quarterly* 41, no. 3 (2000): 443–63.

Plank, George Wolfe. Untitled cover illustration. *Vogue* (US edn) 55, no. 8, October 15, 1919, cover.

Portmann, John. *Women and Gay Men in the Postwar Period*. London: Bloomsbury Academic, 2016.

Postrel, Virginia. *The Power of Glamour: Longing and the Art of Visual Persuasion*. London: Simon and Schuster, 2013.

Potvin, John. *Bachelors of a Different Sort: Queer Aesthetics, Material Culture and the Modern Interior in Britain*. Manchester: Manchester University Press, 2014.

Potvin, John. "Housing the New Dandy, 1920–1924." In *Designing the French Interior: The Modern Home and Mass Media*, edited by Anca I. Lasc, Georgina Downey, and Mark Taylor, 191–201. London: Bloomsbury, 2015.

Prime-Sevenson, Edward Irenaeus [pseud. "Xavier Mayne"]. *The Intersexes: A History of Similisexualism as a Problem in Social Life*. Rome: privately printed, 1908.

Proust, Marcel. *Cities of the Plain*, 2 volumes, trans. C. K. Scott Moncrieff. New York: Albert and Charles Boni, 1927.

Pugh, Martin. *We Danced All Night: A Social History of Britain between the Wars*. London: Bodley Head, 2008.

Punch 167. "The New Coiffure." (1924): 433–4.

Punch 157. "Pretty Play at Putney." (1919): 253.

Purce, Emma. "Scales of Normality: Displays of Extreme Weight and Weight Loss in Blackpool 1920–1940." *Cultural and Social History* 14, no. 5 (2017), 669–89.

Ramos-Gay, Ignacio. "'Partly American!': Sarah Bernhardt's Transnational Disability in the American Press (1915–1918)." *Atlantis: Journal of the Spanish Association for Anglo-American Studies* 40, no. 2 (2018): 63–80.

Rault, Jasmine. "Designing Sapphic Modernity: 1926." In *Networks of Design: Proceedings of the 2008 Annual International Conference of the Design History Society (UK)*, edited by Jonathan Glynne, Fiona Hackney and Viv Minton, 472–6. Boca Raton: Universal-Publishers, 2009.

Reed, Christopher. *Art and Homosexuality: A History of Ideas*. Oxford: Oxford University Press, 2011.

Reed, Christopher. "Bloomsbury Bashing: Homophobia and the Politics of Criticism in the Eighties." In *Queer Bloomsbury*, edited by Brenda Helt and Madelyn Detloff, 36–63. Edinburgh: Edinburgh University Press, 2016.

Reed, Christopher. *Bloomsbury Rooms: Modernism, Subculture and Domesticity*. New Haven: Yale University Press, 2004.

Reed, Christopher. "Design for (Queer) Living: Sexual Identity, Performance, and Décor in British *Vogue*, 1922–1926." *GLQ: A Journal of Lesbian and Gay Studies* 12, no. 3 (2006): 377–404.

Reed, Christopher. "A *Vogue* That Dare Not Speak Its Name: Sexual Subculture during the Editorship of Dorothy Todd, 1922–26." *Fashion Theory: The Journal of Dress, Body and Culture* 10, no. 1–2 (2006): 39–72.

Reed, Edward Tennyson. "Celebrities Out of Their Element.—II. Mr. Sandow in the Throes of Light Verse—Which We Understand He Varies with a Little Needlework or Delicate Embroidery." *Punch* 140 (1911): 13.

Reis, Elizabeth. *Bodies in Doubt: An American History of Intersex*. Baltimore: Johns Hopkins University Press, 2009.

Reynolds, Frank. "The Academy Brightens Cricket (after H. S. Tuke, R.A.)." *Punch* 163, summer number (1922): unpaginated.

Ribeiro, Aileen. *Clothing Art: The Visual Culture of Fashion, 1600–1914*. New Haven: Yale University Press, 2017.

Richards, Cindy, ed. *Society in "Vogue."* London: Condé Nast, 1992.

Richards, David A. J. *The Rise of Gay Rights and the Fall of the British Empire: Liberal Resistance and the Bloomsbury Group*. Cambridge: Cambridge University Press, 2013.

Richardson, Elsa. "New Queer Histories: Laura Doan's *Disturbing Practices* and the Constance Maynard Archive." *Women's History Review* 25, no. 1 (2016): 161–8.

Richlin, Amy. "Eros Underground: Greece and Rome in Gay Print Culture, 1953–65." *Journal of Homosexuality* 49, no. 3–4 (2005): 421–61.

Rodney, Frances [Mrs. James Rodney]. "London Laurels." *Harper's Bazaar* 15, no. 1, October 1936, 52–3 and 122.

Rogers, Stanley. *Freak Ships*. London: John Lane, 1936.

Ross, Charlotte. *Eccentricity and Sameness: Discourses on Lesbianism and Desire between Women in Italy, 1860s–1930s*. Oxford: Peter Lang, 2015.

Ross, Josephine. *Beaton in "Vogue."* London: Thames and Hudson, 1986.

Rowbotham, Sheila. *Edward Carpenter: A Life of Liberty and Love*. London: Verso, 2008.

Russell, John, ed. *A Portrait of Logan Pearsall Smith Drawn from His Letters and Diaries*. London: Dropmore, 1950.

Sackville-West, Vita. "The Edwardians below Stairs." *Vogue* 78, no. 11, November 25, 1931, 55–7.

Samuels, Ellen Jean. "My Body, My Closet: Invisible Disability and the Limits of Coming-Out Discourse." *GLQ: A Journal of Lesbian and Gay Studies* 9, no. 1–2 (2003): 233–55.

Sartiliot, Claudette. *Herbarium/Verbarium: The Discourse of Flowers*. Lincoln, NB: University of Nebraska Press, 1993.

Saville, Julia F. "The Romance of Boys Bathing: Poetic Precedents and Respondents to the Paintings of Henry Scott Tuke." In *Victorian Sexual Dissidence*, edited by Richard Dellamora, 253–77. Chicago: University of Chicago Press, 1999.

Schaffer, Talia. "Fashioning Aestheticism by Aestheticizing Fashion: Wilde, Beerbohm, and the Male Aesthetes' Sartorial Codes." *Victorian Literature and Culture* 28, no. 1 (2000): 39–54.

Schaffer, Talia. "'A Wilde Desire Took Me': The Homoerotic History of *Dracula*." *ELH* 61, no. 2 (1994): 381–425.

Schulz, David. "Redressing Oscar: Performance and the Trials of Oscar Wilde." *TDR/The Drama Review* 40, no. 2 (1996): 37–59.

Scully, Robert. *A Scarlet Pansy*. New York: William Faro, 1933.

Sears, Clare. *Arresting Dress: Cross-Dressing, Law, and Fascination in Nineteenth-Century San Francisco*. Durham, NC: Duke University Press, 2015.

Sears, Clare. "Electric Brilliance: Cross-Dressing Law and Freak Show Displays in Nineteenth-Century San Francisco." In *The Transgender Studies Reader 2*, edited by Susan Stryker and Aren Z. Aizura, 554–64. New York: Routledge, 2013.

Seaton, Beverley. *The Language of Flowers: A History*. Charlottesville: University Press of Virginia, 1995.

Sedgwick, Eve Kosofsky. *Between Men: English Literature and Male Homosocial Desire*. New York: Columbia University Press, 1985, reissued 2016.

Sedgwick, Eve Kosofsky. *Epistemology of the Closet*. Berkeley: University of California Press, 1990, reissued 2008.

Sedgwick, Eve Kosofsky. "Queer Performativity: Henry James's 'The Art of the Novel.'" *GLQ: A Journal of Lesbian and Gay Studies* 1, no. 1 (1993): 1–16.

Sedgwick, Eve Kosofsky. *The Weather in Proust*, edited by Jonathan Goldberg. Durham, NC: Duke University Press, 2011.

See, Sam. "Making Modernism New: Queer Mythology in *The Young and Evil*." *ELH* 76, no. 4 (2009): 1073–105.

Seebohm, Caroline. *The Man Who Was "Vogue": The Life and Times of Condé Nast*. New York: Viking, 1982.

Seitler, Dana. "Queer Physiognomies; or, How Many Ways Can We Do the History of Sexuality?" *Criticism* 46, no. 1 (2004): 71–102.

Senelick, Laurence. "Boys and Girls Together: Subcultural Origins of Glamour Drag and Male Impersonation on the Nineteenth-Century Stage." In *Crossing the Stage: Controversies on Cross-Dressing*, edited by Lesley Ferris, 80–95. London: Routledge, 1993.

Senelick, Laurence. *The Changing Room: Sex, Drag and Theatre*. London: Routledge, 2000.

Shahani, Nishant. *Queer Retrosexualities: The Politics of Reparative Return*. Bethlehem, PA: Lehigh University Press, 2012.

Shannon, Brent. *The Cut of His Coat: Men, Dress, and Consumer Culture in Britain, 1860–1914*. Athens, OH: Ohio University Press, 2006.

Sharpe, Andrew N. *Foucault's Monsters and the Challenge of Law*. Abingdon: Routledge, 2010.

Shepard, Ernest H. "Aren't Their Statues Wonderful." *Punch* 192 (1937): 339.

Shepard, Ernest H. "This Is Not the Culminating Scene from the Seventeen-Reel Film. 'The Modern Cleopatra.'" *Punch* 162 (1922): 213.

Shephard, Sue. *The Surprising Life of Constance Spry*. London: Pan Macmillan, 2010.

Shepperton, Claude A. "If We Ordered Our Lives after the Manner of the Russian Ballet." *Punch* 160, *Almanack* (1920): unpaginated.

Sherry, Vincent. *Modernism and the Reinvention of Decadence*. Cambridge: Cambridge University Press, 2015.

Shildrick, Margrit. *Embodying the Monster: Encounters with the Vulnerable Self*. London: Sage, 2001.

Sigel, Lisa Z. *Making Modern Love: Sexual Narratives and Identities in Interwar Britain*. Philadelphia: Temple University Press, 2012.

Sinfield, Alan. "Private Lives/Public Theater: Noël Coward and the Politics of Homosexual Representation." *Representations* 36 (Autumn 1991): 43–63.

Sitwell, Edith. *The English Eccentrics*. London: Faber and Faber, 1933.

Skelly, Julia. *Addiction and British Visual Culture, 1751–1919*. Farnham: Ashgate, 2014.

Skelly, Julia. "The Paradox of Excess: Oscar Wilde, Caricature, and Consumption." In *The Uses of Excess in Visual and Material Culture, 1600–2010*, edited by Julia Skelly, 137–60. Farnham: Ashgate, 2014.

Sketch. "The Artist Side of Our A.P.H.Orisms." February 2, 1927, 195.

Sketch. "A Bride and Bridegroom in Duplicate." July 25, 1928, 165.

Sketch. "The Chelsea Arts Club Ball: Anna Zinkeisen Impressions." January 9, 1929, 48.

Sketch. "Do We Need the Actress?" June 8, 1904, 272 and supplement 3–10.

Sketch. "A Freak of Fashion." June 23, 1897, 359.

Sketch. "John's Noah and Jack Tars! The Chelsea Arts Club Ball." January 8, 1930, 50.

Sketch. "'Puck. Modes et Robes': Freaks of Fashion." December 18, 1907, 10.

Sketch. "Screen Celebrities—From a New Angle: Unconventional Portraits." March 12, 1930, 505.

Sketch. "Society's Greek 'Freak Party': The Great Urban Dionysia." April 17, 1929, 126.

Skidelsky, Robert. *John Maynard Keynes, 1883–1946: Economist, Philosopher, Statesman*. London: Penguin, 2003.

Skipwith, Joanna, ed. *The Sitwells and the Arts of the 1920s and 1930s*. London: National Portrait Gallery, 1994.

Slide, Anthony. *Some Joe You Don't Know: An American Biographical Guide to 100 British Television Personalities*. Westport, CT: Greenwood, 1996.

Smith, Leonard V. "Paul Fussell's *The Great War and Modern Memory*: Twenty-Five Years Later." *History and Theory* 40, no. 2 (2001): 241–60.

Snow, K. Mitchell. "Does This Fig Leaf Make Me Look Gay? Strongmen, Statue Posing and Physique Photography." *Early Popular Visual Culture* 17, no. 2 (2019): 135–55.

Sontag, Susan. "Notes on 'Camp.'" *Partisan Review* 31, no. 4 (1964): 515–30.

Souhami, Diana. *Gluck, 1895–1978: Her Biography*, revised edn. London: Weidenfeld and Nicolson, 2000.

Spencer, Charles. *Erté*. London: Studio Vista, 1970.

Sphere 101. "Leading Ladies at Cambridge University." June 13, 1925, 318.

Spry, Constance. "And the Church Looked Lovely." *Vogue* 90, no. 23, May 11, 1938, 70–1, and 132.

Spry, Constance. *Flower Decoration*. London: Dent, 1934.

Spurr, Barry. "Camp Mandarin: The Prose Style of Lytton Strachey." *English Literature in Transition 1880–1920* 33, no. 1 (1990): 31–45.

Spurr, Barry. *A Literary-Critical Analysis of the Complete Prose Works of Lytton Strachey (1880–1932): A Reassessment of His Work and Career*, Studies in British Literature 19. New York: Edwin Mellen Press, 1995.

Stampa, George. "'This Is Great. You're Just the Type I've Been Looking for for Years.'" *Punch* 178 (1930): 144.

Steakley, James D. "Iconography of a Scandal: Political Cartoons and the Eulenburg Affair." In *History of Homosexuality in Europe and America*, volume 5, edited by Wayne R. Dynes and Stephen Donaldson, 323–85. New York: Garland, 1992.

Steele, Valerie. "A Queer History of Fashion: From the Closet to the Catwalk." In *A Queer History of Fashion: From the Closet to the Catwalk*, edited by Valerie Steele, 7–75. New Haven: Yale University Press, 2013.

Steenson, Martin. *The Life and Work of Alan Odle*. Stroud: Books and Things, 2012.

Stephens, Elizabeth. "Geeks and Gaffs: The Queer Legacy of the 1950s American Freak Show." In *Queer 1950s: Rethinking Sexuality in the Postwar Years*, edited by Heike Bauer and Matt Cook, 183–95. Basingstoke: Palgrave, 2012.

Stephenson, Andrew. "'Our Jolly Marin Wear': The Queer Fashionability of the Sailor Uniform in Interwar France and Britain." *Fashion, Style and Popular Culture* 3, no. 2 (2016): 157–72.

Stetz, Margaret Diane. "The Bi-Social Oscar Wilde and 'Modern' Women." *Nineteenth-Century Literature* 55, no. 4 (2001): 515–37.

Stevenson, Jane, *Baroque between the Wars: Alternative Style in the Arts, 1918–1939*. Oxford: Oxford University Press, 2018.

Stewart, Mary Lynn. *Dressing Modern Frenchwomen; Marketing Haute Couture, 1919–1939*. Baltimore: Johns Hopkins University Press, 2008.

Stockton, Kathryn Bond. *The Queer Child, or Growing Sideways in the Twentieth Century*. Durham, NC: Duke University Press, 2009.

Stoker, Bram. *Dracula*. London: Constable, 1897.

Stott, Annette. "Floral Femininity: A Pictorial Definition." *American Art* 6, no. 2 (1992): 60–77.

Strachan, John, and Claire Nally. *Advertising, Literature and Print Culture in Ireland, 1891–1922*. Basingstoke: Palgrave Macmillan, 2012.

Stringer, Martin. "Of Gin and Lace: Sexuality, Liturgy and Identity among Anglo-Catholics in the Mid-Twentieth Century." *Theology and Sexuality* 7, no. 13 (2000): 35–54.

Stryker, Susan. "General Editor's Introduction." *Transgender Studies Quarterly* 5, no. 4 (2018): 515–17.

Style for Men 17, no. 5. "The Beau Brummell of Trade Journals." May 1931, 312.

Style for Men 20, no. 5. "The Grotesque in Regent Street." November 1932, 248.

Style for Men 20, no. 6. "Selling with the Hands." December 1932, 326.

Style for Men 24, no. 5. "Britain's Biggest Ready-to-Wear Floor." November 1934, 301.

Style for Men 25, no. 3. "At the BIF Exhibition." March 1935, 217.

Sunday Dispatch. "Greta Garbo's One Ambition—She Wants to Play a Man's Rôle on the Stage." April 21, 1935, 3.

Sunday Post. "Poison among Chocolates." September 27, 1925, 4.

Sunday Post (Glasgow). "Boy's Body Found in Shrubbery." June 27, 1926, 2.

Sutton, Katie. *The Masculine Woman in Weimar Germany*, Monographs in German History 32. New York: Berghahn, 2011.

Sutton, Katie. "Sexological Cases and the Prehistory of Transgender Identity Politics in Interwar Germany." In *Case Studies and the Dissemination of Knowledge*, edited by Joy Damousi, Birgit Lang, and Katie Sutton, 85–103. New York: Routledge, 2015.

Sutton, Katie. "Sexology's Photographic Turn: Visualizing Trans Identity in Interwar Germany." *Journal of the History of Sexuality* 27, no. 3 (2018): 442–79.

Sutton, Katie. "'We Too Deserve a Place in the Sun': The Politics of Transvestite Identity in Weimar Germany." *German Studies Review* 35, no. 2 (2012): 335–54.

Sweet, Matthew. *Inventing the Victorians*. London: Faber and Faber, 2001.

Syme, Alison Mairi. "Bohemians of the Vegetable World." In *Queer Difficulty in Art and Poetry: Rethinking the Sexed Body in Verse and Visual Culture*, edited by Jongwoo Jeremy Kim and Christopher Reed, 10–23. New York: Routledge, 2017.

Syme, Alison Mairi. *A Touch of Blossom: John Singer Sargent and the Queer Flora of Fin-de-Siècle Art*. University Park: Pennsylvania State Press, 2010.

Szreter, Simon, and Kate Fisher. *Sex before the Sexual Revolution: Intimate Life in England 1918–1963*. Cambridge: Cambridge University Press, 2010.

Taddeo, Julie Anne. *Lytton Strachey and the Search for Modern Sexual Identity: The Last Eminent Victorian*. London: Routledge, 2012.

Taddeo, Julie Anne. "Plato's Apostles: Edwardian Cambridge and the 'New Style of Love.'" *Journal of the History of Sexuality* 8, no. 2 (1997): 196–228.

Tait, Peta. *Circus Bodies: Cultural Identity in Aerial Performance*. London: Routledge, 2005.

Talbot, Eugene Solomon. *Degeneracy: Its Causes, Signs and Results*, Contemporary Science Series 35, edited by Havelock Ellis. London: Walter Scott, 1898.

Tamagne, Florence. *Histoire de l'homosexualité en Europe (Berlin, Londres, Paris, 1919–1939)*. Paris: Éditions du Seuil, 2000.

Tamagne, Florence. *A History of Homosexuality in Europe: Berlin, London, Paris, 1919–1939*. New York: Algora, 2006.

Taunton Courier and Western Advertiser. "Boy's Death Mystery." July 7, 1926, 2.

Taylor, D. J. *Bright Young People: The Rise and Fall of a Generation, 1918–1940*. London: Chatto and Windus, 2007.

Taylor, Martin, ed. *Lads: Love Poetry of the Trenches*. London: Constable, 1989.

Tchelitchew, Pavel. "Phenomena." *Vogue* 90, no. 29, August 3, 1938, 26–7.

Tebbutt, Clare. "'The Spectre of the 'Man-Woman Athlete': Mark Weston, Zdenek Koubek, the 1936 Olympics and the Uncertainty of Sex." *Women's History Review* 24, no. 5 (2015): 721–38.

Tenby Observer Weekly List of Visitors and Directory. "Death of the 'Bearded Lady.'" October 11, 1883, 6.

Tennant, Stephen. *Leaves from a Missionary's Notebook*. London: Secker and Warburg, 1937.

Thompson, Sylvia. "The World Where One Amuses." *Vogue* 78, no. 3, August 5, 1931, 19–21 and 59.

Thomson, Rosemarie Garland. *Extraordinary Bodies: Figuring Physical Disability in American Culture and Literature*. New York: Columbia University Press, 1996.

Thorpe, J. H. "Diehard (Stroking His Beard) 'My Dear Girl It's Our Only Chance Left.'" *Punch* 168 (1925): 163.

Timbs, John. *English Eccentrics and Eccentricities*, 2 volumes. London: Richard Bentley, 1866.

The Times. "None Will Grudge Mr. Barnum." November 11, 1889, 9.

The Times. "Pygmies in Piccadilly." November 19, 1880, 8.

Tinkler, Penny. *Smoke Signals: Women, Smoking and Visual Culture in Britain*. Oxford: Berg, 2006.

Tinkler, Penny, and Cheryl Krasnick Warsh. "Feminine Modernity in Interwar Britain and North America: Corsets, Cars, and Cigarettes." *Journal of Women's History* 20, no. 3 (2008): 113–43.

Tinkom, Matthew. *Working Like a Homosexual: Camp, Capital, Cinema*. Durham, NC: Duke University Press, 2002.

Tinkom, Matthew. "Working Like a Homosexual: Camp Visual Codes and the Labor of Gay Subjects in the MGM Freed Unit." *Cinema Journal* 35, no. 2 (1996): 24–42.

Tobin, Robert Deam. *Peripheral Desires: The German Discovery of Sex*. Philadelphia: University of Pennsylvania Press, 2015.

Tromp, Marlene, and Karyn Valerius. "Towards Situating the Victorian Freak." In *Victorian Freaks: The Social Context of Freakery in Britain*, edited by Marlene Tromp, 1–18. Columbus: Ohio State University Press, 2008.

Troubridge, Una. *The Life and Death of Radclyffe Hall*. London: Hammond, 1961.

Troy, Nancy J. *Couture Culture: A Study in Modern Art and Fashion*. Cambridge, MA: MIT Press, 2003.

Troy, Nancy J. "The Theatre of Fashion: Staging Haute Couture in Early 20th Century France." *Theatre Journal* 53, no. 1 (2001): 1–32.

Tumblety, Joan. *Remaking the Male Body: Masculinity and the Uses of Physical Culture in Interwar and Vichy France*. Oxford: Oxford University Press, 2012.

Tyburczy, Jennifer. *Sex Museums: The Politics and Performance of Display*. Chicago: University of Chicago Press, 2016.

Tyler, Parker. *The Divine Comedy of Pavel Tchelitchew: A Biography*. New York: Fleet, 1967.

Tynan, Jane. *British Army Uniform and the First World War: Men in Khaki*. Basingstoke: Palgrave Macmillan, 2013.

Ugolini, Laura. *Men and Menswear: Sartorial Consumption in Britain 1880–1939*. Aldershot: Ashgate Publishing, 2007.

Upchurch, Charles. "Forgetting the Unthinkable: Cross-Dressers and British Society in the Case of the Queen vs. Boulton and Others." *Gender and History* 12, no. 1 (2000): 127–57.

Valentine, Laura. *The Language and Sentiment of Flowers and the Classical Floral Legends*. London: Warne, c. 1860.

Valverde, Mariana. "The Love of Finery: Fashion and the Fallen Woman in Nineteenth-Century Social Discourse." *Victorian Studies* 32, no. 3 (1989): 169–88.

Van Vechten, Carl. *Excavations*. New York: Knopf, 1926.

Variety Weekly. "*Femme de Minuit (Midnight Lady)*". January 7, 1931, 70.

Variety Weekly. "Hollywood's Male Magnolias." October 4, 1930, 1–2.

Variety Weekly. "'Pansy' Palaces on Broadway." September 10, 1930, 1.

Vernon, James. "'For Some Queer Reason': The Trials and Tribulations of Colonel Barker's Masquerade in Interwar Britain." *Signs* 26, no. 1 (2000): 37–62.

Vickers, Hugo. *Cecil Beaton: The Authorised Biography*. London: Weidenfeld and Nicolson, 1985.

Vickers, Hugo, ed. *Cecil Beaton: Portraits and Profiles*. London: Frances Lincoln, 2014.

Vickers, Hugo. "Introduction." In E. F. Benson, *Final Edition*. London: Hogarth Press, 1988), unpaginated.

Vickers, Hugo. *Loving Garbo: The Story of Greta Garbo, Cecil Beaton and Mercedes de Acosta*. London: Random House, 2012.

Viner, Richard. "Ladies Love a Fight." *Vogue* 90, no. 16, February 2, 1938, 44–5 and 70.

Vogue 48, no. 1. "The Triumph of Victorianism." July 1, 1916, 50–1 and 96.

Vogue 52, no. 4. "The High Cost of Dressing." Late August 1918, 42–3.

Vogue 53, no. 7. "The Extreme Importance of Extremities." Early April 1919, 74–5.

Vogue 55, no. 2. "Colour Schemes for the Car." Late January 1920, 82.

Vogue 55, no. 8. "An Ideal Tour of Motor Row." Late April 1920, 72–3 and 102.

Vogue 57, no. 9. "In Paris This Season." Early May 1921, 44–5.

Vogue 60, no. 9. "Public Opinion and Personal Liberty." Early November 1922, 69.

Vogue 61, no. 8. "Wedding Rings, Cakes and Favours." Late April 1923, 50–2 and 118.

Vogue 63, no. 7. "Undergraduates in Tragedy." Early April 1924, 55 and 82.

Vogue 64, no. 6. "Why the Wedding Ceremony Ought to Be Revised." Late September 1924, 48.

Vogue 65, no. 5. "An Economist and Modern Art: The Cambridge Rooms of Mr. Keynes." Early March 1925, 46–7.

Vogue 66, no. 8. "Baring the Secrets of the Turkish Bath." Late October 1925, 66–7.

Vogue 69, no. 5. "The Fur Scarf and the Tailored Suit." Early March 1927, 70.

Vogue 70, no. 9. "Our Lives from Day to Day." November 2, 1927, 57–8 and 76.

Vogue 71, no. 3. "The Frock of the Future: Dresses Designed by Cecil Beaton for a Ball at Claridge's." February 8, 1928, 26–7.

Vogue 73, no. 10. "How One Lives from Day to Day." May 15, 1929, 72–3 and 108.

Vogue 73, no. 12. "Chic: A Defence." June 12, 1929, 61.

Vogue 77, no. 1. "The Victorian Age Returns." January 7, 1931, 56–7 and 68.

Vogue 77, no. 9. "A *Vogue*'s Eye View of the Season." April 29, 1931, 53–5 and 95.

Vogue 81, no. 11. "Lady Melchett." May 31, 1933, 60.

Vogue 82, no. 9. "Weight and What to Do about It." November 1, 1933, 65.

Vogue 82, no. 10. "London and Paris: Recent Events Seen by a Visitor." November 15, 1933, 62–3 and 96.

Vogue 83, no. 5. "Blondes without, Brunettes within." March 7, 1934, 90–1.

Vogue 84, no. 4. "We Hand It to Beauty." August 22, 1934, 20–5 and 70.

Vogue 85, no. 9. "There Are No Beauties." May 1, 1935, 111.

Vogue 85, no. 10. "*Vogue*'s Eye View of the Mode." May 15, 1935, 51.

Vogue 87, no. 9. "Heart-Beats." April 29, 1936, 68–9.

Vogue 90, no. 5. "The Works." September 1, 1937, 38–9.

Vogue 90, no. 8. "Wire, Wax and Plaster of Paris." October 13, 1937, 76–7.

Vogue 90, no. 18. "The Noel Coward Paper Doll." March 2, 1938, 68.

Vogue (US edn) 34, no. 6. "Paris." August 5, 1909, 151–2.

Vogue (US edn) 34, no. 8. "Curious Coincidences of Hat Styles." August 19, 1909, 205–6.

Vogue (US edn) 41, no. 2. "*Vogue* Patterns: French Lingerie Patterns." January 15, 1913, 58–9.

Vogue (US edn) 48, no. 8. "As Seen by Him." October 15, 1916, 57.

Vogue (US edn) 51, no. 1. "What They Read." January 1, 1918: 74, 76 and 78.

Vogue (US edn) 61, no. 1. "Our American Artists in Paris and London." January 1, 1923, 79.

Vogue (US edn) 71, no. 4. "More News of the Sophisticates of Mayfair." February 15, 1928, 60–1, 140 and 142.

Vogue (US edn) 72, no. 5. "Dear Me! These Modern Samplers!" September 1, 1928, 64.

Vogue (US edn) 80, no. 6. "A Circus Party and Dutch Treat Dinner." September 15, 1932, 52–3.

Vogue (US edn) 83, no. 9. "Our Best Families: Party at the Waldorf." May 1, 1934, 54–5.

Vogue (US edn) 87, no. 8. "The Incomparable Mr. Cochran's Stage Revue of 1936. 'Follow the Sun.'" April 15, 1936, 72–3.

Vogue (US edn) 90, no. 10. "Debutante Line-Up—This Is Their Winter." November 15, 1937, 68–71 and 144.

Walkowitz, Judith R. *Nights Out: Life in Cosmopolitan London*. New Haven: Yale University Press, 2012.

Wallace, Edgar. "The Crime in Which Women Specialise." *Daily Mail*, June 13, 1929, 87.

Wansell, Geoffrey. *Terence Rattigan*. London: Fourth Estate, 1995.

Ward, Paul. *Britishness since 1870*. London: Routledge, 2004.

Waters, Chris. "Havelock Ellis, Sigmund Freud and the State: Discourses of Homosexual Identity in Interwar Britain." In *Sexology in Culture: Labelling Bodies and Desire*, edited by Lucy Bland and Laura Doan, 165–79. London: University of Chicago Press, 1998.

Waters, Chris. "Wilde in the Fifties." In *Sex, Knowledge, and Receptions of the Past*, edited by Kate Fisher and Rebecca Langlands, 265–90. Oxford: Oxford University Press, 2015.

Watson, Petra Rigby. "Hannah Maynard's Multiple Exposures." *History of Photography* 20, no. 2 (1996): 155–7.

Waugh, Evelyn. *Brideshead Revisited*. London: Chapman and Hall, 1945.

Waugh, Evelyn. "Let Us Return to the Nineties but Not to Oscar Wilde." *Harper's Bazaar* 3, no. 2, November 1930, 50–1.

Waugh, Thomas. *Hard to Imagine: Gay Male Eroticism in Photography and Film from Their Beginnings to Stonewall*. New York: Columbia University Press, 1996.

Wearing, J. P. *The London Stage 1930–1939: A Calendar of Productions, Performers, and Personnel*, 2nd edn. Lanham: Rowman and Littlefield, 2014.

Weekly Mail. "Father's Appeal." July 23, 1910, 7.

Weeks, Jeffrey. "Inverts, Perverts, and Mary-Annes: Male Prostitution and the Regulation of Homosexuality in England in the Nineteenth and Early Twentieth Centuries." *Journal of Homosexuality* 6, no. 1–2 (1981): 113–34.

Weinberg, Jonathan. *Speaking for Vice: Homosexuality in the Art of Charles Demuth, Marsden Hartley, and the First American Avant-Garde*. New Haven: Yale University Press, 1995.

Weinstein, Deena, and Michael Weinstein. "Celebrity Worship as Weak Religion." *Word and World* 23, no. 3 (2003): 294–302.

West, Mae. *Babe Gordon*. New York: Macaulay, 1930.

Whelpton, Vivien. *Richard Aldington: Poet, Soldier and Lover, 1911–1929*. Cambridge: Lutterworth Press, 2014.

Whitworth, Michael H. "Logan Pearsall Smith and *Orlando*." *Review of English Studies* 55, no. 221 (2004): 598–604.

Wicke, Jennifer. "'Mrs. Dalloway' Goes to Market: Woolf, Keynes, and Modern Markets." *Novel: A Forum on Fiction*, 28, no. 1 (1994): 5–23.

Wild, Benjamin. *A Life in Fashion: The Wardrobe of Cecil Beaton*. London: Thames and Hudson, 2016.

Wilde, Oscar. *The Complete Letters of Oscar Wilde*, edited by Merlin Holland and Rupert Hart-Davis. London: Fourth Estate, 2000.

Wilde, Oscar. *A House of Pomegranates*. London: Methuen, 1911.

Wilde, Oscar. *An Ideal Husband: A Play*, 3rd edn. London: Methuen, 1909.

Wilde, Oscar. "London Models." *English Illustrated Magazine* 64 (January 1889): 313–19.

Wilde, Oscar. *Oscar Wilde in America: The Interviews*, edited by Matthew Hofer and Gary Scharnhorst. Urbana: University of Illinois Press, 2010.

Wilde, Oscar. "Phrases and Philosophies for the Use of the Young." In Oscar Wilde, *Epigrams; Phrases and Philosophies for the Use of the Young*, 139–45. London: Keller, 1907.

Wilde, Oscar. *The Picture of Dorian Gray: An Annotated, Uncensored Edition*, edited by Nicholas Frankel. Cambridge, MA: Harvard University Press. 2011.

Wilks, Claire Weissman. *The Magic Box: The Eccentric Genius of Hannah Maynard*. Toronto: Exile Editions, 1980.

Williams, Tennessee. *Garden District: Two Plays*. London: Secker and Warburg, 1959.

Willoughby, Guy. *Art and Christhood: The Aesthetics of Oscar Wilde*. Cranbury: Associated University Presses, 1993.

Wilson, Elizabeth. *Adorned in Dreams: Fashion and Modernity*, new edn. London: I.B. Tauris, 2003.

Wilson, Elizabeth. "A Note on Glamour." *Fashion Theory* 11, no. 1 (2007): 95–108.

Wilson, Leslie. "The Regeneration of the Johnny." *Physical Culture* 1, no. 1 (1898): 30–1.

"The Window Man." "Display of Sports Shirts." *Style for Men* 25, no. 5, May 1935, 369.

Witchard, Anne. "Sink Street: The Sapphic World of Pre-Chinatown Soho." In *Sex, Time and Place: Queer Histories of London, c. 1850 to the Present*, edited by Simon Avery and Katherine M. Graham, 221–38. London: Bloomsbury, 2016.

Woodcock, Sarah. "Messel on Stage." In *Oliver Messel in the Theatre of Design*, edited by Thomas Messel, 54–83. New York: Rizzoli, 2011.

Woods, Gregory. "British Homosexuality, 1920–1939." In *W. H. Auden in Context*, edited by Tony Sharpe, 88–98. Cambridge: Cambridge University Press, 2013.

Woods, Gregory. *Homintern: How Gay Culture Liberated the Modern World*. New Haven: Yale University Press, 2016.

Woolf, John. *The Wonders: Lifting the Curtain on the Freak Show, Circus and Victorian Age*. London: Michael O'Mara, 2019.

Woolf, Virginia. *Orlando: A Biography*. London: L. and V. Woolf, 1933.

Wynne, Deborah. "The 'Despised Trade' in Textiles: H. G. Wells, William Paine, Charles Cavers and the Male Draper's Life, 1870–1914." *Textile History* 46, no. 1 (2015): 99–113.

Yeats, Jack Butler [pseud. "W. Bird"]. "Hints to Artists and Writers Who Need to Advertise Themselves by Some Eccentricity of Costume." *Punch* 146 (1914): 295.

Yeats, Jack Butler. "Messrs. Hopeful and Boomage." *Punch* 149 (1915): 257.

Yoxall, Harold W. *A Fashion for Life*. London: Heinemann, 1966.

Zinkeisen, Doris. *Designing for the Stage*, How to Do It Series 18. London: Studio, 1938.

Zinovieff, Sofka. *The Mad Boy, Lord Berners, My Grandmother and Me*. London: Jonathan Cape, 2014.

Ziolkowski, Jan M. *The Juggler of Notre Dame and the Medievalizing of Modernity*, volume 4, *Picture That: Making a Show of the Jongleur*. Cambridge: Open Book Publishers, 2018.

Zweiniger-Bargielowska, Ina. "Building a British Superman: Physical Culture in Interwar Britain." *Journal of Contemporary History* 41, no. 4 (2006): 595–610.

Zweiniger-Bargielowska, Ina. "'Healthier and Better Clothes for Men': Men's Dress Reform in Interwar Britain." In *Consuming Behaviours: Identity, Politics and Pleasure in Twentieth-Century Britain*, edited by Erika Rappaport, Mark J. Crowley and Sandra Trudgen Dawson, 37–52. London: Bloomsbury, 2015.

Zweiniger-Bargielowska, Ina. "The Making of a Modern Female Body: Beauty, Health and Fitness in Interwar Britain." *Women's History Review* 20, no. 2 (2011): 299–317.

Zweiniger-Bargielowska, Ina. *Managing the Body: Beauty, Health, and Fitness in Britain, 1880–1939*. Oxford: Oxford University Press, 2010.

Index